INSTRUMENTS OF BATTLE

INSTRUMENTS
OF BATTLE

The Fighting Drummers and Buglers of the British Army
from the Late 17th Century to the Present Day

JAMES TANNER

CASEMATE
Oxford & Philadelphia

Published in Great Britain and the United States of America in 2017 by
CASEMATE PUBLISHERS
The Old Music Hall, 106–108 Cowley Road, Oxford OX4 1JE, UK
and
1950 Lawrence Road, Havertown, PA 19083, US

© James Tanner 2017

Hardcover Edition: ISBN 978-1-61200-369-6
Digital Edition: ISBN 978-1-61200-370-2

A CIP record for this book is available from the British Library

Printed and bound in the United Kingdom by TJ International Ltd

For a complete list of Casemate titles, please contact:

CASEMATE PUBLISHERS (UK)
Telephone (01865) 241249
Email: casemate-uk@casematepublishers.co.uk
www.casematepublishers.co.uk

CASEMATE PUBLISHERS (US)
Telephone (610) 853-9131
Fax (610) 853-9146
Email: casemate@casematepublishers.com
www.casematepublishers.com

Contents

Introduction

See drummers with the fifers come, And Carter with the massive drum; The grand drum-major first doth stalk with gold-knobbed stick and pompous walk, And as he marches o'er the ground he thinks he turns the world around.

There is an enduring image to this day of the British Army on parade, led on to the barrack square or through a town by a band and drums and all preceded by a drum major displaying his magnificent and rightful pomposity. Any tourist visiting London, especially from overseas, will invariably wish to witness the Foot Guards changing guard at Buckingham Palace, with the new guard marching to the Palace and the old guard marching away, both preceded by the band and drums of one of the battalions of Guards. Up and down the cities and boroughs of the United Kingdom an increasingly common sight in the first decade of the 21st century was an infantry battalion, returned from war in Iraq or in Afghanistan, exercising its regiment's freedom by marching through the streets with 'drums beating, colours flying and bayonets fixed'. Within the British Army as late as the 1980s and before the phrase 'over-commitment' became a political tool rather than the simple statement of fact it had always been, the working day of an infantry battalion was still regulated by the sound of the bugle to drag the men out of their beds at reveille, to summon the company sergeant majors, to send the men to their dinners or to end the day's business at 'last post'. Some of this has survived, as will be shown. All of this musical accompaniment was and is military music at its grandest and simplest.

But this book is not about music as such and it is not about true musicians. It is about infantrymen whose weapons of war were the drum and the bugle – musical instruments that were carried in past centuries as essential elements of the battalion armoury. While music will enter this story and some mention of military bands is required for completeness, the main purpose of this book is to describe the British infantry drummer and bugler and how they were, and still are, employed in war and peace. It is essential to put drummers and buglers into context and this book is, therefore, also about the development of command and control and within this the business of signalling on the battlefield at the tactical level – the level of warfare at which business on the battlefield is conducted by platoons, companies, battalions, brigades and divisions. We must consider too how the very tactics used on the battlefield developed over the centuries. What emerges is something of a surprise for there is much mythology that has built up over these centuries and especially about the use of the drum and the age of the drummer. The drum actually had limited utility as a means of battlefield signalling and if the bugle emerged as a rather more useful and handier instrument, it too had its limitations. A modern commentator has concluded, 'For much of military history, drummers and other musicians like fifers and buglers [were] the most effective way for commanders to relay their orders to hundreds or even thousands of troops on the battlefield.'[1] This is actually an over-representation of their utility and effect, for the most effective method was the voice. Nevertheless, drum and bugle played a very important part on the battlefield and the very mythology of their use is a story in itself. Some mention must also be made of the trumpet in as much as trumpet and bugle are largely synonymous in terms of military, as opposed to pure musical, use. Indeed, until the 18th century, no real distinction was made in the family of wind instruments between what would later be defined clearly as bugle, or horn, and trumpet. But the use of trumpet, bugle (and drum, at times) by the cavalry is largely outside the scope of this book. The fife and military flute – again at times interchangeable terms – are also covered here.

There are problems throughout this whole story in unearthing solid fact. Hugh Barty-King, in an excellent little book called *The*

Drum – A Royal Tournament Tribute to the Military Drum, noted that 'Little is known for certain about almost any aspect of the military drum's use in the sixteenth, seventeenth and eighteenth centuries in Britain in spite of the voluminous literature.'[2] The same might be said for the period after this and for evidence of the bugle. But there is enough to put the story together even if, at times, some assumptions must be made. The problem might be that the drum and bugle were in their time so much part of the everyday life of the British soldier and that their calls were so commonplace that they were not worth mentioning. Soldier turned historian Brigadier Peter Young wrote in his introduction to the Napoleonic War recollections of Sergeant Thomas Morris of the 73rd Highland Regiment of Foot: 'The trouble is that memoirists take so much for granted. They assume that we know all about the military organization and tactics of their day.'[3] Indeed, Sergeant Thomas tells us nothing in his description of the battle of Waterloo that would help us understand anything about the employment of drum, bugle or fife. It is only in a sham fight between the Loyal Volunteers of St George's, Middlesex, and the Ratcliff Volunteers that there is a tantalising but equally unrevealing glimpse of 'the thrilling tones of the bugle, and the merry fife and drum.'[4]

The story is important too for our greater understanding of the British Army throughout its history. While other armies feature in the pages ahead, most notably the United States Army and the French Army and to a lesser extent the Germans and others, the drum and bugle – especially the drum – have an iconic status in the British Army that lasts to this day. This status is far less so in any other army. For the British Army:

> The ceremonial duties of the Corps of Drums have remained unchanged and timeless. They march at the head of victorious armies, muffled drums beat and 'Bugles calling from sad shires' (Wilfred Owen) sound when the nation is in mourning. New Colours are consecrated on piled drums and drummers are there, in lofty cathedrals, when the old Colours are laid up, reverently, to rest. Regimental Church Services are still held around drum altars in hollow square. The phrase 'to follow the drum' is still with us, in spite of the jet plane. When in barracks, as regularly as clockwork, throughout most regiments of the line, daily routine bugle calls are still played and at 6 p.m. each night, Retreat is sounded

and as the last note of the call fades, gates are closed and sentries mounted – the Last Post is played before lights out at the end of the day – in this nothing has changed.[5]

While this is something of a romanticised summary and in very recent years much of this regarding barrack routine has fallen by the wayside, that the drum and bugle can still motivate such feelings says a great deal. Most infantrymen felt little affinity to a band of music, even their own regimental band when these existed, but the drummers and buglers are considered their own.

Some words are necessary on definitions. In the Foot Guards and the infantry of the line, whether he carries a drum or a bugle and, at times, a flute, the man is a drummer. With bugle in hand the drummer is often, if erroneously, referred to as a bugler. While this is, technically, incorrect it would be pedantic to continue to labour the point or to call these buglers anything other than buglers, certainly once the bugle became the pre-eminent instrument in the infantry of the line. Within the British infantry, light infantry and rifle-equipped infantry began to emerge properly at the beginning of the 19th century and became regiments in their own right. The original regiments of light infantry also carried drums to begin with and therefore had drummers, but they eventually gave these up for bugles and buglers alone.

Drummer or bugler, they are never bandsmen. British Army bands have always occupied a very different part of the army's structure and even when bands were formally established in 1803 the bandsmen were long considered to be non-combatants. This is a major misconception for once regimental bands did become established the bandsmen were expected to be able to pick up musket or rifle if needed, However, they were more usefully employed as battlefield medical orderlies, a role to which the younger drummers and buglers were also often assigned by dint of fact that these boys were usually placed in the band before they were old enough to take their place in the corps of drums or bugles. Naturally enough drummers and, later, buglers were often grouped with and played alongside their more musical brethren in the band and it can be confusing that drummers and fifers, particularly in the 18th century, were often referred to collectively as 'the musick'. When this term is also used to describe bands and bandsmen it becomes doubly confusing. First and foremost, however, drummers and buglers are all fighting infantrymen.

It is interesting that the British Army, for all the status enjoyed by its drummers and buglers, has never really found a word or phrase that distinguishes them from the bandsmen. The army of the United States has the phrase 'field musicians' for its drummers and buglers, which is particularly helpful. But, while British Army drummers and buglers were often called 'field drummers' or 'field buglers', which described the roles to which they were elevated once they were promoted to drummer or bugler proper, 'field musicians' was not used. Until bands of music started to become increasingly common in the final decades of the 18th century, drummers and fifers, in those days, were the only 'musick' in a battalion and did not, therefore, need to be distinguished from any other type of musician. But once 'proper' musicians were universally established there arose a need, at least in written regulations, to mark the difference. The modern-day musicologists Trevor Herbert and Helen Barlow have produced a helpful summary of this situation:

> During the nineteenth century, terms such as 'instruments of signal' or 'instruments of command' were introduced into the language of British army regulations. Such terms were not previously necessary, because as far as the military authorities were concerned, the only musical instruments that were relevant to the army's principal purpose were precisely those used for communication. However, by the end of the eighteenth century, 'bands of music' with totally different functions had been introduced. This was instigated not by the army centrally, but at the private behest of officers in certain regiments where it was believed that the decorative and aesthetic side of music could enhance military life for members of their class and present a more attractive image of the military.[6]

It must be said, however, that this author has not found either 'instruments of signal' or 'instruments of command' a common feature in any contemporary documents.

At some time in the 19th century the word 'corps' (singular) became the common collective noun for a grouping of drummers or buglers in a battalion. These corps of drums or buglers reflected accurately that there was no formally formed group, no actual platoon of drummers or buglers, on a battalion's establishment as the individuals belonged to their respective companies. At various times in the 20th century there were attempts to have a dedicated drum or bugle platoon in a battalion but, as will be seen, the men were invariably employed on other tasks when not called to beat or blow.

This book focuses almost exclusively on the infantry – the regiments of foot – although there is some mention, for a better understanding of certain aspects of the story, of the cavalry – the 'horse' as originally defined. There was once a third type of combat soldier called the dragoon, who was an early type of mounted infantryman. Unlike the cavalry, which used trumpets, dragoons, like their pedestrian cousins in the foot, carried drums. But dragoons were eventually included in what we tend to understand as cavalry of all types and displaced their drums for trumpets. The history of the organisation of the British Army is a complicated one and the organisation of the British infantry is a particular case in point. The reader will, I hope, permit me to spell out the main features of the system so to better understand the pages ahead.

Our story proper begins in the second half of the 17th century after the creation of the first standing army in the British Isles. There was, of course, no such thing at this time as a 'British' army for England and Scotland were still separate kingdoms and were not brought together until the Act of Union in 1707. Because Ireland also remained a separate kingdom until the creation of the United Kingdom in 1801 the army in Ireland (it would be incorrect to call it the Irish army) was kept on a separate establishment. Throughout these centuries English (and Welsh), Scottish and Irish soldiers, even in identifiably English, Scottish and Irish regiments, were often referred to as 'English' by their own generals and by their enemies.

The principal unit in the infantry is variously referred to as 'regiment' or 'battalion' and they can mean the same thing. In theory at least the battalion is the tactical or fighting unit and the regiment is the administrative unit, for want of a better phrase. They are also often described as 'marching regiments', 'regiments of foot' or simply 'the foot'. For much of history infantry regiments often had just one battalion, so regiment and battalion were invariably one and the same thing and the terms were, effectively, synonymous. There are other common military terms that can confuse. The traditional military hierarchy of the infantry today and going back many years is this: a section (about ten men) is the smallest element (although today they are also divided into fire teams); three or four sections make a platoon and three or four platoons make a company, a rifle company being the term that distinguishes this type of sub-unit from others like support or fire support company, where the infantry's heavy weapons lurk. Three or four or more companies make a battalion (also referred to as a regiment in earlier times) and three or four or more battalions are placed in brigades. Reference is also made to 'battalion companies' and 'battalion regiments'. Both terms were in regular use when infantry battalions/regiments had flank companies – their grenadier and light companies. 'Battalion companies' indicated therefore the 'centre' companies, that is the majority of the companies that stood in line between the flank companies. They were also known as 'hat' companies, although largely in the 18th century, because they wore the three-cornered hat rather than the grenadier's mitre or the light infantryman's cap. 'Battalion regiments' simply meant the battalions/ regiments of the line as opposed to the light infantry regiments or the regiments of Foot Guards.

A number of brigades form divisions and divisions form corps (singular), which is as far as we need to go. In the early chapters of this book it will be seen that the smallest organised unit was the company but until the later 18th century this was an administrative unit, or rather sub-unit, only, all the men being 'platooned' before battle to establish equal fire units in the battalion. For the firings these platoons would also be organised into divisions (sometimes comprising just two platoons) or grand divisions (two equal-sized battalion halves). The higher formation at this time was the brigade – battalions were 'brigaded' before battle commenced – but during the Napoleonic Wars the British Army absorbed the concept of the division, in its modern sense, and the corps. The corps in this sense is, of course, a fighting formation and not an administrative organisation like the Corps of Army Music, or a corps of drums for that matter.

Until 1751 all regiments were referred to by the name of their then colonel, the name of the regiment – always at that time just a single battalion – changing when the colonel changed. Thus the regiment that was raised in 1705 as Lillingston's Regiment and which became the 38th Regiment of Foot in 1751, when numbers according to seniority were imposed on the infantry of the line, changed its name in the intervening years about eight times. Some regiments also had supplementary names by which they were known at various times. The regiment raised in 1680 and which was to become the 4th Regiment of Foot was first called the 2nd Tangier Regiment. Through various name changes it emerged as the King's Own Regiment of Foot in 1715 and when numbered as the 4th in 1751 retained the title of the King's Own. Throughout this book all infantry regiments mentioned are referred to by their names at the time under discussion, or a recognisable abbreviation of them.

Between 1751 and the major reforms finalised in 1881, regiments usually comprised a single battalion but there were frequent expansions in wartime and, in some cases, regiments had three or even four battalions. All regiments had been given county designations in 1782 and the 38th, for example, received the title 1st Staffordshire Regiment (the 64th was the 2nd Staffordshire Regiment). But there was much opposition and regiments clung to their numbers jealously. The 38th's full title was therefore the 38th (1st Staffordshire) Regiment, although it was called simply the 38th Regiment. When, during the Peninsular War, a second battalion was raised for service in Spain it became the 2nd/38th Regiment. The Cardwell/Childers reforms that were finalised in 1881 took away all of the numbers, officially, and allocated full county titles, though very many battalions continued to use their old numbers up to and during the Second World War. In 1881 the 38th became the 1st Battalion the South Staffordshire Regiment and what had been the 80th (Staffordshire Volunteers) became the 2nd Battalion. The 64th became the 1st Battalion the Prince of Wales's (North Staffordshire) Regiment, amalgamating with the old 98th (The Prince of Wales's) Regiment, which became the 2nd Battalion. During the Great War both regiments were expanded considerably, having 19 and 18 battalions respectively, in an amalgam of Regular (that is, full-time professional soldiers), Special Reserve (the old militia), Territorial (pre-war part-time soldiers) and Service (raised for the war) battalions. The Second World War saw rather more modest expansion and in the late 1940s both regiments were reduced to just one Regular battalion and one Territorial battalion apiece. In 1959, while the Territorials survived a little longer, the Regulars of both regiments became a single battalion of the Staffordshire Regiment and in 2007 that battalion became part of the new Mercian Regiment – an amalgamation of the Regular battalions and Territorial elements of the Cheshire Regiment, the Worcestershire and Sherwood Foresters Regiment and the Staffordshire Regiment. Interestingly, the Cheshires had never in their history been subject to any amalgamations and were still called the 22nd (Cheshire) Regiment.

This gallop through the organisational changes of just one regiment is simpler than many! What is, perhaps, surprising is that, throughout often tumultuous change, formed bodies of drummers and buglers have survived and into an age where their very presence seems to be grossly anachronistic. This says much for their iconic status and the very character of the British Army.

Some words too on the construction of the book and its chapters. Progress of the book is largely chronological over the unfolding chapters. The first two chapters set the scene for the main story, which begins around the year of the Restoration of the British monarchy and the birth of the national army in 1660. Subsequent chapters have attempted to parcel up the story through broadly identifiable phases in its development but there are, of course, no actual dividing lines between one chapter and another. All chapters follow roughly similar lines to cover theory and then practice in the matters of tactical developments, application of command and control and drumming and bugling on the battlefield. There is very much more to it than this and some very good stories along the way. Chapter 11 steps aside from the chronology to say something more about the drummers and buglers themselves. More, much more, could be said on the dress and appearance of drummers and buglers but space is limited.

This whole work is crying out for a very liberal use of illustrations but these are limited to the usual 16 pages in the centre, although reference is made throughout to other illustrations and very many of these can be accessed online. All images are credited appropriately. I have used contemporary images as much as possible and a good number of these show drummers and buglers in action. But such images are thin on the ground and some are beyond reach. I am particularly indebted to the Anne S. K. Brown Collection at Brown University, Providence, Rhode Island, for access to this stunning archive and for permission to reproduce a number of images. The collection is entirely accessible online and will absorb many hours.

Throughout I have endeavoured to reproduce anecdotes and quotations as I have found them and, certainly in the early chapters, some of the spelling and description can appear a little esoteric; I hope it is understandable nonetheless. I have avoided extravagant use of the adverb 'sic', confining it largely to avoid any possible confusion when, for example, reference is made to a bandsman when the observer actually meant drummer. I have also steered clear of extensive footnotes, placing all of what is needed in the main body of the text and avoiding, regrettably, going down too many rabbit-holes. However, the text is heavily referenced and the details of all of these can be found at the end of the book. All of my sources are also listed and these include a goldmine of official and unofficial drill books and tactical manuals that help us understand far more of what went on at the time than anecdotal evidence can provide. The reader will see that the practical use in the field of these publications, official or otherwise, is strongly caveated and I am mindful of the Duke of Wellington's words on the matter: 'Nobody in the British Army ever reads a regulation or an order as if it were to be a guide to his conduct, or in any other manner than as an amusing novel.' Or of General Sir Ivor Maxse in 1918: 'They try to cram a Staff College education into a pamphlet ... it is a fine performance but it bewilders our platoon commanders and people like me'.

A number of published works have been highly influential and I cite three in particular. The 18th century has been the most troublesome in separating fact from myth. Of the latter I hope I have succeeded in dispelling the absurdity that stiff-necked British infantry was flogged into battle by popinjay junior officers, often mere boys, and led to repetitive disaster by cruel-hearted generals. First among the three books is Dr John Houlding's *Fit For Service*, which is much more than a study of the training of the British Army during the reigns of the first three Georges. Next, chronologically, is Stephen Brumwell's *Redcoats*, a compelling study of the British soldier in North America during the Seven Years War. And this sets the scene for Mathew Spring's *With Zeal and With Bayonets Only*, covering the American War of Independence. Together all three books establish most clearly how soldiers fought and have allowed me to piece together how the drum and the bugle might have been employed at the time. They help too in our proper understanding of the success of the British infantry in subsequent generations.

★

I am indebted to Major Michael Barthorp for all his assistance many years ago in encouraging me to begin this work and for providing some notes on organisation that led me to seek more. Following a chance meeting in Potters in Aldershot Major Richard Powell provided me with the essays he and Bill Boag had written on the Drum and Fife and gave me a copy of Barty-King's *The Drum*, which has given me much inspiration. Without the help of all of them, effectively setting the framework for much of what follows, this book would not have appeared. My great thanks too to Chris Hobson and the staff of the library of the Joint Services Command and Staff College at Shrivenham for unearthing in their archives, inherited from the old Army Staff College Camberley, practically every British Army drill book and manual published. I have dug deeply too in the Reading Room of the National Army Museum and in the extensive archives of my own regimental museum at Whittington Barracks in Staffordshire.

The British Army today remains reticent when asked to provide information and I hit a void when I wrote to the majority of infantry battalions to ask how they organised their drummers and buglers today. To the rescue came WO1 Ben Roberts of the Coldstream Guards, the Army Senior Drum Major at the Army School of Ceremonial at Catterick. He obtained for me the responses of a good cross-section of a dozen battalions that allowed me to bring this story up to date.

A special word of thanks to my friend, the author and publisher Martin Windrow. His renowned and critical editor's eye over my first published effort for Osprey gave me the confidence to plough on with greater effort. I am particularly grateful for his introducing me to Casemate and there, from the beginning, Clare Litt has shown equal confidence and not a little patience. My editor, Ruth Sheppard, has had to deal with some unfamiliar vernacular and has trusted my guidance fully.

Finally, I must thank my wife Jenny, who has lived with this project for rather too many years and really is the love of my life.

★

I have no doubt that I have missed something here and if any reader can add to this story or correct a mistake in fact I would more than welcome their contribution. Any mistakes within the current text are, it goes without saying, mine.

I owe inspiration for this book's title to Charles Ardant du Picq, the French army officer and military theorist who, as colonel of the 10th Line Infantry, died of wounds received at the battle of Mars-la-Tour in 1870. I was stuck trying to find a phrase that might describe the drum and drummers and the bugle and buglers, and possibly the fife and fifers, all at the same time. Then I came across one of Ardant du Picq's dictums now inscribed above a door at the Palace of Versailles: *L'homme est l'instrument premier du Combat* – Man is the main instrument of Battle.

James Tanner
Armistice Day 2016
Bures St Mary

CHAPTER I

Earlier Times

For if the trumpet give an uncertain sound, who shall prepare himself to the battle?

The drum and the horn, the latter in various trumpet-like guises, are the oldest musical instruments known to man and signalling or communicating a message by means of either are probably as old as the drums and horns themselves. In their natural state – drums made from hollowed-out logs or animal skins stretched over a frame and horns adapted from animal horns and seashells – they were relatively easily obtained by even the most primitive of peoples. Used to amplify the human voice, they lent themselves to religious rituals or to ward off enemies, whether seen or imagined. That they also both readily lent themselves to a military purpose may, therefore, go without saying. As a means simply to put fear in the hearts of foes or courage in the hearts of friends, drums and horns certainly had early military value. These purposes then evolved into a means to encourage a marching army and a beat to march to, to provide communication across the massive din of the battlefield and, in camp, to regulate the activities of the day. The trumpet would appear to be pre-eminent in the ancient world and the Old Testament has a number of references pointing to its military use. The Prophet Moses was instructed in the Book of Numbers that 'if ye go to war in your land against the enemy that oppresseth you, then ye shall blow an alarm with the trumpets ...' And Paul's declamation to the Corinthians in the New Testament has already been seen in this chapter's epigraph. According to the Book of Joshua, the trumpets and shouts of the Israelite army were sufficient to destroy the walls of the city of Jericho. While this cannot be substantiated in fact, such writings certainly serve to support the view that such instruments are almost as old as man himself. There is evidence that drums and flutes date back forty to fifty thousand years. Used in tribal ritual, as man organised himself he would have been quick to realise the value of such instruments in conflict with his neighbours.

The ancient Egyptian armies are known to have combined drum and trumpet, and trumpeters seen in Egyptian works of art are invariably involved in military activities. While their use cannot be ascertained for certain it is believed that Egyptian armies made a great deal of noise with instruments and battle cries as they entered battle and that some simple signals, such as 'advance' and 'retreat', were made by trumpets.[1] The Egyptologist Sir John Garner Wilkinson's various volumes on ancient Egypt, first published in the late 1830s, noted that 'The trumpet was particularly, though not exclusively, appropriated to martial purposes.' Much of his evidence came from the sculptures at the ancient city of Thebes, which show trumpeters in various battle scenes and just one drummer and from which he concluded:

> The only drum represented in the sculptures is a long drum … like the trumpet, it was chiefly employed in the army; and the evidence of the sculptures is confirmed by Clement of Alexandria, who says the drum was used by the Egyptians in going to war. When a body of troops marched to the beat of drum, the drummer was often stationed in the centre or the rear … the trumpeter's post being generally at the head of the regiment except when summoning them to form or advance to the charge.[2]

Two metal trumpets, called *sheneb*, one of silver and one of copper or bronze, found in the tomb of the Pharaoh Tutankhamun in 1922, are inscribed with the names of gods linked to Egyptian martial tradition. Both are modestly sized instruments, a little under 20 inches in length, but capable of producing three or four notes at a surprising volume. This was demonstrated in a live BBC broadcast in April 1939 when Bandsman Jim Tappern of the 11th (Prince Albert's Own) Hussars played them at the Museum of Cairo.[3]

It might seem unlikely, certainly for modern comprehension, but the flute in various forms was also an early aid to signalling in the field and evidence shows that flutes as well as drums and trumpets were used in this manner from early times, whether to signal the impending arrival of an army onto the field of battle or to order some grand movement. All of the ancient Greeks may have used the flute but we know for certain that the Spartans, who dominated Greek warfare for 200 years, preferred the flute to provide martial music to their armies. Their 'flute' was actually a two-pipe reed instrument known as the *aulos* and Nic Fields, in his detailed modern study of the Spartan way of warfare, has written that 'A noteworthy feature of the Spartan battleline ... was that it advanced in an organised and measured way to the wailing music of the *aulos*, flute.'[4] He took as evidence the famous writings of Thucydides, who wrote of the Spartan victory against the Argives at the battle of Mantinea in 418 BC. As battle commenced:

> ... the two armies met, the Argives and their allies advancing with great violence and fury, while the Spartans came on slowly and to the music of many flute-players in their ranks. This custom ... is designed to make them keep in step and move forward steadily without breaking their ranks, as large armies often do when they are just about to join battle.[5]

We can appreciate that the effect was as much psychological as anything else and, while the Greeks as a race had discovered the physical advantage of uniting bodies of lances in the phalanx, the Spartans, with their flutes announcing their 'slow and dreadful advance', had added an ability to strike fear in their foes well ahead of coming to blows. It might be compared to a much later age with the discipline and silence of the British redcoat, of which more anon. The ancient Greek historian Plutarch added that 'It was a sight at once awesome and terrifying, as the Spartans marched in step to the double flute, leaving no gap in their line of battle and with no confusion in their hearts.'[6] It might have been that all organised armies of ancient times, and included in their number are those of the Israelites, Babylonians, Assyrians and Persians, used these instruments mainly as psychological weapons. Scaring the living daylights out of one's opponent even before a physical clash of arms remains a sound principle of war.

The Greeks deployed a second instrument on the battlefield in the form of a long, straight trumpet called a *salpinx*, or 'thunderer', the sound of which has been described as shattering. There is less evidence of how it was used compared to the flute and it is thought that it may have been limited to trumpet calls to initiate a call to battle or an advance, in which case the trumpets would likely have been grouped together for extra effect. Each *syntagma* – the basic unit of the phalanx – included a *salpingktes* (trumpeter) as a supernumerary along with a *semeiophoros* (signaller) and it might therefore be supposed that his function really was to assist with command and control.[7] Evidence is provided by the later Greek author Aristides Quintilianus, but he wrote his treatise on ancient music in the 3rd century AD and referred to the Roman use of the *salpinx*, which is unhelpful. Nevertheless, an idea of the deployment of such trumpets in battle can be ascertained from his description:

> She [Rome] often rejects verbal orders as damaging if they should be discerned by those of the enemy speaking the same language and makes codes through music by playing the salpinx – a warlike and terrifying instrument – and appointing a specific melos for each command. When the attack was by line and the approach was by column, she set down special mele, and a different kind for retreat; and when the pivoting was to the left or right, again there were specific mele for each; and so she accompanies every maneuver one after another by means of codes that are on the one hand unclear to the enemy and on the other hand are both totally clear and easily recognized by the allies. For they do not hear these codes only in part, rather the whole corps follows a single sound.[8]

What is particularly interesting is the point about concealing one's intentions from the enemy by using coded trumpet calls rather than giving away intentions by verbal commands. Two millennia later it was the profusion of bugle calls possibly known to the enemy that gave cause for major restrictions on using bugles in the field, as will be shown.

It should not be a surprise that, given the legendary military organisation enjoyed by later Republican and then Imperial Rome, her armies employed musical instruments for martial use. As with the civilisations that preceded the Roman, it was the trumpet that was used practically exclusively by her armies in the field. Drums seem not to be in evidence in any form and, while we might be forgiven for thinking that the muscled drumbeater of the Roman galleys would bang out the rhythm for 'attack speed' or 'ramming speed', it is the stuff more of Hollywood fiction, good cinema though *Ben Hur* might have been. In ways that would be recognised nearly two millennia later, the late Roman writer Publius Lavius Vegetius Renatus described in his treatise *Epitoma rei militaris* the employment in the Roman armies of three types of trumpet – the *tuba*, the *cornu* and the *buccina*:

> The legion also has its *tubicines, cornicines* and *buccinators*. The *tubicen* sounds the charge and the retreat. The *cornicines* are used only to regulate the motions of the colours; the *tubicines* serve when the soldiers are ordered out to any work without the colours; but in time of action, the *tubicines* and *cornicines* sound together … The ordinary guards and outpost are always mounted and relieved by the sound of the *tubicen*, who also directs the motions of the soldiers on working parties and field days. The *cornicines* sound whenever the colours are to be struck or planted. These rules must be punctually observed in all exercises and reviews so that the soldiers may be ready to obey them in action without hesitation according to the general's orders either to charge or halt, to pursue the enemy or to retire.[9]

Writing even more clearly on the use of the trumpet to govern the activities of the military day, in camp and on the march and in a way that would be familiar to an army in the 17th century and beyond, Flavius Josephus said of the Roman Army in AD 70 that the soldiers' 'times also for sleeping, and watching, and rising, are notified beforehand by the sound of trumpets, nor is anything done without such a signal …' He then went on to explain:

> Now when they are to go out of their camp, the trumpet gives a sound, at which time nobody lies still, but at the first intimation they take down their tents, and all is made ready for the march going out; then do the trumpets sound again, to order them to get ready for the march … Then do the trumpets give a sound the third time, that they are to go out, in order to excite those that on any account are tardy, that so no one may be out of his rank when the army marches.[10]

The signal musicians were called *aenatores* and enough knowledge of the Romans exists to understand that the actual sounds – the calls – made by these trumpeters, whether singly or collectively, were themselves tightly regulated. Forty-three separate calls have been identified and it might be that the legions, or even parts thereof, had their own distinctive calls so that to whom the call was directed could be instantly recognised and acted upon. On the march to battle units certainly repeated their commanding general's trumpet signals on their own *cornus*. But we also know that in the advance to close contact, the Roman legions went forward in silence and at a slow, steady pace in imitation of the Spartan phalanx – a method that could be far more intimidating than a wild charge driven on by a hubbub of trumpeting, drumming and yelling. The modern historian A. K. Goldsworthy has described the moment of battle:

> The Roman advance was normally a silent, steady affair ... Closer to the enemy ... a signal was given to prepare to throw *pila*. It is unclear if this was a verbal order, or a signal on the unit's *cornu*, the unit's horn. Each soldier drew back his *pilum* in his right hand ... On another signal, he would have hurled his weapon at the enemy. This was clearly intended to be an ordered drill carried out under command.[11]

The effectiveness of the Roman Army, its discipline and its complete grasp of the key tenets of command and control – leadership, simple and standardised drills, flexibility and retention of the ability to manoeuvre throughout the battle – is the best chronicled early example of the utility of an effective means of communication on the battlefield, combining the voice of the commander and an audible means of mechanical signalling. The drum was not entirely absent in these times and the Greek-born historian Plutarch, in his life of the Roman General Marcus Licinius Crassus, recorded that:

> The Parthians used hollow drums of stretched hide to which bronze bells are attached. They beat on these drums all at once in many parts of the field and the sound produced is most eerie and terrifying, like the roaring of wild animals with something of the sharpness of a peal of thunder. They have, it seems, correctly observed that the sense of hearing has the most disturbing effect on us of all our senses, most quickly arouses our emotions and most effectively overpowers our judgement.[12]

We need not make too much of the Parthian use of the drum and the fact that Crassus was decisively defeated by the Parthians at Carrhae in 53 BC to prove any superiority of drum over trumpet; it was but an isolated victory against the then might of Imperial Rome; as Aristotle would have said: 'One swallow does not a summer make.' A noteworthy example of a type of trumpet used by peoples who have become known as the 'celts' was the *carnyx*, a large battle trumpet that was held vertically and blown over the heads of troops. A number of these have been discovered across Europe from northern Scotland to southern France and as far to the east as Romania, and there are a number of depictions on Roman coins and on Trajan's victory column in Rome. The most notable and beautiful depiction is on the Gundestrup Cauldron, a large silver vessel discovered in Denmark and thought to date from between 200 BC and 300 AD. The interior shows three *carnyx* players amongst other troops in an obviously warlike array. An early contemporary account by the Greek historian Diodorus Siculus, writing some time between 60 and 30 BC, described the Gauls as having 'trumpets ... of a peculiar barbarian kind; they blow into them and procure a harsh sound which suits the tumult of war.' An earlier Greek historian, Polybius, writing in the 2nd century BC, described the 'terror' of the Romans at the onslaught of the Gallic alliance at the battle of Telamon in 225 BC. The Gauls created a '... dreadful din, for there were innumerable horn-blowers and trumpeters and, as the whole army was shouting their war cries at the same time, there was such a tumult of sound that it seemed that not only the trumpeters but all the country round had got a voice and caught up the cry.'[13]

Trumpets and horns maintained their technical superiority centuries after the Romans had had their day. The late Henry George Farmer, the renowned musicologist, stated that long into the medieval period 'both of these instruments played an important part in time of war, where their potency in conveying signals and in daunting the enemy is often paraded in martial annals.'[14] The drum continued to play little if no part in European armies, even when the concept of nation states began to take form, but it had an important place across the Arab world and Arab use was to influence the Europeans markedly.

The drum had a high and special place for the Saracens and their loss in battle was considered a great disgrace; likewise, the capture of an enemy's drums was a great honour. It would seem that their most important use throughout a battle was to beat as long as the commander and his flags stood firm, thereby signalling to the soldiers that they should keep on fighting. Cessation of the beating would be a clear indication that the commander had fallen and all was probably lost. This practice does not seem to have been adopted by the Crusaders but the use by the Muslim

Arabs of a wider variety of musical instruments in formed military bands did lead to the eventual adoption of these practices in Europe and this does have some further bearing on our main story. These drums were brought back to European countries by returning soldiers and in England the small drum was called a 'naker', a derivation of the French *naccaire*, which had been taken from the Arabic word for drum: *naggara*. A smaller drum still, held in one hand and beaten by a single stick, was the Persian *taburak*, which became the 'tabor' or 'tabour' in England. While the main use for these drums was, certainly initially, to provide stirring musical accompaniment for monarchs and high officials going about their business and pleasure, this gradually migrated from mere pageantry. Edward III, in the first of his great military victories, employed drums as well as trumpets and 'pipes' (that is, flutes), to martial effect against the Scots at Halidon Hill in 1333, an account at the time reporting that 'then the Englische mynstrelles beaten their tabers and blewen their trumpes, and pipes pipedene loude, and made a great chowte upon the Skottes.'[15] The point might have been merely to embolden the English and demoralise the Scots but the drum was now an important part of the field equipment of an English army. Geoffrey Chaucer, writing in the latter half of the 14th century, has told us that, while combinations of instruments such as trumpets, pipes, bells and drums were used by wandering bands of minstrels, they were also 'in the bataille blowen blody sounes.'[16]

There is not a great deal of evidence to tell us exactly how any instrument was used in battle. In legend Roland, champion of Charlemagne, the King of the Franks, used his *olifant* – a ceremonial horn – to summon Charlemagne after Roland's rearguard was betrayed to the Saracens at Roncevaux in 778. Roland, according to the *Song of Roland*, died when he continued to blow his *olifant*, but his king came on with his army, their trumpets announcing their approach and causing the Saracens to flee. The first chronicled evidence of commands being given by trumpet comes from the decisive battle of Bouvines in July 1214 when King Philip Augustus of France defeated the Holy Roman Emperor Otto IV. Roger of Wendover, a contemporary English chronicler (English troops were present on the defeated side), wrote that 'finally, the trumpets sounded on both sides' as battle commenced. And the Minstrel of Reims, writing around 1260, recorded that the 'people of Tournai assembled fully armed with their banners unfurled and their trumpets sounding', the French trumpets later sounding the signal for their final, victorious charge.[17] The least evidence is found for English armies in this whole period. At Stirling Bridge in 1297 it is said that a great blast of his horn signalled William Wallace's attack on the English, but nothing of the English themselves. Most evidence for the later Middle Ages relates to the French but this is helpful if we accept that the English and French armies of the time, their close allies and other foes, conducted themselves on the field of battle in very similar ways. Chroniclers continued to record the use of, mainly, trumpets throughout the medieval period but Jean, or Sir John, Froissart gave a tantalising glimpse of the drum in his description of the Franco-Genoese attack on the Barbary pirate fortress of Mahdia in modern-day Tunisia in 1390. During the approach to the city in the brief Mahdian, or Barbary, Crusade against the 'infidel' defenders, Froissart described the attack on the 'town of Africa' and 'The noise of the trumpets and drums [that] announced to [the defenders] the arrival of the Christians ...', his vivid description, taken contemporaneously at Calais from first-hand accounts, describing too the use of trumpets and clarions (a type of trumpet) in the galleys and ships of the Christian fleet.[18] Of Agincourt on 25 October 1415 the young observer Jehan de Wavrin, son of a Flemish knight who was killed in the battle along with the boy's brother, wrote of the use of trumpets and clarions by the French in their disastrous attack on the English position: 'The Constable [of France] ... and the other princes exhorted their men to fight the English well and bravely; and when it came to the approach the trumpets and clarions resounded everywhere.'[19] This French use of trumpets has long been accepted but Anne Curry, a modern expert on Agincourt, has interpreted de Wavrin as meaning that at this point, when the English army advanced to tempt the French to launch their attack, 'the English sounded their trumpets loudly.'[20] The impact of Agincourt on the English national psyche cannot be underestimated, finding its way most famously to William Shakespeare's *Henry V*, written at the very end of the 16th century. Less well known is Michael Drayton's poem *The Ballad of Agincourt,* written just a few years later. Drayton might well have been influenced by, to him, more contemporary sources, especially in his mention of drums, but his lines, where they impact on our overall story, are still worth showing:

> They now to fight are gone, Armour on armour shone,
> Drum now to drum did groan, To hear was wonder;
> That with cries they make, The very earth did shake,
> Trumpet to trumpet spake, Thunder to thunder.

We might labour a little further with some evidence from the French as it helps complete the picture for the period. David Potter's thorough study of Renaissance France at war contains some extremely useful pages that touch on the whole subject of the use of instruments for military purposes through the Middle Ages.[21] His detailed study notes that 'Music had long played a part in battle, from the "menestrels" of the early Middle Ages' and paraphrases the Italian Renaissance music theorist Giosef Zarlino who, 'in his *Instituzione armoriche* of 1562, remarked that one army could not attack another without the sound of trumpets and drums. Italians, Germans, Swiss and French all used them and they learned from each other.'[22] This is a telling point for the lack of mention of the English, whose armies lost military significance on the European battlefield after Agincourt, consumed as the country was by civil war and religious war for some 150 years. But English and Scots soldiers a-plenty enlisted in foreign armies throughout this time and learnt their business enough for the latest techniques of the battlefield to filter through to the forces of whichever side was in the field in Britain. Potter makes two particularly helpful conclusions, amongst others. One is that war 'From time immemorial was accompanied by noise' and that this appeared to become increasingly so as the Middle Ages progressed, if we are to believe Froissart and other chroniclers. Importantly, there was a point to this din for 'There is evidence enough that by the 14th and 15th centuries a degree of competition in music played a major part in morale boosting and intimidating the enemy (as at Agincourt) and in sieges (as at Melun in 1420 or Neuss in 1474–5).' His second conclusion is that:

> Music was also increasingly used in France in the later Middle Ages as a medium of command and discipline. Froissart evoked a moment which is strikingly close to later modes of command, when 'The trumpets of the marshals sounded after

midnight ... at the second call the men armed and prepared for battle. At the third they mounted up and rode off.' There was nothing new in this.[23]

We might therefore extrapolate further that this use of instruments would also have developed amongst the English, and others. The presence of instruments on the battlefield is clear and it would be wrong to write these instruments off as just a musical accompaniment to the far more serious business of fighting. In simple terms it would seem unlikely that these heavy equipments would have been lugged hither and thither for no better reason than to cheer up the troops or provide a musical backdrop to help drown out the screams of fighting men, as some have postulated. It is likely that their use, limited as it was, was at least to provide the most senior commanders with a means of communicating the most simple and critical signals required, perhaps to halt a vanguard, order a main body to the attack or move a reserve. Henry Farmer was probably correct in stating that 'In the Middle Ages it was the "Kyng's Trompytts" alone that conveyed orders to the armed throng.' He noted that Froissart had written that England's Lord High Constable and Earl Marshal, as King's lieutenants, had trumpeters on their staffs and that during the Agincourt campaign, including at Harfleur, 'there were seventeen of the King's minstrels, under the "King of the Minstrels", a goodly proportion of them trumpeters, present doing fanfare and other services at their old war-service rate of 12d. a day.' That they performed on the morning after the battle we know from the 'old, if not contemporary ballad', as Farmer put it, 'of the "Battallye of Agynkourte," which tells us that "they trompyd up full meryly."'[24] Early trumpets, horns and drums, loud to the ear though they might have been, all had a fairly limited musical range and this, combined with the relative lack of tactical sophistication of most medieval armies would have, in any case, prevented any measure of sophisticated system of communication from developing. These armies often employed flags and banners as additional methods of communicating an order or kept to surer methods of transmitting words of command by use of messengers and the relayed voices of commanders. But we know at least that, during the Hussite Wars of the 1420s and 1430s, the Hussites were known to use their trumpets to sound an attack and their drums to beat the halt. Such was the prowess of their legendary leader, Jan Zizka, that before he died he ordered that his skin be used to make a drum so that it could be beaten as a sign that he continued to lead them in battle.[25]

The true start of the drum's triumph over all others as the principal instrument on the battlefield was a direct result of Swiss tactical innovations during the 15th century. These innovations were to lead directly to the use of the drum in the infantry as its prime means of battlefield communication and of the drummers' ascendance to their special role in all armies of the First World. Farmer, while acknowledging the influence of the Swiss, tended rather more to place the reasoning for this elevation of the drum and, indeed, the trumpet and the flute or fife as actual signalling devices, on a wider resurgence of interest in everything classical during the Renaissance period, including the art of war. Vegetius' maxims, contained in his *Epitoma rei militaris*, certainly appear to have become very influential in military developments in the late 15th and early 16th centuries, and these may have aided the reintroduction of military drum, trumpet and fife players at the lower tactical levels of battalion and company and the use of these 'musicians' as battlefield communicators. Farmer wrote that:

> The textbooks of the art of war of that period are replete with information as to what was required of military musicians. In the Swabian infantry of Maximilian I there were a drummer and fifer in each company of Foot and a trumpeter to each troop of Horse. The drum and fife had been adopted by the famous Swiss troops in the French service, and for a century the Swiss origin of this combination was blazoned in the name of the *Schweizer Pfeife* of the Germans and the *Swache talburn* of the Scots.[26]

But the main answer is much more straightforward and this is where our story really begins, for the manner in which drum, trumpet and flute/fife started to be used at this time would be recognised, with various modifications, over the course of the next five centuries. Simply put, it was the tactics of the Swiss infantry, their discipline and military effectiveness, that led to the universal adoption of many of their methods in other European armies of the time. This period also marked a clear and distinct division emerging between 'true' musicians, even if they could be described as military musicians, and drummers, trumpeters and flautists (or fifers) who were combat soldiers, to use a modern term, in their own right. Potter, taking his evidence from Farmer, has concluded that "'From the late 15th century, although before the era of 'military marches' as understood in modern times, it is clear that drums and fifes played a vital role in the marching order and battle discipline of troops.'[27]

Battle in much of the medieval period had been dominated by the mounted arm. There were some notable exceptions – the English foot at Crécy, Poitiers and Agincourt being perhaps the most famous and certainly the best known to Englishman and Frenchman alike. But for much of the period the infantryman was generally considered a lower class of soldier and the mounted knight the decisive force on the battlefield. The Swiss changed all that in their development of the infantry phalanx, which comprised the combined weapons of pike, polearm, crossbow and firearm and based on the best methods of the Hellenistic *phalanx* and the Roman *maniple*. They also realised that, highly disciplined though they might be, they needed an effective means of communication within the phalanx as well as overall. Written descriptions of the two important Swiss victories of Grandson and Morat in 1476 during the Burgundian Wars detail the make-up of the phalanx and its inclusion, in its centre, of drums and fifes alongside the commanders and their use for signalling on the battlefield. An illustration of about 1485 would seem to confirm this arrangement, showing as it does a drummer and fifer in the middle of a Swiss pike and arquebus phalanx. Moreover, these contemporary descriptions show that the Swiss infantry marched in time to the beat of the drum. We do not know the detail of any words of command or how they might have been transmitted but, submitted to constant repetition of drills, the sounds or calls must have been readily understood by all. Neither do we know, for that matter, why the Swiss chose to give the drum so prominent a part in their tactical methods, as opposed to the trumpet that had reigned for so long. But the drum has always afforded a loud and regular beat and these were large drums, with a diameter of up to two and a half feet. Perhaps more surprising was the incorporation of the flute, but this was a very different instrument compared to those appearing later, often being two feet or thereabouts in length and able to deliver a shrill and very piercing sound. We must assume that it had a technical superiority over the trumpet for the latter to be cast aside.

We are indebted again to David Potter for his thorough investigation of military music during the later medieval and Renaissance periods and his understanding of its effect on the battlefield. Drawing evidence from the French chronicler Jean Molinet, he writes that 'The use of "great drums" by the Swiss suggests the function of rhythmic marching as well as raising the spirits' and that this also began to appear amongst the Landsknecht – the German mercenaries of the Holy Roman Emperor Maximilian I – around 1490. Within the regiments that, for the Swiss, were organised by canton, Swiss and German alike grouped their drummers and fifers as an integral part of each tactical unit's banner party, these *Fähnlein* of between 50 and 150 men each having two drummers and two fifers. Potter quotes Philippe de Comynes, the French diplomat, describing the Swiss troops of the French army after the battle of Fornovo during the First Italian War and how they:

> ... beat their drums during the night. When the army marched out of Fornovo an hour before dawn on 8 July 1495 it did so to the trumpet call of 'Be on guard' but ... there was no other sound at moving off, nor do I think there was any need ... it was to give alarm to the army, at least to men of understanding.[28]

In an effort to improve military efficiency and reduce costs, both problems being inherent in hiring Swiss mercenaries, Francis I of France raised seven provincial legions in 1534. They were not overly successful but their organisation and instructions demonstrated further developments. Each legion consisted of six *bandes* of 1,000 men each and Potter states that every *bande* was to have four *tambours* and two fifers (although R. J. Knecht, in his study of Francis I, gives four fifers rather than two[29]) and that they were to be paid as part of the permanent staff, while the ordinary soldiers were paid only when they were mustered. A document of 1536 – the *Familiere institution* – stated that 'the legions called such musicians "the true joy of the infantryman."' In 1540, Jacques Chantareau, a soldier in the Turin garrison, very helpfully described the infantry on the march:

> Near your standard you should place two drummers and a fife. Of the drummers, one will always be beating, one after another; also after the first three ranks there

should be two drummers who sound all the route of march, and if there are two fifes in the company, one should be there. When the company arrives at its destination, all the drums and fifes should sound.[30]

This is solid evidence of the developing role of drummers and fifers in the ranks of the infantry and begins to provide us with a better feel for their growing importance and how the business of command and control was to be improved. This was also at a time when the professional, disciplined, soldier in large numbers became ever more present in European warfare, and it is not just coincidence that joined him to the 'new' field musicians now showing themselves. These musicians were also becoming soldiers in their own right. Potter cites numerous examples over the whole period of their presence in battles, sieges, marches and assemblies but perhaps his most valuable source is Raymond de Beccarie de Pavie, Seigneur de Fouquevaux, who wrote his *Instructions sur le faict de la Guerre* in 1548. This early book of instructions for his soldiers is of immense value for it set something of a standard and reveals methods that would be similar on the battlefield for the next two to three hundred years. Fouquevaux told his soldiers to: 'Hold ranks steadily in all movement, that is march slowly or quickly; and furthermore learn all the sounds, signs and all the cries by which commands are given in battle and let everyone know their meaning ...' Potter adds:

> He assumes the problem of keeping order in manoeuvre was to be managed by drum beats and it would be drums that would signal advance, halt or retreat: 'the pace of each will therefore follow the beating of the drums, so that all will keep pace together.' ... He notes the common usage of drums for the infantry and trumpets for the cavalry, producing 'sounds to spur on the soldiers when necessary. To this end they were invented to give commands and to be heard from afar.' ... Fouquevaux details some of [the trumpet calls] ... The drummers in turn were to take their tune from the colonel's trumpeters, since trumpet calls were 'heard better' because [they were] 'louder' than drums in a 'great tumult.' This the Swiss, who were the inventors of the 'tabourin', understood.[31]

So successful were the Swiss in battle that their methods were readily copied and exported and it was Henry VII, impressed by the prowess of the Swiss infantry, who first brought the military drum and the fife, in forms that would be recognised today, to England around 1492, Farmer noting that they are mentioned in this year in the King's 'Privy Purse

Expenses'.[32] Indeed, the English military term for the side drum at this time was 'Sweche', meaning 'Swiss', while, as already noted, the Scots were to call their early military drums 'Swasche talburn'. From this time onwards and for nearly half a millennia it would be to the music of drums and fifes (although fifes suffered an interlude of nearly a century) that 'British' infantrymen have trudged many a weary mile and have been instructed, urged and sustained in many a battle.

'Droumes and ffyfers' appear in the musters of the London Trained Bands in the first half of the 16th century and their position and status were consolidated in the armies of Henry VIII. It is thought that Henry had been impressed by the Imperial soldiers of Maximilian I, with whom he was allied at the Battle of the Spurs in August 1513. At some stage in the battle Henry found himself in the midst of a defensive 'hedgehog' of pikemen, whose drummers were beating loudly.[33] The word 'drum' (*drome*, *droume* or *drume* in contemporary spelling) had by now usurped 'tabor', its derivation thought to be an 'onomatopoeic representation of the noise it made when beaten', just as the word 'fife' was derived from the German *pfeiff*, itself 'an onomatopoeia of the sound of air whistling through a hollow tube or pipe.'[34] In Mary Tudor's English battalions at St Quentin in 1557 a drummer and a fifer were attached to each company of foot. An 18th-century historian, Francis Grose, provided an atmospheric description of their deployment:

> In the list of the army employed at St. Quintin's, trumpets and drums were appointed to the different corps, in the proportion of one trumpet to each troop of an hundred men [of horse] ... and a drum and a fife to each company of foot consisting of an hundred men. Besides these trumpets, a drum and a fife made part of the suit or retinue of the great officers.[35]

This was perhaps the earliest example, in English service, of these military musicians being established in pairs in each company, but there is nothing that details their actual employment. What is known is that these first drummers and fifers were more than the battlefield signallers they were to become in the 18th century. Sir John Fortescue, in his great *History of the British Army*, wrote that at the end of the 16th century, the 'two drummers, who, it should be noted, like the trumpeters in the cavalry, were not the mere signal-makers that they now are, but the men regularly employed in all communications with the enemy, and, as such, expected to possess not only discretion but some skill in languages. They received far higher pay than the common soldier, and, if they did a tithe of that which was expected of them, they were worth every penny of it.'[36] Their employment would therefore seem akin to that of the medieval herald and there is at least some association with the decidedly regal duties of the trumpeters of the medieval royal household.

About 1590 there was published a *Treatise of Military Discipline* by one Sir Ralph Smythe and the then duties of drummers and fifers were summed up admirably in its pages; thus:

> All captains must have drommes and ffifes and men to use the same, whoe should be faithfull, secrete, and ingenious, of able personage to use their instruments and office, of sundrie languages; for oftentimes they bee sente to parley with their enemies, to sommen their fforts or townes, to redeeme and conducte prisoners and diverse other messages, which of necessitie requireth language. If such drommes and ffifes should fortune to fall into the hands of the enemies, noe guifte nor force shoulde cause them to disclose any secretes that they knowe. They must ofte practise their instruments, teache the companye the soundes of the marche, allarum, approache, assaulte, battaile, retreate, skirmishe, or any other calling that of necessitie shoulde be knowen. They muste be obediente to the commandemente of theyre captaine and ensigne, when as they shall commande them to comme, goe, or stande, or sounde their retreate, or other calling. Many things else belonge to their office, as in diverse places of this treatise shal be saide.[37]

This is an extremely important passage as it indicates for the first time the full extent of the duties of drummers and fifers and lists the various calls they were expected to sound. It can be safely assumed that these practices were in common usage some time before 1590 for them to be described in a printed work. Two other observations regarding this piece are worth making too. The first, alluded to earlier, is that the drummers and fifers of this period were clearly set above the common soldier (and were paid, as observed earlier, 12 pennies, or one shilling, a day compared to the soldiers' eight pennies) and the second was the special regard in which they were held by both sides in a conflict – a further reflection of their inherited duties of battlefield herald. Both their privileges and their important place alongside their company officers – their captains – at all times are demonstrated in *Compendious Treatise entituled De re militari*, written in London in 1582. This work declared that 'The best Inne or lodging is to be prowided for the Captain, and the seconde is likewise to be given to the Auncient bearer [the ensign], and the Sergeant of the bande [company], next unto them must be lodged the Drumme-plaiers and Fluite.'[38] Over the course of time drummers would lose some of their grander duties and their privileges, but not all. At this time drummers and fifers must have been difficult men to find and enlist in the army, given their many required attributes, and Fortescue, in his *History*, wrote that Henry VIII had had to send to Vienna to procure men of the right quality.[39]

In one hundred years since its first introduction the drum had been established as the pre-eminent musical instrument for use by the English infantry. It was supported by the military fife and the trumpet, but the latter was not viewed as an instrument for the infantry as such, although it was to hold sway in the cavalry and continued, for a time at least, to be favoured by higher commanders, including monarchs. But the drum had established a position here too and such was its importance by the end of this first century of use it had already assumed something of an iconic status. Sir Francis Drake, the English sea captain, took a drum with him when he circumnavigated the world between 1577 and 1580. He continued to have the same drum, emblazoned with his coat of arms, accompany him on all his subsequent voyages. When he died in Panama in 1596 he ordered that the drum be returned to England where, should England ever be in trouble again, the drum should be sounded and he would return to the rescue. In 1897 the poet Henry Newbolt sealed this myth in his famous poem, *Drake's Drum*.

The fife was also fully established as an accompaniment to the drum, having entered the English service some time in the 1530s. Its arrival signalled the removal of the bagpipe from English regiments. While the bagpipe had been a common marching instrument in England and amongst the French and Germans it fell from favour entirely as the fife gained ground, remaining only in Irish service and then being adopted enthusiastically by the Scots. In the days of the Tudors and Stuarts, as with the Swiss earlier, the fife was a cruder and much louder instrument than the small, modern, fife. It was a useful accompaniment to the drum, which was also a much larger instrument than modern drums and, without snares, provided a dull and hollow sound.

A fitting end to this chapter can be provided by Shakespeare, not necessarily for any evidence of historical use of instruments by soldiers contained within his plays but for the fact that he wrote of drums, fifes and trumpets at all. That Shakespeare's theatrical directions to Act II of *Henry VI Part I*, indicate that, before the walls of Orleans, 'Talbot, Bedford and Burgundy [enter] with scaling ladders; their drums beating a dead march' are not evidence as such of the employment of drums in this manner in the English service before the time of Henry VII. But, even if we were to write off Shakespeare's directions as Elizabethan dramatic licence, what this does show is that Shakespeare understood the role of these instruments in the field and this might well have been due to his own experience. Duff Cooper, the Conservative Party politician, wrote an informed and entertaining discourse on Shakespeare's military experience and the effect on his plays in *Sergeant Shakespeare*. Addressing his remarks to 'Diana' (his wife, Lady Diana Cooper), he declared from the start: 'I told you once that Shakespeare had been in the army, that he had served in the Low Countries and had been promoted to non-commissioned rank.'[40] His plays are peppered with directions such as 'Drum sounds afar off – Here sound an English march' (*Henry VI*) and 'Enter with drum and colours' (*King Lear*), so we may assume quite safely that, by Shakespeare's day at least, the drum was a commonplace instrument on the battlefield in his time. The trumpet, it should be said, is even more common in the texts. Othello, the Moor general, may be afforded the final word:

> Farewell the plumed troop and the big wars
> That make ambition virtue! O, farewell,
> Farewell the neighing steed and the shrill trump,
> The spirit-stirring drum, the ear-piercing fife,
> The royal banner and all quality,
> Pride, pomp and circumstance of glorious war!

CHAPTER 2

The New Model

... that upon all occasions you may be ready when the signal shall be given, by the sound of the drumme or trumpet, to repaire to your colours, and so to march upon any service, where and when occasion shall require.

It is fair to say that a revolution in military methods took place in the later Renaissance period. This was not the result of one single factor but a combination of factors and over a number of decades and some of this was identified in the previous chapter. The English national contribution was minor, as has been mentioned. But England benefitted from the changes that were experimented with and fought through, literally, on European battlefields and their lasting effect on English and then British armies by the beginning of the 18th century was fundamental to the eventual supremacy of the British infantry. This will be discussed in the following chapter but for now it is worth focussing on those revolutionary factors as they matured in the latter half of the 16th century and worked their way through to the armies of the English Civil Wars in the middle of the 17th century.

We have already examined the impact of the Swiss and the model initiated by them. The European Renaissance armies all began to appreciate the importance of organisation and training, leading to heightened professionalism and the emergence of national armies on regular pay and terms of service. But in tactical methods there was no great difference between these Europeans and the ancient Romans or Greeks, reliant as they all were on spear or pike blocks and flanking missile-throwers but ultimately requiring the coming to blows at close quarters of a mass of men with edged weapons. The revolution was made more so, and through it the requirement for increased professionalism, by the arrival of hand-held firearms. This was first fully appreciated by the Spanish, whose *tercios* of Spanish and Italian infantry and regiments of German foot held sway through their combination of deep pike blocks, akin to the Macedonian phalanx, and their accompanying 'sleeves' of musketeers. But these were still unwieldy formations, lacking manoeuvrability and under-utilising the infantry's new-found firepower. It was the Dutch, strongly influenced by newly translated Roman texts, who produced a superior tactical formation of shallower pike and shot combinations and greater linear deployments. Their battalion system was advanced by the Swedish brigade system and the best of both were brought together in a German doctrine that became the battle-winning system of the day by the 1640s. These 'fire tactics', while cumbersome to the modern eye, gave the best possible advantage to the firearms of the day and might be seen as the first example of modern battlefield manoeuvre: that combination of fire and movement essential for gaining and maintaining superiority in the field.[1]

England remained abreast of developments but, nationally, lived through a period mainly of isolation while Europe was torn apart by major conflict through the French wars of religion, the war between France and Spain, the Dutch revolt, wars in the Baltic involving Sweden, Russia, Poland and Denmark and the general ruination of the Thirty Years War from 1618 to 1648, to name some. It was the Dutch tactical system that most strongly influenced the English military organisation. The military system within the British Isles at this time, if it can be called a system, was confined largely to local militias but with large numbers of Englishmen, and a number of formed English regiments, serving in the Dutch army. Professional English soldiers thus experienced at first hand the evolution of the various tactical systems and, while Dutch methods guided the training of the English militia at home, including the better trained of the 'trained bands', the German composite system emerged on both sides of the Civil Wars as the preferred tactical method. Overall, as the historian Charles Carlton has observed, 'The tens of thousands of veterans who took part in the Thirty Years' War and then returned to fight in the British civil wars had a profound impact.'[2]

Nevertheless, the overall lack of military experience was very noticeable at the outset of the First Civil War in 1642 and especially with regard to any sort of collective skill above company level. By the time of the creation of Cromwell's New Model Army in 1645 all sides had developed a much higher level of tactical sophistication that, despite the general neglect of the army in the period after the Restoration of 1660, can be seen as an important stepping stone towards a professional British army. As this was the period immediately preceding the appearance of the supremacy of the English line and its fire tactics on the battlefield it is particularly important to our understanding of the use of the drum in the 18th century.

We are helped considerably in our understanding by the appearance, and profusion, of 'drill' books. From early in the 17th century there began to be published military works that gave a far greater understanding of the place of the drum and fife for the regiments of foot, and for the dragoon, who now made his appearance on the battlefield. These works also included instructions on the trumpet used by the horse, but this does not concern us directly. Carlton reckoned there were some 60 drill books or manuals published in England between 1600 and 1634 and a further 37 appearing over the subsequent seven years.[3] One of the more useful appeared in London in 1622 under the title *The Military Art of Trayning*. While there was no such thing during this period as any sort of official training manual for the army – indeed, of course, there was no standing army and largely private arrangements prevailed within the county militias within England – some guidance, written undoubtedly by an officer with much experience of war, would have been invaluable as an aid to training for battle. So, while *The Military Art of Trayning* cannot be taken as official regulation or universal doctrine, its value, like much of what was written and survives over the succeeding hundred years or so, is important to our understanding of the place of the drums and fifes. Of these 'Drums and Phife' it stated:

> There is commonly two Drums to every Company, and one Phife to excite cheerfulness and alacrity in the Souldier: one drum to attend the Colours, another

the Marchings and Troopings as occasion shall call them forth: they had neede be personable men and faithful, expert in Languages, and of good reputation. For they are many times imployed in Honourable Services as summoning the Enemy to a Parley, redeeming and conducting of Prisoners, delivering of Messages, Charges, Retreats, Alarums, summoning to Parleys, Troopings, the stroke for Burials, and suchlike 'Pointes of Warre' necessary to be known.[4]

In the same year Francis Markham published his *Five Decades of Epistles of Warre* and Epistle Five of the Second Decade dealt exclusively with 'Drummes and Phiphes'. Markham very much emphasised the import-ance of the drummer in some splendidly dramatic language:

Valour and courage is necessary in all their employments, for the Drummer's place is ever at his Captain's heeles. It is hee that brings the Battels [meaning, at this time, the tactical formations or divisions of infantry] to joyne, hee that stands in the midst when swords flie on all sides; hee that brings them to pell mell and the furie of execution; and it is hee that brings them both on and off, when they are either fortunate or abandoned or forsaken.[5]

A third example was Henry Hexham's *Principles of the Art Militaire* of 1637. Hexham had served in the Low Countries with the Dutch army for 26 years and he wrote that:

Every company also ought to have two good Drummes, that knoweth how to beate a call, a slow, or a swift march well, a charge, a retreat, and a Reveille: He should also be a linguist, because oftentimes he may be sent unto the enemy, for the ransoming of prisoners, his duty is coming to the campe or garrison of an enemy, having his Generalls passe in his hat, to beate a call, till he is fetcht in, and because he shall not discover the weakenesse of guards, works or trenches, he is led blindfold, and so carried to the Commander, and place where his prisoners are, with whom after he hath ransomed them, he is to returne to the camp or his garrison.[6]

Many of these works appear excessively complicated but they are still important in that they contained the guidance, if not actual approved regulations, for the organisation, training and operation of the regiments of foot as they were to be employed during the Civil Wars. They also, of course, provide further understanding of subsequent developments in the use of the drum and fife. The tactical evolutions of pikeman and mus-keteer of the 17th century were relatively uncomplicated and unhurried, but even so, command and control in battle was hardly straightforward and the noise and confusion on the battlefield gave increased emphasis to the drum to assist the commander. The three publications quoted above make it very clear that each company of foot was expected to have two drummers and a fifer and one, if not both of the drummers, would be stood very close by the captain commanding the company and his ensign, who carried the company colour when every company had its own. If the guidance for the fife given in *The Military Art of Trayning* saw it as largely confined to cheering things up, all three manuals confirmed that one of the main purposes of the drums was to help convey words of command. This point is central to this whole subject: the interaction between the voice of the commander and the sound of some mechanical instrument in assisting with the conveyance of commands and other instructions. It becomes apparent as this story unfolds that the balance between the two changed as weaponry and tactics changed, as might be expected. Commanders at every level would seek to maximise command and control of their troops by whatever means were available and, no matter what any drill book or regulation might have stipulated, this was much easier written than executed, especially on the battlefield.

The point of the matter was described by Captain Thomas Venn in his *Military and Maritime Discipline*. Although appearing in 1672, some two decades after the end of the Civil Wars, infantry tactics were largely unchanged and his advice, given his lengthy military experience from before and during the Civil Wars, remains relevant to this period. Venn noted that 'When by reason of a great noise of guns, men and armes and horses, the commander's voice can neither be heard or obey'd without the beat of a drum, the action of the souldier, whether valiant or otherwise, is to be guided by it.'[7] Venn's point about hearing commands is worth noting for the story of the drum and the bugle in battle was always to be one of finding the right balance between accuracy and confusion. For suppose the drummer were to get it wrong, were to misunderstand the words of his commander? The perils were recognised from the earliest times, which only further emphasised the importance of the drummer in this period. Francis Markham had cautioned in 1622 that the drummer:

> [is] the very tongue and voice of the Commander. He is to have an exceeding careful and diligent ear into all the words of direction (and are called *Vocabula*

Artis) which shall proceede from the Captain, and accordingly to performe and speake it in his beatings.

For to mistake and do contrary as to beat a Retrait when he is commanded to Charge, or to beat a Charge when men are to Retire, were a thing of that danger that the armie might perish by the action.[8]

While so little was written on the drum in battle we can deduce a fair amount from a number of the drill books of the time. A company book of about 1640 described the position of the drummers on the march and gave some indication of their position in battle. Even accounting for its rather archaic language, it is difficult to achieve clarity of intent in the words:

> The first drum[er] beats betwixt the 3 and 4 rank of the first division of muskettiers. The second drum[er] beats betwixt the 3 and 4 ranks of the first division of pikes. Sum causes the first drum beat behind the capitane in the front and the other drum before the enseigne. The drumes beat also in the front but in the sight [meaning when close to the enemy] they must draw asyd to the flankis. The chief drum is to attend the Capitane to delyver his command by tank [tack or tap] of drum quhen the voice cannot be heard.[9]

In referring to a company on the march this book showed that the company was led by its first division of musketeers, with its body of pikes coming next and preceding the second division of musketeers. To place one drummer in the middle of the first division of musketeers and one in the middle of the pikemen and both, therefore, somewhat divorced from their 'Capitane' would not enhance control, unless the purpose of the drummers here is simply to beat a march. It would make far more sense to have one drummer march with his captain and one with the ensign, as the writer then subsequently showed. This drill book also indicated that the drummers stood 'in the front' on the field of battle, probably with their company officers and perhaps beating as loudly as possible, accompanied by the flutes, to daunt the approaching enemy and embolden their own side. Sensibly, the book further warned the drummers to 'draw asyd to the flankis' as both sides closed on one another. Otherwise they would be in the way of their own pikes and muskets as well as in danger of those of their opponents, when they would be needed throughout the battle. This regulation would seem to allude to the practice of centralising the drummers once battle was joined, but it does not make it clear whether all the drummers were centralised or just a number. It would be possible for each company 'captain' to retain one drummer ('The chief drum is to attend the Capitane to delyver his command') while his ensign moved with the second drummer to a central position.

The problem with the detail contained in this drill book is that it dealt exclusively with instructions for a single company of foot which, useful for the purposes of drill, was rarely, if at all, an efficacious tactical unit by itself when in the field. Each company consisted, in theory at least, of two-thirds muskets and one-third pikes, an arrangement common across all European armies. There were nominally ten companies in a battalion of foot, companies being of varying size depending on their commander, whether he was the colonel, the lieutenant colonel, the sergeant major or one of the seven captains (with all ten being referred to as captains of their companies). But a company did not fight as an independent force and, while companies might have drilled on their own, they would have drilled equally as much within their battalion or regiment. Indeed, as Stuart Peachey has observed in his detailed analyses of Civil War tactics: 'There is a strong indication that company and often regimental structures were discarded when forming for battle ... The company, and to a certain degree the regiment, can in reality be, to some extent, viewed as administrative and basic training organisations rather than as necessarily being combat structures.'[10] When it came to forming for battle, the army's field commander would reorganise his available forces to give himself the best tactical combination and, with battalions in the Civil Wars rarely at anything like full strength, he would brigade muskets and pikes in a number of tactical divisions or 'battles', amalgamating battalions as necessary. So, whether a strong battalion maintained its independence or was brigaded with others, as battle was joined all drummers would be centralised to effect greater command and control. For a battalion the drummers (and fifers) would move to co-locate with the colonel's drummer and all of the colours in the centre of the battalion (invariably with the pike block), from where the colonel would control the ensuing activities. From there he would give orders to the assembled drummers, almost certainly through a sergeant drummer or at least the most senior drummer, to beat one of six prescribed 'points of war' or beatings.

There have already been references in this chapter to these beatings or calls and it becomes evident that they were fixed as specific tunes and therefore readily identifiable by those trained to understand them. The phrase 'point of war' appears at least as early as 1578 in a document translated from the French as 'When threatnying trumpet sounde the points of warre.'[11] Some think the phrase applied only to the trumpet but 'to beat a point of war' became common enough after this time and Francis Markham wrote in his *Epistles of Warre* that 'In Horse-Troupes the *Trumpet* is the same which the Drum and Phiph is, onely differing in the tearmes and sounds of the Instrument.'[12] It would appear an unusual phrase, but in music 'point' was defined in the revised (1929) edition of the *Oxford English Dictionary* as 'A short strain or snatch of melody: especially in phrase *point of war*, etc., a short phrase sounded on an instrument as a signal.' Gervase Markham's second, 1635, edition of *Souldiers Accidence, or an Introduction into Military Discipline* described six 'Soundings which we generally call *Poynts of Warre*' as pertaining to the trumpet and for use by the 'Horse-troope'. While they are directed specifically at the trumpet alone, they tell of the development of these calls and their universal application. The language is also entertaining and some of it is worth repeating here:

> The first is − 1. *Butte Sella*: or Clap on your Saddles. Which as soone as the Souldier heareth (in the morning or at other times) he shall presently make readie his Horse, and his own person, trusse up his sacke of necessaries, and make all things fitting for Journey.
> The second is − 2. *Mounte Cavallo*, or Mounte on Horsebacke.
> The third is − 3. *Al'a Standardo*, or Goe to your Colours. Whether it be *Standard*, *Cornet*, or *Guidon*, upon which sound, the Souldier with those of his Fellowship, shall trot forth to the place where the *Cornet* is lodged, and there attend till it be dislodged. Also, this sound in the field, and in service, when men are disbanded, is a Retrayt for the Horseman, and brings him off being ingaged, for as oft as heares it, he must retire and goe back to his Colour.
> The fourth is − 4. *Tucquet*, or March. Which being heard simplie of it selfe without addition, Commands nothing but a marching after the Leader.

The fift is – 5. *Carga, Carga,* or An Alarme, Charge, Charge. Which sounded, every man (like Lightning) flyes upon his enemie, and gives proofe of his valour.

The sixt and last is – 6. *Auquet,* or The Watch. Which sounded at night, Commands all that are out of dutie to their rest and sounded in the morning, Commands those, to rest that have done dutie, and those that have rested, to awake and doe dutie. And in these Sounds, you shall make the Souldier so perfect, that as a song he may lanquet or sing them, and know when they are sounded unto him.

Other Soundings there are; as *Tende Hoe,* for listening, *Call* for Summons, a *Senet* for State, and the like. But they have reference to the greater Officers, and those have no need of my Instructions.[13]

These trumpet calls and their definitions are actually quite different from those applied to drum and fife and seem to have co-existed with the latter, for the aforementioned *Military Art of Trayning* of 1622, in referring to drum calls, indicated that 'The several Beates or poynts of War are: 1 – A Call; 2 – A Troope; 3 – A March; 4 – A Preparative; 5 – A Battalia; 6 – A Retreit' and added that 'Besides these six there are two other beats of the drum: 7 – A Ta-to; 8 – A Revally.' These eight calls do appear to be, given later evidence, fairly standard for the time but it is important to understand here a fundamental principle of any set of instructions: that the definition for any specified call must be clearly understood by all those who should be receiving it. If trumpet calls and drum calls were different, notwithstanding the obvious differences between the two instruments, the differences between the calls had simply to be understood by every officer and soldier, although the word 'simply' might well underestimate the difficulty of putting this into practice. Nevertheless, although it is not stated in any of the books or accounts of this period, any company of infantry drilling independently would, of sheer necessity, conform to the calls of its parent regiment. Going further, given the need to reorganise and amalgamate companies and regiments prior to battle, there must have been a standardisation of calls across an army. This was alluded to in the previous chapter but it is possible that, when referring to the Call, each regiment had its own distinctive sound in order to differentiate between units and prevent one regiment acting on the orders designed for another. But it is more probable that the divisions or battles organised for the fight were allocated a distinctive call once they were so organised, using calls already familiar to the assembled men and to the drummers and perhaps combined with the day's password so that it could not be utilised by the enemy to cause confusion. Each significant signal given to the division thereafter on the battlefield would likely be preceded by the day's distinctive call. This would all negate the need for any system of regimental calls, especially on the field of battle.

By far the most important printed manual at the time of the English Civil Wars and for some time beyond was that of William Barriffe, a Parliamentarian officer who died in 1643. He based his work on his observations of the Thirty Years War and the tactical innovations of the Dutch and Swedish armies. First published in 1635 and going through six editions until its final printing in 1661, his *Military Discipline or The Young Artilleryman* included the most straightforward instructions so far of the various beatings required of the drummers as well as indicating the importance of their clear understanding by the soldiers. The fourth edition, as an example and published in 1643 and thus at the height of the first Civil War and almost certainly used universally by both sides, described these beatings and the reason for them. The six calls that Barriffe detailed actually very closely reflected those laid out in the 1622 *Military Art of Trayning*. In Barriffe's words:

> Our Souldiers being sufficiently instructed in the Postures of such Armes as they carry … the next thing they are to learn is the knowledge of the severall beats of the Drumme, which is as requisite to be learn'd of the Souldier, as any thing else in this way. For the Drum is the voice of the Commander, the spurre of the valiant, and the heart of the coward; and by it they must receive their directions, when the roring Canon, the clashing of Armes, the neighing of Horses, and other confused noise causeth, that neither Captain, nor other Officer can be heard. Therefore it will be necessary that every Souldier should learn these six Beats, viz. 1. A Call. 2. A Troop. 3. A March. 4. A Preparative. 5. A Battell. 6. A Retreit.
>
> By a *Call*, you must understand to prepare to heare present Proclamation, or else to repaire to your Ensigne.
>
> By a *Troop*, understand to shoulder your Musquets, to advance your Pikes, to close your Ranks and Files to their Order, and to troop along with (or follow) your Officer to the place of Rendesvous, or elsewhere.
>
> By a *March* you are to understand to take your open order in rank, to shoulder both Musquets and Pikes, and to direct your March either quicker or slower, according to the beat of the Drum.

> By a *Preparative* you are to understand to close to your due distance, for
> skirmish both in Rank and File, and to make ready, that so you may execute
> upon the first command.
>
> By the *Battell* or charge, understand the continuation or pressing forward in
> order of Battell without lagging behind, rather boldly stepping forward in the
> place of him that falls dead, or wounded before thee.
>
> By a *Retreit*, understand an orderly retiring backward, either for reliefe, for
> advantage of ground, or for some other politicall end, as to draw the enemy into
> some ambushment, or such like.[14]

It might seem that the complications of the battlefield could hardly be
regulated by just six beatings, but they were not in any way intended
to wholly replace the spoken word of command and were developed
as a practicable means of assistance to the field commander. While
we do not know what these beatings sounded like, being just six in
number they would have been simple enough. These drill books do
not provide much further help and, while Barriffe enticingly concluded that 'Much more might be written concerning the Drum,'[15] it
is still not easy to discern from these various instructions exactly how
the drum (and the fife) were used to direct the actions of a body of
infantry in battle. Neither, sadly, do any of the surviving contemporary
accounts. Joshua Sprigge, eyewitness to the battle of Naseby in 1645
and chaplain to the Parliamentarian commander Sir Thomas Fairfax,
provided a detailed account of the battle in his *Anglia Rediva* but, as
Stuart Peachey has observed, it 'tells us almost nothing about the way
the infantry fought. [And] In this Sprigge is typical of the military
commentators of the day.'[16]

Nevertheless, William Barriffe described in Chapter 72 of his *Military
Discipline* how a formed body should prepare for a skirmish, which can
be taken to mean the close contact battle:

> Now the Drums beat a March, the Ensign flying at the head of the Pikes, the
> Pikes and Musquets shouldered, marching at their distance of Order in File, at
> Open-Order in Ranke: presently, by a sign from the captain, the Drums beat
> a Preparative, the Pikes advance, the Ranks close forwards to their order, the
> Musquittiers make ready, and every man prepares himself for Battell or Skirmish.
> And here the eyes of the Drum must be very vigilant to observe his Captain
> or Commander, that by the least signe, either of his hand, leading-staffe, or
> whatsoever else hee carries, he may either continue his Charge, Retreit, or else

Charge home, and every Souldier ought to be so well trained and practised that in the Time of Battell he may receive ample instructions from the sound of the Drum.[17]

What was missing from Barriffe and all the aforementioned manuals was any mention of the fife as a field instrument. There is one important reference discovered by Maurice Cockle who noted that one John Roberts, writing at the same time as Barriffe and Hexham, witnessed 'Certain Gentlemen of the Artillery Garden' taking part in a display of drill at the Merchant Taylors' Hall in London in 1638. Cockle wrote that:

> The march past was followed by the manual and firing exercise, to the time of the fife and drum. There were three calls, the *Posture Tune*, the *Falling Off Tune*, and the *Tune for the Motions*. The Posture Tune … was played during the Firing Exercise, once through to each posture. The Falling Off Tune … was for the Manual Exercise, and was played once to every rank. The Tune for the Motions … was played for all parade movements, such as Facings, Doublings, etc.[18]

A body of opinion has long held that it was the more extremist and puritanical Parliamentarians who banned the fife for its apparent frivolity but the instrument's popularity was already failing and well ahead of its formal removal from the English infantry later in the century. Farmer reckoned that the fife of the time had not commanded universal respect from the outset and used as evidence William Shakespeare referring to its 'ear-piercing' shrillness in *Othello* (*c.* 1596), having already 'pilloried it for all time when he spoke of the "vile squeaking of the wry-necked fife[r]."' in *The Merchant of Venice* (*c.* 1603).[19] The French cleric Jehan Tabourot (alias Thoinot Arbeau), who, in his *Orchésographie* – a study of French Renaissance dance published in 1589 – declared that the fife was to be used for marching only, and 'not on the field'. He added that 'Those who play [the fife] improvise to please themselves and it suffices for them to keep in time with the sounds of the drum.'[20] There had been a corruption of the important drum marches before the onset of the Civil Wars, the proper beating having fallen into decay. In 1632 King Charles I issued a warrant deprecating the 'negligence and carelessness of drummers' in the beating of the English March – 'the march of this our nation so famous in all the honourable achievement and glorious wars of this our kingdom in foreign parts.' To rectify this the Royal warrant expressed specifically:

> Willing and commanding all drummers within our kingdom of England and principality of Wales exactly and precisely to observe the same, as well in this our kingdom, as abroad in the service of any foreign prince or state without any addition or alternative whatsoever. To the end that so ancient, famous and commendable custom may be preserved as a pattern and precedent to all posterity.[21]

But, while the reason for the poor drumming of marches was being placed at the hands of the negligent drummers, Farmer reckoned:

> One suspects that the reason for the desuetude or vulgarization of [the English March] was the use of the fife as an accompaniment to the fundamental drum beats. We read elsewhere that it was customary for fifers to be allowed to play according to their own pleasure, so long as they kept time with the drum. Could it be wondered that drummers should catch the contagion of indifference to note and rote?[22]

There was a growing body of criticism amongst the contemporary military writers, with Francis Markham concerned 'lest the "air of a whistle" should divert the soldier's attention.' 'Yet', as Farmer has concluded. 'notwithstanding the sneers of highbrows and the opposition of commanders, the fife won the ear and foot of the army as an incentive to the march.'[23]

Taking Barriffe's definitions of the six beats of the Drum, his instructions for preparing for a skirmish and what is known of the various tactical motions and manoeuvres of the period, it is not too hard to conjure up a description of the application of command and control and regulation of tactical formations by drum and voice. It is harder to imagine the usefulness of the fife at the same time and, while it might have been a common augmentation to exercising by drum before the Civil Wars, the fife's use on the battlefield for this purpose cannot have survived long.

We can picture that in practice the day of a battle would have begun with the drummers beating reveille to summon the soldiers from their slumber, company drummers taking up the call from those of the senior commanders, perhaps walking their beat on the ground occupied by their companies and through any lodging places that the lucky few had found. More serious intent would have been announced by the beating of the call – a 'call to arms' in other words. At this sound the soldiers of every company would know that they must assemble under their colour and await the orders given by their captain. This might well have been a regimental call or at least a call unique enough for the soldiers to know it applied to them, but once gathered by their captain they would receive the necessary instructions for the forming of the various divisions into which the assembled army would be organised for the coming fight. Perhaps too they would be given the call for that day, by which they would understand that the beatings that followed such a call applied to their division alone. Some idea of the scene unfolding and the seriousness of the tasks ahead can be seen in the famous painting *The Night Watch* or *The company of Captain Frans Banning Cocq* by the Dutch Master Rembrandt Van Rijn. Although this is a Dutch scene and pertaining to one of Amsterdam's notable civic guards, the date – 1642 – and the great similarity of English with Dutch tactical methods of this period makes this a contemporary, relevant and particularly atmospheric rendition. Under their company colour and to the beat of the company drum the musketeers and pikemen assemble round their captain to hear his orders.

The troop was therefore the signal for the assembling of the tactical divisions and at that signal each captain would take his men to their proper place within their allocated division. The beating of the troop is, to this day, associated with some show or display, and in the 17th century would have provided some opportunity for officers to show off their men as they assembled in their proper places. From the beating of the call onwards, and especially from the beating of the troop, there was need for many words of command to have the soldiers carry their weapons as appropriate and arrange themselves in their ranks and files and there was clearly no attempt to use drumbeats to regulate what were necessarily detailed spoken instructions. As the troop progressed the commanders of the divisions would be able to see for themselves what the condition of their assembling men was and make adjustments to their formation, although rank and seniority of the various officers would play their part in the final layout. It is likely too that at the culmination of the troop the drummers would be grouped or massed, as with all the colours, within the pike block of each division. With no requirement for captains to retain their own drummers, the drummers would be grouped and placed so as to have greatest effect and certainly close enough to hear the divisional commander's drummer and repeat his calls.

The divisions in their tactical formations would march forwards to meet their foe on receipt of the word of command and then possibly to the beat of the drum. Barriffe indicated that the speed of the march was regulated by the beating of the drums and companies were to 'March either quicker or slower, according to the beat of the Drum.' There is no particular reason to disagree but, as will be seen in later periods, marching into battle (as opposed to route marching) to the beat of the drum was not, for English and British armies at least, a common practice. And we know that at Naseby the Parliamentarian Army advanced silently and in good order and 'no drum or trumpet was heard'. Barriffe, as we have seen, emphasised the importance of the drum to spur on the valiant and give courage to the heart of the coward, and commanders of English Civil War armies are almost certain to have used drums to these effects. But at the same time the almighty din of massed drums could be a hindrance and the increasingly better organised and disciplined Parliamentarian forces may well have ignored Barriffe's instructions to show their Royalist enemy that they had courage enough. Not for the last time would the theory of the drill book and what was practised on the field of battle differ in application.

The other matter was that of marching in step, something that would seem extremely unlikely and preserved perhaps at most for a formal review or parade of troops, if at all, given the generally low state of training of the armies and the altogether *ad hoc* tactical formations for much of the war. As the march was conducted in open order in rank it was not difficult for soldiers even with pikes to keep their distance from their fellows and not tread on one another's feet whilst still maintaining the tempo of the march, whether or not it was to the beat of the drum. Michael Pfeil, in his excellent little study of drumming in the Civil Wars, has noted that 'Marching in step and at different speeds was definitely known in Elizabethan times' and added that Arbeau had 'described [this] as essential for the orderly marching and attacking of soldiers.' Arbeau had explained 'You will concede that if three men are walking together and each one moves at a different speed they will not be in step, because to be so they must all three march in unison, either quickly, moderately or slowly' and concluded that 'The custom of marching to the drum looks very fine when well executed.'[24] He further explained that a march always began with men placing down their left foot first and, whether marching in step or not, 'The French make use of the drum to beat the rhythm to which the soldiers must march, especially as the majority of soldiers [that] march, are no better trained in this than they are in other branches of the military art.'[25]

Arbeau's *Orchésographie* was much more than a discourse on dance and, accompanied by a number of fine woodcut drawings that depicted various musicians, continues to be a valuable source for understanding military music at the time. The drawings showed drummers with two types of drum, one large and one small, and both long and short flutes or fifes. These drawings were accompanied by some very simple music notations and with these Arbeau intimated that the drum was used as 'a pacemaking instrument ... for marching, attacking and retreating' and that there was no occasion for their use as signalling instruments.[26] Pfeil, having studied all of the contemporary drill manuals and applying a good dash of common sense, has concluded 'that drum beats were not used for initiating drill movements [that is, weapon handling], although some drum signals (preparative, troop, charge) entailed meanings for the posture of the arm (musket and pike) and the distances of the soldiers.'[27]

The first large-scale battle of the Civil Wars took place at Edgehill on 23 October 1642. It was a muddle of a battle, unsurprising given the scant experience of both sides, but has been subject to some detailed study and from this we can draw some fairly accurate assumptions on how the infantry and its drummers operated. The infantry battle was relatively well organised to begin with and a modern account by a trio of Civil War historians – Christopher Scott, Alan Turton and Eric Gruber von Arni – has provided some helpful guidelines for us to create a picture of how the drummers would have operated.[28] We know that the Royalist infantry was formed up in the Swedish manner, with three brigades in the first line and two in the second, each brigade in four 'squadrons' of pike and shot and in six ranks. The Parliamentarian infantry stuck more closely to the Dutch model in two lines of battalions, each battalion being in eight ranks, which was an English variation of the traditional Dutch formation of ten ranks. Parliament's eight ranks gave its infantry a significant advantage in the static firefight in the middle of the battle as this provided for a greater ability to keep fire going.

Sharing a common military heritage, infantry regiments on both sides were organised very largely in the same way. Most commonly the regiments each had ten companies, although pre-war there were examples of regiments with 12 or 13 companies. However many companies, the army of the Earl of Essex, who was the principal Parliamentarian field commander in 1642, was known to have regiments at Edgehill whose companies were of unequal size and this was another common factor. A 1,200-man regiment of ten companies would, in theory at least, comprise the colonel's company of 200, the lieutenant colonel's company of 160, the sergeant major's (meaning 'major's') of 140 and seven captains' companies of 100 men each.[29] However, Civil War regiments rarely, if ever, reached anything like these numbers. Each company had its own colour, which conformed to a regimental design, and two drummers, with a drum major on the regimental staff. The drummers appeared on the muster rolls of the time but, while the presence of fifers is known, the latter appear to have had no formal status and may well have been appointed and paid for personally by their colonels. Nevertheless contemporary statuettes representing soldiers of the trained bands of about 1638, which are on display at Cromwell House, Highgate, include a fifer as well as a drummer.

The Earl of Essex produced a set of orders for his army at Worcester a month before the battle that set down a number of principles for how he wished the army to be handled. This chapter's epigraph is part of one of eight specific articles contained in these orders and, in reproducing the article in full below, it is also worth providing some important elements of the Earl's preamble. While the orders contain no detail about how the army was to be organised and fought they do demonstrate, even in their gentility, some evidence of the then concepts for tactical manoeuvre. The Earl began:

> 1. ... I shall desire all and every officer to endeavour by love and affable carriage to command his souldiers, since what is done for fear is done unwillingly, and what is unwillingly attempted can never prosper. Likewise 'tis my request that you be very careful in the exercising of your men, and bring them to use their armes readily and expertly, and not to busy them in practising the ceremonious forms of military discipline, onley let them be well instructed in the necessary rudiments of warre, that they may know to fall on with discretion and retreat with care, how to maintaine their order and make good their ground: also [that they] should answer my expectation in the performance of these ensuing articles. ...
> 2. That you take special care to keape your armes at all times fit for service, that upon all occasions you may be ready when the signal shall be given, by the sound of the drumme or trumpet, to repaire to your colours, and so to march upon any service, where and when occasion shall require.[30]

When the time came for the Royalist infantry to attack at Edgehill, Sergeant-Major General Sir Jacob Astley, having uttered his famous words 'Oh Lord, Thou knowest howe busy I must be this day. If I forget Thee, do not Thou forget me' rose to his feet and cried 'March on boys!' Scott, Turton and von Arni felt, from the evidence available, that the advance would have been preceded by 'A preparative roll ... sounded from the drums of each of the five brigades followed shortly by each unit stepping off in their own time to begin the advance on the Parliamentarian line "with a slow and steady pace and a daring resolution"'. It was much more likely that what was beaten was the march as prescribed by Barriffe, rather than the preparative, as the march was the proper beat to initiate the advance. It was well understood that control and order were fundamental to achieving victory in the infantry fight and that this fight would likely decide the whole matter. Whether this decision would be achieved by fire superiority or the brute strength of 'push of pike', or a combination of the two, keeping each unit together and maintaining the cohesion of the whole were critical. An infantry attack, if unmolested by cavalry or dismounted dragoons, had little to stop it given the meagreness and very slow rate of fire of cannon and the short range of temperamental matchlock muskets. But once close in, to below one hundred yards, musket fire by well-drilled troops would tell. Scott, Turton and von Arni reckoned that:

> It would have been impossible to co-ordinate the stepping off of individual regiments, let alone those of an entire brigade, although some cohesion may have been achieved with the help of the drums beating a regular rhythm, their cadence swinging into the period march-pace of around seventy to the minute. There appears no evidence to suggest any attempt was made to have the men march in step although there would be a natural tendency for the body to fall in with the beat and rhythm of the drum.[31]

It might have been that, given the very steadiness of the Royalist advance, with regular halts and dressing of ranks, and 'the effect of the merging rhythm of the various company drummers [which would] have told on the soldiers' corporate feeling of togetherness ... whole regiments marching to the same step may have been achieved.'[32] But no evidence has emerged either way that the men marched in step, or even tried to, and it seems unlikely. They were vastly inexperienced soldiers, the ground crossed was difficult and broke up formations, and the very business of halting to keep formation would have disrupted the march and the rhythm. Even if a regiment, or even just a company, could keep its own drummers in hand to maintain a step, further disruption would have been caused, especially to inexperienced soldiers, by the noise of drummers from adjacent units. But it must have been an imposing and daunting sight nonetheless, added to by the large number of colours, the noise of the drums and fifes and the likely chanting of the Royalist foot. They took their time and then halted again for the final time, beyond effective musket range (so about 100 yards out) to bring all five brigades into line – 'all in Front' in the words of the official account of the day.[33] There was no identifiable drumbeat so the word of command to halt would have been bellowed at the appropriate moment and repeated across the brigades.

Then would have come the preparative, which would have initiated the attack proper. The six-deep Royalist foot would have marched forward again and for the next 60 to 80 yards, the pikemen – by now carrying their pikes – levelled, or 'charged', while the musketeers stepped out by each rank in turn, firing a volley and then halting or slowing to allow the next rank forward to fire. This was a complicated enough movement by experienced troops and reloading in this situation would also seem highly unlikely. They were met by the Parliamentarian foot, maintaining its ground by each rank of musketeers, having fired, turning and moving to the rear to reload while the next rank stepped forward. Again, the advance continued to be slow and methodical, the maintenance of formation being even more critical at this point for any chance of victory. Assuming Parliament's infantry did not flee, which it did not, the matter would be settled ultimately by mass and stamina. This final advance was almost certainly accompanied by vigorous drumming, essential now to maintain rhythm and momentum, and just some 20 yards or so out the order would have been given to beat the 'Battell', or charge, and 'fall on'. There might have been time for a final salvo of shot by the Royalist infantry but the 'Battell' was the signal to increase pace and bring pikes and clubbed muskets crashing into the stationary Parliamentarians. It is likely that the 'Battell' continued to be beaten, and perhaps by both sides, while the melee continued so that those in the midst of it could be confident that their side had the uppermost hand. If that were the case though, the call would have needed to be distinguished between one another in some way. As these slogging matches could go on for some time, with elements of each side drawing back, battalion by battalion, to fire a salvo or to bring their pikes crashing into their foes once more, the 'Battell' might have been preserved for each renewed clash. And when the Parliamentarian foot did, eventually, gain that upper hand, the Royalist commander would have had no option other than to order the 'Retreit' to be beaten to pull his surviving men back in as orderly a manner as possible.

As the Civil Wars progressed the tactical adeptness of the armies improved, more so for Parliament than for the King. One of the valuable letters of Neremiah Wharton, a sergeant in Denzil Holles' Parliamentarian regiment of foot, described a number of details of the battle of Naseby, fought on 14 June 1645. This, the decisive engagement of the First Civil War, demonstrated the supremacy of Parliament's New Model Army. The forces of Parliament had been gaining the upper hand by 1644 but failure to exploit tactical victory at the Second Battle of Newbury in

September 1644 demonstrated once and for all that Parliament's armies needed major reorganisation if they were to win the war. The result was the New Model – a national army under Sir Thomas Fairfax that proved to be the foundation of Britain's standing army. From Wharton's letter we can deduce that the infantry of both sides were well-handled, with the more experienced veterans of Sir Bernard Astley's Royalist foot gaining the upper hand early but not being able to break through to the second line of the well-disciplined Parliamentary foot. Sir Philip Skippon, who commanded the latter, had initially partially concealed his foot behind high ground. Then,

> Upon the Enemies approach, the Parliaments army marcht up to the brow of the hill, having placed a Forlorne of Foot (musquetiers) consisting of about 300. down the steep of the hill towards the enemy, somewhat more than Carbine shot from the Main battail, who were ordered to retreat to the battail, whensoever they should be hard pressed upon by the Enemy.[34]

We have no detail of any signals or uses of the drum during the battle but we might suppose something along the lines of what was described earlier. We might even imagine that Skippon's forlorn hope was ordered to make its timely withdrawal in the face of the Royalist foot by a pre-arranged drum beat. We know at least that the attack by Henry Ireton's Parliamentarian cavalry on the left, the defeat of which so nearly created the conditions for a Royalist victory, was 'sounded [by] a Charge ...'[35] One final piece of evidence, albeit a snippet, does show that drums were at least present on the field. Joshua Sprigge, chaplain to Fairfax, wrote, in 1647, his *Anglia rediviva: being the history of the motions, actions and successes of the army under the immediate conduct of His Excellency Sr. Thomas Fairfax*. In describing the attack of the New Model Army on Bridgwater on 20 July 1645, Sprigge, as related by Charles Carlton, recorded that "'Mr Peters preached a preparatory sermon to encourage the soldiers to go on." ... Then, after another homily from the Reverend Bowle, the drums beat, the troops attacked, and with "fresh exhortation to do their duties with undaunted courage and resolution' from the indefatigable Mr Peters, the Roundheads took the town."[36]

The Civil Wars were fought to their conclusion in 1651. Despite its hard-won and new-found professionalism the New Model Army eventually fell victim to the stigma associated so closely with the Commonwealth and the perception of dictatorship of the Lord Protector. When the monarchy was restored in 1660 there was a determination by Parliament to destroy Cromwell's army. But a good degree of sense prevailed and sufficient elements survived to create the foundation stones of a standing army. That military professionalism had also found its way into the ranks of the army's drummers and their roles and responsibilities were to expand, with them becoming one of the best recognised symbols of the British soldier in the centuries to come. The oft-assumed dignity of the drummer of the time and later was no better demonstrated than at a military funeral, the simple solemnity of the music played adding much to the solemnity of the moment. When a Royalist officer died in battle in 1643:

> They buried him in a warlike manner, with his sword upon his coffin, and a drum beating before him to the church, where he was buried … men giving two volleys of shot there for him and afterwards the same drum beat before them home again.[37]

CHAPTER 3

The English Line

Drum and drummer were in the centre of every British square in Marlborough's day. The drum taps carried the orders to the soldiers in the line and the sound of the drumming behind them gave them the encouragement and strength required to face and overcome the fears and horrors of the battlefield.

The above epigraph was penned by His Royal Highness The Duke of Kent as part of his preface to Hugh Barty-King's *The Drum* in 1988. In these simple lines he described the place of the drummer and his drum in the heyday of the instrument in the British Army in the 18th century. This chapter seeks to show how the drum attained its position in the 100 years or so from the formation of a full-time, Regular, army through to a peak of professionalism at the end of the Seven Years War. This period coincided with the early and continued supremacy of the English line in battle and this had an impact on our main story as will be shown.

While the origins of Britain's professional army can be found in Parliament's New Model Army, 1660 marked what is acknowledged as the founding of the Regular army. While a few regiments can claim their date of formation as being earlier – the oldest was the Holland Regiment, raised in 1572 and later becoming the 3rd Regiment of Foot – 1660, the year of the Restoration of the English monarchy, is generally recognised as the British Army's year of birth. That army continued to enjoy if not a poor reputation then poor comparison to other European armies of the time but this was to change markedly in the first decade of the 18th century. During the course of that century the 'English' infantry achieved a formidable reputation and one that it has on the whole maintained. By 1706, four years into the War of the Spanish Succession, King Louis XIV of France cautioned Marshal Villeroi before his defeat at the battle of Ramillies that May, to 'Have particular attention to that part of the line which will endure the first shock of the English troops.' Against Villeroi stood the English line under General John Churchill, 1st Duke of Marlborough. Two years before, at Blenheim, 'Corporal John' and his English infantry, despite their small numbers, had secured their respective future reputations.

While the drum was not the panacea for command and control that it can be made out to be, as an instrument of battle and supported at various times by the fife, the 18th century did indeed witness its heyday. The drum's effectiveness was enabled by the tactics of the time. Certainly in the years after the restoration and during the first half of the century up to and including the Seven Years War (1756–63), the regulated, rather stilted, manoeuvres and close-order motions of the men, and the relatively short distance between one unit and another, allowed command and control by beat of drum to remain practicable. Movements of troops on the field also tended to be in full view of an opponent's army, success being dependent upon the skilful handling of battalions and brigades by the army commander and his ability to take advantage of his opponent's mistakes. Marlborough created success in this way, combined with the only major tactical innovation of the time – the platoon fire system. This is not to say that regiments of foot were otherwise handled in battle through hide-bound and unresponsive manoeuvres. The impression has been gained of this time of lines of redcoats being driven unintelligently and inflexibly towards the cannons and muskets of their enemies. But it is a false impression overall, driven largely by the strategic failure experienced in the later American War of Independence. The various drills and evolutions of the infantry were certainly a slow and seemingly complex process, if we are to believe the drill books. But intelligent, tactical manoeuvres by often well-led infantry developed over the decades by dint of evolving practice and practical experience, the British becoming particularly adept at combining firepower and movement.

An evolution of tactics also took place as a result of experience outside Europe and especially to meet the conditions of fighting in North America, where regiments of foot were trained to move and fight in open or extended order and appreciate the utility of skirmishing. At the same time the drum's utility began to wane. Experience in the fight against Frenchman and Indian in North America up to and during the Seven Years War had initiated some changes but it was not until the struggle with the American colonists that the horn, or bugle, began to make its appearance among light infantry in the late 1770s. It eventually superseded the drum for signalling purposes in all regiments in the 19th century, though the drum still had a place, if diminished, in the battle line. Evidence shows that, as a signalling device, the drum had had its day by the time of the Peninsular War.

But the drum dominated through much of the 1700s, its beat enlivened in the second half of the century by the reintroduction of the fife. The publisher's introduction to *The Drum* accurately summarised the story of

> ... how the colonel depended on his drummer to beat out his commands to the front line, to keep the drum rolling to tell them the colours were safe; to walk fearlessly towards the enemy beating a chamade to seek a parley; to raise morale on the march; and in garrison to beat the Camp Calls that signalled the sequence of events, to stir the spirit on ceremonial parades, to mark with muffled drumhead solemnity of burial, to humiliate with the Rogues March the offender drummed out of the regiment; to administer the flogging by which the colonel kept discipline; to help Recruiting Sergeants enrol villagers at the market cross By Beat of Drum; to warn shopkeepers against giving soldiers credit and see their debts were paid.[1]

Generally speaking this was how drummers were utilised throughout the period covered by this chapter and for some years beyond. Together with the fife, referring to these two instruments as 'music' was absolutely correct for it was the only music available to the army at this time. This book has just cause to make a clear distinction between drummers and fifers on the one hand and bandsmen on the other but that distinction was not so clear in the latter half of the 17th century. What might be called proper bands of music with instruments other than the drum began to appear from the 1760s onwards. But eighty or ninety years earlier drums and fifes were joined by increasing numbers of oboes, variously referred to as *hoboys*, *hautbois*, or *hautboys* at the time. This demonstrated their French origin and French influence on King Charles II, who had these instruments introduced to his army and who may be seen as the instigator for the establishment of the first bands of music. These *hautboys* began to appear on the establishments of regiments of dragoons in the 1670s and about 1678 the Horse Grenadiers − mounted troops of newly raised grenadiers attached to troops of Horse Guards − were shown as having two drummers and two *hoboys* per troop. The oboe 'then found its way into the foot guards and regiments of infantry, and completely ousted the fife from its old position.'[2]

The oboe had no signalling purpose and could only have been introduced to provide musical augmentation to the drum. We must not, however, think of the oboe at this time in a modern sense. Farmer declared that 'we must remember that the oboe of that period was a very coarse thing compared to our modern instrument … Such an instrument was well adapted to military purposes … and gave a tone louder than all other instruments, except the trumpet.'[3] The complete replacement of the fife by the oboe would suggest that the fife had no or very little practical purpose other than musical accompaniment to the drum on the march or on parade. This statement adds further substance to our consideration in the previous chapter of the disappearance of the fife. There is some possible substance in attributing this to the more extreme Puritan elements who dominated the years of England's republican Commonwealth between 1649 and the Restoration and who considered all musical instruments as frivolous. Farmer observed that, while many Puritans viewed music other than psalms and hymns as profane, 'the army … could not very well dispense with such important offices as the trumpeter and drummer, upon whom they relied for their "sounds" and "signals" … [but] That almost indispensable appendage to the march − the fife, was banished from the service.'[4] Whatever the reason, the fife had disappeared as a military instrument by the closing years of the 17th century, having been entirely usurped by the oboe. The status of the oboe players is not clear but it might be assumed that they enjoyed a similar ambiguous status as bandsmen when bands were first authorised. Their numbers are, therefore, also difficult to ascertain but early evidence shows that the 1st Regiment of Foot Guards was authorised by Royal Warrant to have 12 *hautbois* on strength in 1685.[5]

Between the Restoration and the War of the Spanish Succession the English army was not idle and a short review of this period, albeit over-simplified, helps to set the scene and explain why Dutch military methods were an early influence. The army was hamstrung for some time by politics and the determination of Charles II to destroy the Cromwellian army and James II to return his kingdom to Catholicism. But under William III, once he had secured the throne and destroyed the Jacobite threats in Scotland and Ireland, the army began to build its skills as it became increasingly engaged on the European continent against the expansionist policies of King Louis XIV of France. In the final years of the Stuart kings English soldiers had been involved in various ventures as England's first empire began to emerge and garrisons had been established in Virginia, New York, the Caribbean and Bombay. English troops also supported Portugal as she fought successfully to separate herself from Spain. And English, Irish and Scottish regiments also fought for their king in the service of France. But with the Glorious Revolution of 1688 came the beginning of real political and religious stability and the affirmation of lasting alliances. It was in Flanders during the Nine Years War between 1688 and 1697, where William used his army in support of the Dutch, that an English-cum-British fighting tradition emerged. It was in this final decade of the 17th century that England began to emerge as a great power and the war proved to be for the army a 'worthwhile apprenticeship. When Marlborough took over command in 1702, the British army knew its trade well enough to take on the armies of the great powers of Europe on equal terms.'[6]

Infantry tactics evolved gradually over the 40 years that separated the Restoration from the ascendancy of Marlborough. The matchlock musket and pike combination gave way equally gradually to flintlock and bayonet so the infantry continued to be guided by what lessons could be remembered from the Civil Wars. Later editions, the last in 1661, of William Barriffe's *Military Discipline* and of Lieutenant Colonel Richard Elton's *The Compleat Body of the Art Military*, first published in 1649,[7] remained highly influential. Whether exercised using Barriffe's guidance on formations of eight ranks or Elton's six ranks, the fire effect of infantry was on the increase and the position of honour of the pikeman began to give way to the technical expertise of the musketeer. He was increasingly armed with the flintlock, or firelock as it was more commonly known, even before the invention of a practicable bayonet. Barriffe's and Elton's were never official works and the extravagant verbiage of the latter must have tested even the most enthusiastic of soldiers. The text, for all its lengthy dissection of postures, positions of dignity, doublings, wheelings and the many various ways to draw up a regiment in the field, gives little clue to fighting a battle. But Elton, while he appeared to assume a degree of tactical knowledge from his readers – for example, he did not provide any detail about the meanings of the various beatings for the drum – did provide some useful guidance on command and control during what might best be described as the approach to and engagement in close combat; the 'Battail' in the continued common vernacular:

> Having thus briefly set down severall *firings* … with their uses either marching, or standing, I hold it convenient in the next place to give some short directions in time of Battail, both to the Officers, and their Souldiers.
>
> First, that the *Drummers* have a vigilant eye upon their Commanders, whose voices are drown'd by the loud thundering of the *Cannon,* or *Muskettiers,* as also by the *neighing* of Horses, or the lamentable cries of the *maim'd* and wounded Souldiers, at which time the *Leaders Staffe, half-Pike,* or whatever he carries in his hand may be sufficient for to inform them to continue their charge, retreat, or else to charge home.
>
> … Fourthly, their [that is, the soldiers'] eyes ought likewise in times of Battail to be fixed stedfastly upon their *Captain,* always conforming to him in Posture when he shall prepare to charge or retreat, and likewise they ought to be knowing and well verst in the severall *beats* of the *Drum,* which if well observed by all, there would not be so much confusion in time of Battail amongst them, as many times by sad experience hath been found, when disregarding their Officers commands, and the beating of the *Drums,* they ignorantly and [illegible] run on in a disorderly manner.[8]

This passage appears to assume a common understanding of what the 'Battail' entailed and that the drummers were expected to recognise at all times, by observing their commanders, what was required of them in the various beatings and despite the cacophony of the moment. It states explicitly too that all soldiers needed to understand and act upon the beat of the drum.

Elton did not say very much at all about the role of the drummer in either regulating the day or on the march. But there were some useful, if brief, words on the position of the drummers when companies were organised for the march and when they were formed 'a Brest', that is, in line. Here they were placed in pairs in the front rank either side of the central division of pikes, thus flanked by the left and right divisions of muskets, if, of course, this was how the company was itself organised.[9] As to the actual number of drummers in a company – and the emphasis on company organisation has to be seen in the light of it being the essential building block of the battalion/regiment – Elton provided somewhat contradictory evidence. Being in pairs either side of the pikes would imply four drummers in the company while his diagram for the march showed three, with one behind the second rank of the three divisions.[10] It does appear that around the time of the Restoration and for some years after, companies of foot did have as many as three drummers on their establishment but there is also evidence that three drummers were allotted to the colonel's company, it being larger in numbers of men, while the remainder had two drummers. The Lord General's Regiment of Foot was shown in the Army Establishment of 1661 as having three drummers for each company, each drummer receiving three shillings pay a day, a tidy sum at the time. The regiment is significant in that it was the one regiment of the New Model Army retained by the Crown, its colonel being General George Monck. The regiment attained the title of the Coldstream Regiment of Foot Guards upon his death in 1670. The British Museum has in its collection a drawing of the funeral of Monck as the Duke of Albermarle, showing four drummers and a fifer, but this should not be taken, necessarily, to indicate their numbers in a company. Within a few years the establishment appears to have settled at two drummers per company, generally coinciding with the reduction of companies in each regiment from 12 (13 when the grenadier company was added in 1677/78) to ten, when the pike was finally abolished around 1706. Details for the English regiments at the battle of Almanza in Spain in 1707 show that three of them were still on the 13-company establishment and therefore had 26 drummers in total on the strength.[11]

That the ten-company establishment, which prevailed throughout much of the 18th century, permitted two drummers per company is amply demonstrated in contemporary inspection returns. A review of five regiments of foot (3rd, 4th, 11th, 12th and 13th) in 'North Britain' for 1738 showed 20 drummers on the strength for each regiment.[12] However, it should be noted that battalions on the Irish establishment were considerably weaker than those in Britain and on active service – just 297 men compared to 497 respectively, until both were brought onto the same establishment of 442 in 1770. As both establishments maintained the same number of companies the number of drummers in an 'Irish' regiment totalled just nine until 1770. Inspection reports for the 38th Foot showed that the regiment in Ireland in 1769 had nine drummers on establishment, and two of these were away on 'recruiting duty', while in 1771, still in Ireland, the establishment had been raised to 20, and 'mostly boys'.[13] Battalions were reduced to nine companies (eight 'hat' companies and one grenadier) by the time of the Seven Years War, but the number of drummers remained fixed at 20 (and nine for the Irish) and this met the needs of the expansion in companies when a tenth, light, company was added in 1771 (1772 for Ireland).

Mention should also be made here of the emergence of drum majors in the infantry. Barty-King has recorded that one 'Gerat Barry referred to one in the *Militarie Discipline* he wrote in 1634 … [and that] Sir John Hepburn certainly had one in his regiment in 1637.'[14] While their principal job was to 'appoint, train and superintend the regiment's side-drummers'[15] they appear in contemporary records to have had much more authority than that held by their senior non-commissioned officer descendants in the 19th century and beyond. Similarly a regiment's sergeant major, in his original form, held a position that can be likened to an adjutant or a chief of staff. The drum major would stand with the regiment's colonel and alongside the senior drummer so that both could act immediately on the colonel's orders as required. Drum majors were finally ordered to be on the strength of all regiments in

1659 and Elton, in his second edition of the *Art Military* published that same year, wrote:

> There ought to be in every Regiment a Drum Major, being skilfull in his profession, instructing the others in the true beating of a march, with all other points of war. A Drum-Major must likewise be well skill'd in severall languages, and tongues, and to be wise and courteous when he shall be imploy'd or sent to an enemy; He is in a discreet manner upon the marching of a Regiment to order part of the Drums where they shall beat, seeing them timely and duly relieved by the others for the better performance of their service. For upon the march if all the Captains Drums should beat together, it would quickly tire them out ...[16]

Elton also provided guidance on all the duties expected of every rank in a regiment, including the drum major just described and, in considering drummers, noted that 'Every Captain ought to have two good Drummers that know how to beat the several points of war before mentioned.' It was in this section that he noted 'A Private *Souldier* ... upon the beat of the Drum ... is to repair to his Colours ...' and 'He must informe himself of all the severall beats of the drum, as first of a Call, second a Troop, third a March, fourth a Preparative, fifth a Battle or Charge, sixth a Retreat, and also of the Revalley and the Tattoo.'[17] This was very similar to Barriffe's list but it should be noted that in defining the 'Battle' further as a 'Charge' (Elton changed the spelling of the word 'bataill' to 'battle' in his third book) he did not mean the final rush at the enemy at a fast pace or run but rather that quickening of pace with pikes levelled (that is, 'charged') and muskets ready to give their final firing or clubbed, ready to lay about their foe. Another writer, Captain Thomas Venn, who had considerable military experience from before and during the Civil Wars, wrote in his *Military and Maritime Discipline* in 1672 perhaps the clearest description of the six essential beatings:

1. *A Call*: By a call you must understand to hear your present engagements [that is, orders].
2. *A Troop*: Shoulder your muskets, advance pikes, close ranks and troop along [that is, follow] your officer to the rendezvous.
3. *A March*: By this you understand to take open order in rank. Shoulder muskets and pikes. To direct your march quicker or slower according to the beat.
4. *Preparative*: Close to due distance for skirmish in rank and file, to make ready that you may execute on first command.

5. *A Battle*: Battle or Charge. Pressing forward in order of battle, without lagging behind, rather boldly stepping forward into the place of him who drops dead or wounded before thee.
6. *A Retreat*: Understand an orderly withdrawal backward for advantage of ground or other politic reason, to draw the enemy into some ambushment or the like.[18]

Venn is particularly important and we might also see his writing as an accurate description too of battle in the Civil Wars. His *Discipline* contained the clearest evidence of soldiers at this time marching into battle at the beat of the drum, as described for the 'march', and that the beat could be quickened or slowed according to circumstance. That there were just six basic orders regulated by drum beats would help to emphasise the relative simplicity of battlefield tactics for the period being considered. In practice, of course, battles were never simple and Venn and all the authors mentioned above could describe how things ought to be but the reality would be very different. Nevertheless, the writings do suggest that trained soldiers could manoeuvre to beat of drum as the voice of the commander, albeit the actual voice was just as important if it could be heard. Venn emphasised further that it was every captain's duty 'to teach his souldiers distinctly the several beats of the Drum that they may be better able to perform their respective duties whenever they shall be commanded by the drum.'[19]

The drummers themselves continued to be, or were meant to be, quite different to those who were to make their mark under Marlborough and beyond. They were certainly not young boys, given their extra responsibilities, but still maintained the role of messenger and herald. These roles were detailed in the previous chapter and their continuation into the later decades of the 17th century were described by Elton:

> It is likewise expedient that he should be a good linguist in respect sometimes he may be lent unto an enemy for the ransoming of prisoners. His duty is coming to the camp, or garrison of an enemy, having his Generals Pass in his hat to beat a call, till he is fetcht in, and because he shall not discover the weakness of guards, works, or trenches, he is led blind-fold, and so carried to the Commander, and place where his prisoners are; With whom (after he hath ransomed them) he is to return to his own quarters, giving an account of such things he hath seen or heard, which may prove advantaged to his own party, or of any other thing he had opportunity by their neglect to take notice of.[20]

Before it fell entirely out of use at the end of the 17th century, the fife continued to accompany the drum in the beatings. Drum and fife combined, and voice of course, were thus used 'to synchronise those motions in exercises for which our pikemen and musketeers were famous' and, importantly, 'to enliven and regulate the march.'[21]

As the drum increasingly came into its own the number of beatings used to enable a unit or larger formation to manoeuvre in the field were expanded. The use of the drum to regulate the soldier's day also expanded and the earliest evidence of it governing the domestic circumstances prevailing in encampments and garrisons was in the daily procedure of beating reveille and retreat. Hexham made the point in 1637, described in the previous chapter, about the requirement for drummers to beat the reveille to order the troops to rise and the daily routine to begin. Elton, as shown above, recorded the necessity of beating the 'Revally and the Tattoo', the latter to mark the end of the day, at least as early as 1659. But the first recorded mention of beating a retreat, as distinct from beating the retreat as a point of war, was around 1690, although the beating of the tattoo then meant much the same thing (both terms appearing to be interchangeable in this period) was mentioned by Venn in his 1672 work. Retreat in this context was beaten originally to indicate the time soldiers were to retire to their billets. Humphrey Bland's *Treatise of Military Discipline* of 1727 described that:

> The Retreat, or Tat-too, is generally beat at Ten-a-Clock at Night in the Summer, and at Eight in Winter. It is perform'd by the Drum-Major, and all the Drummers of that Regiment which gives a Captain to the Main-Guard that Day. They are to begin at the Main-Guard, Beat round the Grand-Parade, and return back and finish where they began ... They are to be answer'd by the Drummers of all the other Guards, as also by the four Drummers of each Regiment in their respective Quarters ... The Tat-too, is the Signal given for the Soldiers to Retire to their Chambers ...[22]

That, in its original intention, beating retreat was also intended to indicate when garrisons should close up and assume their night-time routine was demonstrated by Venn when he wrote that 'The Ta-to is beaten when the Watch is set at the discretion of the Governour; after which ... none are to be out of their houses.' The two beatings – tattoo and retreat – became distinctly separate activities in the first quarter of the 18th century and more or less how we understand them today – tattoo being the time for soldiers to retire (today in garrison, normally at 10.00 p.m. when 'Last Post' is sounded) and retreat being the earlier (today at 6.00 p.m. at guard mounting). The drummers of the regiment were key to these activities, as Bland further described about the Retreat:

> … the Drummers of the Port-Guards are to go upon the Ramparts and beat a Retreat, to give notice to those without, that the Gates are going to be shut … As soon as the Drummers have finished the Retreat, which they should not do in less than a quarter of an Hour, the Officers must order the Barriers and Gates to be shut.[23]

The English/British armies at this time developed a tactical superiority over their foes that had much to do with the technical superiority of deployment and manoeuvre in line – largely in three ranks under Marlborough and for a while beyond – and the speed and efficiency of platoon fire tactics. This is not the place for a thorough discourse on these developments. They can be traced in Dr John Houlding's most excellent study of the training of the British Army between 1715 and 1795[24] and David Blackmore's more recent book on the development of British infantry firepower between 1642 and 1765.[25] In short, an English battalion prior to battle was told off into a number of equal-sized platoons, each of which was numbered and then allocated to a firing, the aim being to ensure that a number of platoons would always be able to deliver fire throughout the firefight and the battalion would never be left entirely unloaded. There were various methods and whichever was then in vogue it is difficult to conclude other than that such a system would break down the further into the fight the battalion got. Controlling the firings by drum beat becomes even more difficult to imagine but there is much evidence that this was the intention and English/British platoon fire tactics certainly had the upper hand in battle. There was inherent flexibility in the system as long as the soldiers were trained well enough, and whole ranks or whole battalions could fire at once if required or platoons could be grouped into a number of grand divisions within the battalion. There was also inherent chance of confusion and the system was not helped by the soldier's company – his most familiar 'home' – being broken up into these fighting platoons prior to battle. Eventually it was recognised that the whole thing could be simplified by establishing the company as the tactical fire unit, making it much more permanent, and there is evidence that this was being done as early as 1728 under the influence of the new drill manual published that year.

The other key feature of the English infantry was this deployment in three ranks and this was certainly in place when Marlborough took command. When 'locked up' – that is, when all three ranks closed up, with the front kneeling, the centre stooping and the rear standing, – they could deliver fire all at once in their platoons. By these methods the infantry 'repeatedly achieved a high level of effectiveness and superiority over their enemies in firepower and relied on that firepower to win battles.'[26] This is an accurate assessment but an army requires much more than just technical superiority to win and, certainly for the British Army, leadership and morale provided just as much for the infantry's renowned steadiness. The drummers were an important facet of a growing culture of rock-steady infantry and the development of their employment on the battlefield in the 18th century was further indication of a different and superior way of fighting. British drummers were very tightly controlled and while, as elsewhere, evidence is very slim, an impression is gained of increasingly limited use of anything like massed drumming in battle as much to heighten the effect of the drums when they did beat as well as to better preserve command and control.

The very first official book of regulations was published in 1676. *An Abridgement of the English Military Discipline* was, like so many of its successors, not really a tactical manual but we can conclude from this fact that, in its emphasis on the handling of arms and the formations and movements of bodies of foot in review, these various instructions were the very basis for manoeuvre on the field of battle. There was, therefore, no need to say more in print. The 1676 manual offered some relief from the flowery language of its unofficial predecessors, although its instructions appear extraordinarily complicated to the modern eye and ear. The drum beats were not listed so we have to assume the six to eight described by Barriffe and Elton were well known. We might deduce further that there was no attempt to over-complicate drill movements by adding any further beatings, especially as there was much emphasis in the manual on the usefulness of the voice.

A good example of how command and control were managed is shown in the instructions for the 'Fireings'. The manual dictated that:

> The Commander in Chief gives no Command nor Direction besides Make ready. Present. Give fire. And the first of these he uses but once. The Souldiers are to be instructed and minded by subaltern Officers, that when the first two Ranks make ready and advance forward, the Body of Musqueteers is to make good the Front of Pikes, and the next two Ranks unshoulder and make ready, without any Word of command; and when the last Rank presents, or both, if both fire together, to advance, and this also without any Word of Command …[27]

Apart from some words on the placing of drummers on each wing of the battalion for musters and parades they received barely a mention so we must also assume that Barriffe's and Elton's guidance remained largely extant. Usefully, however, the 1676 manual provided some guidance on 'Orders for Battel', which included a sensibly pragmatic preamble warning that 'there can be no certain Rules given for any Order of Battel, which depend chiefly upon the circumstances of Place, and other Accidents that may happen …' In this, while we cannot know if the drums beat out during the advance, there is some intimation at least of the assured steadiness and order that was to become the trademark of the British infantry:

> You must then first of all Command Silence; next to March very Leisurely. To observe the right in Marching, and preserve the intervals … None to speak but the Commander in chief, or the Major by his Order. Advancing against the Enemy in Battel, out of Musquet Shot, the Captains and other Officers at the head of the Battalion, are all to March in Line … two good paces before the Men, and are often to look behind them; Because otherwise they may insensibly get too much before the Body; and the Souldiers by following too fast, fall into disorder, whereof great care is to be taken in Marching against an Enemy.[28]

While the 1676 manual went through a number of editions, the 1685 edition, under the authorship of the Duke of Monmouth (beheaded that same year following his failed rebellion against King James II), represented a far more extensive set of instructions that also showed that the drum was used more widely in battle than the earlier manual implied.

Monmouth had been a very experienced soldier who had commanded English troops in three wars against the Dutch before rebelling against the Catholic Stuarts. The final pages of his new manual covered the use of the drum to beat reveille, tattoo or retreat, to beat to mount the day's new guard and, during review, to accompany the salute. These practices were well established but the manual also mentioned for the first time the employment of grenadiers (first mentioned in English service in 1684) and, having been issued firelocks, their use of the bayonet. The 1690 edition of the *Abridgement of the English Military Discipline* called these early bayonets 'daggers', which serves as a helpful indicator that they were plug bayonets in this period, having to be screwed into the muzzles of their firelocks.

Over a number of pages there appeared a detailed description of the 'Battle'. While the confusing profusion of words does not help to garner that clear an understanding of sequence, the several mentions of the drum are helpful. With an army drawn up in its various divisions and ordered to march 'As soon as ever the Drums beat the Preparative, every Division (except the first) is to march up with all the speed they can, keeping their Order ...' Typically, this army might be in three main divisions and the Preparative was the signal for the second and third to close up on the first while the first division maintained its steady pace. Some confusion comes from the next main instruction that states 'When the Battalion has Marched (so near that the Granadiers may throw their Granaldo's so as to fall among the Enemy) ... the Commander in Chief gives the Command to *alt*, at which word of command the Drums are to cease from beating'. What is difficult to ascertain is the sequence then of the firings of the musketeers in their three ranks and there is no instruction to beat the Battle or Charge. But what is clear is that at a close distance from the enemy the front rank of musketeers was commanded to kneel, the two rear ranks to close up and present their arms and the pikes to be charged. Following the firing musketeers were to 'Recover your arms. Club your muskets. [and] Fall on. Which they do with an *Huzza*, and the Pikes are to continue Charged, and the Drums to beat the *Preparative* again.' Until the further command was given to 'alt. At which time the Drums are to cease Beating.'[29] While instructions to beat the Battle or

Charge are noticeably absent, that the drums did beat during this stage of the attack seems apparent, the Preparative being used ahead of each use of the command to halt.

It would be tedious to continue to dissect these manuals without attempting to examine the use of the drum in practice. Indeed, while a number of unofficial publications covering *The Exercise of the Foot with the Evolutions* appeared in the 1690s, none of these had anything illuminating to say about the use of drums and no new official publication was issued until the *Exercise for the Horse, Dragoons and Foot Forces* appeared by order of King George II in 1728. Sadly, one can scour contemporary accounts of Marlborough's campaigns and find little to add to our knowledge, and there are few accounts to scour. Private John Marshall Deane, likely a 'gentleman centinel' of the First Guards, left a splendid personal narrative of his service between 1704 and 1711. His account is almost devoid of any mention of drums except in instances of 'routine': of marching after tattoo had been beaten, of beating a parley or chamade or, when speaking of the French, when their garrisons surrendered their fortresses of Douai, Bethune and Aire in 1710 and 'marcht out wth. Cullers flying [and] drums beating ...'[30] But, while the reference was to a grand review of his whole army by the Duke of Marlborough on 30 May 1707, Deane did record further that 'all the English foote exercised by signall of coulers & beat of drum, and every brigade fired in platoons before his Grace.'[31] John Millner, 'Serjeant in the Honourable Royal Regiment of Foot of Ireland' (later the 18th Foot) was also witness to this review and expounded in his extensive journal, completed at Ghent in 1712, that:

> The Duke of *Marlborough* review'd all the *British* Corps, who exercised and fired four Rounds gradually before him ... attended by each Drum-Major, with a Drum, in the Front of their respective Regiments, who, at each wave of the Colours, gave a Tap on his Drum, answerable to and for each Word of Command; the which each Regiment observed to perform accordingly ...[32]

One brief mention in the tortuous poetry of John Scot, a soldier in the Scots Brigade in the service of the Dutch States-General, would suggest that they did march in to the attack to the beat of the drum. For the bloody Battle of Malplaquet in September 1709 he recorded that, in the fight on the Allied left 'Our Granadiers march we boldly did beat.'[33]

That the use of the drum in battle received no mention by Millner or any of his contemporaries sits alongside the lack of any mention of how the armies or their component parts were organised or commanded or of the tactics involved. We might suppose therefore, for lack of any other evidence, that the manoeuvring of Marlborough's foot was controlled by voice and drum in the fashion described in the published manuals. 'Control' might be a loose term: on the approach to the battle of Ramillies on 23 May 1706 Tom Kitcher, who had been a Hampshire farm labourer and had joined Meredith's Regiment (later the 37th Foot) 'told of his march to battle that Sunday morning: "When the call to arms sounded, he and his comrades made many complex movements the purpose of which he understood nought and which he and his companions, grumbling, derided but carried them out without fault."'[34] The regimental officers and sergeants would have been conspicuous as they encouraged and cajoled their men towards their victory. While we have nothing written of British drummers in battle we do have what might be seen as an associated example, and evidence of drummers in the field, provided by Colonel Jean-Martin De La Colonie. He commanded the Grenadiers Rouge in the army of the Elector of Bavaria, standing alongside the French against Marlborough in the Blenheim campaign of 1704. The Grenadiers Rouge were something of a penal battalion of ex-French and Italian deserters and when they began to run as the Allied infantry broke onto the Schellenberg at Donauworth on 2 July De La Colonie, already wounded, 'looked on all sides for my drummer, but he had evidently thought fit to look after himself, with the result that I found myself at the mercy of the enemy and my own sad thoughts.'[35]

It would seem perhaps strange that, given the success of the British infantry in the later years of the reign of William III and throughout the reign of Queen Anne, that no new complete work on infantry drill was published until many years after the War of the Spanish Succession. John Houlding has ascribed this to the 'wholly admirable Stuart drill-books [which] ensured the survival of the core of practice that they laid down.' While the intelligent leadership of Marlborough and his officers must also have created a pragmatic application of the drills in the field – and the origins of the platoon fire system were not founded in any of the existing drill books – the fundamentals were well established. Even by the time of Blenheim the new British fire tactics were in place and nothing else required change: 'almost everything else – the evolutions, manoeuvres, and marches of the army – had changed hardly at all by the end of Marlborough's campaigning, so strong was the tradition of basic practice already established.'[36]

The British Army did not fight another major battle between its success at Malplaquet in 1709, three years before the withdrawal of British troops from Flanders, and the battle of Dettingen in 1743. The intervening years of peace had a deleterious effect overall on the efficiency of the British infantry, the army being much reduced in strength and spread about Britain, Ireland and foreign garrisons in often little more than company-sized groups. But they were important years nonetheless in the infantry's development. King George II demonstrated considerable interest in his army and its improvement and he had ordered the production of the 1728 *Exercise* because 'every Colonel alters or Amends [the drills] as he thinks fit.'[37] Inspecting officers specifically tested regiments on their ability to conduct the official drills and it is therefore relatively safe to assume a fair degree of standardisation in practice and to remember that these various drills were intended for use on the battlefield. The 1728 *Exercise* was an altogether different work in its breadth and detail. It described, for example, 64 vocal commands and 185 separate motions for the manual exercise, which were the various movements a soldier was required to master as an individual. Even the platoon exercise, the next step which brought all men in a platoon into the position to fire their muskets, contained around 63 motions although, unlike the manual exercise, the platoon exercise, as Houlding has concluded, was designed to be 'performed very quickly and to only [four] words of command or to commands relayed by the drums.'[38]

We are helped greatly in our understanding of how the infantry were to be managed in the field, at least in theory, by the publication in these years of two highly influential works: that of Brigadier, later Lieutenant General, Humphrey Bland in 1727 and mentioned above and that of Brigadier General Richard Kane in 1745; Kane will be considered later. Bland had been commissioned in 1704 and was later to fight at Dettingen and to command the cavalry at Culloden in 1745. His *Treatise of Military Discipline*, touched on earlier, was of great influence. For the first time the individual and sub-unit exercises – referred to as the manual and platoon exercises respectively – were explained in detail and in clear prose and it is little wonder that the official 1728 *Exercise* simply copied the entire regulations for the Foot and made it regulation across the army. With very little written elsewhere about the application of drum to battle, Bland (and Kane) contain valuable pointers. Bland, while not free himself from over-complicated drill movements, certainly alluded to the 1690 regulations being unsatisfactory and that he was using experience in the field to produce a better manual:

> The Evolutions of the Foot, which were formerly practised, being found not only of very little Use, but likewise of such a Length, that they had not Time to perform the more essential Parts of the Service, (the Firings) without over-fatiguing the Soldiers … I shall insert no more of them here than what was practised by the Foot during the late War in *Flanders*.[39]

Bland described no material difference from what had gone before in the way the drummers were to be deployed in the line or for the march. But their role and the importance of the 'musick' were certainly enhanced in his writing and we might assume that this was very long-established practice but now detailed for the first time. His first chapter was dedicated to forming the battalion in line and he described how the colours were to be called for:

> The major is to order one of the Granadier Drummers to beat the Drummers Call; upon which the Ensigns who are to carry the Colours, and the Drum-major with one Half or two Thirds of the Drummers, are to repair to the Head of the Company of Granadiers, where the Drummers are to be form'd into Ranks in the Rear of the Ensigns … [The Colours are marched into the regiment] the Drummers, with the Drum-major at their Head, marching in the rear of the Ensigns, beat the Troop, and the Granadiers … march immediately after the Drummers … when the Colours are brought to the Regiment, they are receiv'd with rested Arms, and the Drummers, who remain, beat a March, which is the Reason that one Third of the Drummers, at least, remain with the Battalion.[40]

This is but one small example of the detail for parading. For the officers to take their posts he directed, in part, that:

> First, the Major is to direct the Orderly Drummer to beat a Ruff (one being to attend for that Purpose) to give the Officers Notice. After that a Flam, or double Stoke; at which the Lieutenant Colonel ... and the rest of the Officers, face to the Right about on their left Heels. At the second Flam, they are to advance their Half-pikes, and the Serjeants on the Flanks their Halbards. At the third Flam, the Officers, Serjeants on the Flanks, the three Divisons of Drummers, and the Hautboys, are all to march to their Posts, beginning with the left Feet.[41]

It was in Chapter VI, which consisted of 'Directions for the different Firings of the Foot' that Bland provided solid evidence of the application of drum beats to tactical manoeuvre. The battalion's major had to take care before the firings commenced to let the battalion know 'what Signals by Beat of Drum he intends to make use of, and what they are to perform at each Signal.' These directions, while intended also for a general review, were clearly intended too for application in the field. They are worth showing in some detail:

> The usual Beatings made use of on these Occasions, which are performed by the Orderly Drummer attending the Major, are as follows:
>
> At the Beating of the March, the Regiment is to march strait forward ... and when the Drum ceases they are to halt.
>
> When a Retreat is beat, the battalion is to face to the Right-about ... and march towards the Rear: and when the Drum ceases, they are to face to their proper Front ... But that the Men may not mistake the Time of their facing to their proper Front, by the short Pauses which the Drummer must of Course make in the beating of the retreat, another Signal may be added when they are to do it, such as a short Ruffle, by which Means the Facing will be perform'd with the more Exactness, and prevent the least Disorder.
>
> At the beating of a Preparative, all the Platoons of that Firing which is to come next, are to make ready together, as is explain'd in the Platoon Exercise.
>
> A Flam, or double Stroke, is the Signal for the Platoons to begin to fire ...
>
> [When ordered] To go through the Firings standing ... The major is to order the Drummer to beat a Preparative; at which all the Platoons of the first Firing are to make ready ... then the Major orders the Drummer to beat a Flam; at which the Officer commanding the first Platoon of that Firing, gives the following Words of Command. *Present. Fire.*
>
> As soon as the Word *Fire* is given to the first Platoon, the Officer commanding the second Platoon is to give the Word, *Present*, and then *Fire*. The Officer

commanding the third ... fourth and fifth Platoons of that Firing, are to follow the same Directions.

As soon as the first Firing is over, the Major orders a second Preparative to be beat; at which the Platoons of the second Firing make ready ... After this a Flam; then the first Platoon of the second Firing, presents and fires, and the other Platoons of that Firing follow in their Order.

The same Method must be observ'd for the Platoons of the third Firing, as also for those of the Reserve.

Bland provided additional instructions for firing advancing, retiring, when attacked by Horse, from parapets, in streets and by ranks, with extensive instructions on firing in square. In all cases the drum was used to control the firings and for any movement the order to beat a march was given to set the battalion moving, the halt being brought about by the drums ceasing to beat. If the platoon firings were not to be used and an entire rank was to fire at once, such as in the advance, no Flam was beaten to initiate the platoon firings.[42]

All of these directions would appear to indicate that the drums beat out the march and for their actual use in the field Bland added an entire chapter of 'Rules for Battalions of Foot when they are to engage in the Line.' Here he emphasised that threatening silence of voice for which the British infantry was to become well known for 'In marching up to attack the Enemy, and during the Action, a profound Silence should be kept, that the Commanding Officers may be distinctly heard in delivering their Orders ...

> ... lest He should not be distinctly heard by the Whole, they are to regulate their Motions by the several Beatings of the Drum; for which End, the Drummers in the Center Platoons are to be very attentive to the Words of Command, and to Beat, on the Delivering of them, according to the following Directions.
>
> When the battalion is order'd to march Forward, they are to beat a march; and when the Word Halt is given, they are to cease.
>
> When they are to Retire, as soon as the Battalion has faced to the Right-about, and the Word March is given, the Drummers are to beat a Retreat; and not to cease 'till the Battalion is order'd to Halt.
>
> The Drummers on the flanks are to govern themselves, both in their Beatings, and in Ceasing to beat, by those in the Center; by which Means, those Men who could not hear the Word of Command, from their being at too great a Distance from the Center, or the Noise of the Drums, will know by the different Beatings, what they are to perform.

The Drummers in the Center must be ready to beat a Preparative for the whole Battalion to Make ready, if the Commanding Officer thinks proper to have it perform'd in that Manner.[43]

Bland further directed that for the attack 'the Line should move very slow ["as slow as foot can fall" as he states elsewhere], that the Battalions may be in Order ...' This would be sensible advice for control of the line, especially in the attack, was critical if the full force of the attack was to be effected. But the directions appear ponderous, especially in the very deliberate control of the firings by drumbeat. There was perhaps a supposition that battles would be conducted in a relatively stately manner, as long as both sides were following similar rules, but the conditions prevalent during the firefight could not have been conducive to continued steady regulation by drum. The observer might draw from this that theory, as contained in the manual, was getting the better of practice but that the drum was to be used in battle the way Bland described was certainly the intention. The *Treatise* contained a great deal of common sense. Drawing from his own experience in Flanders Bland gave very pragmatic direction on siege operations in which he stated that 'The Relief of the Trenches is always made without Beat of Drum, and with as little Noise as possible, that the Besieged may not know the exact Parts you are in, by which means their Fire can only be given at Random; whereas, if the Drum was to Beat, or a considerable Noise made, they could direct it with more Certainty, and thereby make your loss greater.' He added that it had been common practice to enter trenches with colours flying and much ceremony but that by the end of the war in Flanders this show had been abolished and even the colours left in camp. He noted too, with a hint of derision, that the French persisted in this absurdity.[44]

We need not dwell too long on the additional directions provided by Bland on the various beatings in garrison and in camp. There is a great deal within his *Treatise* that provides a good understanding of the organisation of an army in the field and Bland's consideration of drums can conclude with his direction for an army about to march:

The Reveille is never Beat the Day the Army Marches, unless particularly Ordered, but the General instead of it.

At the Beating of the General, the Officers and Soldiers Dress and Prepare themselves for the March.

At the Beating of the Assembly or Troop, they are to strike all their Tents, pack up and load the Baggage ... [the Guards are drawn in] ... the Troops and Companies to Draw up in their Streets, and to be Told off, that they may be ready to Form into Squadron and Battalion at the next Signal.

At the Hour appointed for the Army to March, the Drummers are to Beat a March at the Head of the Line; and as soon as they cease Beating, the Squadrons and Battalions March out and Form at the Head of their Incampment, Compleat their Files, and tell off the Battalions by Grand or Sub-Divisions, as it shall be Ordered: And when the March is beat a second time on the Right or Left of the Line, all the Squadrons and Battalions are to Wheel towards the Flank, where the March was beat, and begin the March as soon as wheeled.[45]

The great amount of detail provided by Bland made his manual, given its almost official sanction by way of the 1728 regulations, the tactical textbook of the day. Both works had their critics and the most well known was Brigadier General Richard Kane. An officer of even more experience than Bland – he had begun his service in the defence of Londonderry in 1689 and was severely wounded at Blenheim – he had compiled by the time of his death in 1736 his *Campaigns of King William and Queen Anne*. Included in this volume was *A New System of Military Discipline, for a Battalion of Foot on Action* in which he roundly criticised the lack of any instructions on 'how they are to act when they come to face the Enemy' and derided the 1728 regulations by name as a 'poor ... Performance.'[46] Kane's *Discipline* may have had a posthumous effect but this would have been beyond the War of the Austrian Succession for it was not published until 1745. It was also a very minor work, consisting of just 30 pages compared to Bland's 400. Nevertheless, we can look at Kane in the light of his experience and of other officers of his day and reckon by this that his guidance reflected practice at least in part in the army.

Kane's illustrations showed clearly the presence of the drummers in a battalion and he wrote that, in forming for battle: 'The Drums are to be divided into three Parts, on the Right and Left, and behind the two Centre Platoons, all to range in a Line with the Serjeants, but not to Beat without Orders.'[47] This was no different to before but it is particularly interesting that Kane felt the need to recommend greater use of the drum over the voice, feeling that the efficacy of the drum had not been fully realised. In forming up the battalion and 'Before we enter upon Action' Kane thought it necessary to 'Take Notice of one Thing, hitherto overlook'd by all; that is, the Use of the Drum on many more Occasions than is generally made of it.' He was concerned that some commanding officers might not have the voice to exercise effective command and was therefore 'for introducing the more frequent Use of the Drum, as well upon Action, as in the common Exercise of a Regiment, to assist the Voice.' To add emphasis he added:

> Suppose the Commanding Officer should happen to be killed, the Voice of him that supplies his Place may be different from the other's, that it may occasion a Confusion; whereas the Drum is always the same, and much easier heard and understood, especially when the Men are train'd up by, and constantly us'd to it. A great deal more might be said in Favour of this warlike Instrument; however I would not be so understood, as that the Drum is wholly to be depended on. No, I am only for introducing the more frequent Use of it purely to assist the Voice … [but] I see no Reason why our Infantry should not be train'd up by the Drum, as well in their Firings, or rather more, than the Manual Exercise; so that, as it often happens in the Hurry of Action, when it is not possible for the Voice to be heard, that then the Drum will be of the greatest Consequence.[48]

Were things so simple! This debate must have been a constant one for there were times when the beat of drum was also not loud enough to convey an intended signal. Barty-King quoted an un-named Royal Dragoon at the British capitulation at Brihuega in Spain in 1710 (dragoons, of course, fighting on foot at this time) who declared 'Thare was orders for our drum-major to beet a parley but it was not heard the first nor second time, but third time it was heard and the enemie stood before all the time & when the parley was heard they came to our breastwork & talk'd with us …'[49] Pragmatically, Kane had made it very clear that it was a combination of voice and drum that was being recommended and not the dependence wholly on one method or the other. He then obliges us with full descriptions of how the drum and voice were combined in directing the drills and manoeuvres of the battalion in action:

> Suppose that the Signal for battle is given: Upon this the Colonel orders his Drum to beat a Ruffle, which is as much as to say, *Take Care*; and then saying something to encourage and excite the Men to the Performance of their Duty

> ... he then gives the Word, MARCH; at which time the Drum beats to the March; and when the battalion has got to within four or five paces of him, he turns to the Enemy, and marches slowly down ... till he finds they begin to fire upon him; upon which he orders his Drum to cease beating, and turning to the Battalion, gives the Word, HALT; and then orders his Drum to beat a Preparative, upon which the six Platoons of the first Firing make ready ... The Platoons being presented, the Colonel orders the Drum to beat a second Flam, on which they fire, and immediately recover their Arms, fall back, and load as fast as they can ...[50]

Kane actually had much the same to say as Bland, if the former was more economical with words, in the use of the drum in the firings but added some further words on what to do should the enemy 'obstinately maintain their Ground.' Here the commanding officer would order the drum to beat the Preparative for the platoons of the next firing to make ready and would then command the battalion to march, presumably with drums beating. If the enemy continued to stand its ground the battalion would close until ordered to halt again,

> On which the Front-Rank kneels, and the Rear-Ranks of the Platoons that are to fire, close forward; he then orders the Drum to beat a Flam, on which the Front-Rank drop their Muzzles, and the Rear-Ranks present; and on the next Flam they fire; and so he continues his Firings as fast as he can, until he obliges them to give Way ...[51]

So much for the theory. We have little enough to tell us how Marlborough's infantry utilised the drum on the field of battle but, given the experience of Bland and of Kane, it is fairly safe to assume that use of the drum was pretty extensive.

CHAPTER 4

Infantry without Parallel

... the redcoats stepping out to the rub-a-dub-dub-dub of the drums.

The latter part of the previous chapter described at some length the theory at least that would bring an infantry battalion to battle. If Richard Kane propounded a far more pragmatic approach, the publication of his *New System of Military Discipline* came much too late, in 1745, to have any effect on the preparation of the British Army for its next great test. When this test came between 1743 and 1746 the army attracted criticism that left the infantry with a record of inadequacy. This is, overall, a misconception for the infantry fought in the main with great determination and no little skill, if not according to the book. Colonel H. C. B. Rogers concluded in his study of the British Army in the 18th century that, 'Although a defeat, there is no battle in history that throws more lustre on British infantry than that of Fontenoy.'[1] However, for all its gallantry, the British infantry was poorly prepared for its battles, a direct result of its lack of battlefield experience after 1709 (if we ignore the inconclusive action at Sheriffmuir in 1715). As in every age, without practical experience to temper them the writers wove increasingly intricate exercises into their manuals. This caused Kane to pose in his criticism of the 1728 regulations, 'Is it possible for young Gentlemen that never saw any thing of Action (of whom the Army in a short Time will be composed) to form an Idea of Action, out of this Book of Discipline?'[2] Nevertheless, the 1728 regulations and Bland remained extant and it might be surmised that their collective guidance were authority enough for colonels of regiments of foot and their captains to conduct their commands in battle.

The five decades between the end of the War of the Spanish Succession and the end of the Seven Years War saw Britain emerge as the world's leading imperial power. By the end of the Seven Years War Britain's infantry had also sealed its position as practically undefeatable on the battlefield. When the army was finally committed to the European continent in 1743 the narrow allied victory of King George II at Dettingen on 27 June owed itself to the guts and discipline of his British infantry. That infantry's lustre has already been commented on in relation to the battle of Fontenoy on 11 May 1745. In both cases British fire and movement proved far superior to that of the French, even at Fontenoy when the British and Hanoverian line was forced to withdraw, having taken and occupied the centre of the French position, due to the failings of the Dutch infantry. A withdrawal in contact is a perilous movement in any circumstances but Lieutenant General the Earl of Crawford, commanding the Household Cavalry, observed that the retirement 'was carried out in as good order as the advance.' He added that the infantry 'retired by succession of battalions, facing about and firing at every hundred yards by word of command as steadily as if they had been on parade.'[3] The French cavalry tried repeatedly to break the Allied infantry but were repulsed with heavy loss.

Here, and at Dettingen, it might be supposed that the British infantry owed its prowess to the movement and fire discipline bred from the stipulations of the drill book and carried out its evolutions to beat of drum. What little we know of the infantry fight at Dettingen suggests the contrary and that platoon fire tactics broke down almost immediately. That is not to say that the drums were silent for the British infantry regiments had spent a year on the Continent in cantonments so that they might improve their collective training. But to suggest that the drum was used to control the firings is to fly in the face of evidence. At Dettingen the British infantry proved itself to be inexperienced and inadequately prepared and caused problems from the start for firing much too soon and to so little effect, and without orders. The young James Wolfe, later the victor of Quebec but then adjutant of Duroure's

(12th) Regiment of Foot, spent a great part of the day 'begging and ordering the men not to fire at too great a distance ... but to little purpose. The whole fired when they thought they could reach [the French] ... We did very little execution with it.'[4] When the British line did gain sufficient ground, whether or not it did this to beat of drum (and it is probable that it did), when faced by the advance of the French cavalry, one battalion commander enquired of Lieutenant General Clayton 'whether he shou'd Fire at them by Platoons or Ranks' and received the response that 'as to Platoon or rank firing I shall be glad to see you perform either in Action, but I own I never did yet on a Field day or at a Review.'[5] The reality, as observed by Lieutenant Colonel Charles Russell of the 1st Foot Guards, was that the infantry 'were under no command by way of Hide Park firing, but the whole three ranks made a running fire of their own accord ... without waiting for words of command.'[6]

It seems patently obvious that the drum was superfluous throughout for controlling the platoon firings according to the book for the simple reason that the platoon firings were not executed. But the drum might well have been controlled centrally to beat executive orders such as to march or to retire. Fortunately, the running fire used by the infantry throughout the day proved remarkably effective at close range and, while the discipline of the French infantry showed itself particularly wanting, the British infantry finished the day with its honour intact. Fortescue described the confusion as the British infantry tried to keep itself together during the advance, not helped by the gesticulations and shouts of King George. After numerous halts and dressing of ranks it met the 'fitful and disorderly fire' of the French:

> The British, now thoroughly in hand, answered with a regular, swift, and continuous fire of platoons [although we know this to be unlikely], the ranks standing firm like a wall of brass and pouring in volley after volley, deadly and unceasing ... The French Guards staggered under it and the British again raised an irregular cheer. 'Silence,' shouted [Field Marshal The Lord] Stair imperiously, galloping up. 'Now one and all together when I give the signal.' And as he raised his hat the British broke into the stern and appalling shout which was to become so famous on the fields of the Peninsula. The French Guards waited for no more when they heard it, but shrank back in disorder in rear of their horse ...[7]

We might imagine the drummers beating a march at the ordinary step of about 75 paces to the minute, ceasing to beat at every halt and dressing, and beating again as the march continued until silenced by their officers on the command to halt the line. If control had been established over the firings a preparatory, perhaps just the one, might well have been beaten ahead of the command to re-commence firing but, given the evidence, there was little opportunity for such formality.

Lessons were learned and, while the Duke of Cumberland later proved to be a poor Commander-in-Chief as the war developed, he did at least ensure much improved training that saw marked improvement in the handling of his infantry. It required tight control but the officers at all levels had learned their business and exercised it, ensuring that, according to one infantry officer, the commanding general was heard 'frequently giving direction to [his] Officers, to tell their men to preserve their Ranks & keep their line; and to direct them to observe the word of Command, & not to fire till they were order'd.'[8] One later description of the battle of Fontenoy described, when touching on the part of the 13th Foot, 'The whole line, with drums beating and shouldered arms, deliberately advance[ing] across the open space of half a mile...'[9] This would fit well with our understanding of the steady and methodical advance uphill of the British and Hanoverian infantry, the drums helping to weld their discipline and spur them on as they approached the steadfast French and Irish regiments, which showed no sign of yielding until close-range musket fire drove them from their position.

The failings evident from the War of the Austrian Succession and the initial problems encountered by British infantry during the Jacobite Rebellion of 1745–46 resulted in a simplification of exercises in new regulations issued in 1748, at the instigation of the Duke of Cumberland, and in their 1756 and 1757 amendments. The main purpose of the 1748 set was to simplify the firings but elsewhere there was little change from the 1728 manual with regard to the exercises and evolutions. With regard to drums there was no change and the dispositions of the drummers in line was as before. Significantly it was the 1757 *Manual Exercise* that ordered a tightening up of the rank and file and an emphasis on close-order drill at speed. The inherent confusion in having what was in effect two sets of instructions – one for the manual exercise and one for the platoon exercise – was done away with and there were increasing efforts to make the company both the administrative and the tactical entity under the same officers. It will be recalled from the previous chapter that, prior to battle, the companies hitherto were 'platooned' within the battalion in order to equalise the size of the fire units.

A contemporary observer in the *London Magazine* noted that, with the propensity for battalions to disperse their fire platoons to cover their ground, centralised control of the firings was not practicable. He wrote 'I should think that it must also be impossible for the scattered divisions, in action, to hear their signals, whether they be given by drums, or voices' however the firings were organised.[10] James Wolfe also recognised this problem and in his *Instructions* to the 20th Foot, which he compiled as commanding officer at Dover Castle in January 1755, he demanded decentralisation, in imitation of the best-disciplined troops in Europe. In so doing he flew in the face of officialdom, 'making every platoon receive the word of command, to make ready and fire from the officer who commands it; because in battle the fire of the artillery and infantry may render it difficult to use any general signals by beat of drum.'[11] It would seem evident that if every platoon was to receive its orders to fire from its officers and in effect independently of battalion control, drums would add great confusion through their incessant beating at different times by numbers of platoons in close proximity. Wolfe later confirmed his direction when he issued additional instructions at Canterbury in December that year 'in case the French land'. Here he made it clearer still that 'The soldiers are to take their orders intirely from the officer of the platoon.'[12] Wolfe possessed great powers of discipline, organisation and common sense as is evidenced by a whole series of orders written and issued by him over the years. His instructions at Canterbury were a model of clarity for a battalion in action and put the official manuals in the shade. Wolfe also provided early evidence of the British infantry being ordered to 'maintain a "nobly awful" silence on the battlefield', a custom with which they were to become readily identified. Captain John Knox of the 43rd Foot, who served in North America in the late 1750s, had commented on this and that shouting and whooping like the French was unusual. Wolfe's orders in 1755 ordered that the 20th 'is not to hallo, or cry out, upon any account whatsoever ... till they are ordered to charge with their bayonets ... [when] the battalion may give a warlike shout and rush in.'[13]

It was the experience of battle in the Seven Years War that led to a formal simplification of the platoon firing system, putting into regulation what had become practice, that trained men readily abandoned the platoon firings and fired by companies. This allowed for faster loading and firing in the ranks, which, in turn, would see formations increasingly in two ranks rather than three and a larger regular space between files with no resultant loss of firepower. Some of these simplifications were embodied in the 1764 *Manual Exercise*, drawing on all the diverse experiences of British soldiers in the Seven Years War.

That war marked significant victories for British arms across three continents, covering battles in Germany, Canada, the Caribbean and India. In Germany it marked a particularly astonishing success for British infantry at the battle of Minden on 1 August 1759, a success born of a mistaken order. Britain had been slow to send troops to support her German allies following the outbreak of war in 1757, preferring to focus efforts on securing her enlarging empire elsewhere. But setbacks for the allied commander, the able Prince Ferdinand of Brunswick, brought a British contingent to Germany at the end of 1758.

Ferdinand led his army to the open plains before Minden in Westphalia, the city being occupied by the French and of strategic importance as it controlled the River Weser and threatened the state of Hanover. The allied army was encamped when it got news in the early morning of 1 August that the whole French army was on the move. Hospital Assistant William Fellowes described that morning, as they were stripped off and washing their shirts, that 'suddenly the drums began to beat to arms; and so insistent was the summons that without more ado we slip't on the wet linen ... hurrying to form line lest our comrades should depart without us.'[14] General Friedrich von Spörcken commanded the allied infantry in the centre, which comprised two brigades formed in two lines. Major General Waldegrave commanded the first line of the 12th, 23rd and 37th Regiments and Major General Kingsley the second line of the 20th, 25th and 51st Regiments, a battalion of Hanoverian line infantry and two battalions of Hanoverian Guards. It was a modest force and faced the centre of the French army, which was made up, unusually, entirely of cavalry.

Ferdinand gave orders that, at the appropriate time, the infantry should advance with drums beating and then saw, to his utter surprise, that the advance was under way. Lieutenant Montgomery of the 12th Foot and in the leading brigade wrote of 'the redcoats stepping out to the rub-a-dub-dub-dub of the drums.'[15] The solidity of the British line during what then ensued when, against all odds and expectations, the French cavalry and then its supporting infantry were shattered, might be assumed, therefore, to have been assisted by the steadiness and discipline imbued by the methodical martial cacophony of so many beating drums. Ferdinand had tried to halt the advance by sending further orders but the only halt occurred when the first line stood its ground for some minutes to allow the second line to close up. If Ferdinand had been relieved to watch the line halt his relief was fleeting:

> … suddenly to the general amazement the drums again began to roll, and the first line stepped off once more, advancing rapidly but in perfect order, straight upon the French horse. The second line, though its formation was still incomplete, stepped of likewise in rear of its comrades, deploying as it moved, and therefore of necessity dropping somewhat in rear.[16]

Waldegrave's leading brigade had been enfiladed by 60 French cannon as it crossed about 700 yards of open ground but did not halt again until the huge body of French horse thundered down on their front and at 30 yards was shot to pieces by British musketry. The drums would have been silent as the order for the volley – quite possibly an entire two ranks to provide for the third rank to be held in reserve – was given; there was certainly no attempt at platoon firing. Reloading was done rapidly and without order and then, to further astonishment, the advance was renewed. The French brought forward four brigades of infantry and additional cannon against the British right and a second line of cavalry was then committed. This too was beaten off with great loss and Waldegrave then turned his attention to the French infantry.

A third wave of French cavalry finally broke through the thinning first line but was shattered by the fire of the second British line. At last von Spörcken's dauntless infantry received support and the day was won despite the appalling failure of Lord Sackville to commit his British cavalry at any stage. The French commander, Marshal Louis Contades, was quoted as saying:

> I have seen what I never thought possible, a single line of infantry break through three lines of cavalry ranked in order of battle, and tumble them to ruin.[17]

While the victory of von Spörcken's infantry was total and the actions of the French cavalry look all the more inept, although it must be said that cavalry did not commit itself solely due to an assumed superiority of the equestrian over the pedestrian, as had often been the case in earlier times. The French cavalry knew well that it could not just ride down disciplined and resolute infantry, even if in the open. Nevertheless, the sheer numbers involved gave a distinct advantage and one that heavy cavalry had always tried to exploit. The British and Hanoverian battalions received three attacks by three successive divisions of cavalry, each of them comprising 20 or more squadrons and thus about 2,000 horse at a time. A heavy cavalryman with horse and equipment came in at about half a tonne so for exposed infantry to stand its ground each time against about 1,000 tonnes of charging mass would take utter confidence born of training, experience and good leadership.

The success of the composite battalions of grenadiers at Warburg in Germany on 31 July 1760 showed how responsive and manoeuvrable trained infantry could be. Warburg is known mainly for the decisive attack by the allied cavalry under the Marquis of Granby but the conditions for victory were set by an infantry assault on the far left of the French line, which occupied the high ground of the Heinberg. For this assault two columns were formed of British and German infantry, the column on the right comprising two composite battalions of British grenadiers drawn from the 11 British battalions present; five of these battalions had been at Minden. The right-hand column also included the 87th and 88th Highlanders and three battalions of Hanoverian grenadiers. Speed and surprise were essential and, while it must be assumed that the drummers accompanied their battalions, it takes little imagination to see that the approach and rapid deployment would not have been to the beat of the drum. If the drummers kept pace with the lead grenadiers as they deployed into line at the trot and uphill and swept through the left flank of the French defence on the hilltop then they did a good job. But it might have been that for such a nimble achievement the drum was more of an encumbrance and could be dispensed with on such occasions. It takes even less imagination to see that, in the conditions prevalent throughout much of the fighting against French and Indian in North America at the same time, the drum would be of little use. This will be addressed in the next chapter.

It is interesting to note that at Minden the British set off to win their glory by reason of that mistaken order, the brigades advancing prematurely by obeying an order to advance *to* the beat of drum when they should have waited to advance *on* the beat of drum. While this was an example of a mistaken word of command and not of a mistaken beating of drum, the latter was clearly possible in the noise and chaos of battle. Another order by Wolfe, issued at Winchester in late 1755, sought to avoid any confusion by limiting any beating of drums, even simply to sounding the alarm to be beaten only when absolutely necessary:

> As beating to arms in the night or upon an alarm is apt to create confusion and disorder, it should be practised as seldom as possible; but when there is a necessity for calling the troops suddenly under arms, either to resist an enemy or to march and surprize them, or for any purpose of war, the officers and non-commissioned officers of companies should call their own men out of their respective quarters, and assemble them silently and quietly at their place of parade, to march from thence in good order to the general alarm post of the regiment.[18]

A useful example of the need for caution occurred in 1758 when drums ordered to beat to raise the spirits had an unfortunate effect. In September that year a British expedition under General Thomas Bligh against Cherbourg was faced by increasing opposition and required to re-embark with some haste. Security became paramount and, as Tobias Smollett later recounted, 'Had the troops decamped in the night without noise, in all probability they would have arrived on the beach before the French had received the least intelligence of their motion … but, instead … the drums were beaten at two o'clock in the morning, as if with intention to give notice to the enemy, who forthwith repeated the same signal.'[19] The result was a near catastrophe with much of the rearguard being killed or captured.

The enduring legacy of the Seven Years War, demonstrated in the 1764 regulations, was the further emphasis on close-order drill and, even more significantly, of marching to a cadenced step. The efficacy of light infantry tactics, especially in North America, would not be entirely forgotten but success in the war in Europe had owed much to the manoeuvrability and discipline demonstrated by Prussian troops, a model copied readily by the British and, indeed, the French. When Wolfe mentioned 'the best disciplined troops in Europe' (above, in 1755) he was referring specifically to the Prussians and the successes they had enjoyed on the battlefield under King Frederick the Great. Translations of the Prussian infantry regulations strongly influenced the updating of British methods and organisation in the 1750s and 1760s and the continued set-piece battles on the Continent gave significant advantage to the side that could control its line of battle and its manoeuvres tightly.

British regulations, when they did mention the drum, had done so largely in relation to its use only as a signalling device. Its use on the march, in the advance and the attack and despite its ability to spur the valiant, were still not fully regulated, although drums were clearly used extensively in this manner. Closer adoption of 'Frederickian' methods helped to further the place of the drum in the line where it was to reach its apogee, if briefly, to beat out the march *in* step. There is precious little written record from soldiers of the time but the remarkable journal of Corporal William Todd of the 30th and then the 12th Foot, while it spreads little light on the use of the drum in battle, does provide plentiful evidence of its universal presence in the field. Todd served between 1745 and 1762 (but, unfortunately, not at Minden) and wrote numerously about the drum beating reveille and other orders and, notably, when he was corporal of the regimental pioneers, the drums beating the pioneers' march to assemble these men for various duties. His best example of the utility of the drum in controlling field operations comes from the misbegotten Cherbourg expedition in 1758. Engineers had emplaced a number of mines under a French battery and when these were ready to be exploded 'As soon as the Match is Lighted & Laid at the train, the Drum Beats out a signal for every one to keep out of the way & go some Distance of[f].' Todd was lucky not to be injured or killed when this occurred for he was taking 'a very Fine Little Cow' down to the quayside 'And I narrowly Escaped, for just when I got there the Drums Beat as a Signal that A mine was a going of[f] ... [and] I was afraid to leave the Cow ...'[20]

While not extensive in number, there are some contemporary artworks that help show what drummers and fifers looked like in this period and one or two that demonstrate their use in the field. The most important of the latter is probably David Morier's painting of the battle of Culloden on 16 April 1746 entitled *An Incident in the Rebellion of 1745* and in the Royal Collection. It was probably painted around 1753 and depicts the grenadier company of Barrell's Regiment (the King's Own Regiment of Foot and, from 1751, the 4th (The King's Own)) receiving the Highlanders' charge on the far left of the Duke of Cumberland's line. Directly behind the grenadiers stand two drummers in their reversed coats and mitre caps, one of them clearly beating his drum. Morier had already been commissioned by Cumberland to paint a series of studies of grenadiers and two of these are of interest, one of a drummer of the 18th (The Royal Irish) Regiment and one of a drummer and fifer of the 49th Regiment. A further useful work is William Hogarth's *The March of the Guards to Finchley*, painted in 1750 and housed today in the Foundling Museum in Brunswick Square in London. This satirical depiction of the Foot Guards mustering at the Tottenham Court Turnpike as they prepare to defend London from Bonnie Prince Charlie shows a drummer beating, accompanied by an adolescent fifer as the guardsmen march towards Finchley.

Another popular myth has arisen that would have us believe that all infantry had always marched in time and in step to the beat of the drum. While marching in time to a regulated beat had been in evidence during the English Civil Wars, as detailed earlier, and beating the march was common in the 17th century, the development of marching in step to music was altogether new and came to the British Army at about the same time as the re-introduction of the fife. The main influence for this innovation appears to have been Maurice de Saxe, Marshal of France and one of her most successful generals, who had defeated Cumberland at Fontenoy. Saxe held great store in the manoeuvrability of infantry, which he held could be 'attained by training the troops to march and manoeuvre in close order, to a cadenced step.'[21] Houlding evinces that 'Marching in step, to a musical cadence, was probably the most widely adopted of the reforms suggested by Saxe' in his *Reveries, or Memoirs upon the Art of War*, which appeared in translation in Britain in 1757. He adds that 'this device made possible speedy and flexible manoeuvring by ranks at close order, and was one of the most significant developments in the drill of the armies of the eighteenth century.' He quotes a particularly significant point from Saxe, who wrote that:

> ... the manual exercise is, without doubt, a branch of military discipline necessary to render a soldier steady and adroit under arms; but it is by no means of sufficient importance in itself to engage all our attention ... The principal part of all discipline depends upon the legs, not the arms: the personal abilities which are required in the performance of all manoeuvres, and likewise in engagements, are totally confined to them.[22]

The Duke of Cumberland, clearly impressed by his experiences on the Continent, was also influenced by the use of the fife amongst his Hanoverian and Hessian allies and re-introduced the instrument to the Foot Guards in 1745. The first regiment of the line to follow was the 19th, the Green Howards. Francis Grose, who served in the 19th later, noted that the regiment adopted the fife in 1747 and that 'Fifers were afterwards only allowed to the Grenadier Company ... [but] most of the drummers were taught the use of the fife as well as the drum ... Fifes afterwards, particularly since the practice of marching in cadence, have been multiplied.'[23] The Reverend Percy Sumner, a leading member of the Society for Army Historical Research from its first days, once noted that a return of accoutrements for the 33rd Foot stated that 'The drums need not be completed above 16, as H.R.H. [Cumberland] was graciously pleased in 1748 to allow the regiment to keep up 4 Fifers in room of 4 Drummers.'[24] In fact the fife was not allowed on the infantry establishment, officially, until 1764 and then only two for each grenadier company. In July 1750 the review of the 20th Foot 'noted the absence of "3 Drummers at Berwick learning the Fife"'[25] and in 1759 the 67th and 72nd Regiments were seen at Hilsea in England drilling 'to the sound of the fife; keeping the most exact time and cadence ... The effects of the musick in regulating the step, and making the men keep their order, is really very extraordinary.'[26] Colonel Samuel Bagshawe had raised a new regiment of Foot – the 93rd – in Ireland in 1760 and his lieutenant colonel reported to him most enthusiastically in a letter in September that year:

> I am teaching four pretty large Squads, & the Grenadiers, the method of Firing, Advancing, & Retreating, ... with the Officers superintending, & the Serjeants & Corporals paying attention to their own Squads, so that, by this means, every Squad is sure to do alike, to step together, & all must do it with the same signal of the Drum, & keep the same time.[27]

It seems perhaps counterintuitive that having soldiers march in step to the beat of drum aided manoeuvre and provided added tempo rather than reduced everything to over-control. Stephen Brumwell has provided a useful definition of why this was the case:

> The tactical flexibility of the infantry was enhanced further by the revival of the cadenced marching last practised by the hoplites and legionaries of the classical world. Here, as in many other aspects of military science, the lead came from the Prussia of Frederick the Great. Before the adoption of cadenced marching, troops had manoeuvred in open-order formations, only closing their file intervals prior to the linear confrontation; stepping forward in unison to the sound of fife and drum, the infantry now proved capable of swift and coherent movement in close order.[28]

Whatever the apparent efficacy of the use of the drum and the fife in this way, musical accompaniment to infantry manoeuvres appears to have been relegated relatively quickly to a training role and for parades and reviews of troops. It would be all very well having bodies of troops perfect their manoeuvres to the sound of drum and fife during a review and without any fear of shot and shell interfering, but another thing to demand such precision in battle. It would demand also that the drummers and fifers could keep the time while conscious of the fight they too were about to face. In 1778 General Jeffery Amherst, then commanding the army in Britain, had the 1764 regulations thoroughly revised in light of experience. Amherst possessed considerable experience, having been present at Dettingen and Fontenoy and commanding the army in Canada that ousted the French from the territory during the Seven Years War. Perhaps cognisant of his experience in Canada – he was instrumental in the establishment of the first light infantry in the British Army – he had laid down that:

> … henceforth all infantry manoeuvres were to be performed by vocal commands only, and that 'Drums should be used as little as possible in manoeuvring of Regiments & Musick [i.e. bands] never'.[29]

★

This is an opportune moment to consider military marches in this era and the arrival on the scene of bands of music. Both should be viewed as supporting elements to the central theme of this story but consideration is important nonetheless in view of, with regard to marching music, the essential business of effective marching to an army on the move and, with regard to bands, the blurring of lines between 'field musicians' and musicians 'proper' that was to occur over time.

A most thorough study of 'war music' by Lewis Winstock was published in 1970. He made a point at the very beginning of his book *Songs & Music of the Redcoats* that, in his writing, he had not touched on 'signalling music … the blowing and beating of a charge, or reveille' but was focussed on 'the songs and music that were an integral part of military events – that were played on the march, in camp, sometimes even in combat … [of] the instrumental music that was actually played in war – by fifes and drums, and by bands.'[30] With undeserved self-deprecation, Winstock felt that he had barely touched on the whole subject of military music altogether but he certainly allows us to see that music and song were of great importance to the British Army throughout its history. The need for music was the very reason behind the retention of numbers of drummers, fifers and buglers in the ranks for so long and well beyond the necessity to have just one or two for signalling purposes. The same need led to the establishment of bands of music that were to feature so prominently in the history of the British Army for the best part of 250 years.

Chapter 2 mentioned, if only in passing, the English March and the use of the drum and fife. In Chapter 3 we noted that, with the doing away of the fife, the oboe provided additional music to the army until it was replaced again by the fife, as described above and if thenceforth limited to the grenadier companies. Together all of these instruments constituted the only 'musick' available to the foot, the one constant being the drum. We probably underestimate the importance of the drum march to the armies of the 16th and 17th centuries but Farmer described it as 'one of the main features of martial discipline, and every nation had its own particular national type.'[31] We also noted earlier that the French cleric known to us as Thoinot Arbeau wrote in 1589 that 'The custom of marching to the drum looks very fine when well executed.' However, 'The mere sound' of drums beating a military march had much wider application. According to Winstock the sound of the Scots March was so ominous that it 'could frighten off an enemy not anxious to try conclusions with the fierce Scots.' At the important Swedish/Saxon victory at the battle of Breitenfeld near Leipzig in 1631 Robert Monro, commanding the Scottish contingent alongside the Swedes, ordered the march to be played in the middle of the battle so that, in the dust and smoke, 'his position should be known to both friend and enemy.'[32] This provides a clear reference to the use of the drum in one of its original purposes of demonstrating resolve to friend and foe alike. The English March might be as old as the Hundred Years War and there is a famous story, also related by Winstock, 'that at the end of the 16th century the French Marshal Biron had criticized the march for being slow, and had been sharply reminded by Sir Roger Williams [the renowned Welsh soldier] that slow or not it had been heard through the length and breadth of France.'[33]

Probably the most famous English march of all, and originally very much a drum march, was *Lilliburlero*, known to this day as the signature tune of the BBC World Service. The tune is attributed to the English composer Henry Purcell but it might have been known as early as the Civil Wars. The fame and popularity of the tune were established in 1688 when its anti-Papist words were used to mould public opinion and raise support for William of Orange; indeed, Farmer reckoned that it even helped precipitate the Glorious Revolution that same year.[34] *Lilliburlero* very quickly became the army's song and helped maintain William III's forces in the Irish War between 1689 and 1691. A contemporary ballad entitled *The Battle of the Boyne*, quite possibly written by an Enniskillen man in William's army, declared:

> ... the hautboys played.
> Drums they did beat and rattle.
> And *Lilliburlero* was the tune
> We played going down to battle.[35]

We have well established that music at this time, and before, was provided in the infantry by the drum and, for a time, either the fife or the oboe, however short-lived the latter. *Hautboys* appear to have disappeared from service very early on in the reign of King George I and quite possibly as a result of Marlborough's attitude that money spent on such instruments was wasteful. Francis Grose, in his *Military Antiquites*, wrote that the Duke, when asked by King George as to the whereabouts of the regimental oboes during an inspection of a regiment of dragoons, struck his pockets until the golden guineas in them jingled and replied 'Here they are, your majesty. Don't you hear them?'[36]

The subject of whether or not music, as distinct from the points of war, was played by drums, fifes and oboes on the actual battlefield is an elusive one. It would seem very unlikely unless by exception and except for beating the march, the evidence for which establishes this fairly well. The fife's re-introduction from the late 1740s brought to the infantry a much-needed musical addition, but it was not enough. At about the same time and, like the fifes, owing their introduction to German influence, bands of music began to make an appearance. While the decades of the 1760s and 1770s saw their proliferation, the first recorded infantry band has been identified as that of the 3rd Foot in 1754, with Parliament authorising in 1757 the establishment of bands of six musicians for each marching regiment.[37] However, there is evidence that some regiments at least had a few instruments other than the oboe early in the 18th century, and these included clarinets, French horns and bassoons. Definitively, there is a reference to the 1st Foot Guards having had a band established by the 1740s, for the *London Evening Post* reported in 1749:

> We are informed that on Sunday last the ENGLISH Band of Musick, belonging to the First Regiment of Foot Guards, Commanded by His Royal Highness the Duke of Cumberland, receiv'd their Dismission, to make room for a Band of *Germans*, who mounted Guard on Monday last.[38]

Other than the drummers and fifers and, for the cavalry, the trumpeters, other musicians and their instruments were found in regiments entirely by private arrangements and were funded by the colonel and his officers. Unlike field musicians these 'bands of music were introduced ... not through necessity, but by desire on the part of the officer class'[39] and originally had no direct military or ceremonial function. Hence their being paid for by the regimental officers and the emergence of increasing numbers of bands throughout the second half of the 18th century did not change this arrangement. Their arrival, however, does seem to have signalled attempts to regularise the position of the bandsmen as soldiers rather than simply hired musicians. Fortescue observed that at this time 'sufficient deference was paid to the popular love of military music to relieve colonels in part of the burden of hiring bandsmen, who, in some regiments at any rate, were after 1749 enlisted as soldiers and placed under military discipline.'[40]

What is also evident is that the role of these early bands changed rapidly from providing entertainment for officers to wider military roles. The bandsmen, and especially their bandmasters, might not have been soldiers in the proper sense and might have worn regimental uniform, or a more decorative version of it, by association. But their utility for ceremonial functions led to their early combination with the drums and fifes for parades and reviews. Together they could also have a major and positive effect on the public, which would aid recruiting and what we would call today public relations. As the modern musicologists Trevor Herbert and Helen Barlow have concluded:

> ... it takes little imagination to appreciate how smartly dressed soldiers marching to the sounds of music and drums impressed their beholders ... The sonic and visual effect of a band was clearly inspiring, and for the mass of ordinary people at this time there was no other sight or sound in public display to match it. It afforded regiments a colourful and attractive face that rendered their law-keeping role a little more palatable to the populace and made military service an exciting prospect for some.[41]

We shall examine later how the roles of the drummers, fifers and buglers and that of the bandsmen became blurred. Until bands were formally established for all regiments and while bandsmen were still very much civilians there was a great separation in roles but the army was quick to recognise that bands 'were soon so conspicuous and ubiquitous that it was necessary to embrace their existence into the formal regulatory framework of the army.'[42] The first attempt to do this occurred in 1803 but the blurring of distinctions between the two groups was by then already underway.

CHAPTER 5

American Scramble

Do you know where a drummer is? A drummer was quickly found, and ordered to beat to arms. The throb of the drum began to reverberate across the Common.

Governed though the army might have been by official regulations, the wars in Britain's North American colonies in the second half of the 18th century provided a number of distinct and different examples of fighting techniques that led to a distinguishable evolution in organisation and tactics and changes to the role of drummers. Soldiers had long understood the need to adapt to local conditions but the nature of much fighting in America required new techniques to be adopted across the deployed army as a whole. In America, facing as it was the *petite guerre* of irregular warfare against Indian, Frenchman and, later, American 'patriots', the British Army faced the problem 'of opposing an enemy that avoids facing you in the open field' which was 'totally different from what young officers learn from the common discipline of the army.'[1] One notable effect of this type of warfare was the creation of the British Army's first companies and then battalions of light infantry and with them appeared the bugle horn.

Nevertheless, the formalities of drumming and fifing as established at this time were prevalent and evidence of some of the more set-piece fighting in the colonies also helps us to better understand the application of drumming in battle. The official regulations and the writings of both Bland and Kane were well known and it is important to understand that the militia and provincial corps in all the colonies provided ready audiences for the various manuals. By extension, of course, the colonists who rebelled against Britain's government in 1775 were drilled and manoeuvred in exactly the same manner as the redcoats. General George Washington's Continental Army was no different, Washington having been very active in the militia against Frenchmen and their Indian allies in the Seven Years War. An abstract of Bland's *Military Discipline* was printed in Boston and New York no fewer than eight times collectively between 1743 and 1759. In the 1754 New York edition Governor William Shirley ordered 'that all corps of foot within the province were to conform to this drill.'[2] Notwithstanding the presence of the extant manuals the fact that battalions of foot were frequently moved to and from the American colonies – there were 15 there in garrison in 1764 – meant that the latest instructions soon found their way across all military forces. An official imprint of the important 1764 regulations was certainly in circulation by 1766 and Houlding has identified at least 26 such imprints in America between then and 1780, noting that this 'boded no good for the British Army … in the circumstances prevailing by 1774 the sincerity of emulation can hardly have seemed flattering.'[3]

The colonies of New England had been poorly garrisoned by Regular troops since their beginnings in the early 17th century, security being largely in the hands of locally raised militia and provincials. In 1750 there were just three Regular battalions in North America and these were based in Nova Scotia, with seven so-called independent companies spread across the 13 New England colonies. The frontiers of these colonies experienced never-ending skirmishing with Indians, but the main menace was posed by the French from their Canadian stronghold. Fighting intensified in the early 1750s and the spark that eventually ignited the Seven Years War can be said to have happened in 'the backwoods of the Upper Ohio during the summer of 1754.'[4] The theatre of operations was truly vast and British forces were for most of the time severely under-resourced despite Britain's strategic aims. The British soldier proved to be markedly adept at adapting to new conditions and new methods yet he has received scant praise for his successes. The victories of Louisburg in July 1758 and Quebec in September 1759 over the French in Canada and the numerous tactical victories during the American War of Independence are still too often seen as won by men who 'were no more than automatons – faceless components in a rigid military machine ... [with officers who] were largely fops and fools'.[5] If this was the case, and it was far from so, they were all the more remarkable for it.

Warfare in North America posed a particularly difficult dilemma for the redcoat. The historian Stephen Brumwell has noted that 'once the redcoat had overcome the difficulties of terrain and climate, and survived the attentions of the enemy's irregulars, he still needed all his traditional training to tackle the disciplined battalions of Old France.'[6] General James Wolfe's victory at Quebec on 13 September 1759, which sealed the fate of the French in Canada, was achieved by disciplined movement and firepower by infantry trained according to the book and well handled by the inspirational Wolfe. Much debate continues to this day over whether Wolfe deployed his five battalions of British Regulars and single battalion of Louisburg Grenadiers on the Plains of Abraham in two ranks or the traditional three. A formation three deep was still customary but the enlightened Commander-in-Chief in America, Major General Jeffery Amherst, had issued orders to his army on 9 July 1759 that:

> regulars were to be 'drawn up on all services two deep' because 'the enemy have very few regular troops to oppose us, and no yelling of Indians, or fire of Canadians, can possibly withstand two ranks, if the men are silent, attentive, and obedient to their Officers.[7]

By this order it has been assumed that Wolfe complied; it was a sensible reaction to local conditions. But the order had also made it clear that two-rank formations were not necessarily intended for use against enemy regular troops and that all troops were to be proficient in forming two deep and three deep. A very recent in-depth study is probably nearer the mark in concluding that Wolfe's battle line was actually three ranks deep but acknowledges that forming two ranks deep was well established by 1759.[8] The important point is that Wolfe's battalions would have been very able to handle any orders given them and that the drummers, having hauled their loads up the steep cliff paths, would have been beating commands as ordered. We know the drummers were present because Drummer John Fawcett, a 32-year-old drummer in the 47th Foot, was shot through the knee during the battle.[9] The 47th occupied the centre of Wolfe's line.

The experience at the beginning of open warfare between the two countries had not boded well for British soldiers' adaptability. In June 1755 Major General Edward Braddock set out with a force of two British battalions – the 44th and the 48th – and units of provincials to capture Fort Duquesne from the French. They stepped off with drums beating and in high spirits. Even as catastrophe crept up on them on 9 July on the Monongahela an officer's batman, who survived the subsequent massacre, wrote that that morning 'we began our March again, Beating the grannadiers March all the way, Never Seasing.'[10] This is not as absurd as it may seem, and it is not to suggest either that the men marched to a beat or in any way in step. Braddock's army took just under a month to cut its way through over 100 miles of thick forest and over mountain and river and exhausted itself in the process. However, a Royal Navy midshipman, Thomas Gill, one of a small group of sailors employed by Braddock to assist with the hauling of cannon and wagons over the formidable terrain, wrote of the distinct moral effect on their Indian allies of the drums and fifes that, together with a firepower demonstration, 'astonished and pleased the Indians greatly.'[11]

The disaster that befell Braddock's force that day was at least in part due to the failings of the European style of tactics in the forests and swamps. Braddock and his officers had done as much as they could to ensure the protection of the British column but the British regulars proved unable to cope with the intelligent Indians and their use of cover. It was not the fault of the drill book or its adherents but the tactical ineffectiveness of line and column led to rapid and utter rout. When parties of Indians, despite lacking any numerical advantage, began to envelop Braddock's army, the men would not stand. David Preston's recent outstanding work *Braddock's Defeat* describes the end. One British officer, who survived the ensuing massacre, wrote that '"As if by beat of Drumm" the remaining men collectively executed a right-about face, pivoting 180 degrees and fleeing for their lives.'[12] Further disasters followed, such as that experienced by the 42nd Highlanders against French regulars and colonial troops at Ticonderoga in 1758. Increasing numbers of British regulars in America seemed impotent in the face of 'skulking tactics'. But they were learning and, as Captain George Washington, who had been present as one of Braddock's aides at the Monongahela, remarked later:

> The folly & consequence of opposing compact bodies to the sparse manner of Indian fighting, in woods, which had in a manner been predicted, was now so clearly verified that from hence forward another mode obtained in all future operations.[13]

It was recognised by late 1757 that a counter to the French and Indians in the forests and on the rivers could be acquired by employing 'rangers', or light infantry, able to operate in a widely dispersed manner. Independent companies of rangers had existed for some time to range into the forests and scout against French troops and their Indian allies. But they were ill-disciplined and unreliable and even the most famous – Rogers' Rangers, later His Majesty's Independent Companies of American Rangers – owed their reputation more to Major Robert Rogers' exaggerated journal than their military utility. In 1758 Amherst, sent to America to command the expedition to Louisburg, had ordered that every regiment of foot should 'provide active marchers and men that are expert at firing ball.'[14] This post-dated the formation by Colonel Thomas Gage – who had led Braddock's advance party at the Monongahela and survived the ordeal – of a specialist battalion of light infantry to be known as the 80th Regiment of Light Armed Foot, or Gage's Light Infantry. In the campaigns that followed where stealth and tactical skill were paramount, British forces proved increasingly skilled at engaging the enemy on their own terms. The utility of light infantry and the grouping of battalion light companies into light battalions were demonstrated at the seizure of Louisburg and at Quebec, where the light infantry under Lieutenant Colonel William Howe scaled the heights and was first to occupy the ground before them. Howe's older brother, George, had also been involved in training and equipping his men better for service in North America. He had ordered the shortening of the soldiers' coats, removal of pigtails and various modifications to equipment and was killed while scouting Fort Ticonderoga with a party of

Rangers in July 1758. It is inconceivable that units such as Rogers' Rangers, Gage's Light Infantry or the light infantry battalions would find any use for the drum in the type of operations and fighting they were engaged in. But it is interesting too that there is no evidence of any other mechanical means of signalling, reliance being placed, it would seem, entirely on the voice at this time.

We noted earlier that in 1770 the distinctions between marching regiments on the British and Irish establishments were removed, both being equalised and fixed at 442 men each. Then, as a direct legacy of the finishing off of Old France and the success of British forces in the field, each regiment was ordered to increase its number of companies from nine to ten by finding a light company of 44 men within the new establishment. This took place in Britain in 1771 and in Ireland in 1772.[15] The formation of light companies clearly owed much to the success of light infantry in America but light infantry had also been noticeable in the armies of Prussia, Austria and other German states on the European Continent during the Seven Years War. The work of these *jäger* (hunter) units was confined initially to reconnaissance but they were to prove increasingly important when deployed as screens of skirmishers to blunt, if not break up, large bodies of line infantry. The introduction of light infantry in the European armies did not represent a revolution in military ways and means but they were an important adjunct to the battlefield and provided a major step towards universally greater tactical dispersion once mass-produced rifles were introduced.

It was mentioned in the previous chapter that a new set of regulations for the infantry was published in 1764 and we have observed too that these regulations received very wide circulation in the American colonies. They survived practically unchanged for the next 30 years but an analysis of them adds no more than we know already about the use of drum and fife. We have identified too that enhanced manoeuvrability of infantry was to be attained by imitating Frederick the Great's Prussian infantry, 'by training the troops to march and manoeuvre in close order, to a cadenced step.'[16] While this all coincided with the raising of bands of music in the infantry regiments, bands never had a role in regulating manoeuvre, that role being retained entirely by the drum.

That the 1764 regulations remained extant and largely unaltered for three decades did not mean that no changes took place and, in light of the major conflict that erupted in Massachusetts in 1775, this should not be surprising. The intervening years also gave rise to further private publications and, before examining the impact of the American War of Independence, one example will help show how theory could so quickly outstrip practicality. This example is, nonetheless, important in identifying the evolution of the use of the drum at a time when its use was at its very peak. It is important too in showing what was expected of the British Army at least in peacetime training.

Thomas Simes had been an officer in the 2nd (Queen's Royal) Regiment of Foot and in the 1760s and 1770s he published a profusion of works governing every possible detail supposed. Much of this he had plagiarised from others. While Houlding described Simes with some accuracy as 'without doubt the most long-winded drudge'[17] the bulky volumes were certainly of some use to officers learning their profession. Simes recorded in *A Military Course for the Government and Conduct of a Battalion* in 1777 various details for the use of infantry battalions and it is worth showing three particular examples. The first, under the title 'Of the Public Beatings of the Drum in Garrison' provides a very useful summary of the development of the original Points of War and also shows a conclusive difference established between Retreat and Tattoo:

> To beat the General, is an order for the whole to make ready to march; the Assemblee, to repair to their colours; and the March commands them to move; the Reveille, at day-break, warns the soldiers to rise, and the centries to cease challenging; the Troop assembles them together, to call over the roll and inspect the men for duty; the Retreat is beat at sunset, for calling over the roll again to warn the men for duty, and read the orders of the day; the Taptoo beats at ten o'clock every night in summer, and at nine in winter; the soldiers must then repair to their quarters or barracks, when the non-commissioned officers of each squad call over the rolls, and every man must remain there till reveille beating next morning. A Beat to Arms, is to advertise them to stand to their arms, or to repair to their alarm posts; and a Chamade, is to desire a conference with the enemy.[18]

These would seem straightforward enough instructions but Simes proceeded to describe in the 'Street Firing' how he saw it, or imagined it to be, and it is hard for us to imagine to what degree of training the soldiers of the day would have had to be subjected to master such a complicated series of evolutions, and harder still to believe that such evolutions to the prescribed beatings would survive contact with the enemy. The beatings are combined with words of command from the company officers, thus:

'To fire the Street Firing. March.'
The fifers and the drummers play and beat a march: the whole step off with their left feet; and upon the preparative, the first company gets the word from their own officer,
'Halt. Make Ready. Present. Fire.'
After which the men recover their arms, and face outwards from their centre. 'March'.
They go down the flanks by files, form in the rear; load, shoulder, and keep marching to the front, till they are ordered to fire again. When one company has fired the next takes up its ground, fires, and files off in the same manner: when the General beats the firing ceases. N.B. This firing is to be performed retreating, by each company firing without advancing to the ground of the one that fires before. The usual notice for this fire is preparative, and the retreat beating immediately after.[19]

Very usefully, Simes also described a comprehensive list of the various signals used to control the evolutions of the men and the way in which they were beaten on the drum:[20]

Turn or face to the right	One single stroke and slam
Turn or face to the left	Two single strokes and slam
To the right about	Three single strokes and slam
To the left about	Four single strokes and slam
To wheel to the right	Roll, one single stroke and slam
To wheel to the left	Roll, two single strokes and slam
To wheel to the right about	Roll, three single strokes and slam
To wheel to the left about	Roll, four single strokes and slam
To front	Strong double slam
To make ready	Preparative
To cease firing	General
To march	March
Quick pace	Quick march
To charge bayonets	Point of war
To form battalion	To arms
To ease your arms	Tow-row-dow

To secure your arms	First part of the tat-too
To shoulder your arms	Last part of the tat-too
To call the Adjt	First part of the troop
To call a Sjt and Cpl of each coy	Three rolls, six slams
To call all Sjts and Cpls	Three rolls, nine slams
To assemble pioneers	Pioneers' march
To assemble the drummers and fifers	Drummers' call

It is easy to see why there appears to be no evidence of the majority of these evolutions and their accompanying beatings being put into practice in the field because they must have been simply unachievable. The intended effect would be much more readily achieved and without confusion through voice commands. But a number of the beatings, such as those to call sergeants and corporals, do identify a growing propensity to establish routine calls in garrison or in camp.

★

The American War of Independence – the American Revolutionary War as it is called in the United States – provides us with some very clear evidence of the use of the drum and of the fife on the battle-field. As we saw earlier, whether they were deemed patriots or rebels, or whether they were colonial militia, state troops or the Continental Army, much of their original knowledge of soldiering owed itself to the British tradition. Therefore, examples from the American infantry can also be cited. The authors of the thoroughly researched *Military Music of the American Revolution* noted that the 'Revolution was essentially a civil war. Americans had the same cultural heritage as their British adversaries. Therefore, the same musical tunes could be heard in both British and American camps.'[21] We are helped by vast bodies of research into every aspect of the war, especially in the United States. Sadly, and this point has been mentioned earlier but is worth re-emphasising here, much of the literature persists in characterising the British infantry as 'serried ranks of grim-faced, pipe-clayed, red-coated automata advancing relentlessly in perfect cadence to thudding drums and squealing fifes, with regimental colours snapping at their heads.'[22] This is utter nonsense, as is the other side of the coin that has American success down to swarms of green-coated riflemen. In *With Zeal And With Bayonets*

Only Mathew Spring has done much to put this record straight. In this predominantly infantryman's war the reality was that 'the King's troops won the vast majority of their battlefield engagements in America because they tailored their conventional tactical methods intelligently to local conditions – very much as they had done in similar circumstances during the French and Indian War.'[23]

Military music, in all its guises, was an important feature of the war. Washington, who had served ably in the Virginia militia and had been present at the disaster on the Monongahela in 1755, when Commander-in-Chief of the Continental Army in 1777 declared that 'Nothing is more agreeable, and ornamental, than good music; every officer, for the credit of his corps, should take care to provide it.' We might assume this refers to bands of music but Gary Vorwald, Inspector of Music of the Brigade of the American Revolution, summarised the state of things by the 1770s:

> The main function of the field music was communication. It was the musician's duty to relay signals in camp, on the march, and in battle. In camp music served as the soldiers' clock to regulate their activities. Reveille was beat at sunrise to wake the men, the Troop was beat in the morning to assemble the soldiers for roll call and inspection, and Retreat was played at sunset to signal the end of the day's duty, and Taptoo was beat by 10:00 pm as a signal for 'lights out.' The sounds of drums and fifes assembled the men and informed them to dismiss. The march was regulated by fifes and drums which kept an even cadence or pace. On the battlefield there were signals to prepare to fire, to advance, and to retreat. In that way, music helped to maintain discipline and made it possible to move large bodies of soldiers in an orderly fashion and on time.
>
> In addition to those duties, music was also a major part of military ceremonies such as parades and reviews, the receiving and lodging of colours, punishments, and funerals.[24]

This is a correct assessment but the practicalities of campaigning over such vast distances, near-impossible maintenance of supply chains and major manpower shortages would have seen a great deterioration of formalities for both sides. While there were a number of general engagements the war was also characterised by near-continuous skirmishing on various scales. Light infantry were to prove indispensable in dealing with what were seen as the skulking tactics of the American militia.

This and the need for the infantry to cover far greater frontages than on the European Continent saw all British infantry become increasingly adept at deploying in open order or even more widely. They could do this with relative impunity as cavalry played, largely, no role other than reconnaissance throughout the war, which negated the need experienced by all infantry hitherto to manoeuvre in closed ranks as the best defence against a cavalry charge. But this dispersal of men and their firepower was to have unfortunate consequences when faced by Washington's trained Continentals.

Drums and fifes would have been a very evident and common feature of the King's regiments in Boston, the city then being the seat of the British government in New England. At the outbreak of the war in 1775 there were 16 infantry regiments based in and around Boston, the garrison there having being steadily reinforced since the previous year. Until 1770 regiments in America had been authorised the same number of drummers as for the old Irish establishment, that is, nine. But that year the number of drummers was doubled to 18, providing two per company plus the additional two fifers for the grenadier company. The following year the establishment was changed again when light companies were ordered to be formed, with the number of drummers being reduced once more to one per company, which included the light company, thus making a total of ten, plus the two fifers as before. In late 1775 regiments in America were augmented with an additional sergeant, 14 private soldiers and a drummer, providing two drummers per company once more.[25] Orders to raise regiments of foot in 1777 and 1778 for service in America showed that battalion, grenadier and light companies were all authorised to have two drummers each, the grenadier companies to have in addition to their drummers two fifers (and, for the Highland regiments, two pipers instead of the fifers).[26] That each light company of a line battalion had drummers rather than buglers is also evident in a *General Order* of May 1776 for the 1st Battalion of Light Infantry in the American Colonies. The light companies from each line regiment that contributed to this composite battalion were required to provide a captain, two subalterns, three sergeants, three corporals, 35 rank and file and one drummer.[27] There is some evidence to suggest that bugle horns were already in vogue for the light infantry in America even before the war commenced but all regiments raised on higher establishments in Britain for the American war continued to be provided with two drummers. The emergence of bugle horns is discussed below.

In garrison the work of the drummer was as before. Lieutenant John Barker of the 4th Foot – the King's Own – recorded in his diary on 12 July 1775 at Boston: in 'Camp on the Heights of Charlestown ... The Orderly Drummers of every Corps to Continue at their respective Quarter Guards from Gun Firing in the Evening, 'till after Reveille beating, and the Non Commissd. Officers Commanding these Guards to be answerable the Drumrs. are Attentive to the taps and beat the Reveille regularly.'[28] British soldiers marched to and fro to the sound of their drums and fifes, the mere sound able to cause alarm amongst those conspiring to open rebellion. When Bostonians gathered on 6 March 1775 on the fifth anniversary of the Boston massacre to hear an address by the political leaders of the approaching rebellion they were severely unsettled by the sound of approaching redcoats. This turned out to be 'the Forty-Third Regiment, its fifes and drums blaring outside the front door.' But 'As it turned out, the soldiers had just returned from a brief march into the countryside and had no interest in what was going on inside the Old South [Meeting House].'[29]

Young Fifer Samuel Dewees, who served in several Pennsylvania regiments during the war, left us with a splendid summary of a drummer's camp duties. His very clear discourse is worth showing in some detail as it gives us a very good idea of a drummer's routine:

> Each morning we had to play and beat the Reveille at the peep of day, and then the Troop for roll call. After roll call a number of men would be called out of each company as camp and piquet guards, and so many for fatigue duty ... A drummer was also chosen and was called 'Orderly Drummer' of the day. This drummer had his drum constantly lying on the parade ground during the day. Its place was generally where the colours were planted ... When the Sergeant of the fatigue men called out 'Orderly Drummer,' this drummer repaired to the Sergeant immediately, who ordered him as follows: 'Orderly Drummer beat up the fatigue's march.' We having had a name for every thing, or rather tunes significant of duties of all kinds. To beat the 'Point of War' *'out and out,'* or through from beginning to end, which embraces all tunes significant of *Camp Duties,* ADVANCES, RETREATS, PARLEYS, SALUTES, REVEILLES, TATTOOS,

&c. &c., would consume nearly or altogether half a day, and to beat the Reveille properly, 'the Three Camps,' which constituted the 1st part, 'the Scotch, Hessian, and Drags Single and Double,' which constituted the 2d or middle part, and 'the Three Camps,' which constituted the 3d or last part, would consume from the peep of day until after sun rise.

    … Early in the evening we had to beat up 'The Retreat.' We played and beat the *Retreat* down and up the parade ground as far as our regiment extended, for 'roll call.' We had many tunes that we played and beat for the Retreat. '*Little Cupid*' was often played and beat for Retreat. At bed-time we had to beat the '*Tattoo*.' For Tattoo, we had many tunes also. For roll call in the morning we had many tunes that we played and beat as the 'Troop.'[30]

There are some evident 'Americanisms' but both sides were happy to use one another's music, as is shown here by inclusion of a 'Hessian' piece, the 'Scotch' being perhaps assumed as just as relevant to an American army. Hessian was the common collective name for all German troops who fought for the King and elements of their tactical and musical methods were to influence the British Army.

Fifer Dewees related that 'There was always a great difference manifested in the manner attending the calls … the soldiers at the Fatigue's call generally turned out slowly and down-hearted to muster upon fatigue parade … [But when the] Orderly Drummer beat up "the Roast Beef," the soldiers would be seen skipping, jumping and running from the tents, and repair to where the rations were to be issued out.' This should not be wondered at, as Dewees noted. He added that 'Often the "Orderly Drummer" would be ordered to beat up "the Adjutant's call"' and the Adjutant would then attend to his superior officer. If the 'Drummer's' or (Musician's) call was beaten the drummers and fifers 'would have to "*drop all*," and answer by our presence. Our duties upon such calls were various. Sometimes we would be required to play and beat the Long Roll, Roast Beef, the Troop or the General, and sometimes "the Rogues March," and sometimes "the W[hore]'s March."' The rogues' march was used to drum a disgraced and discharged soldier out of camp. The meaning of the whores' march is rather more obvious but Fifer Dewees provided us with a descriptive example of the procedure. Having mustered at the sound of the drummers' call and marching to the parade ground:

    A woman of ill-fame was brought in front of us. In a few minutes afterwards we received orders to march. As we started off we commenced playing and beating

up the 'W[hore]'s March' after her until we arrived at the bank of the river ...
she was then conducted by the Corporal into the river ... Quite a scuffle ensued,
when the Corporal attempted to 'duck' her by plunging her head under the
water. The Corporal after a number of trials, at last succeeded in executing this
part of the sentence ... He plunged her '*head and all*' three times under water and
then let her go. When she started off after coming out of the water, we gave her
three *cheers* and three long rolls on the drum, and then marched back without
our fair Delilah ... Such frolics as these were often made a part of our duties, and
which (being young as some of us were) we enjoyed very well. It was not only
viewed as a necessary conduct of severity to this class of unfortunate women, but
it became necessary, at least that they should be removed from the camp.[31]

Evidence of the use of the drum in battle during the war is contradictory.
Notwithstanding printed regulations and the numerous private publics-
ations (*Military Music of the American Revolution* shows half a dozen or
so, including Simes, and all give varying versions of the same thing) the
likelihood was that there was but limited use for the drum on campaign
once the war developed beyond the abandonment of Boston in March
1776. The widening of the war and the ever-increasing distances and
logistic problems would make it seem unlikely that drums were used as
extensively as they might have been had similar fighting taken place at
that time on the European Continent. There would always have been
occasions when drums and fifes enlivened the march and orderly drummers were almost certainly retained by commanding officers. A 1775
American manual by the New Englander Lieutenant Colonel Timothy
Pickering – *An Easy Plan of discipline for a Militia* – was pragmatic enough
to suggest that 'Whenever the battalion marches, in order to perform
the firings, advancing and retreating, the fifes are to play some tune to
regulate the step, And tunes, which have some grandeur and solemnity
in them are undoubtedly preferred. The light airs, frequently played
for a march, would appear to me as unnatural and improper to be
used when a battalion is advancing towards an enemy.'[32] But, given the
increasingly difficult conditions that prevailed during the war, retaining
large numbers of encumbering drums and fifes as a general means to
regulate all manoeuvre might well have been deemed unnecessary and
unwanted. The drum was not replaced by the bugle as a general alternat-
ive, although increasing numbers of bugle horns were certainly adopted

by light infantry, as will be shown. That prolific writer Thomas Simes in his *Military Guide for Young Officers*, a copy of which was published in Philadelphia in 1776, wrote that 'In action, save the two orderly drummers, drummers and fifers were to "stay with their respective companies, and to assist the wounded."'[33] Given Simes' propensity to plagiarise the work of others this stipulation might well have been adopted fairly universally by this time and especially in America. If this was the case then it was the first evidence of drummers providing this important secondary role. This is supported by the memoir of Private Thomas Burke of the 45th Regiment who wrote of the battle of Brooklyn on 27 August 1776: 'In this engagement my colonel was wounded. He had two balls shot through his body, and was taken from the field, supported by two drummers.'[34] To add further explanation as to why drummers were available for duty as medical orderlies we also have the point made by Lord Amherst in his regulations issued in Britain in 1778 and mentioned in the previous chapter, 'that Drums should be used as little as possible in manoeuvring of Regiments ….'

The challenges of the terrain and the dispersal of infantry over it might also have limited the effectiveness of drum beats. However, the sound of the drum, especially when grouped together, could carry a remarkable distance. American re-enactors of His Majesty's 64th Regiment of Foot of the American War of Independence have demonstrated this by responding to drum beats above the noise of battle, albeit simulated, at well over one mile distant.[35] But manpower shortages, which were a constant problem for the British Army, also meant that drummers were also required to serve in the ranks. Steven Baule's investigations of drummers during the war have uncovered orders in Boston in March 1776 that make it apparent that some drummers were then serving as privates and that all drummers and fifers 'were to be thoroughly schooled in the manual of arms and be able to serve in the ranks when necessary.' On 13 March 1776 General Howe ordered that all drummers unable to carry arms were to be put on board ship in Boston harbour ahead of the evacuation. And the Orderly Book of the 17th Foot showed that at the end of that year a number of drummers had served in the ranks but were to be returned to duty as drummers while the regiment was in winter quarters.[36]

That drums and fifes continued to provide 'musick' for the purpose of an additional injection of courage and confidence is also shown from the very start of the American war. In February 1775, ahead of the rebellion itself, the 64th Foot was ordered from Boston to Salem to seize illegally held powder and shot. '... confident that nothing could stand in their way [the Regulars] decided to announce their presence. The fifes and drums of the 64th Foot suddenly shattered the stillness of the Sabbath with a raucous rendition of Yankee Doodle.'[37] This had long been a redcoat tune, originating around 1755 and whose words derided the unmilitary-looking colonial militias. Once the Revolution was underway American troops soon picked up the tune and used it to mock, in turn, the British Regulars after their losses at Bunker Hill.

In the exhaustively researched fights at Lexington and Concord on 19 April 1775 there is rather more evidence of both fife and drum, some of it usefully described by the American militiamen. One of them, 19-year-old drummer William Diamond of the Lexington Militia 'had been trained in the art of military drumming by a kindly British soldier'[38] at Boston and was ordered by his company commander to beat to arms to call out the militiamen. As the redcoats approached Lexington they could hear a drum beating the militiamen to arms and one of the Concord Minutemen remembered hearing 'our drums and fifes a going, and also the British. We had grand musick', although many were 'panic-struck at the first sound of the British drums.'[39] When discipline broke down amongst the British advanced guard (and one British drummer was killed there and another wounded) it was quickly re-established when Colonel Francis Smith arrived with the main body of British troops. He rode into the centre of the fight and demanded of Lieutenant Sutherland of the 38th Regiment:

> 'Do you know where a drummer is?' A drummer was quickly found, and ordered to beat to arms. The throb of the drum began to reverberate across the Common. The Regulars had been trained in countless drills to respond automatically to its commands. The British infantry heard the drum's call, steady and insistent even above the rattle of musketry.[40]

Having dispersed the rebels on Lexington Green Colonel Smith decided to strike out for Concord as planned. Smith wrote later that they marched 'with as much good order as ever troops observed in

Britain or any other friendly country'[41] and we can be certain that the drummers and fifers played throughout to announce their superiority. A local woman, Mary Hartwell, despite her husband being a sergeant in the militia, watched them come and later told her grandchildren 'The army of the king was coming up in fine order ... their red coats were brilliant, and their bayonets glistening in the sunlight made a fine appearance.'[42] In the contemporaneous sketches by the Loyalist Ralph Earl of the fighting that day it is difficult to discern drummers but he represented the formations of the British infantry very well and it is easy to see their battlefield deployments and their attempts at maintaining order. When the redcoats pulled back in some disorder from Concord Bridge to Lexington the sound of Lord Hugh Percy's approaching 1st Brigade would have been a great relief. They too had departed Boston that morning with their fifes and drums playing 'a spirited version of "Yankee Doodle" as a taunt to the inhabitants.'[43] The awfulness for the British soldiers of their subsequent long withdrawal to Boston would not have allowed for much in the way of drumming and the drummers would have been conspicuous and easy targets for the American militia hanging on the flanks and the heels of the redcoats.

Few images quite sum up how it is supposed British soldiers fought their battles during this war than Howard Pyle's 1898 painting *The Battle of Bunker Hill*. It is a superb canvas and its depiction of the British line carrying out an assault in accordance with the 1764 regulations may not be as fanciful as once supposed. We know that in this hard-fought battle on 17 June 1775 the assaulting redcoats were not handled particularly well initially, their commanders assuming they would be able to sweep away the rebel rabble in front of them. But such images have helped feed the myth of British military stupidity when, in fact, such a deliberate execution of Frederickian methods, even down to the drummers beating out the march, would serve to intimidate an ill-disciplined foe in to early submission. It did not work at Bunker Hill and, while a British victory was gained eventually, tactics had to change.

As an example of how the sound of the drums could help turn disadvantage to advantage, at Princeton in January 1777 the outnumbered and encircled 17th Foot, 'with drums beating and colours flying, charged into the midst of the encircling enemy, and by sheer courage, and fierce bayonet work fought their way through.'[44] Later that year at the important battle of Brandywine Creek on 11 September a captain of the 2nd Grenadier Battalion recorded just how the drums and fifes struck up the Grenadiers' March and set moving the whole of the British line into the exposed American flank: 'Nothing could be more dreadfully pleasing than the line moving on to the attack ... Believe me I would not exchange those three minutes of rapture to avoid ten thousand times the danger.' As the author Mark Urban has written, little wonder officers and men would succumb to the 'intoxicating reverie of power' resulting from drums ringing in their ears.[45]

The British Army was to experience significant change in the way it conducted itself in battle and this change was to have a lasting effect on the use of the drum. When General William Howe replaced the inadequate General Thomas Gage in late 1775 the British Army had found a commander who recognised that the prevailing fighting conditions demanded organisational and tactical changes in order to take on the American militia and Continentals at their own game. As we have seen, Howe had learnt by experience in America in the earlier war and, while there is little doubt that British regiments would have adapted their fighting methods in any case, Howe gave official sanction from the outset. The result was a return to two ranks and more widely spaced files and the speedier manoeuvres and firings that had proved so effective against the French. The drum would still play its part here, as the example of Brandywine showed, but for the companies and formed battalions of light infantry, operating in much looser and dispersed formations and appreciating the need for stealth and fieldcraft, the drum was an unneeded encumbrance. It has been noted already that drummers were on the strength of all light companies at this time but – taking their example as before from the *jäger*, the light infantry of the regiments of German infantry employed in the British service – they put aside their drums and took up the hunting horns of their Hessian allies. For the spread-out bands of light infantry the bugle horn had far greater utility than the drum. Those light infantry soon gained a reputation for fighting skill, which the sound of the bugle seemed to herald. At Washington's first victory at Harlem Heights on Manhattan Island on 16 September 1776 his adjutant, Joseph Reed, described the approach of the British and Hessian light infantry: 'The enemy appeared in open view, and sounded their bugles in a most insulting manner, as is usual after a fox chase. I never felt such a sensation before – it seemed to crown our disgrace.'[46]

Exactly when this change to bugle for the light infantry came about is not known. Hunting horns had been around for centuries and something similar to a post horn is purported to have been used by light dragoons in Germany in the Seven Years War. When the first German infantry regiments arrived in America in August 1776, they brought with them their light infantry equipped with bugle horns. So named because of their origin in natural animal horns, these large copper instruments have been described as Hanoverian horns or Hanoverian *halbmond* due to their half-moon shape. The 2nd Battalion of Light Infantry was using horns as early as the battle of Germantown on 4 October 1777, an officer of the light company of the 52nd Foot recording that the 2nd Light Infantry 'was so reduced by killed and wounded that the bugle was sounded to retreat.'[47] And there is early pictorial evidence in the contemporary drawings of the Italian artist Xavier Gatta, likely on the instructions of a British officer who was present at Germantown, of a bugler, also of the 2nd Light Infantry, sporting a large brass instrument very like a *halbmond*.[48] The further development of the light infantry arm and the evidence of its intelligent handling throughout the rest of the war may lead us to suppose that, given its later use amongst the specialist corps of light troops raised to fight Napoleon, the bugle proved of much benefit. The requirement for some handier means of battlefield communication than the drum was now well recognised amongst the troops themselves due to their experiences in battle. Indeed, one advanced practitioner of light infantry went a step further by employing a whistle to relay signals, anticipating their general use amongst rifles and light infantry some twenty years later. This was Major Patrick Ferguson of the 71st Foot, perhaps most famous for inventing the Ferguson Rifle – a rifled breech-loading musket well ahead of its time. Ferguson trained a provincial corps of Loyalists to move and fight in response to whistle blasts and when he and his provincials were destroyed at the battle of King's Mountain in South Carolina on 7 October 1780, 'Many patriot fighters later recalled hearing the sound of Ferguson's [silver] whistle over the sound of the rifle fire' during the course of the battle.[49]

Ferguson's is the best-known example of this early use of the whistle but it is apparent that from the onset of light infantry in the British Army the whistle was being considered as a means to exercise command and control over much more widely dispersed troops. As early as May 1772, shortly after light companies were formed on the Irish establishment, Lieutenant General Lord George Townsend, the Lord Lieutenant for Ireland, issued instructions on their training and equipping. These instructions made a clear requirement for 'officers commanding companies or battalions of light infantry to establish particular signals (which the "stoutest of the drummers" was to convey via a whistle or horn) for particular maneuvers, such as advancing, retiring, or extending or contracting the frontage.'[50] A subaltern in the 46th Regiment observed at the battle of Harlem Heights in September 1776 that Captain Mathew Johnson, who commanded the regiment's light company, which then formed part of the 3rd Battalion of Light Infantry, 'goes through his maneuvers by a whistle, for which he has often been laughed at … [but with] which his men are as well acquainted with as the battalion [companies] with the word of command.'[51] It is noteworthy too that the subaltern, Loftus Cliffe, did not mention the drum.

The men of the Continental Army were, originally at least, ambivalent towards the adoption of the bugle horn. No matter that the American colonials had something of an affinity with the methods of light troops, the bugle horn was too closely associated with the British light infantry and therefore disliked.[52] There might also have been a shortage of instruments to provide for any kind of general issue and some improvisation was certainly at large to fill the gap. The patriot Colonel Daniel Morgan, who commanded a company of riflemen soon after the start of the war and later a battalion of trained light infantry, was known to have used a 'turkey-call' to aid him in regulating the movements of his scattered troops. At the battle of Freeman's Farm on 19 September 1777, which was one of the two battles instrumental in the disastrous defeat of Burgoyne's British army at Saratoga, Morgan used his turkey-call to help rally his men after they had been flung back by British volleys. An American eyewitness was the controversial Colonel James Wilkinson who wrote that 'my ears were saluted by an uncommon noise, when I approached and perceived Colonel Morgan … who, with a turkey-call [an instrument made from a turkey-bone for decoying a wild turkey], was collecting his dispersed troops.'[53]

The Americans began to assume their own style early on. While the militia was very strongly influenced by British teaching, as it had been their own, the proper training of the Continental Army was established following the arrival of Friedrich Wilhelm, Baron von Steuben, an experienced Prussian officer who offered his services to Washington at Valley Forge in early 1778. His *Regulations for the Order and Discipline of the Troops of the United States* regularised training throughout the American forces and this included instructions regarding drum calls. These showed no major differences to British ways although in organisation, while light infantry also became a feature of the Continental Army, they were not as distinct as they were amongst the redcoats. American regiments often had light companies early on in the war and, in similar fashion to the British, Washington began brigading them into light infantry battalions from 1777. Despite their apparent ambivalence the bugle horn was certainly adopted by some of the units. For June 1778 Lieutenant Bernadus Swartout of the 2nd New York Regiment noted:

> 24 June A detachment was ordered out to act as light infantry …
> 25 June The Horn blowed (a substitute for a drum in the Infantry corps) we marched about four miles … and halted for the day.
> 26 June At the sound of the horn we marched eight miles and halted …[54]

When, in the summer of 1779, the American force was sent against the Indians in western New York, orders stated that, because 'the Bugle horns have not arrived, officers commanding columns [are] to provide two conk shells for their respective columns in lieu.'[55] But what is also interesting is that American regiments, certainly the Continentals, assumed a greater number of fifes than the two authorised for a British regiment. On 1 January 1781 Congress ordered that regiments were to have each ten drummers and ten fifers and also a fife major as well as a drum major. Reality was another thing and the five surviving *Returns of the Music of the Army* compiled by Lieutenant John Hiwell, Washington's Inspector and Superintendent of Music, show that regiments averaged five or six fifers in 1781 and nine drummers in 1782.[56]

The American War of Independence, while better documented than any war hitherto, provided few contemporary soldier-chroniclers and none of these, as in earlier wars, included any illuminating details of drums, fifes, horns or whistles on campaign. The best chronicle of a British soldier is that of Sergeant Roger Lamb. Lamb enlisted in the 9th Foot in Ireland in 1773 and was at Saratoga when Burgoyne surrendered his army in 1777. After his 'desertion' (escape) from the Convention Army he joined the 23rd Royal Welch Fusiliers, going into captivity again at Yorktown in 1781. His detailed account provides helpful insight into Major General William Howe's new tactical exercises in England in 1774 and the development of more advanced infantry manoeuvres in America. Of drums there is but one mention. On 8 June 1776 at Three Rivers Lamb recounted: 'At three o'clock this morning our drums beat to arms, and we soon marched out of the village to meet our foe.'[57]

What Sergeant Lamb does tell us is that General Howe's 'new exercise … consisted of a set of manoeuvres for light infantry … [which] were chiefly intended for woody and intricate districts, with which North America abounds, where an army cannot act in line.' Later on he made the comment that 'In fighting in the woods the battalion manoeuvring and excellency of exercise were found of little value. To prime, load, fire and charge with the bayonet expeditiously were the chief points worthy of attention.'[58]

Despite the lack of direct evidence we can deduce from close study of the changed fighting conditions, to which Sergeant Lamb pointed, how British soldiers operated in the field and thus make some fairly safe assumptions about the use of instruments to help exercise command and control. Mathew Spring's book referred to earlier is an invaluable modern-day guide to the British Army on campaign at this time, especially by way of deciphering tactics. What becomes abundantly clear in Spring's work is the rapid appreciation by senior British officers early on that the conditions of campaigning in North America required modifications to tactical methods. The dilemma for infantry for all time has been to concentrate sufficient force as quickly as possible to effect a decision, which usually meant to defeat the enemy, being able to survive the enemy's fire in the meantime, which would indicate the need to being dispersed. In Europe infantry had to be alert to the constant threat of massed cavalry, which required close-order formations, but close order exposed infantry further to cannon fire. Close order also exposed infantry at close range to enemy musketry but the discipline and firepower it enabled amongst one's own infantry provided major advantages. In America the threat from cavalry was negligible and close order made British infantry particularly vulnerable to the 'running fire' and fleeting targets usually posed by the Americans. None of the battles during the war, not even Bunker Hill, could be described as 'set-piece'. In the campaign against Savannah in late 1778 in the southern colony of Georgia, Lieutenant Colonel Campbell, who led the expedition, issued intelligent tactical instructions directing that 'the ceremonials of parade [should] give way to the essentials of the service' and that an 'army, battalion or detachment ought to be ready to meet or fight an enemy at all times and in every direction.'[59] While codified by Campbell, this was not new advice and experience had shown already that deploying in unbroken lines for battle was both impracticable and unachievable; moreover, it invited failure in the field. American topography and American tactics required something else: 'British battalions did not deploy, advance, and engage in strictly linear fashion but instead fought fluid and ragged combats that defy detailed sequencing.'[60]

General Gage had insisted in orders at Boston in August 1774 that 'troops are always to form three deep unless ordered to the contrary' but the lessons of Lexington and Concord and certainly the lack of rebel cavalry had him order two ranks henceforth on 3 June 1775, two weeks before Bunker Hill. Gage's order stated that 'The troops will draw up two deep on their regimental parades as well as on the general parade' and for the morning of 17 June Captain Charles Stuart wrote later to his father that the 'men were drawn up two deep on the beach in one line.'[61] They still retained close order but on 29 February 1776 General Howe, now in command, had ordered ahead of a planned but subsequently aborted assault on the American lines, that 'Regiments when formed by companies in battalion ... are always to have their files 18 inches distant from each other, which they will take care to practice for the future, being the order in which they are to engage the enemy.'[62] This was open order – 'the common open order of two deep' as described by Major General Philips on the Chesapeake in April 1781 that, as Spring states, 'remained the standard fighting formation for British infantry in America for the duration of the war.'[63]

While this was also deemed expedient due to manpower shortages it proved to be the best formation for infantry in battalion to manoeuvre over the broken ground they encountered. It was accompanied by a quickening of pace to a recommended 120 paces per minute for all standard movements. This would not have been difficult for drummers to keep up with and beat as required and manoeuvre might well have been accompanied by the drum on occasion. At Brandywine an anonymous chronicler recorded that when the 1st Battalion of Grenadiers opened their attack 'The line moving on exhibited the most grand and noble sight imaginable. The grenadiers beating their march as they advanced contributed greatly to the dignity of the approach.'[64] Lieutenant William Hale of the 2nd Battalion of Grenadiers reported 'when the line first formed, the Hessian Grenadiers were close in our rear, and began beating their march at the same time as us.'[65] German troops had a reputation for ponderous manoeuvre but the point about drums is well made. The Germans probably clung to music longer than the British. An American eyewitness at the action at Hubbardton on 7 July 1777, during the promising initial stages of the ultimately disastrous Saratoga campaign, recalled the reinforcement of the lead elements of Brigadier General Simon Fraser's Advance Corps by Major General Frederick von Riedesel's 'Brunswickers':

> At that moment, over the noise of gunfire came the surprising and unmistakable notes of a military band [sic] – a small one, to judge from the sound – bugles blaring, fifes tootling, drums beating the grenadiers' march.[66]

Von Riedesel's grenadiers and light infantry had been ordered to make as much noise as possible on their approach so as to give the impression of larger numbers. They might even have been singing psalms, although this seems extremely unlikely.[67]

From open-order manoeuvring at a quickened pace British infantry rapidly developed further celerity. Infantry could never afford to get out of hand by breaking formation. Resulting loss of control would quickly negate any chance of concentration of force and such disorder greatly reduced effective firepower. British infantry also had a much-feared reputation for firm steadiness and composure even under the most galling fire, as demonstrated at Bunker Hill, and this provided for further advantage over less steady troops such as militia. While the bulk of the infantry in their battalions did not seek to emulate light infantry, strict dressing of ranks was abandoned and companies learnt increasingly to operate separated from others on their flanks and, within the companies, to maintain the integrity of each file rather than each rank. After 1775 and therefore demonstrating a very responsive understanding of the tactical challenge, British battalions would quicken their pace as soon as they were under effective enemy fire – about three hundred yards – and accelerate into a run with bayonets charged. A further appreciation had been that American infantry would not stand in the open and fight it out by musketry volleys but, frustratingly, would fire from cover before scattering to concentrate again beyond range, making engagements endlessly inconclusive. If a stand was to be made it was done from 'behind fieldworks and walls, where they were nearly impervious to British musketry.'[68] To counter this skulking Spring states that 'the redcoats commonly accelerated to a kind of trot or jog long before they broke into a run for the bayonet charge.' That they could maintain their order at the same time is confirmed by a rebel militiaman at the battle of Cowpens on 17 January 1781 who recalled that 'the British line advanced at a sort of trot with a loud halloo. It was the most beautiful line I ever saw.'[69] We can probably conclude with some safety that, apart from the retention of orderly drummers, having drums deployed and grouped behind the twin ranks to regulate these manoeuvres would have been unwarranted and burdensome. The same can be said for the colours. Some regiments did continue to take their colours into the field and they were certainly present with the 17th Foot at Princeton, as shown earlier, and at the start of the Saratoga campaign in July 1777. At a 'desperate moment' at Vigie in December 1778 'Brigadier General Medows made a dramatic appeal to the 5th Regiment: "soldiers, as long as you have a bayonet to point against an enemy's breast, defend these colors"' and a few days later 'he instructed the soldiers of the reserve that, in the event of another French assault, the drums and fifes were to assemble around the colors of the 5th Regiment and play "The Grenadiers' March".'[70] But the importance of the colours became diminished, alongside the role of most of the battalion drummers, through sheer impracticality for much of the remainder of the war.

There is a possibility too, and quite a strong one, that even the orderly drummers were dispensed with. As early as 1768 the military theorist Captain Bennett Cuthbertson 'had recommended that troops should be trained to respond to vocal commands only, "because in action, the noise of the artillery and musketry generally renders it impossible to use any signals by drum, and therefore it can answer no purpose to have soldiers trained to what can never be attempted on real service."'[71]

Cuthbertson was, of course, speaking of rather more conventional procedures than those provided by conditions in America. But Spring cites a Horse Guards circular of June 1779 that regularised this recommendation. The restriction was clearly common practice by then for in February 1776 Howe ordered that British regiments at Boston were 'not to use the drum or fife for marching *or signals* [author's emphasis] when in the field' and a further directive for the 4th Brigade in May 1777 demanded 'No fifing or drumming but when ordered.'[72] This is not to say that the application of these orders was universal or final. The stipulation 'or as ordered' applied too and we have already seen examples, if a little sparse, of drums in the field throughout the war.

Shock tactics rather than fire tactics were therefore prosecuted and evidence suggests too that this was done with the bayonet alone, no shots being fired by the British infantry so that they could close with the enemy as fast as possible. No firing, no drumming, but shouting: 'the speed, vigor, and noise with which the redcoats came on with charged bayonets was often quite enough in itself to send all but the best rebel troops into a panic.'[73] That this method was employed early on was shown by Howe's victory at Long Island in August 1776. An anonymous British officer wrote:

> It was the General's orders that the troops should receive the rebels' first fire, and then rush on them (before [the rebels] had recovered their arms) with their bayonets; which threw them into the utmost disorder and confusion, they being unacquainted with such a manoeuvre.[74]

As the war progressed the battalion companies, now well used to not operating with their flank companies, were increasingly able to operate in effect independently, the battalion commander leading one company and the remainder conforming as best they could, 'it being impossible [in thickly timbered country] to maintain a properly connected line during the advance.'[75] This might have enhanced the role of the orderly drummer as the battalion commander would find it near impossible to shout orders that could be heard across his dispersed command. Control of the battalion and the larger formations remained critical to prosecuting a successful attack. A set of tactical instructions issued in August 1780 by Lieutenant Colonel Henry Hope, commanding the 1st Battalion of Grenadiers, emphasised the necessity of maintaining control during the bayonet charge:

> When the line is ordered to charge, either by word of command from the commanding officer or by signal of drum, each officer will repeat the word to his own company, and will endeavour as much as possible in rushing forward to prevent his men from breaking their order, that, either upon being ordered to halt, or after coming up with and forcing the first body of the enemy, the line may be reformed again with as little confusion and loss of time as possible, so as to throw in a fire upon such of the broken, flying enemy as they can't come up with, or to be in order to charge any second body that may present itself.[76]

Retaining control was always easier said than done and all too easily infantry could get out of hand as they drove ever more deeply into woodland in pursuit of their fleeting enemy. But sometimes too speed was deemed the critical factor, no matter what formation of order the infantry was in. As early as Monmouth (June 1778) the 2nd Battalion of Grenadiers found itself facing broken American infantry and Lieutenant Hale wrote to his parents that the matter was finally settled when General Clinton came up and cried out '"Charge, Grenadiers, never heed forming!" [and] We rushed on amidst the heaviest fire I have yet felt. It was no longer a contest for bringing up our respective companies in the best order, but all officers as well as soldiers strove who could be foremost …'[77] The same problem of control went for light infantry too and, while the sound of the bugle could carry much further than the drum, it did not mean that the light infantrymen were able to respond to a summons on the instant of a call, even if they knew where they were.

It must be added too that, while British infantry had often proved to be tactically superior to the Americans, once the Continental Army had gathered sufficient experience it began to show itself able to stand and face the redcoats in open battle. The return that this brought to fire tactics found British battalions, often much reduced in numbers, wanting. The new-found cohesiveness of Washington's regiments owed a great deal to von Steuben's training and the effect was that 'A British bayonet charge no longer assured a British commander a vista of fleeing Americans.'[78] Of course, no matter how well the British infantry proved itself on the battlefield, the army was in the end thoroughly outman-oeuvred in the strategic sense. When Lord Cornwallis surrendered to his American and French besiegers at Yorktown on 19 October 1781 the act of surrender was preceded by drummers being used in one of their more traditional roles: to beat a chamade or parley. Major Ebenezer Denny of the Continental Army witnessed the events and wrote on 17 October:

> In the morning, before relief came, had the pleasure of seeing a drummer mount the enemy's parapet, and beat a parley, and immediately an officer, holding up a white handkerchief, made his appearance outside their works; the drummer accompanied him, beating. Our batteries ceased. An officer from our lines ran and met the other, and tied the handkerchief over his eyes. The drummer sent back, and the British officer conducted to a house in rear of our lines. Firing ceased totally.

The following day he was able to record:

> Several flags pass and repass now even without the drum. Had we not seen the drummer in his red coat when he first mounted, he might have beat away till doomsday. The constant firing was too much for the sound of a single drum; but when the firing ceased, I thought I never heard a drum equal to it – the most delightful music to us all.[79]

CHAPTER 6

'That Article' and the Great War with France

… at length the bugles sounded the 'advance' and a hearty 'hurrah' announced to the spectators that we had gained an advantage.

Of all the wars fought between Britain and France the greatest of these struggles was brought on by Revolutionary France in 1793 and culminated in Napoleon Bonaparte's final defeat at Waterloo in 1815; this settled the matter once and for all. The reasons that the British Army began that war in traditionally poorly prepared style have been reckoned as very much a legacy of the late American war. The Army was certainly exhausted by 1783 and in the intervening decade suffered from major economies – it was barely 40,000 strong when the Revolutionary War began – and lack of political interest. But it is much too simplistic to say that the poor performance of the British Army in the first few years of the new war with France was due to the failure to heed the lessons learned from often extremely hard-fought battles in the American Colonies. It is true that British tactical successes in America were rather forgotten in the immediate aftermath and, while the fighting prowess of the British infantry remained unsullied, criticism was heaped by many on an apparent failure in the system of manoeuvre that had developed. That system, so disparagingly called the 'American scramble' – the two ranks and loose files that had proved itself very well in America – was now identified with strategic failure. Particular criticism was saved for the 'light infantry fashion', seen by many, and not just those who had sat out the war elsewhere, as systemic of poor discipline, lack of order and wasted resources. Further development of light infantry was certainly curtailed after the war and this did not help British armies when they took to the field once more in the 1790s. But the very different fighting conditions experienced during much of the war in America, combined with limited resources, did require different fighting methods as we have seen. As Philip Haythornthwaite, a major authority on the British Army at this time, has remarked: 'tactics suitable for North American conditions were not necessarily ideal for European warfare.'[1] The large armies of France presented more traditional challenges. It was correct, therefore, that the British military authorities embarked on a process of relearning what had been forgotten. The end result was further unsurpassed respect for 'that article' – the British infantryman with whom the Duke of Wellington, never easily pleased, reckoned at the end of the Peninsular War he could have done anything with. Before Waterloo, while strolling through a park in Brussels with Thomas Creevey, a Member of Parliament, Wellington pointed at a British soldier and exclaimed 'There, it all depends on that article whether we do the business or not. Give me enough of it and I am sure.'[2]

The state of the army by 1783 certainly required putting right, not the least of which was the great irregularity of drill that had developed amongst the marching regiments. The remedy was seen as a return to the Prussian system and the regulations published after the end of the American War of Independence and, indeed, well towards the middle of the following century, tended to return time and again to enforcing regularity and solidity in the movements of bodies of troops. An attempt was made at this sought-for regularity in 1786 when the Adjutant General at that time, Sir William Fawcett, updated the existing regulations by drawing on Prussian methods and especially General Friedrich von Saldern's *Taktik der Infanterie*. But the most influential British officer proved to be Colonel, later General, Sir David Dundas who, significantly, was also one of the foremost critics of the tactics used in America, which he viewed as suitable at most for 'colonial conditions'. Dundas had witnessed the extensive Prussian field exercises of 1785 (as had the then up-and-coming Duke of York) and was so impressed that he based his *Principles of Military Movements*, published in 1788, on the uniformity and regularity he experienced when viewing the perfect manoeuvres of the Prussian infantry. He has often been viewed as the epitome of a reactionary senior officer in his dismissal of open and extended order and the looser formations used in North America. But when examining his preamble to his *Principles* we may discern some advanced thinking on training and methods of command, albeit based on traditional methods of 'Superior order, regularity and weight of fire' as discerned by him of the Prussians. When viewed as his attempts to establish a system to fight in a more conventional manner he was correct in summarising the problem by saying that 'Our ranks are so thin, our files so open, and such intervals [are] permitted between companies of the same battalion when in line; that all idea of solidity seems lost.' The cause of this he deduced, again correctly, was the lack of cavalry found in America. Had the infantry 'seen and been accustomed to the rapid movements of a good cavalry, they would have felt the necessity of more substantial order, of moving with concert and circumspection, and of being at every instant in a situation to form and repel a vigorous attack.'[3]

This was a very important work and, while it is easy to criticise Dundas' somewhat dogmatic insistence on close order and manoeuvring on pivots, it brought some standard back to the training of the British infantry. Experience in the war that followed against Revolutionary France and then Napoleon showed up his system and the drill books on which it was based as over-rigid, but only if the system was rigidly applied, which was not the purpose. Ultimately the British infantry would adapt as it had before and produce battle-winning tactical methods.

What is most significant for the story of the drum is that, judging by Dundas' directions, its days as a primary means of signalling on the battlefield really had passed. The set of interim regulations published in 1786, 'by His Majesty's Command' stressed most explicitly that they were 'a Foundation for establishing amongst His Troops that Uniformity and System ... which are so essentially requisite for Military Operations ... [and] To remove the various Defects in Discipline, which may have been introduced through Negligence, or Prejudice, and confirmed by long Practice ...'[4] These modestly sized regulations gave a brief but clear order: 'The Use of Drums, or Trumpets; and of Musick, is to be avoided, as much as possible; the former may be had recourse to sometimes, for the Circulation of general Signals; but the Voice is the best, and safest Engine to be employed, in the immediate Communication of all Orders to Troops under Arms, so as to prevent Disorder, and Confusion, in the Execution of them.'[5] Dundas added further explanation, showing clearly the balance required between voice and other signal:

> Words of command, for all movements of lines or columns, must be given in such manner, and in such extent of voice, that every individual should be apprized of what is to be done ... All alterations in carrying arms, change of pace, facing, inclining, halting, marching, and in general every operation of the battalion, whether in line or column, which ought to be executed by the whole, at the same instant, are made in consequence of one word from the commanding officer.
>
> ... Signals [i.e. drum beats] are improper in exercise, because dangerous and apt to be mistaken in service: every direction ought to proceed from the voice, which is explanatory to the understanding. But a few well distinguished signals of the drum or trumpet, may on some occasions be permitted as expressive of the alterations of pace, and as preparation to a march – halt – quick step – slow step – forming line from column.
>
> ... On all occasions of parade, the drums and music add much to the appearance of the troops; but they are improper in manoeuvre, and counteract the regular movements of great bodies. They are constantly varying the times of march, they create noise, prevent the equal step which habit alone can give to troops, and tend to destroy the very end they are meant to promote; for the uncertain time of an instrument, can never regulate the cadenced march; and the same sound is progressively heard at different instants ... The tact or cadenced march, can be preserved from the eye and habit alone, and troops must be accustomed to maintain it, notwithstanding drums, music, or other circumstances may be offering a different marked time. Their general use therefore is on occasions of show and parade; at the moment of the charge, they may however be allowed, as inspiriting and directing the attack, and also in the column of march; but in most movements of manoeuvre, during every transition from line to column, or from column to line, in all formations, and in the march of the line in front, they must be sparingly used, and never as directing the cadence of the step, or in the instruction of the recruit, officer, or battalion.[6]

This was all thoroughly pragmatic and it should be noted that the drum was allowed for when deemed necessary, including during the charge. But the all-important cadenced step would be learnt by constant practice and without the drum providing the timing, which confirmed earlier regulations. In order to add even more regularity, Dundas directed that 'It has been customary from the halt, when to march in front to step off with the left foot ...' which, again, confirmed a relatively long-established practice.[7] That the drummer still retained an important role was clear and Dundas instructed that in formation, as before: 'The drummers of the six battalion companies, are assembled in two divisions, six paces behind the third rank of the second and fifth companies.' Note the definite statement of there being three ranks and just six battalion companies rather than eight, these stipulations also being evident in the 1786 regulations. On numbers of ranks these regulations were also specific:

> The regular, established Order, in which the Infantry in general, is to be formed, is three deep; – This being considered therefore, as fundamental Principles, respecting its Formation, every Regiment of Foot, when assembled for Exercise, or on any other Occasion, is to be drawn up in three Ranks.[8]

As if to emphasise even further a return to the order that prevailed before the disruption of the North American experience, there was no mention by Dundas of the bugle; rather 'The grenadier and light company drummers and fifers, are six paces behind their respective companies.'[9] He reserved special criticism for the light infantry. He did not doubt their gallantry and their conspicuous service, but their 'showy exercise, the airy dress, the independent modes' flew in the face of the need for greater solidity. They had drained battalions of their best men and had almost become 'the principal feature of our army'. He recognised the importance of light infantry but demanded their regularity and, where they might be battalioned, that they 'conform to the same principles of order and movement' as the marching regiments.[10] This was a further important point – that light infantry should perfect the entirety of the battalion exercise before they advanced to practising light infantry tactics – and it was a point that would be repeated well into the 19th century.

One year later in 1789 Dundas, on being appointed Adjutant General in Ireland, redressed his passing over of the 'light bobs' – a nickname increasingly applied to all light infantry – when an amended version of his work was published in Dublin in which he provided much more detailed direction on the use of light infantry. In fact the Dublin amendments represented detailed guidance for light infantry both for light companies operating with their battalions and when companies might be assembled together in light battalions. He still emphasised the requirement to keep light infantry in hand and especially if ever required to run, when 'the utmost care is to be taken that confusion do [sic] not ensue; for which purpose the velocity must never exceed that at which divisions can keep together and dressed ...'[11] It must be remembered that this was all ahead of the formation of proper light infantry but recognition was also given to the utility of the bugle which, from 'Old Pivot', was recognition indeed. Under 'Signals' he identified five, and provided the music to go with them: Advance, Retreat, Halt, Cease Firing and Assemble and directed that these

> ... signals are to be always considered as fixed and determined ones, and are never to be changed. The bugle horn of each company is to make himself perfect master of them. All signals are to be repeated. All of those signals made from the line or column are to convey the intention of the commanding officer of the line to the officer commanding the light company who will either communicate them to the several companies or detachments by word or signal.[12]

That no major set of new regulations was published throughout the Revolutionary and Napoleonic Wars says much for Dundas and the 1786 regulations being fit for purpose. The latter were amended in 1792 and a newer set were published in 1801 but both showed very little material difference and would have us conclude that these were all good enough as a basis from which to operate in the field. The 1801 *Rules and Regulations for the Formations, Field Exercise, and Movements of His Majesty's Forces* reiterated that 'The drummers of the [again] eight battalion companies are assembled in two divisions, six paces behind the third rank of their second and seventh companies – The grenadier and light company drummers and fifers are six paces behind their respective companies ... Drummers in column of march, or close column, are with their companies, and on the flank, not the pivot one.'[13] This shows that the impact of war had allowed for battalions to rise once more to ten companies in total, and that light companies were still, officially, provided with drummers. Three ranks also remained 'the established order of formation for the infantry' and this was further stipulated in 1804 when the Adjutant General signed off *General Orders and Observations on the Movements and Field Exercise of the Infantry* on 1 September. Three ranks were 'not to be departed from except in light infantry battalions, or in small or detached corps acting as such.'[14]

These 1804 orders also made a particularly strong point about conducting movements without music, so strong a point that we might think similar previous orders were being ignored by some commanding officers. The orders stated that, except for parade or other similar occasions, 'The use of music or the drum in instruction, or to regulate the time of march of troops in movement, is positively forbid ...'[15] This must be set alongside a further order that provided for the following:

> When a line halted is to be put in motion, and before the word march, a drum may beat a march, or give a roll from whatever battalion is to direct: such signal will be considered as announcing the directing battalion, and such battalion, during the march, will occasionally repeat. If necessary, during the march, from obstacles of ground, to change the directing battalion, the drum from the new battalion will announce such change. Every battalion in line will always have a drum in readiness behind its colours, for the purpose of giving such signal when so ordered.
>
> In the exercise of a brigade or line of infantry ... no signal of the drum, or bugle ... are to be given or repeated by individual corps. They alone come from the battalion ... of direction ... The only exceptions are signals to cease firing, which can never, when given, produce inconvenience, as it can immediately be ordered to proceed if necessary.[16]

This can only show that universal drumming in infantry battalions and across the whole length and depth of infantry in the field had been suppressed. While every battalion appears to have had its drummers in the line in the field the active drummers seem to have been limited to an orderly drummer or two with the commanding officer or stationed with the colours. The remaining drummers probably had their drums with them but all drummers were to remain silent except for the orderly drums of the directing battalion, except when the order to cease fire was given, whence they would all beat.

This order would seem pretty conclusive: there was no cacophony of British drums on the battlefield at this time. Nevertheless, all orders were invariably caveated with the proviso that such-and-such was to happen unless otherwise ordered by the commanding general or appropriate commander. There may still have been occasion when, for effect and stimulus, drumming as we might imagine it and as was established in the previous century was used. Professor Richard Holmes provided a splendid description in his book *Redcoat* of a regiment of foot, in this case the 37th (North Hampshire), preparing to receive the attacking French in an unnamed battle in the Iberian Peninsula in 1808. The 37th was an unfortunate choice as the regiment did not serve in Portugal or Spain at any time but the writing is nevertheless powerful in demonstrating the formality of a set-piece battle and this is certainly how we imagine the British infantry fought, if the reality was somewhat different.

Holmes described the 37th formed in line on the reverse slope of a hill as they waited for the British and Portuguese skirmishers to withdraw in contact as the French assault, still unseen but clearly heard, came on. The commanding officer of the 37th then gives the order to march 'And they step off, as one man, with their left foot, boots swinging low over the earth in 30-inch steps at 75 paces to the minute. The drums tap out the step as the lines move forward ...' On reaching the crest and with the French infantry coming on apace,

> Raising his voice against the din, the colonel gives a long drawn-out preparatory command of 'Thirty-Seventh' and follows it three paces later with 'Halt'. The drums cease on the instant, lending emphasis to the order, and the battalion stands ready. ... The colonel ... shouts 'Front rank: Make ready'. The drummers beat the short roll of the 'preparative'; captains step back behind the second rank; the front rank's muskets come up .... [The French] are only fifty yards away ... when the command 'Present ... Fire' rings out. The British front line fires a volley of shattering precision.[17]

This is an opportune moment to consider the French approach to drumming at this time. Without delving too deeply into French tactics, which would be a book in itself, the use of drums by the French infantry might be summarised as somewhat unsophisticated and showy, certainly when compared to the British infantry. The noise generated during a French assault and the often inevitable breaking of that assault by British discipline and firepower went hand-in-glove with respective use of the drum in battle. One of Napoleon's young officers in Spain, Thomas Bugeaud, who later rose to be a marshal of France, wrote a stirring comparison of the two to his aide-de-camp in Algeria in the 1840s:

> Arrived at a thousand yards from the English line, our soldiers began exchanging their ideas in agitation, and hastening their march so that the ranks began to waver. The English, silent, with grounded [that is, ordered] arms, presented, in their impassable immovability, the aspect of a long red wall; an imposing aspect that never failed to impress the novices. Soon, the distances becoming less, repeated cries of 'Vive l'Empereur! En avant! A la baïonette!' sounded from our ranks; the shakos were raised on the muzzles of the muskets, the march became a run, the ranks got mixed, the agitation became tumult; many fired as they marched. The English line, still silent and motionless, with arms still grounded, even when we were not more than 300 yards off, seemed not to be aware of the storm about to burst upon it ...
>
> At this moment of painful expectation, the English wall moved. They were making ready. An indefinable impression fixed to the spot a good many of our soldiers, who began an uncertain fire. That of the enemy, concentrated and precise, was crushing. Decimated, we fell back, seeking to recover our equilibrium; and then three formidable hurrahs broke the silence of our adversaries. At the third they were on us, pressing our disorderly retreat.[18]

No mention of drums here but we know that much drumming accompanied a French infantry assault. The nine platoons in a French battalion each had two or three drummers and in battle these were concentrated in one large group to the rear of the colour or eagle, there to concentrate their drumming so that it could be heard above the sound of battle. Indeed, there is evidence that the French drummers were concentrated with the regimental band, for no less a witness than Michel Ney, Marshal of France, wrote: '*La Musique du regiment, durant le combat, sera réunie en arrière du regiment et jouers de airs guerrière pendant le combat ou la bataille.*'[19] The drummers, forward or rearward, were controlled by their drum major, described by the historian Paddy Griffith 'as a sort of human flag on the battlefield: while the drums beat under his control, the battalion is still a living force.'[20] This statement implies a much more primitive status to drumming in the French army where the emphasis was on emboldening the men more than in exercising command and control. The French held little regard for the use of the horn and, while horns were not unknown in their light infantry, the drum was also predominant in these units.

If French drumming was also meant to intimidate the British it did not work. British infantry spoke disparagingly of the French infantry as 'old trousers', especially when executing their attack. This expression was derived from 'The ominous drum roll for ordering the 'charge' ... rendered by the French as the rhythm "PLAN rat a PLAN rat a PLAN (etc)", which British witnesses famously remembered as "OLD trousers, OLD trousers, OLD trousers (etc)."[21] A British officer of the 5th Division at Waterloo, writing some 20 years after the battle, recalled seeing the day following the battle the field strewn with French drums and noted that 'The French drummers make a great noise when they advance to the attack, – striking up a beat which was well known to our old soldiers, and called "old trousers," from its resembling in sound the pronunciation of these words. They are said to be more active in carrying off the wounded than ours, who are notorious plunderers.'[22] The officer's point about the plundering activities of British drummers is worth noting, as is the point made about French drummers also acting as medical orderlies. In his *Random Shots of a Rifleman* Captain Sir John Kincaid of the 95th Rifles, in writing of old trousers, recalled 'I have, when skirmishing in a wood, and a French regiment coming up to the relief of the opposing skirmishers, often heard the drum long before we saw them, and, on these occasions, our riflemen immediately began calling to each other, from behind the different bushes, "Holloa there! look sharp! here comes old trousers!"'[23]

Returning to the fictitious account of the 37th Regiment, being early in the Peninsular War a British regiment may well have been handled in this way, especially if steadiness and discipline required additional guarantees. But it is very unlikely they marched in step to beat of drum and there is every indication that British infantry had far greater ability to move and handle their weapons at speed, responding to simple words of command down the lines and acting with celerity. It would be called tempo today – the ability to respond and manoeuvre at greater speed than one's enemy and, given the speed that Napoleon's generals could bring on their infantry columns, this would have been of acute necessity.

No matter what Dundas might have prescribed about pivots and fronts, the reality of the situation was another matter and there would be little place here for lengthy commands and orders transmitted by drum (with which Dundas would have concurred). Certainly a commanding officer would retain his orderly drummer by his side, to use as the situation might permit, but the orderly drummer would just as likely be gripping a bugle. In one of the best memoirs to emerge from the Peninsula, William Grattan, a young officer of the 88th (Connaught Rangers), recalled how well Colonel Wallace, his commanding officer, handled the battalion at the battle of Bussaco on 27 September 1810. With, it would appear, a few simple words, Wallace threw out the battalion from line into column, filed out the grenadier company and two of the centre companies to get at the French flanks and then, dismounting from his horse, led the charge of the 88th and the 45th.[24]

While the drum would still be used on appropriate occasions to regulate the day and issue some commands – Reveille, the Alarm, etc. – and to add emphasis to commands such as the Cease Fire, it was giving way increasingly to the bugle. Whatever shortcomings there were in Dundas' work, there was a practicability to his direction on use of voice and drum that endured for 100 years or so, as will be seen. To emphasise the points again, drummers still retained an important place in garrison and for regulating the day but once deployed and on the battlefield their playing of field signals was increasingly given over to buglers. Those not retained for this role found themselves grouped with the bandsmen and involved in bringing succour to the wounded as temporary medical orderlies, a matter expanded on below.

That drums continued to be present on campaign is not doubted but it would seem that their use was confined much of this time to regulating the day in camp and garrison and enlivening the march. There are plentiful examples of the drum in routine use and two will suffice. The Standing Orders for the 33rd (1st Yorkshire West Riding) Regiment in 1798 provided the following:

> The orderly Drummer of the Day will beat the Drummer's Call twenty minutes before the morning and evening Parades, on which each Company is to assemble … When there is no Parade a ruffle will beat after the Drummer's Call.

> There must be an 'Orderly Drum and Fife' to beat all duties, the former to be warned by the 'Drum Major', the latter by the 'Fife Major'.[25]

General Lake's orders for his Grand Army encamped near Agra in India in September 1804 during the Second Maratha War stated that:

> ... officers [for duty] are to mount on Marching days at General beating, and on Halting days, at troop beating.
>
> When the Assembly beats, the picquets on duty are to assemble at such a place in front of the centre of the line as shall be pointed out by the Field Officer on duty.
>
> The taps for the General and Assembly beating are always to be given from the Park, and to be taken up by the corps to the right and left, and the drummers' call to be returned from the flanks. When the drummers' call reaches the Park, the General Assembly is to be beat off.[26]

But even in camp the bugle was supplanting the drum. While the following example is taken from the Light Division in the Peninsula it does demonstrate the point. Captain Jonathan Leach, commanding the 2nd Company of the 95th, later recalled General Craufurd's Standing Orders for his division as issued in July 1810 and which included regulations 'to govern troops' behaviour from their first waking moment to their last. Reveille, the blowing of a bugle horn, would sound an hour and a half before any intended march got under way. The Standing Orders set out what had to happen before a second horn blast an hour after the first, noting, for example, "the baggage must be loaded at least ten minutes before the second horn sounds". A quarter of an hour later, at the third horn, companies were to form, ready to set up. On the fourth blast, the head of the column would begin its march.'[27]

As the principal means of signalling on the battlefield the role of the drum had certainly been fairly brief and was near its end. Barty-King summed up the position by stating that by the turn of the century 'Gradually less and less reliance was placed on The Drums for signalling in the British army.'[28]

We have seen already that the situation was not clear-cut. That change and, perhaps, confusion were abroad may be indicated by the fact that in 1798 the Secretary of State for War had ordered an enquiry into the use of the drum, fife and bugle so that some measure of standardisation could be imposed on the army, and especially with regard to signalling. Trumpet Major James Hyde of the London and Westminster Light Horse Volunteers was commissioned by the Duke of York to study the problem and make recommendations. While these recommendations, published in December of that year, were confined mostly to the use of trumpet and bugle in the cavalry, an addenda provided 'The Bugle Horn Duty for the Light Infantry as used in the Foot Guards.'[29] This work had a direct effect on the work that immediately followed in regulating bugle sounds for the light infantry as a whole and as described below.

The evolution of light infantry in the British Army had been largely ignored after the American War of Independence, as we have noted above. However, early experience against the armies of Revolutionary France and their use of skirmishers, almost in swarms ahead of their attacking columns, showed the British Army that it needed an effective counter. Whether poorly trained and organised *grandes bandes* or what were to become formidable *tirailleurs* and *voltigeurs*, French light infantry could ruin an attacking or defending formation and could only be dispersed effectively by other well-trained light infantry.

It will help here to explore, if briefly, the development of British light infantry from the 1790s due to the direct link this had with the development of bugling in the army as a whole. The line regiments had continued to maintain their light companies but they were to prove inadequate to the task. This was demonstrated early on when the Anglo-Hanoverian Army at the battle of Hondschoote on 6 and 8 September 1793 showed itself completely outmatched by French *tirailleurs*, neither British or Hanoverian infantry having anything but poorly trained light companies. The lesson taught by the French in the close country of Flanders was largely lost on a British Army then struggling for more universal improvement and in a campaign where it suffered various humiliations. The threat of invasion provided further impetus and in 1798, in examining the enclosed country of eastern England, General Sir William Howe, by then commanding defences in the east, wrote to Lord Cornwallis, then Master General of the Ordnance that 'A large body of infantry with a considerable force of light infantry, are, I think, essentially necessary for the defence of Essex.'[30] Both men, of course, had

had considerable experience in America. Major General John Moore had also served there as a young officer and supported Howe's points by adding that 'To prevent the progress of an enemy marching to Colchester when landed would require a great superiority of light troops … The country … is much enclosed and flat.'[31]

The Army had experimented a little with light infantry in the mid-1790s. Large numbers of light infantry had actually been utilised in the crippling campaign in the West Indies between 1793 and 1798. Here the battalion flank companies had again demonstrated poor performance, not helped by the hostile terrain and climate. The Army resorted to establishing corps of rangers composed entirely of 'released' slaves, who proved remarkably effective and who had a marked influence on officers like John Moore. The Flanders campaign of 1793–94 had also seen the raising somewhat hastily of additional foreign units to be used as skirmishers, and these too were despatched to the West Indies in 1795. These units were made up almost exclusively of Germans, with one Dutch corps, demonstrating the much-held view in the British Army that the work of light infantry was best left to foreigners. None of these experiments provided a proper solution to the army's overall problem and in December 1797 the remnants of the foreign corps, now returned from the West Indies, were pulled together at Cowes on the Isle of Wight to create the 5th Battalion the 60th Foot. The 60th, the Royal Americans, had been raised in the American colonies in 1756 specifically to operate in the close American terrain against the French and their Indian allies. Unusually, the regiment had four line battalions, none of them being designated light infantry as such. Its new 5th Battalion was composed entirely of Germans and placed under the command of Lieutenant Colonel Baron Francis de Rottenburg. It was the first unit in the British Army to be armed exclusively with the rifle but it was despatched to Canada, after a brief period of service during the Irish rebellion of 1798, as was the 6th Battalion, raised in July 1799.

Next on the scene was the Experimental Corps of Riflemen, ordered to be raised by the Commander-in-Chief and to be under the direction of Colonel Coote Manningham, who had gained much experience of light infantry in the West Indies. Command was delegated to Lieutenant Colonel William Stewart, another experienced light infantry officer and it was he, after considerable early trouble in putting the corps together, who took his battalion – now the 95th Regiment and soon to be the 95th Rifle Regiment – to a new camp established by Moore at Shorncliffe in Kent in January 1803. At the same time Moore recommended the conversion of his own regiment, the 52nd (Oxfordshire), to light infantry, and this was followed in July by the conversion of the 43rd (Monmouthshire) Regiment. During the course of the war five further line regiments were to be converted to light infantry: the 68th (Durham) and 85th (Bucks Volunteers) in 1808, the 51st (2nd Yorkshire West Riding) in 1809, the 71st (Glasgow Highland) in 1810 and the 90th (Perthshire Volunteers) in 1815.

None of this would have occurred without the enthusiastic support of the Commander-in-Chief, Prince Frederick, the Duke of York. While often much maligned, he possessed a decent amount of military experience and a determination that the British Army should undergo major improvement. Having experienced at first hand in Flanders major disadvantages in the field at the hands of French light infantry he responded energetically to calls for strengthening the British light infantry arm. In August 1798 he had authorised the publication of *Regulations for the Exercise of Riflemen and Light Infantry*, which was a direct translation of Colonel de Rottenburg's drill manual for his newly formed 5th Battalion of the 60th. The experiments in light infantry conducted subsequently and most influentially by John Moore at Shorncliffe drew heavily on de Rottenburg's work, and these experiments clearly utilised bugles. The 1798 regulations contained explicit instructions on the use of the bugle when appropriate and were combined with clear words of command. They included two pages of regulated bugle signals to be sounded (a distinction from drum calls, which were to be beaten). These were: to Extend, to Close, March, Skirmish, Fire, Cease Firing, Retreat, Incline to the Right, Incline to the Left, Alarm, Halt, On Discovering an Enemy, The Enemy is Infantry, The Enemy is Cavalry, The Enemy has both Infantry and Cavalry, Assembly of Officers.[32] But the body of the text also contained much about the words of command and their combination with bugle signals. Part of the instructions for extending and closing files directed, for example, that:

> On the signal to extend, the files open from the spot where the commanding officer has placed himself with the bugle ... On the signal from the bugle to close, every man faces and closes briskly to the point from whence the signal is given. When firing in extended order and skirmishing the commanding officer then orders the horner to give the signal to commence firing ... In firing in advancing, the commanding officer first orders the signal to march to be sounded, and immediately after the signal to fire ... If the firing in advancing is to cease, the commanding officer orders the signal for halt, after which not a shot must be heard.[33]

A detailed examination of these regulations can only conclude that the light infantry arm was actually a well-developed concept, if insufficiently established in practice, and that the use of the bugle in controlling most of the movements of light infantry in the field was taken for granted. It is of note too that the 'horners', as buglers were sometimes described, were augmented by whistles carried by the sergeants.[34]

The main obstacle for light infantry companies elsewhere, as Moore remarked in a letter to the Adjutant General in September 1803, was that 'At present Buglers are not allowed upon the establishment of regiments [meaning those other than the 43rd, 52nd and 95th], so the Light Companies have drums, the same as the battalion. The Buglers, which many have, are by sufferance, not by Order. Should not the establishment be so far altered, and each regiment directed to have eighteen drummers, two fifers, and two buglers, the latter to belong to the Light Companies exclusively?'[35]

This is also very significant. It makes clear reference to the need for buglers, albeit confined to light companies as the drum was still shown as preponderant (and the fife confined to the grenadier companies). Indeed, Moore's earlier instructions for light infantry, which he produced in Ireland in 1798–99, emphasised that when light infantry were operating in close order as a company or as a whole battalion, it was the drum to which they were to respond. At this early time, when Moore was experimenting with a battalion of light infantry of the Irish militia, he not only drew on the work of de Rottenburg (who was then commanding his battalion of the 60th within Moore's command in Ireland) but also on Dundas. While Moore, an impatient and ambitious officer, might later have despaired at the constraints Dundas' system seemingly imposed on the training and handling of the infantry, he also recognised the value and need for close-order manoeuvres and, by extension, the continued application of the drum, when appropriate, because it worked.[36] Moore could not have been clearer in emphasising that all infantry, whatever their final persuasion, must be trained to manoeuvre and fight in close order first and foremost: close-order drill was the basis of extended-order drill. Just as significant was that Moore also noted in his 1803 letter that the bugle calls printed in the 1798 rifle and light infantry regulations were used by buglers in most regiments. This would indicate that the light infantry companies of the line battalions, or some of them at least, and possibly a majority, had long adopted the bugle at their own expense and despite regulations to the contrary.

The eyewitness accounts of battle in these wars against the French provide plenty of evidence that, as a means of controlling troops, the bugle was now to the fore. It is not surprising that examples of the light infantry regiments and the 95th Rifles should include references to the use of bugles, but examples from the line regiments also do this, and to the exclusion of the drum. It is probable that the light infantry regiments still carried their drums for use in camp and on the march, although the Connaught Ranger William Grattan observed that at the assault on the fortress of Ciudad Rodrigo in January 1812 the 43rd Light Infantry's band preceded the storming party and 'they had no drums, and there was a melting sweetness in the sounds that touched the heart.'[37] But if light infantry regiments did still carry a number of drums the same must be said for the line regiments. Captain Sherer of the 34th Foot recalled in his memoirs of the Peninsular War that just after Talavera in July 1809 'Our drum beat two hours before dawn of day and at an early hour we reached Niza.' Later that year, in close proximity to the French on the River Tagus, his regiment, which had remained unmolested for nearly three months, was still prepared for a fight: 'We should never have been surprised had the alarm drum at midnight roused us from our beds.'[38] It is then particularly telling that by 1810 he mentioned that the drummers' calls were becoming unfamiliar enough for the company drummer, when hearing the halt beaten by the orderly drummer and repeating the call, would have to tell his company commander what the call meant. This example and other evidence would thus indicate that, as a means of signalling in battle, the drum would appear mostly defunct across the whole of the British infantry.

Again, this is not to say that the drum did not have its place on the battlefield at all and there is every likelihood that there were occasions still when commanding officers would employ their drummers for moral effect. We have noted already that Napoleon's infantry had taken this to something of an extreme, perhaps in direct support of Napoleon's maxim that 'the moral is to the physical as three is to one', by often grouping their drummers in massed 'batteries' with the deliberate intention of spurring on the attacking columns and striking fear in the hearts of their opponents. Veteran British infantry remained unimpressed by the approach of old trousers, as has also been noted. Captain Kincaid of the 95th, mentioned earlier, wrote of the moment at the onset of the battle of Waterloo in June 1815 when Napoleon appeared to review his regiments, who greeted him with:

> ... shouts of 'Vive l'Empereur,' nor did they cease after they had passed; but backed by the thunder of their artillery, and carrying with them the *rubidub* of drums, and the *tantarara* of trumpets, in addition to their increasing shouts, it looked, at first, if they had some hopes of scaring us off the ground; for it was a singular contrast to the stern silence reigning on our side, where nothing as yet, but the voices of our great guns, told that we had mouths to open when we chose to use them.[39]

British regiments would invariably stand in silence, demonstrating in their obdurate calmness a far more unnerving method than any noise could achieve, as Thomas Bugeaud recalled. Nevertheless, British infantry may at times have responded in kind. While an example from the outset of the Revolutionary War and when the drum might still have been expected to be used, the 14th (Bedfordshire) Regiment gave the French a taste of their own music at the battle of Famars near Valenciennes on 23 May 1793. The assault by the 14th was checked by the French, whose drummers were banging out *Ça ira!*, the anthem most identified with the revolution. The commanding officer of the 14th, 'seeing the invigorating effect that the tune had on the enemy' ordered his drummers to take up the rhythm. Lieutenant Thomas Powell wrote in his diary 'Attacked and carried a Battery of 16 Guns with the band [sic] playing "Ca Ira", for which we received publick thanks from the Duke of York ... Had the Duke's order to play "Ca Ira" in future for our quick march.'[40] This survives today as the regimental quick march of the Yorkshire Regiment, the descendants of the 14th Regiment. Much later, at the very end of December 1811 at the siege of Tarifa in southern Spain, the 2nd Battalion the 87th (Prince of Wales's Own Irish) Regiment stood impassively enough as they awaited the approach of 2,000 French grenadiers towards the city's gate. As the 87th's volleys shattered the French they gave 'three cheers and their fifes and drums began to play "Garryowen to Glory Boys" and "St Patrick's Day"'.[41] At Vitoria in northern Spain in June 1813 the 88th (Connaught Rangers) and, it might be assumed, the whole of General Picton's Division, went forward in line with drums beating to close up to and present their muskets in the faces of the French. The important contemporary letters of Private William Wheeler of the 51st Light Infantry add further substance to the presence of drums at times. In July 1813, when the French sallied out of the Pyrenees and attacked General Sir Rowland Hill's position at Basta, Hill, characteristically, counter-attacked with vigour. Two regiments of light infantry – the 51st and the 68th – were engaged alongside the 82nd (Prince of Wales's Volunteers) and the Chasseurs Britanniques, a regiment composed largely of Frenchmen and originally royalists but latterly deserters and ex-prisoners-of-war now in British service. Wheeler wrote 'Now fifty buglers were sounding the charge, and the drums of the 82nd and C.B.'s were beating time to the music. A general rush was made by the brigade, accompanied by three tremendous British cheers.'[42]

It may have been the case too that, at times, British regimental bands accompanied soldiers in battle in the manner reported by Marshal Ney of the French. Henry Farmer recounted a number of episodes where a band 'On entering battle [would be placed] in the rear of the regiment, where it played strenuously so as to encourage those who were taking the shock of arms in front.' But evidence is scanty and, indeed, Farmer had conveniently passed over examples of drummers playing, such as those of the 14th Regiment at Famars in 1793, and injected bandsmen in their place.[43] One cannot imagine Wellington in later years tolerating bandsmen playing in the midst of battle when the requirements of total command and control were paramount and the bandsmen had rather more important duties to perform with the wounded. Indeed, with bandsmen now soldiers proper, the situation might demand that they take up arms. The romantic novel *Mary Anne Wellington* by the Reverend Richard Cobbold, published in 1846, related the actual experiences of Bandsman Hewitt of the 48th (Northamptonshire) Regiment at the battle of Talavera in the Peninsula in July 1809. Here they had to lay down their instruments for, as Hewitt stated, " 'We had a dreadful hand-to-hand engagement, for even the band had to fight in the ranks with their companions that day.'[44] The 48th certainly played a pivotal role in the battle throughout.

Herbert and Barlow's study of British military music, in tracking the rise of British Army bands, concluded that by the beginning of the 19th century, 'They were soon so conspicuous and ubiquitous that it was necessary to embrace their existence into the formal regulatory framework of the army.'[45] Bands and bandsmen had been governed by various rules since their inception but were still either civilians, by way of bandmasters and some musicians, or men 'borrowed' from the ranks. In 1803 the Commander-in-Chief issued an order that regularised their number and military duties:

> It is H.[is] M[ajest]ys. pleasure, that in Regiments having Bands of Music, not more than one Private Soldier of each Troop or Company shall be permitted to act as musicians, and that one non-commissioned officer shall be allowed to act as Master of the Band. These men are to be drilled and instructed in their exercises and in the case of active service are to fall in with their respective Troops or Companies, completely armed and accoutred.[46]

Commanding officers would still interpret this regulation in imaginative ways but bandsmen were now, officially, soldiers and could be treated as such.

There are rare examples of drums on the battlefield. The presence of the drummers of the 57th (West Middlesex) Regiment on the bloody field of La Albuera in Spain in May 1811 is confirmed by the fact that they suffered one killed and three wounded. However, we have no way of telling what the drummers were actually doing, and they might have been carrying bugles of course. Lady Elizabeth Butler's famous painting *Steady the Drums and Fifes* of the 57th at the battle – and it really was a bloody affair, the 57th earning the nickname the 'Die Hards' – may be a glorious representation of the adult and boy drummers but it is late Victorian romanticism at its best. Drummer Richard Bentinck's story of his service in the 23rd (Royal Welsh Fusiliers) between 1807 and 1823 (they were not 'Welch' until 1920) is an atmospheric account of the time but tends to confirm the presence of bugles in place of drums as means of control on the battlefield. In 1809 at the siege of Fort Desaix on the island of Martinique the 18-year-old Bentinck recalled the French making an attempt on the British besiegers. Alert and quickly under arms, the British 'bugles rang out the advance and the French, on seeing this, hesitated and then halted.' However, Bentinck clearly had his drum with him at some point for he then related that when the French resumed their attack and a French drummer sprang forward from their ranks to beat the *pas de charge*:

> ... a noted shot in the Company, turned and said to him, 'Bentinck, you want a new pair of drumsticks don't you?' 'Aye, I could do with 'em, why?' replied the lad. 'Because you shall have 'em, by God ... [and levelled] his musket at the French drummer ... [who] fell flat on his face and the fatal drum sticks dropped from his nerveless grasp. 'Run and get them,' shouted his slayer to Bentinck ... [and] the little drummer, forgetful of the French muskets, of all but the French drumsticks, put down his drum and ran like a deer to the dead Frenchman.[47]

Tellingly, Bentinck later wrote that at Albuera, when the 23rd were formed in square, he 'and his brother bandsmen [sic] dragged inside the square those who were only wounded, to be carried off when there was time to the rear.'[48] This would indicate that some or all of the drummers, especially the boys and even numbers of buglers, may well have been told off to help assist the wounded, as their brothers in the band would almost certainly have done. As early as the 1780s instructions were being issued that 'In action the drum-major puts himself in the rear of the battalion, with all the drummers, except the orderley, to assist the wounded.' This is taken from John Williamson's third edition of his *Elements of Military Arrangement* published in 1791 and quoted in Philip Haythornthwaite's recent work on British Napoleonic infantry tactics.[49] This instruction was reinforced in *The Regimental Companion*, a manual published by Charles James of the 60th Regiment in 1799 and in which he declared that, while 'as many drummers are usually sent for duty as there are officers ordered for that duty ... In battle the drummers are to assist the wounded men of their respective companies.'[50]

He could not have meant for all drummers to be assigned to the role of medical orderly but bandsmen were now certainly employed in this task and conclusive evidence that some drummers and buglers were so assigned to help the wounded can be found in Edward Costello's memoirs of the 95th Rifles in Portugal and Spain between 1809 and 1812. In these he wrote that '... the care of [the wounded] alone devolved upon our buglers and bandsmen.' When one of the 95th's officers was badly wounded during a skirmish 'two buglers took him to the rear.'[51] It was the presence of drummers and buglers amongst the wounded and the slain that caused the officer quoted earlier to refer to them as 'notorious plunderers'. We have to conclude that large numbers of drummers and buglers were simply not required to assist with command and control.

We cannot tell for certain when, during the Napoleonic Wars, the bugle became the principal adjunct to signalling across the infantry. It may well have been very early on and concurrent with the establishment of the light infantry arm and it is apparent too that the use of the bugle in place of the drum was not confined just to the marching regiments converted to light infantry. One of General Moore's officers at Shorncliffe in 1803 was Major Kenneth Mackenzie. He had seen much service as a light infantry officer in the West Indies and in 1794 joined the newly raised 90th, the Perthshire Volunteers. This was, officially at least, a line regiment (it was not to be classified as light infantry until 1815) but quickly adopted light infantry methods, which Mackenzie ensured whilst the regiment occupied Minorca in 1798–99. The 90th established an early reputation for excellence, with Mackenzie as second-in-command, and at the battle of Mandara in Egypt in March 1801 General Sir Ralph Abercromby placed the regiment in his advanced guard alongside the 92nd Highlanders. It is likely that in this position both regiments intended to operate in extended order against the French skirmishers and this provides an indication that all line regiments were beginning to be trained to operate in this way. The 90th certainly began the battle in a conventional manner as it initially marched against the French in column of companies, led by its light company. The then Lieutenant Colonel Rowland Hill, commanding the regiment, wrote very tellingly in his despatch dated 4 April 1801 that, having formed line 'We advanced and drove the French from the first position. I then, with the bugle-horn, halted the regiment and ceased firing, and, correcting our line, advanced with the greatest regularity to the second hill …'[52]

As it had always done, the British infantry adapted to the reality of conditions on the battlefield and we must not therefore take Dundas' *Principles* or the 1792 and 1801 regulations as proscriptive. Their main achievement, as intended by both Dundas and the Duke of York, was to impose a common system of 'military movements' across the infantry as a mandatory base line so that all infantry could fall back on that system, if necessary, and one that every soldier understood. This base line was a system described by Dundas as 'Eighteen Manoeuvres' and was expected to be achieved in training, to be performed in review and 'encompass much of what would be required on the battlefield.'[53] Officers like John Moore were quick to modify the drills to suit local conditions or as a result of experience. And whatever the criticisms of the drills by some, including Moore, they endured largely unchanged until the demise of the smoothbore musket. As we have seen, Dundas quickly remedied his earlier ignoring of light infantry requirements when he updated his Principles, which was also reflected in the 1792 regulations. The need, supported by the Duke of York, to suppress the loose tactics prevalent in America was essential in dealing with the greater challenges imposed by huge French armies with their 'combined arms' of infantry, cavalry and artillery.

The regulations also witnessed the final demise of the platoon firing system and all its complications. Platoon firing had ensured a continuous fire but a firefight of this nature against hordes of French skirmishers would have been a very costly affair. Officially, three ranks were also insisted on, but experience also showed that two ranks had far greater utility. In a modern detailed study of Wellington's army in the Peninsula it has been concluded that 'British infantry seem to have adopted the two-deep line as their standard formation much earlier in the war'[54] than otherwise thought previously. Evidence has been found from as early as 1793 when, despite the new regulations, Major General the Earl of Moira ordered his troops assembling at Portsmouth for the campaign in Flanders to adopt two ranks in the field. Two ranks were certainly the norm in Portugal and Spain for Wellington stipulated 'the use of the two-deep line almost in passing' in his General Order dated 3 August 1808 and this can be seen 'as the confirmation of an accepted norm [rather] than as the introduction of a significant innovation.'[55] Interestingly, the British infantry reverted in many ways to the aggressive tactics of North America, if delivered in close rather than extended order. Aggression was key. Stuart Reid has provided a fitting summary of the situation in the Peninsula:

> … now the British infantryman was being handled much more aggressively, and even in a defensive situation he would normally act offensively by giving an attacker a volley in the teeth and then following it up with an immediate, but intimidatingly steady, bayonet charge through the smoke.[56]

The battalion volley or two, perhaps delivered a whole single rank at a time or even both ranks together, became the norm, followed by that terrifying bayonet charge. All light infantry regiments were expected to fight in the same way and evidence of this might be taken from Major General 'Black Bob' Craufurd's Light Division on the Rio Côa in July 1810. The division, made up entirely of light infantry battalions – the 1st/43rd and 1st/52nd and two battalions of Portuguese Caçadores – along with the 1st/95th Rifles, must have deployed in close order to stand any chance of slowing Marshal Ney's corps as it did. Even the battalion of the 95th (minus one company, which might have provided the skirmish line), holding Craufurd's right, appear to have acted in close order in line. When French cavalry threatened to turn Craufurd's left it was the buglers of the 1st/43rd who sounded the retreat.

At the same time line infantry regiments showed a growing ability to act in the same way as light infantry. After all they all carried the same smoothbore musket and having sufficient light infantry, or line infantry that could also operate in a skirmish line to screen its main battle line, was a battlefield winner. It would appear therefore that once the British had also provided proper light infantry from 1803 onwards and these regiments were seen to have great utility and to excel in their new roles, that it was only natural that the line regiments would then seek to emulate the light battalions.

All depended for their success on order, on discipline and on good leadership. While the British line was at its greatest advantage in defence – and here the infantry was often kept below the crest and in cover, sometimes lying down and emerging only when their retiring skirmishers indicated that the time was right – well handled it was unstoppable in the attack, and could combine both. The Marquis de Chambray described the British infantry at Sorauren in the Pyrenees in July 1813 as at first concealed on the reverse slope, when they appeared suddenly,

> ... fired, charged with the bayonet, and overthrew them [the French], but did not pursue; on the contrary, after having remained some time near the crest ... they retired in double quick time [and] resumed their position ... [The French were] astonished at being repulsed, almost without having fought [so rallied and re-ascended the hill, but] as before, received a discharge of musketry, and were again charged and over-thrown.[57]

We might imagine that the commanding officers of the British infantry regiments had their orderly buglers close to hand but would have given the order to advance the line to the crest by word of mouth alone, perhaps retaining a single bugle call to retire back on the position once the French had been scattered. Use of drums at this stage in this manner would seem very unlikely and, of course, the bugle could be heard far more easily and over longer distances and was capable of delivering a greater variety of sounds. In *A Practical Guide for the Light Infantry Officer* of 1806 by a Captain Thomas Cooper of the 56th (West Essex) Regiment it was noted that 'A good bugle may be heard at the distance of three miles.'[58]

It will be recalled that another effective method in the War of Independence was to concentrate flank companies into formed battalions of light infantry (and grenadiers) but this method was not reverted to on the whole and certainly not on a permanent basis in the Revolutionary and Napoleonic Wars. At the stunning British victory at Maida in southern Italy on 4 July 1806 Lieutenant Colonel James Kempt (later another of Wellington's trusted generals) of the 81st (Loyal Lincoln Volunteers) was given command of a composite light battalion drawn from the light companies of the six British regiments present and Louis de Watteville's Swiss Regiment. Kempt's battalion bore the brunt of the fighting and demonstrated its experience in operating in line in close order by delivering two devastating volleys against the French attack on the British right, then followed these up by a bayonet charge that swept the French away. But the normal state of things was provided in a general order dated 4 May 1809. This noted most specifically that for the line of battle:

> The light infantry companies belonging to, and the riflemen attached to each brigade of infantry, are to be formed together … under the command of a Field Officer or Captain of light infantry of the brigade … Upon all occasions, in which the brigade may be formed in line, or in column, when the brigade shall be formed for the purpose of opposing an enemy, the light infantry companies and riflemen will be of course in front, flanks, or rear, according to the circumstances of the ground, and the nature of the operation to be formed. On all other occasions, the light infantry companies are to be considered as attached to their battalions …[59]

Wellington opposed the older arrangement and emphasised in a letter in March 1810 to Major General William Stewart, soon to command the 2nd Division in the Peninsula, that 'I disapprove of detaching flank companies from the battalion to which they belong, and I have not allowed of such detachments in this army.' Line battalions therefore retained their light companies even if they were deployed in a common skirmish line under brigade or divisional arrangements ahead of battle being joined. A good example of light companies being brigaded for battle was seen at Fuentes de Oñoro in May 1811 when all of the light companies of the 42nd, the 2nd/83rd, the 2nd/84th, the 92nd and the 5th Line Battalion of the King's German Legion were grouped with the 5th Battalion the 60th Regiment to hold the town itself. Light infantry numbers were also augmented by additional men selected as battalion flankers, to operate on the flanks, front and rear of their battalions when the light infantry companies were pushed out further. We might imagine correctly these companies and the 'flanker units' out beyond the main line, with their officers having a bugler close to hand to call men in when necessary. Such means of control would have been necessary in the dispersed battlefield and the difficult terrain of Fuentes.

By this stage too the bugle calls prevalent in the army were well regulated and established. The 1798 listing of *The Bugle Horn Duty for the Light Infantry as used in the Foot Guards* and the same year's *Regulations for the Exercise of Riflemen and Light Infantry*, published at Horse Guards, both reproduced de Rottenburg's calls verbatim. These numbered 16 useful calls in all and a copy of them was found amongst Sir John Moore's letter to the Adjutant General of September 1803, referred to earlier and in which he wrote that 'The sounds at present used by the 52nd and 95th are de Rottenburg's – which are the sounds I believe most generally used by the Light Companies of the Regiments.'[60] When the aforementioned Captain Thomas Cooper wrote his *Practical Guide for the Light Infantry Officer* in 1806 he showed no fewer than 57 different calls. 14 were intended as 'Barrack Sounds' and the remainder as 'Field Sounds'. These included, amongst others, calls for shoulder arms, order arms, form company, form column, form line, form Indian files, form two deep, form sections. The very number of these calls might have us reflect on why Cooper was on half-pay, that is, not employed! However, he did emphasise that there were just five 'Signals for the Bugle ... which are to be considered as fixed and determined ones ... To Advance, To Retreat, To Halt, To Cease Firing, To Assemble.' A little surprisingly he also defined the same signals for the drum (and thus also for application to light infantry), and these were, respectively, the 'Grenadiers March, The Retreat, Troop, The General, To Arms.'[61] Definitively, the 1798 Regulations were republished in 1814 by the War Office and showed de Rottenburg's original 16 calls unchanged.

Some final examples of bugling by the Rifles, light infantry, line infantry and Foot Guards in the Napoleonic Wars will help provide a conclusion to this period. At Roliça in Portugal, in the very first battle fought by the British in the Peninsula in August 1808, Rifleman Benjamin Harris of the 95th Rifles recalled a difficult moment for the 29th (Worcestershire) Regiment. The 95th, out in a skirmish line, were also under some pressure and awaiting reinforcement or the call to retire. '"Fire and retire" is a very good sound' he related 'but the Rifles were not over-fond of such notes.'[62] Bugler William Green, also of the 95th and who was later wounded, bugle in hand, at the storming of the fortress of Badajoz in 1812, but telling earlier of the retreat to La Coruña in January 1809, wrote that 'Our bugles sounded the advance; away went the kettles; the word was given "Rifles in front extend by files in chain order!"'[63] Private Wheeler of the 51st made numerous mentions of the bugle in camp and in the field. Of particular value was his letter covering a skirmish in front of Salamanca on 22 June 1812 when Wellington tried to provoke the French into attacking. The 51st were ordered forward to deploy on the 1st Division and Wheeler wrote that

> We was soon within point blank distance of [the French] line. Sir Thomas [Graham] then gave the word double quick, in a moment thirty buglars was sounding the charge and off we dashed in double quick time with three cheers, and away went the enemy to the right about. We had now gained the ridge without discharging a single musket, our bugles sounded the 'halt' and 'fire'.[64]

All elements of the Light Division became just as versed in the use of the bugle as their brothers in the Rifles. Mark Urban drew on the letters of one George Hennell, a 'gentlemen volunteer' of the division, when describing the advance through the Pyrenees in 1813. Colonel Hobkirk, commanding the 43rd Light Infantry, was sent forward with two of his companies towards the French positions to cover them with fire. Their subsequent poor handling began when Hobkirk ordered his bugler to sound the advance, which brought the British light troops out of the covering of the trees and into the greater fire of the French. When the bugler did at last sound the retire the men had to expose themselves again to make their escape – all clear evidence of the ability of the light infantry to understand and respond to commands sounded by bugle.[65]

The bugle would have been of far more use than the drum during assaults on fortresses. In the failed second attempt on Badajoz in May 1811 an unknown private soldier in one of the Irish regiments (probably the 88th but possibly the 83rd) recorded that 'our gallant leader ... having fallen, and the enemy moving into the fort [of San Cristobal], the bugles sounded a recall, and we retired into the trenches.'[66] Just over a year later on 6 April 1812, when Badajoz finally fell, Lieutenant 'P.K.' of the 88th wrote in his journal of his regiment's struggle for the ramparts of the castle:

> ... the cheering of our men, and the animating bugles sounding the charge, made those below so anxious to share the glory of their comrades ... The enemy's fire meanwhile continued with unabated fury ... At this point, also, the uproar in the town exceeded all description; great guns roaring, musketry blazing; men shrieking ... bells ringing; and dogs barking ... Add to this, the sounding of bugles in all directions, and the French drums beating with hurried and redoubled violence the pas de charge ...[67]

That the Foot Guards were also responding to the bugle was demonstrated by Ensign John Aitchison of the 3rd Guards, who wrote that at the storming of San Sebastian in July 1813, in attempting to force their way into the breach, a delay ensued due to the fire of the defenders. Once sufficient reinforcements had been gathered, '... at length the bugles sound[ed] the 'advance' and a hearty 'hurrah' announced to the spectators that we had gained an advantage.'[68] Nor were such examples confined to the Peninsula. William Bell of the 89th Regiment included in a letter of 4 December 1810 from Coopers Island near Mauritius that 'At about eleven o'clock in the forenoon we heard a firing to the front of the lines. The bugle sounded the turn out and before we had got formed up, I saw the two Generals ... returning at full gallop and making signs for the lines to form.'[69] At least one bugler received a gallantry medal of some sort for his part in the battle of Waterloo. One Heinrich Steinweg, a bugler of the 'Black Brunswickers' – the Brunswick Ducal Corps – 'with men falling all around him ... lived gloriously on, winning a medal for bugling without faltering in the face of battle.' This bugler survived to become Henry Steinway, creator of the famous pianos.[70]

It would be safe to conclude that the bugle had become the main means of tactical battlefield communication, combined of course with the voice and now the whistle. In practice, adherence to the written regulations, however clear and simple they might seem, was unlikely to have survived the realities of battles and campaigns, and battalions, brigades and divisions would have adapted them to suit the reality of the situation. Again, as in previous wars, the British infantry proved well able to adapt as circumstances changed and to modify tactics and methods to defeat its foes on the battlefield. Published drills and the theories that supported them should, as in previous wars and later ones, be seen as a start point and an easily understood commonality from which more complicated tactical manoeuvres could be developed and methods of command and control modified. Quoted by Richard Holmes, the historian Paddy Griffith, whose various works on tactics have offered plentiful accurate insights into their practicalities, observed that, while 'drills in this period were "really no more than an ideal to be aimed at," and which rarely survived first contact with broken or uneven terrain, ... "battlefield manoeuvres could normally be achieved faster with drill than without it."'[71] This was really the nub of the matter: well-practised drills, with every man knowing his place, and balancing speed with order and thorough control all aided communication and, together, provided for far greater tempo in battle. These were not constraints. As Howie Muir has concluded and quoting the 1803 *Regulations*: 'In order to achieve victory in close order combat, "it is necessary to reconcile celerity with order; to prevent hurry, which must always produce confusion, loss of time, unsteadiness, irresolution, inattention to command, &c."'[72]

In so many of the battles of the Napoleonic Wars the British Army proved time and again, by means of its training and the leadership of its officers, to be so well handled as to be able to survive and win amidst adversity and often against the odds. By comparison the French, and the Spanish it must be said, are to be viewed unfavourably. Drummers and buglers played their part but the British infantry had developed well beyond any requirement for their instruments to be of any universal use in controlling manoeuvre. Indeed, such universal use would have limited manoeuvre severely, although there were always occasions when the orderly buglers retained by the tactical-level commanders were still an asset. Flexibility, born of experience and confidence, were paramount. Perhaps echoing General Clinton's appeal to the Guards at Monmouth in 1778, in 1809 at the hard-fought battle of Talavera, General Rowland Hill, commanding the 2nd Division, 'seeing the overwhelming force that was coming against us, gave orders that the light troops should be recalled, and the bugles sounded accordingly. The skirmishers were closing in and filing to the rear with the regularity of field-day and parade exercise, which the general observing, called out "D[am]n their filing, let them come in anyhow."'[73]

CHAPTER 7

Beyond Wellington's Legacy

By the time British regiments were being sent to fight in the Crimea in 1854 most military drummers were also buglers. There were men and boys who could beat a drum, play a fife and blow a bugle. Some probably were only drum-beaters and buglers; others maybe purely fifers.

The British Army changed very little in the first 50 years or so of the 19th century and in the just under 40 years from Waterloo to the Crimean War, battlefield tactics in particular were recognisably similar; the armies looked more or less the same too. That character – long lines of red-coated infantrymen delivering volleys of musket fire – changed markedly in the course of the second half of the century during a very different period of warfare marked too by major technological change. But there were some changes underway already by the time of the Crimean War and the army also began to deal with the challenges of some very different enemies as the Empire widened its bounds. Major Michael Barthorp has written extensively of the British Army on campaign between Waterloo and the Great War and has calculated that, in addition to the major war in the Crimea and the second war against the Boer Republics in South Africa, British soldiers fought in 'some 80 other campaigns and expeditions of varying scale all over the world' between 1815 and 1902.[1] Nevertheless, the two halves of the century, roughly speaking, need to be dealt with separately with some justification and it serves our purpose too to interpose the 1850s between these two halves. This decade saw both the war in the Crimea and the Indian Mutiny and these two major campaigns are not just a dividing point between what went before and what came after but provided too an impetus for much wider changes in the army.

The new types of foe being met after Waterloo as the British Empire expanded were reminiscent to some extent at least of the challenges that faced the British Army in the French and Indian wars in North America in the previous century. They will be considered in this chapter but more extensively in Chapter 9 in the context of what is often called 'colonial warfare' or 'small wars' in the later 19th century. Ian Knight, who has studied Queen Victoria's soldiers in great depth, has summarised this period up to the major challenge presented by the Crimean War and states that '... until the middle of the century [the British Army was] faced only with minor campaigns which did not unduly test them. Weapons, uniforms and tactical theory were all based on those that had smashed Boney.'[2]

Given this preamble, it would be expected therefore that there was very little distinction between the regulations governing the employment of British infantry in the Napoleonic Wars and those in the Crimean War. A number of factors contributed to this state of affairs and Professor Hew Strachan has dissected this period in detail and the effects of Lord Wellington's reactionary influence up until his death in 1852.[3] It was not just the supreme victories gained by the British infantry against Napoleon and the assumption that the tactics used were therefore proven beyond the need for change. The simple fact that firearms remained practically unaltered, in that the smoothbore musket continued to reign supreme for much of this time, provided little incentive to alter successful fighting methods. Add to these the lack of opportunity to fight any foe other than those armed and organised in the same way, such as the Sikhs or the Russians, or those ill-equipped to compete, such as the Burmese or Maoris, it was little wonder that 'A Field Officer' was able to write in the *United Service Journal* in 1845 that 'The system laid down by Sir David Dundas, after the lapse of half a century, still remains in use almost unchanged.'[4]

The dilemma for this period, and for some time beyond, was that posed between 'Frederickian' methods and the new experience of fighting native enemies in less than orthodox ways; seen by many as an aberration and akin to the arguments of the previous century regarding American methods. But, as Hew Strachan has also described, although orthodoxy largely held sway, 'colonial campaigning did ensure that skills of skirmishing … were tested in advance of the supplantation of the musket for the rifle.'[5] With regard to the drum and bugle, study of the period shows at least the confirmation of the practices that had evolved in the 20 years or so preceding Waterloo and, importantly, the continuing evolvement of light infantry. Bugles more often than not supplanted drums for all calls in camp and in the field but the drum and the fife retained an important role. In completing this chapter's epigraph, Hugh Barty-King summarised in a particularly accurate way the prevailing situation:

> By the time British regiments were being sent to fight in the Crimea in 1854 most military drummers were also buglers. There were men and boys who could beat a drum, play a fife and blow a bugle. Some probably were only drum-beaters and buglers; others maybe purely fifers. But in the line regiments there were no separate corps of buglers who played nothing else. 'The Drums' remained the section of the regiment, quite separate from The Band, which consisted of drum-beaters, fifers and buglers. And Drums and Fifes retained their indispensable role on the march … [and] played regiments to action in the Crimean War.[6]

The field regulations for this whole period that might shed more light on the use of the drum in battle are, sadly, almost mute on the subject; indeed, they show very little change in almost all respects from those that started with Dundas and which governed the wars against France. But an examination of them serves our purpose because, from the publication of the 1824 *Field Exercise and Evolutions of the Army*, the detailed instructions therein, and thereafter, for the man, the company, the battalion, the brigade and the line – and for the very first time for light infantry – were orders! It was the same old story of attempts by central authority to impose regularity but is worth here emphasising this particular point, made most emphatically by the author of the 1824 regulations. The then Adjutant General was Major General Sir Henry Torrens, a relatively young infantry officer (he was but 44 when the 1824 regulations were published) who had had much first-hand experience of battle from the start of the French Revolutionary War onwards. In his General Order, which prefaced the regulations and was written at Horse Guards on 10 March 1824, he declared that:

> The King having been pleased to decide that one uniform system of Field Exercise and Movement shall be established throughout His Army, the Commander-in-Chief has received His Majesty's Commands to direct, that the Rules and regulations, approved by His Majesty for this important purpose, and now detailed and published herewith, shall be strictly adhered to, without any deviation whatever; and such Orders, hitherto given, as may be found to interfere with, or to counteract their effect and operation, are nullified.
>
> All General Officers, Colonels, and Commanding Officers of Corps, are therefore held strictly responsible for the due and accurate performance of every part of these Regulations ...[7]

The point made above – that the 1824 regulations did not differ greatly from those used in the preceding 30 years – was explicit in Torrens' introduction, with specific mention of the continued relevance of 'Old Pivot's' system:

> Thirty-three years have elapsed, since the late General Sir David Dundas conferred upon this country the essential benefit of introducing a System of Tactics, calculated to combine and unite the Field Movements of the Forces; the fundamental principles laid down by that distinguished veteran, must ever form the basis of subsequent systems ...[8]

Nevertheless, the 1824 revision also emphasised that improvements had been incorporated, based on 'practical experience ... during the late eventful war' and that much had actually been done during the war, especially by way of simplifying drills and movements and thus improving 'celerity', even if all this was achieved hitherto but partially and 'without adherence to any general or fixed principle or formation.'[9] The platoon firing system was long a thing of the past and companies long established as a tactical as well as an administrative unit but the regulations still stipulated that they should be equalised in strength before forming for battle. Additionally, instructions were given for a firing system by 'divisions' – a continuing useful if confusing word for the fire-units. These instructions allowed for 'firing by companies from right to left – from left to right – from flanks to centre, and from centre to flanks' or even by battalions at once. Sensibly, it would all 'depend much upon circumstances, and the discretion of commanding officers.' Most notably 'File or independent firing from the right or left of wings, or from the right or left of sub-divisions … [is] the most essential and usual mode of firing upon actual service.'[10] This was some change.

Of great significance, and one cannot help but think that the establishment of file firing as the norm was at least part responsible, was the formal recognition within the regulations of light infantry, whose methods were to become increasingly adopted across all infantry as standard practice within a couple of decades. This is really where the main difference lies between the 1824 regulations and Dundas. Torrens' foresight might have been aided by the fact that he had been commissioned originally in the 52nd (Oxfordshire) Regiment, which became one of those original regiments of light infantry in 1803. At this stage, however, two ranks in close order (defined, as before, as 'the files lightly touching, but without crowding; each man [occupying] a space of about 21 inches') remained 'the chief and primary order in which the battalion and its parts at all times assemble and form – *Open order* is only regarded as an exception from it … In close order, the rear rank is closed up to within one pace …'[11] This was also the first time that two ranks rather than three was formally stipulated for the line although, as we have also seen, in practice this had been the norm for some considerable time.

If the 1824 regulations said very little about drummers and drumming, let alone buglers and bugling, it might be supposed that it was unnecessary to say any more on the subject than Dundas and this was because drumming was now relegated by practice and necessity to a supporting role. Drummers were certainly reduced in number for the 1824 regulations provided for just one drummer per company in the, now, eight companies of the battalion: one grenadier, one light and six 'battalion'. The battalion, or centre, companies increased again to eight in the 1833 regulations. In line, that is in the field and not just while exercising, and in the firings, the drummers were to stand six paces behind the third, or supernumerary rank occupied by the company officers and covering sergeants. The detail in the regulations stated specifically that 'The drummers of the six battalion companies are assembled in two divisions, six paces behind the third rank of their first and sixth companies. The grenadier and light company drummers and fifers are six paces behind their respective companies.'[12] Note again that light companies were still supposed to have drummers and not buglers.

It should be noted too that fifers had crept in here and are not otherwise mentioned and thus their place on the organisation table of the battalion was now determined. It might be assumed too that the commanding officer, mounted and also in the rear in the line, retained an orderly drummer. The musicians – the band – were also mentioned as being placed in a single rank to the rear of the battalion pioneers, themselves in the centre and to the rear of the third rank; their role in the line was also not mentioned. Additional instructions were included for drummers when the battalion was to take open order and resume close order but, noteworthy for its absence, there was no instruction for the drummers to beat when the line moved or charged. All movements and all activities were subject to words of command, which were to 'be given short, quick, and loud, so as to be heard and understood from right to left of a battalion in line: or from front to rear of a battalion in column … In the midst of the surrounding noises, the eye and the ear of the soldier should be attentive only to his immediate officer; the loudness of whose commands, instead of creating confusion and unsteadiness, ought to give confidence in the hurry of action.'[13]

Much of this helps us understand further the method of command and control of a battalion and of larger formations during the Napoleonic Wars and it should go without saying that the competence of the officers is also proven. The almost mind-boggling number of movements and formations would have demanded ability and professionalism to ensure that their soldiers were tightly managed in battle and were confident in their company and battalion officers. We might wonder how any body of troops, especially in the heat of battle, might execute, with the required celerity, a change of position 'to the front on the right halted Company, by throwing forward the whole left, and by the flank march of Companies by Threes' using the words of command: 'Remaining Companies Threes Left. Form Open Column in front of the Right Company. Right Counter-March, Quick March. Halt, Front, Dress. Right and Left Wheel into Line.' There were 144 pages of instructions for the battalion alone in the 1824 regulations and these contained detailed instructions for 43 battalion evolutions, some of these covering a number of pages. Despite General Torrens' clear instruction regarding strict adherence to the regulations one suspects that, while the evolutions might have been perfected for inspections and reviews, they would prove impractical in the field. It must also be clear that no drum beat could possibly provide a signal for the example shown above and the myriad of other orders. But let us remember too that the drills and evolutions were always designed as a start point and their practise and perfection were intended to be a baseline on which commanders in the field could act with flexibility.

Because it was not mentioned whatsoever we might conclude therefore that the drum for anything other than parade and regulating the day was to remain silent. Its presence – for it does seem that it was present – on the battlefield at all could, therefore, seem entirely superfluous but for Dundas' comment from those three decades before that 'a few well distinguished signals of the drum ... may on some occasions be permitted', and we might imagine that commanding officers would retain close control of all their drums to provide immediate impact when requiring actions such as assembly or halt or cease firing.

But it might also have been the case that the general adoption of light infantry formations and methods by all line infantry was well enough advanced by 1824 that the bugle had become absolutely pre-eminent and we must remember that all line battalions still had their light companies. While the 1824 regulations made clear to all eight light infantry battalions – the 13th (1st Somersetshire) Regiment had been added to the list in 1822 – that they had to be 'thoroughly versed and well grounded in the prescribed exercise and movements of a battalion of the line' they also stated that 'When battalions of the line are in perfect order in all the detail of line movements, it is essential that they should be practised in certain extended formations.'[14] The principal object of light infantry remained to protect the advance or retreat, with additional duties in protecting flanks and marching columns, forming advanced guards and posting piquets and these duties were to become increasingly commonplace for line battalions as campaigns against 'irregulars' increased. Due to the dispersal of men inherent in skirmishing, 'Signals and sounds for regulating Movements' were deemed necessary to enable better command and control, although only as substitutes for the voice. The regulations recognised that 'as they are liable to be misunderstood, they should never be resorted to, excepting when the voice cannot reach' and that 'they ought to be as few and as simple as possible.'[15]

The regulations provided full details on the use of the bugle and the various sounds, amounting to some 15 in all in addition to 'the light infantry call and the officers call', which were described as 'as established'. Again, it might be assumed that all these calls had become common practice and in universal use in the Napoleonic Wars and the list of calls certainly had major similarities with the 1814 regulations which, it will be recalled, were first issued by Horse Guards in 1798. The 1824 list showed calls for the Extend, Close, March, Halt, Fire, Cease Firing, Retreat, Assembly, Disperse, Skirmish, Incline to the Right, Incline to the Left, Alarm, Lie Down and Rise. All of these were in use in 1814 except that Disperse had been added in 1824 and Assembly in the earlier regulations had been specified for officers only. The four earlier calls regarding the enemy – On Discovering an Enemy, The Enemy is Infantry, The Enemy is Cavalry and the Enemy is Infantry and Cavalry – were dispensed with. The music for the bugle sounds was identical to the earlier regulations and showed two more sounds for quick time and double time.

This might all seem relatively simple, on paper, and the 15 or so sounds were described as appearing to be 'sufficient for every situation in which light infantry can be employed.'[16] But even the descriptions for each sound or call – the terms were interchangeable – appeared over-complicated and one can see that the voice just had to be the preferred method of giving instructions. The list of calls was further preceded by the instruction:

> No movement should ever be executed until the bugle sound is perfectly finished; and in the combinations of the sounds with the 'Fire,' that sound should always be the *last*, otherwise the company might immediately commence a fire upon the spot; and if the march or retreat were to follow, it would not be heard.[17]

This seems thoroughly sensible. But for the Fire alone the definitions for calls provided for various options and complications, or over-complications. Sounding Fire demanded 'If when halted, they fire upon the spot, skirmishers selecting their objects. If on the march, whether advancing or retiring, it will be by alternate *ranks*, if in single files; by alternate *files*, if in double files, unless otherwise ordered.'[18] There were actually 42 pages dedicated to the formations and evolutions of light infantry and throughout there were details on when the bugle might be sounded. There is not space here to describe in detail everything that these pages contained but we might note that two further calls could be derived from the halt and from the march, the former being used to annul all previous sounds except the fire and the latter being used to signify forwards after an incline to the right or to the left. Six calls – the March, Retreat, Halt, Fire, Cease Firing and Disperse – were the only sounds that had to be 'repeated by all buglers on every occasion' and no signal by bugle sound applied to bodies of troops in reserve. If all of this did not seem to be enough, sounding the note 'G' or a number of them, which was a method that had also developed at the beginning of the century, could add further meaning; thus: 'The use of the bugle [could] be considerably increased by adopting the use of three simple G's, as distinguishing sounds':

> One G to denote the right of the line.
> Two G's, the centre.
> Three G's, the left.
> This, preceding any sound, denotes the part of the line to which it applies. For instance, two G's before the EXTEND, signifies to extend from the centre. One G followed by the CLOSE, signifies to close to the right. When no G is prefixed to the EXTEND, it will mean from that part of the line where the bugle sounds.[19]

That, despite their apparent complicated details, the instructions in these pages had common utility is proven by their continuation almost unchanged for decades to come.

The penultimate part of the 1824 regulations addressed general principles for the movements of the brigade or line and, recognising that the voice of the commanding general might not be heard across the breadth of his command, stated that 'The execution of a command may be regulated by signal, such as a trumpet, or any other method for effecting simultaneous movement ... it is particularly essential that the commands to HALT, or to MARCH, should be communicated by a signal, upon which the battalion commanders may act simultaneously.'[20] And it might just have been the case that drummers, especially orderly drummers for commanding generals and battalion commanders, were retained for this purpose. We have no particular evidence to help us but this might well account for the continued presence of drummers with their drums on the battlefield and we might assume too that all drummers also increasingly carried a bugle.

The final part provided instructions for inspection or review. The instructions for the music and drums would be recognisable today, particularly for the 'present arms', as an accompaniment for the inspection by the reviewing officer and in marching past in slow and quick time. We should note too that Part One of the 1824 regulations, in its instructions for the training of recruits, made a very strong point about the use of 'music'. Similar to previous orders, these instructions were repeated in the next edition of the *Field Exercise and Evolutions of the Army* published in 1833. The following quotation from 1833 repeated the 1824 instruction verbatim in the first paragraph but added an entirely new, second, paragraph as further emphasis:

> Neither fife, nor music, must on any account be used; it being essential to confirm the Recruit by habit alone in that cadence of step which he is afterwards to maintain in his march to the enemy, amidst every variety of noise and circumstance that may tend to derange him.
>
> The habit here adverted to, is acquired by impressing the time upon the Recruit's mind by tap of drum, and no Recruit or squad of Recruits must therefore be permitted to exercise in marching, without the constant use of plummet, drum, and pace stick; the drum to beat the time *only* when the squad is halted, never when in motion: when the superintendent of the drill sees it necessary to give the time, every squad will instantly be halted at the first tap of the drum, and the recruits required to give their whole attention to the proper cadence.[21]

The 1833 regulations, unsurprisingly, showed little alteration in principle to what had gone before, it being noted in the introductory

General Order that the board of officers composed to revise the earlier regulations 'in no instance, lost sight of the principles inculcated, originally, by the late General Sir David Dundas, and, subsequently, by the late Major General Sir Henry Torrens.'[22] Nevertheless, close comparison between the two does show the 1833 regulations as bearing areas of material revision in order to simplify the movements and reduce the words of command. These were still complex evolutions and to the modern eye they do seem so over-convoluted as to stifle any agility and tempo on the battlefield. Enough has been said about the 1824 regulations and there is no need to emphasise further the points made by trawling through the 1833 publication. What is important is to understand that both editions of the *Field Exercise* were designed to provide a base line for the training of battalions scattered all over the world so that, in the words of another reforming general, Lord Frederick Fitzclarence, this 'mechanical portion, or ABC, [could be learned] in time of peace on the level surface of the parade ground, with a view of applying such knowledge in broken undulated ground.'[23] The reformers adjudged that battalions trained in this way could take their place in the line and 'manoeuvre with comfort' should necessity arise.[24] Nevertheless, years of general peace and the presence of continued conservatism, combined with the obligatory rigid drills, did not make for 'comfortable manoeuvre' in practice.

Of greater significance to this particular study were the words used within the section of the 1833 regulations that laid down the formation of the battalion, showing that 'The drummers, fifers *and buglers* [author's emphasis] of the battalion are assembled in two divisions, nine paces behind the supernumerary rank [that is, the third rank] of the first and last battalion companies.'[25] While the position of these men differed little from earlier and there is no mention of the flank companies (so we must assume no change to them retaining their own drummers, fifers and buglers), buglers for the battalion companies got their first, subtle, mention in regulations. Again, it is difficult to ascertain what the intended role for the drummers and buglers was to be from this position. But it was unlikely to be for the purposes of signalling, a role given now solely to the commanding officer's orderly drummer or bugler, that of his superior or a bugler acting in the same role for a company on independent or detached duty. To add emphasis to this new-found or, rather, properly recognised position of the bugle, when considering the commands necessary for the brigade or when in line, the 1833 regulations directed more or less as before that 'The execution of a command may be regulated by a signal, such as a *bugle* [author's emphasis – the instrument replaced trumpet in the earlier work], or any other method for effecting simultaneous movement'[26] and stressed that commanders should use what they found as most effective, a signal being of particular use over longer distances. Clear instructions were provided to effect the halt:

> Whenever the bugle sounds the halt, the head of each battalion [when brigaded or in line] is to stand fast … When it is intended that the whole should close up, the head will be halted without sound of bugle, and the word of command … will be passed from front to rear; and when the rear is closed up, the bugle of the rear battalion will sound the halt as a notice.[27]

The 1833 regulations did therefore represent better recognition of the practicalities of field soldiering. They also continued the work of the 1824 regulations in demonstrating the evolution of light infantry. By about 1830 there was a growing body of opinion recommending that all infantry regiments should take their light infantry skills more seriously and that the distinction between light infantry and line infantry should be removed altogether as unnecessary. This momentum was driven by experience, which could only have a further impact on the drummer/bugler argument. The light companies of the regiments of the line had at last been provided with two buglers on their establishment and the light infantry regiments were to have buglers only, like the two rifle regiments. In the line regiments there were again two drummers to each company and two fifers in addition to the drummers for the grenadier company, but all regiments were ordered by the Commander-in-Chief in 1830 to instruct their men in light infantry practice and this was confirmed in the 1833 regulations. The reason behind this momentum was summarised neatly in the *United Service Journal* of 1830:

> The employment of light troops is as much, or even more, called for in the British army than in that of any other nation, on account of our numerous insular

colonial possessions, where, from the mountainous and intricate nature of the country, it is almost impossible for troops to act in a body.[28]

The unknown correspondent went on to deplore the continued distinction between designated light infantry and line infantry regiments, the commanding officers of the latter being cautious of exercising light infantry skills should they be seen to be ignoring the common evolutions required of the line. He went on: '... if the infantry were all considered as troops of the line, there would be sufficient to stimulate them to acquire a perfect knowledge of the movements and duties of light troops ... Every regiment ought to consider light movements to be as much its province as battalion ones.'[29]

Opposition to this change throughout the military hierarchy, including at regimental level, continued for many years but the requirement for all infantry to be capable of operating in extended order and in skirmishing eventually broadened so that all British infantry showed itself capable of operating in this way in the Crimea as well as in the increasingly numerous colonial campaigns. Therefore, the 'Signals and Sounds for regulating Movements' as contained in the 1833 regulations may be considered to have had, from this time onwards, universal application. These were now reduced to 11 calls plus the officers' call. These were very largely as before except Advance replaced the order March and Skirmish was deleted in recognition of the fact that skirmishing was largely what all light infantry did. The other three that were lost were Disperse, Lie Down and Rise. All of the additional instructions were as before, including the use of the 'G', but there was an added note that stated 'Every regiment should have a well-marked and simple regimental call.'[30] The need for all calls within a regiment to be preceded by that regiment's unique regimental call, so that their companies could understand that a particular call was meant for them, had likely been the case for a long time. But the 1833 order presaged the development of a host of individual regimental bugle calls. The regulations ended with a cautionary note, whose application was to become increasingly relevant as weapons, tactics and methods of warfare changed:

> It will be often prudent to communicate orders to a line of skirmishers, by passing them along the rear, instead of betraying an intended movement by bugle. For

'*the retreat*' to one party is the '*advance*' to their opponents, who are generally well acquainted with the sounds and prepared to act upon them. Too much bugling under any circumstances is to be avoided, as tending to distract the attention of the soldier, and to cause confusion.[31]

Our understanding is further assisted by the increasingly vocal military press in Britain, which began to get into its stride from the late 1820s onwards and allowed regimental officers to voice their views. There was plenty of anonymous comment on drill in the *United Service Journal* in the three years or so before the publication of the 1833 revisions and one in particular exposed the problem for the common soldier of the complications inherent in the evolutions:

> We have at present so many authorised modes of doing the same thing, that it is quite astonishing how the common soldiers can be brought to recollect them … for instance, a soldier standing in our ranks as the flank man of a subdivision has to remember as follows: that he is the left hand man of the right subdivision of *such* a company, which company is a right or a left company, and which company is in the right or in the left wing; that he is, farther, the left hand man of the second section; that he is a *left* file in forming four deep; that he is No. 3 file, perchance, in forming threes; No – for piling arms; and that as each of the above he is to act in a prescribed and different manner.[32]

One of the better-informed correspondents was Major C. Leslie of the 60th King's Royal Rifle Corps. He published in Dublin in 1831 *Instructions for the Application of Light Drill to Skirmishing in the Field* and it is interesting to speculate on this publication's influence on the 1833 regulations. He made particularly clear that his instructions had universal application for all battalions as well as for companies acting in the light role and, while instructions on bugle sounds and light infantry evolutions bore close similarity to the official manual in 1833, Leslie made some additional points:

> All [bugle] sounds made from the battalion are intended to convey the intention of the officer commanding the line to the officer in command of the Light Troops, therefore when the commanding officer's bugle sounds, such sound is to the person in command of the company or skirmishers to which it applies, and the sound for execution will be ordered by the person commanding each body.
>
> Every officer in command of skirmishers will have a bugler attached to him. When the commanding officer's bugler sounds orders, the bugler will instantly

repeat it, and the officer in command on the spot will give the necessary orders for the execution to the skirmishers.

When a company is ordered out to skirmish, its own bugler will invariably accompany it.

When the commanding officer's bugle sounds the distinguishing call of any particular company, it must be instantly repeated by the bugler of that company; after which, the commanding officer's bugle will sound what the company is to do, and the officer will give the necessary word of command. The succeeding sounds will all relate to that company, until the regimental call, or that of some other company, is made.[33]

Little detail at all has been given above about the drum and fife but we have seen that they were not forgotten entirely. It is of note that a standard for the drum was established, actually for the very first time, by the publication in 1815 of Samuel Potter's *The Art of Beating the Drum*. Potter was then the senior drum major in the Coldstream Guards and was also to publish *The Art of Playing the Fife* and *The Bugle Horn-Major's Companion*. Samuel Potter's son, Henry, was to give his name to the company established first in London and later in Aldershot that has provided drums, bugles and fifes/flutes to the British Army and others since. The importance of Potter's manuals was demonstrated when a *General Order* dated 28 December 1816 directed that:

> The mode of Instruction for the Drum and Fife, practised in the Coldstream Regiment of Foot Guards, having been referred to several Regiments in order to ascertain whether adoption would be attended with advantage, and the reports which have been received appearing satisfactory, the Commander-in-Chief, with a view of assimilating the respective 'Calls and Beats' throughout the several Regiments of Infantry, is pleased to command that the System of Instruction for the Drum and Fife, introduced by Drum-Major Potter, of the Coldstream Guards, shall be considered as the established System, and be adopted accordingly.[34]

Usefully, Potter's manual listed 19 drum calls under various classifications. The calls themselves included Retreat, Taptoo, The General and To Arms and a number of marches that included The Rogues' March, The Grenadiers' March and The Dead March. As this author can find no further reference to some of the calls, such as the three listed within 'The Raising of the Troop' and 'The Camp Taps', it is difficult to discern their intention.[35] However, as *The King's Regulations* of 1837 and *The Queen's Regulations* of 1844 repeated the 1816 order verbatim, we might assume that all of these calls remained extant at these dates.[36]

Nevertheless, there is evidence below, if only by omission, that the drum was carried less and less in the field. What becomes most apparent is that the drum was usually retained for close-order evolutions by all infantry, except the rifle regiments but probably still including the light infantry regiments. However, those close-order evolutions were to become of decreasing utility in the field, especially once the rifle was widely adopted, and the bugle gained its place not just for companies and units deployed in extended order and in skirmishing but also for the commanding officer's orderly signaller in all circumstances. This *de facto* situation was sealed in the Crimea. The following correspondence from the *United Service Journal*, quoted of necessity at length, summed up the situation precisely. In 1839 'A Battalion Officer' wrote:

> I have never yet been enabled to find out how it is supposed a regiment of ten companies is capable of being efficient as a Light Infantry Regiment, with the assistance of 'two buglers.' I am well aware that there are always boys employed as 'acting buglers', but the Ordnance do not find instruments for them; and besides whom, there generally are an endless lot of boys (comparatively speaking, a useless set) being brought up acting as drummers. Now ... would it not be an advantage to the Service, if drummers were altogether abolished, and buglers (buglers only) instituted in their place? We find Light Infantry Regiments doing duty as Battalion Regiments very well without drums, but I do not see how a Battalion Regiment is to act as a Light Infantry one without bugles; but they are expected to do so by the regulations of the Service. I am quite aware that some regiments make all their drummers learn the 'duty calls', and carry a bugle (which must be supplied from some private source); but what a pretty figure a drummer would cut skimming over a country intersected with hedges and ditches, with a drum swung on his back. ... Again, of what little service is a single drummer to a detachment? Able to beat the taptoo and dinner-call, certainly; but were he a bugler he may be of service to the officer, if he thought proper to practise Light Infantry drill with his small detachment, which he is entirely precluded from doing for want of his musical assistant. I think it will be apparent that a regiment can do all duties perfectly with bugles, and without drums, but that no regiment possible can do so with drums, and without bugles; and, therefore, if the drum and the fife were superseded by the bugle, two sets of actors would be got rid of, namely, acting buglers, and their brother actors on the drum; by which all regiments would become more efficient ...[37]

It is important to remember that the 1833 regulations were the last full set to be issued before the Crimean War and, devoid of any wider experience, their strictures were in place for the Army of the East. Given their harking back to Dundas and Torrens the great similarities between the tactical handling of the infantry in 1815 and in 1854 are not surprising. They were re-emphasised for the infantry in an abstract published by Horse Guards on 1 March 1847 entitled *The Infantry Manual* in which the Commander-in-Chief desired 'that every Serjeant of Infantry be provided with a Copy ... in order that a perfect uniformity of system ... may be maintained throughout the Service.'[38] But we should remember too that there were influences of other campaigns, however poorly their lessons and their relevance filtered through to the army as a whole. And there was the impact of the new rifle. *The Infantry Manual* contained no changes from the 1833 regulations but had a new section covering 'The Manual and Platoon Exercise of Riflemen' for all to see and absorb, for within a decade all British infantrymen were to be riflemen.

Contemporary illustrations provide helpfully supportive evidence of the evolution of the infantry and the employment of drum and bugle during these years. While we might expect, given their important ceremonial role, that the regiments of Foot Guards retained drummers an illustration of the drummers of the Scots Fusilier Guards in 1838, published in Dublin that year, demonstrated the point well. The artist was Michael Angelo Hayes, an Irishman whose watercolour depictions of many regiments from the late 1830s to the mid-1850s are very important records of dress and procedure. This particular painting of the Scots Fusilier Guards showed drum major, bass drummer, two side drummers and a fifer, all dressed correctly for the time and with the Royal lace of blue *fleur-de-lys* on a white ground of all the Foot Guards regiments.[39] Slightly earlier, in 1832, one of A. J. Dubois Drahonet's beautiful paintings showed Drummer Cann, also of the Scots Fusilier Guards, lugging his drum over his shoulder. The continued presence of drums in the regiments of the line – the 'battalion regiments' referred to by the battalion officer above – is also demonstrated in, for example, a watercolour of the 8th (The King's) Regiment in Guernsey in 1840. This painting depicts 'The guard falling in at the head of the column' and includes a drummer beating what must be the assembly.[40] A further and finer example was painted by Hayes of the 5th (Northumberland Fusiliers) and published in 1846. This showed a quarter guard presenting arms to an inspecting officer, the guard being accompanied by a pair of drummers.[41] We can therefore assume from these examples that drums continued to play an important part at least in regulating the day and in the numerous routine ceremonial activities of an infantry battalion.

Of further help are the various depictions of line infantry with both drummers and buglers although, while these demonstrate the presence of both instruments in the line, the buglers all appear in contemporary pictures to wear the green ball tuft in their shakos to indicate that they were on the strength of their respective light companies. Reginald Augustus Wymer, who painted in the late 19th and early 20th centuries, depicted a young drummer of the 57th (West Middlesex) Regiment around 1820. The boy, in a reversed jacket of yellow cloth carries a bugle only and his shako plume has a white over red plume – the plume giving way to ball tufts for light infantry in 1830 and for all others in 1835. The white over red plume showed clearly that the boy came from a centre company and not from the light company, but it must be remembered that Wymer painted the picture much later. Of more value are Hayes' detailed illustrations of the 46th (South Devonshire) Regiment executed in Ireland in 1837.[42] One plate shows five figures of the regiment's drummers with the drum major and a fifer in bearskins, the latter presumably because he was in the grenadier company, and a side drummer from one of the centre companies. The bugler's shako bears a green ball tuft, therefore indicating his position in the light company.

The point hardly seems worth proving further but there are numerous illustrations to show that rifle regiments and light infantry regiments carried bugles and the same can be said for light companies of line regiments, as just mentioned, and light companies of battalions of Foot Guards. For the latter there exists a sketch of the light company of the 3rd Foot Guards completed in 1828, three years before they became the Scots Fusilier Guards, and in this is a clear depiction of a bugler in the field and 'equipped for service.'[43] An example for the regiments of the line is one of the lithographs after E. Hull showing a bugler of the 17th (Leicestershire) Regiment in 1828.[44] For the light infantry regiments a splendid painting by David Cunliffe of the 68th (Durham Light Infantry) Regiment, known as the Paulet Group, may be seen as representative. This was painted at Weedon in England in 1846 and has been described in full in the *Journal of the Society for Army Historical Research*. Of special interest are the commanding officer, Lieutenant Colonel Lord William Paulet, and his accompanying field bugler, Bugler Jepson. Also shown is a man dressed as bugle major and who carries what can only be a ceremonial bugle as this instrument is of the type of circular horn that originally equipped light infantry in the 18th century. This fellow is known to have been Private Jock Edwards who, as one of the tallest men in the regiment, was dressed for ceremonial occasions as bugle major until the practice was discontinued in the regiment when it went to Dublin, also in 1846.[45] Hayes also showed the 90th (Perthshire Volunteers) – one of the light infantry regiments – in the late 1840s. This is a good depiction of light infantry skirmishing with an officer, sword drawn, and his accompanying orderly bugler, and provides a good idea too of infantry in action a few years later in the Crimea. To complete the picture, a Rifle Brigade group of about 1834 is shown in a lithograph after S. Eschauzier, which has a bugler blowing a call alongside a mounted field officer and officers during a field exercise.[46]

Of solid and irrefutable written evidence of instruments in battle there is precious little but, as before, there are snippets that provide for some sensible conclusions on functions in the field. There is certainly little actual mention of drums at all, save for some occasions in regulating the day and accompanying the march, but we are better served with references to bugles, as might be expected. Difficulties posed by extraordinarily challenging terrain and weather in countries on the fringes of the Empire were certainly no bar to the carriage of the bugle as an essential piece of equipment. The jungle of the Arakan in Burma posed immense difficulties to the British army fighting there against the Japanese in 1943 and 1944. An earlier expedition against the Burmese between 1824 and 1826 posed similar problems. In the fighting to take the city of Arakan in 1825 Captain Edward Evanson, commanding the Light Company of the 54th (West Norfolk) Regiment, was badly wounded in the attack on the Burmese stockade. He wrote later '... I was very sick and hardly able to crawl, which however I succeeded to do, with the assistance of my bugle boy, who brought me through a shower of stones and bullets to the rear.'[47]

During the civil war in Spain, fought between 1833 and 1839 and generally known as the First Carlist War, large numbers of Britons joined the British Auxiliary Legion after the suspension of the Foreign Enlistment Bill, which had, hitherto, forbidden enlistment outside the British and Indian armies. The legion included experienced British officers and, as a rare example of British soldiers in action on the European mainland at this time, we have some useful examples of battlefield techniques. An officer of the 10th Regiment of the legion – the Munster Light Infantry – writing in the *United Service Journal* in 1838 and 1839 recalled that 'we had the satisfaction of perceiving the 4th Regiment [Queen's Own Fusiliers] marched down to the quay for embarkation, their drums and fifes playing their favourite step, "Poor Mary Anne."'[48] Originally there were 11 regiments of infantry, all of single battalions. Eight of these were modelled on line battalions, two on light infantry and one on rifles, the line battalions each containing, in theory at least, six centre companies, a grenadier company and a light company. The officer of the 10th, echoing other voices in the British Army at the time, recorded his dissatisfaction with the training his light infantry battalion received: '... it was the opinion of our old hands, that when so little time was likely to be afforded for organisation, good skirmishing tactics ought to have been inculcated at once, in preference to battalion drill. A parade on level ground is one thing and a fight on the hills another.'[49] This officer provided a particularly useful description of an action during the advance from Bilboa in late August 1835:

> ... we proceeded along the high road to Vittoria. The legion had advanced some five or six miles when a hurried movement was observed among some of the General Staff that came galloping up, conveying orders to the commanders of the brigades. Some companies of Chapel Gorees [highly regarded Spanish irregulars], acting as rear-guard, were ordered to the front, while the emphatic 'halt' sounded by the bugles of the 'advance', and carried along the column of troops by the

voices of commanding officers, augured a rather unusual movement, and it was immediately rumoured that we were about to be engaged with a Carlist force in our front.[50]

In May 1836, in describing an attack on the Carlist lines, this same officer wrote that 'With the "advance" sounding, our regiment commenced descending the heights of the first, for the attack of the second line along which the enemy's fortified houses stood in formidable number.' While brief, this does at least provide good evidence of the use of bugles in the line of battle.

The now pre-eminent role of the bugle can be seen in two further examples drawn from campaigns at this time, examples that also demonstrate some of the difficulties inherent in field signalling and which were to attract increasing criticism. Britain embarked upon its first war in Afghanistan in December 1838, the fighting involving a number of assaults on fortresses. In the attack on the city of Ghuznee in the first year of the war the assaulting troops had to advance in silence to within a few hundred yards of the walls during the night of 23 July. The orders made very clear that all 'movements must be made without the sound of *Bugle*, or *Trumpet*' in order to preserve surprise and an eyewitness affirmed that 'The quiet and silent manner in which every thing was done was really awful … Not a bugle was allowed.'[51] The key to the assault was for the army engineers, protected by a company of the 13th (1st Somersetshire Light Infantry) Regiment, to blow in the gate and the orders added that 'On the chief Engineer finding the opening practicable, he will have the *advance* sounded, for the column [actually for the storming party] to push on.'[52] The attack by the storming party, consisting of the Bengal European Regiment, the 2nd (Queen's Royal) Regiment, the 17th (Leicestershire) Regiment and the remainder of the 13th, was a great success and the following day the army commander, Lieutenant General Sir John Keane, wrote in his despatch to the Governor General of India that:

The different troops of Horse Artillery, the camel and foot batteries, moved off their ground at twelve o'clock that night, without the slightest noise … and in the most correct manner, took up the position assigned them, about two hundred and fifty yards from the walls; in like manner, and with the same silence, the Infantry soon after moved from their ground, and all were at their post at the proper time. A few minutes before three o'clock in the morning, the 'explosion' took place, and proved entirely successful ... On hearing the advance sounded by the bugles (being the signal for the gate having been blown in), the Artillery ... all opened a terrific fire upon the citadel and ramparts of the fort.[53]

Subsequent reports however alluded to some difficulty with signals. A report on the engineer operations by George Thomson, the Chief Engineer of the Army of the Indus, noted that the engineer commander, Captain Peat of the Bombay Engineers, was thrown down and stunned by the explosion and that 'There was some delay in getting a bugler to sound the advance' but that 'this was the only mistake in the operation.' The report added that 'the foolish story, hazarded in the Agra Ukhbar, of [Captain Peat] having seized a bugle, and by mistake sounded a *retreat*, is without a shadow of truth ...'[54] But an officer of the 2nd Queen's also wrote later that in the confusion 'the engineer who had fired the train ... unfortunately ordered a retreat to be sounded [and this] was but too readily obeyed.'[55]

The First Afghan War is remembered today mainly for the disaster that befell General Elphinstone's force as it withdrew from Kabul in the winter of early 1842. Just one European, Assistant Surgeon William Brydon, and a few Indian sepoys reached safety at Jalalabad. For several nights,

> Unwilling to give up hope, the commanding officer at Jalalabad instructed his buglers to take post on the city walls at dusk to play the Advance and Assembly, in order to let any other stragglers and survivors know that there was safe haven to be found. In the words of Sergeant Teer of the 13th Light Infantry, then serving in the garrison, their task was 'To send a message of welcome and safety ringing over those barren plains and amongst those pitiless hills, to sound those clear and stirring notes which would have been so gladly heard by those whom death had made silent for ever.' For six nights the 'resurrection bugles', as they were dubbed in the garrison, played their lonely, pitiful call ... until ... 'we ceased to hope that stragglers from the vanished army would answer the call, and after that the bugles rang no more.'[56]

A number of European soldiers and their families and larger numbers of sepoys survived as prisoners of the Afghans, many of the sepoys being sold into slavery. Sita Ram Pande was one such soldier and whilst in bondage must have yearned for the sound of a British force coming to free him. He was eventually able to obtain his freedom at Ferozepore in late 1843 and recalled, when approaching the city, that he 'could hear the drums and bugles of the garrison, and I was overcome with delight.'[57]

The two wars fought against the Sikhs in 1845–46 and 1848–49 and which led eventually to the annexation of the Punjab were very serious affairs, the Sikhs proving to be well-trained and formidable foes in their own right. The Anglo-Indian Army of the Sutlej found itself extremely hard-pressed by the sheer size of the Sikh armies and by the terrain but fought a conventional set of battles in both wars, well able to recognise in turn the European-style tactics of the Sikh infantry in particular. The regular soldiers of the *fauj-i-ain* carried out similar manoeuvres to the British, if trained largely along French lines and in methods that used line and column but with little experience in open order and skirmishing. Their methods also utilised the drum as an adjunct to command and control and also in what might be described as outdated fashion.[58] There is no particular evidence that the British or East India Company European and native regiments used the drum in the field, but we might suppose that drums were carried universally throughout the infantry. That the bugle was employed is confirmed by Lieutenant Robertson of the 31st (Huntingdonshire) Regiment, who wrote a letter describing his regiment's part in the battle of Moodkee in December 1845. He recalled that during the advance their brigade commander, Brigadier General Bolton, who had commanded the 31st at the commencement of the campaign, was:

> ... mounted on his grey Arab, with his orderly bugler by his side, [and who] rode in front of the colours of the regiment under which he had been wounded at Albuera ... On we went into the jungle, with a tremendous fire of musketry and guns in front of us. Of course we were much broken by the bushes, which would have done well for light infantry ... The last words I heard Bolton say were 'Steady, 31st, steady, and fire low for your lives!' Cockins, the bugler, was trying to hold the grey horse, when they were all three hit and went down together.[59]

This demonstrates clear evidence of the place and importance of the orderly bugler alongside his commander and it should be noted that, as was often the case, Bugler Cockins was on foot while the officer was on horseback. Evidence that the bugle could also be out of place was taken up by Robertson as he wrote on, amusingly:

> After it was quite dark the firing was kept up, the men blazing away at nothing, or at each other, and the bugles sounding 'cease firing' in all directions. At last they left off firing, and we got something like a regiment formed at quarter distance, but no colours or bugler to sound the Regimental Call, so we got a nigger [that is, an Indian sepoy] bugler to try it, and just as he got out a squeak someone nearly knocked the bugle down his throat; this was Sir Harry Smith, who asked what on earth we were making such a row for.[60]

CHAPTER 8

Armies in the East

In those days a regiment on parade could perform all the movements by bugle call.

It could be argued that, until the onset of the Crimean War, the British Army had no need for major change to its tactical methods, except as required by local experience against 'natives'; this was until the impact of new weaponry began to be felt, and such weaponry was nowhere in evidence, certainly not universally, within the Empire at this time. Even the Russian Army – an army of a great power – was still largely equipped with smoothbore muskets in 1854. Indeed, some British regiments began the war similarly equipped. The lessons that emerged might therefore have been ignored had they not been so profound due to the shocking inadequacies of the British Army as a whole. Even said, there was no need for any particular tactical innovation during the course of the fighting, for the Crimean War 'was fought entirely according to European conventions of war. There were no great disparities of outlook, organisation or tactics between the opposing armies, and … the fighting was conducted with weapons and methods which had altered little since the Napoleonic period.'[1] Drummers and buglers were certainly present with the fighting battalions during the war, employed in broadly similar fashion as they had been by the time of the later fighting in the Peninsula and at Waterloo. What is also apparent is that, at least to some extent, a further merging of the roles of drummers/buglers and bandsmen was taking place, encouraged by the relative peace of the years up to 1854.

The administrative depravations of the British Army in the Crimea were a scandal of the time and it is worth noting the effect of the poor state of the army on the regimental bands as this also had an influence on the employment of military musicians in general. Farmer recorded that 'In the infantry, the acting bandsmen, who were privates, were naturally absorbed by their respective companies, whilst the regular bandsmen, numbering twenty per battalion, accompanied their regiment in their official capacity.'[2] There is much ambiguity in Farmer's statement as the acting bandsmen and regular bandsmen had been, or had meant to be, since the *General Order* of 1803 and referred to in Chapter 6, one and the same thing. There were still numbers of civilian bandmasters, many of them foreigners, and there might have been a few musical specialists in some regiments, provided at the whim of a commanding officer and paid for by his officers, but no civilians were permitted on campaign. There may also have been a number of men from the ranks still acting as bandsmen and there were still numerous boys being held on the strength of the band before they came of sufficient age to be drummers, buglers or rank and file. It will be recalled too that the 1803 order demanded that all bandsmen were to take their place in the ranks of the infantry as required. Reacting to pressure in 1823 the Commander-in-Chief authorised an increase in band establishments from one sergeant and ten bandsmen to one and 14 but commanded that 'any excess of the prescribed numbers shall be strictly applied to the establishment now authorised.'[3] *The King's Regulations* of 1837 made it more than clear what was expected of commanding officers and their bandsmen:

> The Establishment of a Regimental Band is to consist of a *Serjeant*, as *Master*, and *Fourteen Privates*, as *Musicians*; but these Men are to be effective to the Service as Soldiers, – to be perfectly drilled, – and liable to serve in the Ranks on any emergency; – this number is not to be exceeded under any circumstances, excuse, or arrangement whatever.[4]

That all regimental officers were still paying for the upkeep of their respective bands was also made clear in the same orders. These orders had noted that 'The Formation of a Band of Music upon an economical Scale, being considered essential to the Credit and Appearance of a Regiment, every Officer (married or single) is required, on entering a Regiment, to pay towards the maintenance and support of a Band.' This was set, by order at '*A Subscription of Twenty Days' Pay*, on Appointment – and an *Annual Contribution*, at the discretion of the Commanding Officer, *but not exceeding Twelve Days' Pay* ...' This was a large sum indeed and was added to further by every officer when promoted paying the difference between the 20 days' pay of his former rank and his new rank. In 1846 there was another increase to one sergeant and 20 privates, authorised that April by circular memorandum to all commanding officers.[5]

By the time the British Army of the East had arrived in the Crimea the effects of disease, which tore through the ranks of the army through-out its journey, meant that maintaining numbers of bandsmen as well as drummers and buglers as actual musicians became a very low priority. Farmer quoted a 'Regimental Officer' recalling in an article written in 1859 and entitled *Our Veterans of 1854*, the march from Scutari to Varna at the onset of the land campaign when the effects of disease became evident amongst the drummers: 'As we crossed the bridge, and neared the French guard, our drummers [and here Farmer added 'and fifers'], with but feeble wrists, poor lads, struck up "Partant pour la Syrie", but that spirit-stirring air fell flat now.'[6]

There was another knock-on effect that depleted the numbers of all musicians still further. Medical facilities and the means to transport the wounded and the sick proved totally inadequate for 'We had invaded without means of transporting the sick and wounded beyond a few stretchers in the hands of bandsmen and drum-boys.' While the army was still concentrated around Constantinople in May 1854 a general order was issued that stated unequivocally that:

> At the recommendation of the principal Medical Officer, Medical Officers in charge of Corps who may not have instructed the Band and Drummers of their respective Regiments in the application of tourniquets, and other such duties as may be required of these men as auxiliaries in the field will, at such hours as may be approved of their Company Officers, do so without delay ...[7]

The provision of medical orderlies by re-assigning bandsmen and many of the drummers and buglers was, of course, long-established practice and it is interesting that the orders to this effect had to be given at all. It was almost as if this requirement had also been forgotten. Prior to the opening battle of the war at the Alma on 20 September 1854 Major General Sir Colin Campbell, commanding the Highland Brigade, gave the following clear warning:

> Remember this: whoever is wounded – I don't care what his rank is – whoever is wounded must lie where he falls till the bandsmen come to attend him. No soldiers must go carrying off wounded men. If any soldier does such a thing, his name shall be stuck up in his parish church … Keep silence. Fire low.[8]

The author of *Our Veterans of 1854* knew from experience that the secondary duty of bandsmen and the younger drummers was to act as medical orderlies and stretcher-bearers but noted too that 'These lads being physically unequal to the duty expected of them, we endeavoured to supply their places with the heavy-weighted soldiery.'[9] Farmer also quoted the author of a piece written in 1855 who stated that 'The fifteen or twenty bandsmen with each regiment had been provided with stretchers to carry the wounded to the rear … a mile from where our troops were fighting, so that … the bandsmen were soon inadequate for the performance of their melancholy task.'[10]

That drummers were also told off for this task was confirmed by the famed correspondent of *The Times*, William Howard Russell, who reported that 'the very first to be killed [at the Alma] was "a drummer who was carrying a litter."'[11] Farmer added that 'It was this duty which hushed the bands [and drums and bugles] of the British army for many months to come.'[12]

Yet another factor at play was that General FitzRoy Somerset, more usually known as Lord Raglan and commanding in the Crimea at the start of the war, appeared to have no enthusiasm for military music of any sort. Whether this was simply personal preference or recognition of the practicalities of the time and the problems experienced by the musicians, as just discussed, is not known. Lord Raglan was certainly annoyed by 'the infernal toot-toot-tooting of [the] bugles' by the French as they prepared to attack the Russians at the Alma.[13] But added to the army's administrative troubles were the enormous difficulties of supply in the field and musical instruments would have been way down the list of priorities for movement. Long the scapegoat for the poor state of his army in the Crimea, Raglan was also blamed for forbidding the playing of any music and thus depriving the soldiers of this potential boost to morale at a grim time. On 19 September, the day before the Alma, Raglan ordered that 'The Army will get under arms to-morrow morning without signal from Bugle or Drum.' This was followed by a further order that 'Whenever a Division or portion of the Army is in the immediate presence of the enemy, no sound of Bugle or Drum is to be made. In all cases the Reveillé may be discontinued.'[14] Our 'Regimental Officer' added that 'A command was issued that no orderly drum or bugle should sound ... for fear of informing the enemy of our whereabouts; accordingly, directions about the assembly of parades, fatigue parties, etc., had to be given *viva voce* by drummers, who ran from tent to tent screaming "It's time to fall in."'[15] This might seem pragmatic and a common-sense response to changing tactical conditions, and it was hardly a new phenomenon. But these regulations ignored the critical needs of the moral component: failure to maintain morale could be as decisive a decider of a battle as any tactical innovation. Russell reported that 'The silence and gloom of our camp are very striking. No drum, no bugle call, no music of any kind, is ever heard within our precincts ... the want of music in camp is productive of graver consequences than appear likely to occur at first from such cause ... The military band is not meant alone for the delectation of garrison towns ... the men are fairly entitled to its inspiration during the long and weary march in the enemy's country, and in the monotony of a standing camp ere the beginning of a siege.'[16] Farmer's comment on this was telling: 'The soldier had heard the drum taps and bugle call from "Reveille" to "Last Post" all the days of his soldiering ... it was part and parcel of his being, and to shut all that out of his life was disastrous.'[17] This was in marked contrast to the French, who had shown no such timidity in the face of the Russians and, as another commented, 'never cared a straw for the Muscoves ... the *rappel* and the *générale* were sounded in their camp without let or hindrance.'[18] The day after the victory of the Alma, Russell reported that:

> Soon after dawn the French assembled all their drums and trumpets on the top of the highest hills they carried, and with a wild flourish and roll, repeated again and again, and broken by peals of sound from the horns of the infantry, celebrated their meeting ere they departed. It was spirited, stirring, and thrilling music, and its effect, as it swelled through the darkness of the early morning down over the valley, can never be forgotten.[19]

By November 1854 Raglan had corrected his earlier order, allowing drums, bugles and bands to 'play whenever commanding officers think fit.'[20] It may well have been just a misunderstanding, later exaggerated, and the bandsmen and younger drummers and buglers had been most certainly needed to tend to the wounded. There is enough evidence too that the drummers and buglers (and even fifers) who had retained these duties, however few in number they might have been, continued to be used in their original role as battlefield signallers. Certain calls, such as the alarm, represented immediate authority and were critical to effectiveness and could not have been dispensed with. We know too that, while perhaps an unusual example, the sound that bugles gave could not be bettered in certain circumstances. Daily, beyond the harbour at Balaclava, 'At nine, infantry bugles in vessels three miles at sea blew the Last Post to recall stragglers, with as much regularity as if still in barracks at Winchester or Portsmouth … and at midnight the silver trumpets from the cavalry transports wound clear and long their melancholy notes, proclaiming to the assembled squadrons that none of their men were absent.'[21]

While, in obeying Raglan's order, the 4th (The King's Own) Regiment might have reported on the morning of the Alma that 'At 6 a.m. the troops fell in without sound of drum or bugle',[22] the 2nd Battalion the 60th Regiment − the King's Royal Rifle Corps − found itself in much difficulty because of bugles during the mass Russian attack to recover the Great Redoubt. The Russian defenders of the heights above the River Alma had been astonished at what appeared to them a thinly supported attack by the British line against their cannon and strong infantry columns. But they were also impressed by the steady and remorseless advance by the two forward divisions − the Light and the 2nd Divisions − and especially when they gained their objectives, having suffered appalling casualties. The Russians were quick to react and counter-attacked to recapture their redoubts. The commanding officer of the 60th described that:

> At this juncture a most untoward mistake occurred. Some Officer [he did not say from which regiment] believed the advancing column to be French, & called upon a Bugler to [sound] cease firing, & shortly after the mass [referring to the

British defenders] began to give way … In vain Col Saunders of the 19th exhorted his men both by voice & manner not to retire. In vain Genl Codrington rode up to the left where I was, & made every effort under this murderous fire to check the rolling mass. But it slowly retired, and our voices were unheeded in the din.[23]

Alexander Kinglake added in his extensive history of the war that a never identified staff officer cried as the Russians approached 'The column is French, don't fire men! For God's sake don't fire' and that, simultaneously, bugles took up the calls to cease fire and retire, the latter call being for the 7th, the Royal Fusiliers, who were already engaged in a fire-fight with the Russian regiments.[24] The supporting 1st Division was certainly too far away to be of immediate assistance and both divisions were forced to give way. We have to imagine that no bugler could be found to blow a more positive sound on his bugle or that the noise and confusion were just too great to be corrected simply. Russell thought that the basis of the story was ridiculous and that only 'The stupidest lout alive could not have thought that a French column … was marching out from the Russian lines with bayonets at the charge to attack us.' But added that 'it is certain that an order to sound the "retire" was given by some officer on horseback to a bugler of the 19th Regiment! The bugler obeyed, whereupon the call to retire was sounded along the line by all the buglers!'[25]

It is worth reflecting here on the fighting and the tactics experienced by the Army of the East in what might best be understood as the final flourish of Napoleonic-style methods. In the previous chapter we noted some gradual evolution of tactics and might further emphasise that, notwithstanding the effects on field evolutions of the experience being gained by fighting irregular forces in difficult terrain, conventional tactics were being forced to change anyway with the universal issue of rifled weapons to the infantry. Raglan's divisions might have looked much like Wellington's and they might have manoeuvred in similar fashion but they were armed almost universally with the rifle, whose range and accuracy tipped the balance in battle in favour of the British (and the French) with devastating effect. The new Rifle Musket, Pattern 1851, better known as the Minié rifle, began to be issued to the British infantry at the end of 1851. It was approved by Wellington in one of his

The English drumming and fifing tradition owed much to the influences of the Swiss in the early Renaissance period and, later, the mercenary armies as epitomised by the Landsknecht. This engraving of about 1540 by Zasinger shows two Austrian drummers and a fifer of the time. Henry VIII's soldiers would have been similarly dressed and equipped. *(Anne S. K. Brown Military Collection, Brown University Library)*

This spirited contemporary engraving by N. van der Meer dated 1572 provides a realistic depiction of battle at this time. Here infantry can be seen attacking a fortress with a drummer in the foreground beating out a command or simply a march to embolden the attackers. Such a scene would be common in the late 16th and early 17th centuries. *(Anne S. K. Brown Military Collection, Brown University Library)*

Left: A modern interpretation of a drummer of the British Army at the beginning of the 18th century by the artist Charles C. Stadden. Typical of drummers over the decades from the Restoration and throughout Marlborough's campaigns, this drummer of the Earl of Donegal's Regiment (later the 35th Foot) in 1702 wears a 'reversed coat' of orange with red facings and carries a drum adorned with the earl's coat of arms. *(Author's Collection)*

Right: Another Stadden painting, this one of a drummer of the 70th Foot in about 1758. The drummer's reversed coat is in grey, the coat and sleeves adorned with regimental lace. He wears a typical drummer's mitre cap, shorter than that worn by the grenadiers, and the drum bears a now-standard emblazon of the royal cypher and regimental number. *(Author's Collection)*

An Incident in the Rebellion of 1745: detail from David Morier's near-contemporary painting of the grenadiers of Barrell's Regiment, later the 4th (King's Own), facing the Highland charge at Culloden. Note the pair of drummers behind the line, where they should be standing, and on the left flank, both wearing the shortened mitre cap *(Royal Collection Trust © Her Majesty Queen Elizabeth II 2016)*

The Battle of Bunker Hill. While completed in 1898, Howard Pyle's oil painting of the British line attacking the American rebels on Bunker Hill in 1775 is a magnificent portrayal of manoeuvre according to the drill book. While the lines are probably too perfect and maintaining the step would have been impossible, this execution of Frederickian methods at this stage in the war is not wholly unrealistic and tight control of the line and a deliberate and steady pace were essential. Note the groupings of drummers in the centre and on the flanks. *(Delaware Art Museum, Institutional Archives)*

Left: Edward Dayes produced a number of watercolours depicting drummers of the Foot Guards that were published by Hewgill in 1792. This drummer of the Coldstream Regiment of Foot Guards is typical, showing the additional lace worn on the arms by drummers at this time. *(Anne S. K. Brown Military Collection, Brown University Library)*

Right: A drummer of the 77th (East Middlesex) Regiment of about 1808 by Charles Stadden, in dress typical of drummers of line regiments throughout the Napoleonic Wars. The facing colour of the 77th was yellow, hence the yellow of this drummer's reversed coat. Evidence suggests that due to drummers being singled out as targets by the French, many regiments dressed them in standard red coats. *(Author's Collection)*

This semi-caricature by Johann Ramberg, executed in 1783 and showing British infantry attacking French infantry in the American colonies, is nearer the mark when it comes to realism. Confusion is evident, together with an abandoned French drum. Abandoned drums are far more common than carried drums in contemporary pictures over the centuries. *(Anne S. K. Brown Military Collection, Brown University Library)*

Field Day, aquatint by John Augustus Atkinson. Published in 1808, this depiction of grenadiers in line, three ranks locked and delivering a single volley, provides a fine impression of an evolution about to be superseded in the field by two ranks and in a slightly more loose order as common. Note the two drummers who can just be discerned behind the rear rank. *(Anne S. K. Brown Military Collection, Brown University Library)*

A contemporary print of the mid-1850s of the 90th Light Infantry by Michael Angelo Hayes. Hayes was a keen observer of the British Army of his time and this is an accurate depiction of infantry skirmishing, with company officer and bugler, and representative of infantry in action from the Napoleonic Wars to the Crimea. The uniform has also seen little change in the intervening years. *(Author's Collection)*

An important role for drummers since their earliest days was to assist with recruiting. This delightful contemporary caricature by Denis Dighton is titled *Recruiting Scenes, 1821* and shows a recruiting sergeant and his accompanying drummer assessing potential recruits in a stable-yard. *(Anne S. K. Brown Military Collection, Brown University Library)*

Right: A photograph by Roger Fenton of the Grenadier Guards at the Curragh in Ireland in 1861 provides valuable contemporary and irrefutable evidence of a battalion's corps of drums for the time. Note the age range of the drummers and the extreme youth of the small boys. Despite their presence in the photograph and thus in the drums the boys would not have been employed as drummers in the field. *(Author's Collection)*

Left: Detail from a contemporary painting of the charge of the 22nd (Cheshire) Regiment at the battle of Meeanee during the conquest of Scinde in 1843. The loose order of the men is well shown, with a company bugler at the centre of things. *(Mercian Regiment Collection)*

Right: *Blowing Up of the Cashmere Gate at Delhi.*
A near-contemporary print showing Lieutenant Salkeld and his demolition party when they forced the gate at Delhi in 1857. On the right, Bugler Robert Hawthorne of the 52nd (Oxfordshire Light Infantry) prepares to sound the regimental call of the 52nd. He was awarded the Victoria Cross for his gallantry. (Author's Collection)

Close detail of a watercolour by Orlando Norie of the 24th (2nd Warwickshire) Regiment skirmishing in close country in the late 1860s. Norie's huge output demonstrated much realism of soldiers in action and here a field officer is closely followed by his orderly bugler, ready to blow any calls required. *(Anne S. K. Brown Military Collection, Brown University Library)*

In this detail from a contemporary print of about 1850 of a painting by Hayes of fusiliers in various scenes, a company is shown in close order with its drummer in attendance. Such close-order drill continued to be practised at this time and the men have all the appearance of the Napoleonic era. *(Anne S. K. Brown Military Collection, Brown University Library)*

While near-contemporary, this detail from Richard Simkin's fanciful depiction of the Grenadier Guards on manoeuvres in 1879 is far from the reality of the time. The close order and closed ranks of the Guardsmen owe more to Napoleonic era drills than those post-Crimea. Note, however, the company buglers, the orderly bugler to the rear and the group of drummers on the rear flank. *(Anne S. K. Brown Military Collection, Brown University Library)*

Closer to reality is one of Orlando Norie's atmospheric contemporary watercolours, here of the 72nd (Duke of Albany's Own Highlanders) on manoeuvres in the 1860s. The detail shows a skirmish line with an orderly bugler standing close to his officer. *(Anne S. K. Brown Military Collection, Brown University Library)*

The Guards at Tel-el-Kebir. Richard Caton-Woodville's splendid painting of the Guards Brigade in Egypt in 1882. Just to the right of the Duke of Connaught on his white horse can be seen his orderly bugler and note the drummer in the bottom left corner, sitting amongst the stretcher-bearers. *(Royal Collection Trust © Her Majesty Queen Elizabeth II 2016)*

Another Norie, this one of a company of the Dorsetshire Regiment in a firing line during manoeuvres somewhere in England in 1890. Note the company commander and his orderly bugler standing to the rear. While khaki uniforms were now almost universal for foreign service, battalions at home continued to wear Home Service Dress in the field, as here. *(Anne S. K. Brown Military Collection, Brown University Library)*

The drums of the 2nd Battalion Royal Sussex Regiment in Crete in about 1906. The sheer size of the corps should be noted, representing numbers typical for a battalion on foreign service. Seated either side of the base drum can be identified the sergeant drummer and the adjutant, the latter on the right of the picture. Standing far right is the battalion's mascot and handler. *(Author's Collection)*

Left: Drummers, 2nd Scots Guards. A postcard dated about 1910 providing a fine depiction of typical young drummers of the Foot Guards in full dress. The uniform is practically unchanged today. *(Author's Collection)*

Right: By comparison, this postcard of a similar date shows a typical drummer of the infantry of the line, here the Princess of Wales's Own (Yorkshire Regiment), later the Green Howards. It is noteworthy that when all non-Royal English infantry regiments adopted white facings in 1881, in some regiments drummers retained their old regimental facings which, in this case, were green. *(Author's Collection)*

The artist Richard Caton-Woodville's illustration of the battle of Paardeberg in South Africa in February 1900. While over-dramatised, the depiction of the commanding officer with his orderly bugler is not unrealistic. *(Author's Collection)*

A contemporary print of a sketch by Lester Ralph, almost certainly gleaned from a still from cinematographic film, of General Hector MacDonald directing the Highland Brigade at an action near Koedoesberg in South Africa in January 1900. Note the presence of the various items of signalling equipment, including the orderly bugler. *(Author's Collection)*

Four paintings by Caton-Woodville dating from the Edwardian era and showing drummers and buglers of Territorial Army infantry battalions. Top left 4th and 5th Battalions Royal Scots; top right 4th and 5th Battalions the Devonshire Regiment; bottom left the East Yorkshire Regiment; bottom right Infantry Skirmishing. There is an incongruous mix of home service frocks and headdress in the field, with the depiction of skirmishing showing the 1902 service dress and how it was supposed infantry would operate on campaign. This was not far from what occurred in the opening weeks of the Great War, before reality struck. *(Author's Collection)*

While all instruments had practically disappeared from the battlefield, bar a few exceptions, a common enough sight on the Western Front during the Great War was a battalion marching to or from the front led by its drummers and buglers. Here the 8th Battalion The Prince of Wales's (North Staffordshire) Regiment is photographed near Estaires in France in 1915. Both drums and bugles are evident. *(Author's Collection)*

We're marchin' on relief over Injia's coral strand: Kipling's words help immortalise a sight common in India for much of the late 19th and early 20th centuries. Here the 1st Battalion the Dorsetshire Regiment, marches into Landi Kotal in the Khyber Pass in 1936, led by the drum major and drummers with the band in tow. *(The Keep Military Museum)*

Above: The semi-religious status of drums is evident in this photograph of an army padre arranging the Colours, themselves religious icons, of the 2nd Battalion the Duke of Lancaster's Regiment on their return home from Afghanistan in October 2010. The drums – here the battalion's silver drums – form the centrepiece of a drumhead service at Catterick Garrison. (Stuart Walker Photography)

Below left: There has been little occasion for the use of bugles in the field for more than one hundred years but here Corporal Timmins of the 1st Battalion the Staffordshire Regiment calls for B Company's reserve platoon to deploy while on exercise in Canada in 1990. *(Author's Collection)*

Below right: Last Post being blown by a drummer of the 2nd Battalion Royal Anglian Regiment at a repatriation ceremony in Afghanistan in 2014. *(Royal Anglian Regiment Collection)*

last acts as Commander-in-Chief although, in typical style, he insisted on the inclusion of the word 'musket' in the weapon's description, 'lest the whole of the infantry should clamour to be clothed in green.'[26] While the Minié equipped many of the British regiments in the Crimea, it was already being superseded by the more superior 1853 Pattern Enfield Rifle. But both provided a technological edge that, with the already evident ability of all British infantry to adopt open order and to skirmish in extended fashion, gave the British infantry a battle-winning formula.

None of this would have been worth a jot without training, discipline and courage and all were in evidence at the tactical level in the Crimea. This was the case despite a lack of overall experience in the field that marked the army of the early 1850s. But it was probably extremely fortunate too that neither Russian nor mutinous sepoy later in India carried a more effective firearm. The previous chapter tracked the various modifications to the regulations in the years after Waterloo and noted that the effects of colonial warfare helped, at least in part, to maintain an adherence to the need for all infantry to be trained in the light infantry manoeuvres. Without this the army would simply have embraced its Peninsula experience and, almost certainly, have gradually reverted to concentrating on close-order manoeuvre and nothing else. In fact, with the light infantry regiments continuing to be armed as before with the smoothbore musket, there was even a danger that none but the rifle regiments would adhere to the light infantry drills. Fortunately some senior officers continued to ensure that their line regiments absorbed these drills and it was fortunate too that in 1852 General the Lord Hardinge succeeded Wellington as Commander-in-Chief. Hardinge had considerable field experience gained in the Peninsula and in the First Sikh War and, while no great reformer – and he did not live long enough to initiate reforms following the lessons from the Crimea, the overall conduct for which he was responsible – he established, in 1853, the first divisional camp of exercise at Chobham. It was here that the major faults of the official manual were at last exposed and acknowledged. Hew Strachan has reckoned that, 'although unrevised by 1854, drill had in practice undergone a process of gradual evolution.'[27] The more conservative and reactionary officers in the army abhorred the apparent neglect by some officers of the established drills but there had been a gradual chipping away by more pragmatic officers and some of these of considerable seniority, such as General Sir Charles Napier, another Peninsula veteran and the conqueror of Sindh in 1843. Certainly that propensity for many commanding officers in the British Army to do their own thing and ignore officialdom helped and they were able to use common sense in the face of modern reality to circumvent the more ridiculous absurdities demanded by the drill book.

The main obstacle was really little more than recognising once and for all that there was the need for just one type of infantry and thus removing any remaining distinction between line, light and rifle, and Guards for that matter. While the full effect of the issue of the rifle to all infantrymen was not to be realised until its impact was demonstrated in the Crimea, it was evident to many already that every infantryman really did have to be thoroughly versed in the skills of the light infantry. It is of some note that in 1845 General Sir George Murray, who had been Wellington's Quartermaster General in the Peninsula and was then Master General of the Ordnance, wrote to the Prime Minister, Sir Robert Peel, 'that Sir John Moore had told him that "his wish [at Shorncliffe] had not been so much to form regiments of Infantry differing from those of the rest of the Army, as to introduce into the British Infantry in general a system more suitable than the unnecessarily slow and formal system which Sir David Dundas had copied from the Germans."'[28] This, as we have seen, is to over-criticise Dundas' intentions somewhat, but the point is still important. Yet, while it might seem that sticking to the seemingly ponderous stipulations laid down by Old Pivot was flying in the face of reality, we have to remember also that the apparent need for everyone to be a light infantryman was being driven by the experience of the 1830s and 1840s and that experience was confined to colonial campaigns. If Britain were to face a 'real' enemy, the prevailing view into the early 1850s was that this would be the French since the period was witnessing another of Britain's periodic invasion scares. In what seemed to many a repeat of history another Bonaparte – Louis-Napoléon, nephew of Boney – now ruled across the Channel and it was deemed that, when the time came, his rapidly moving columns would have to be dealt with as before, by infantry in line and in close order. What was really needed was for all infantry to be able to operate in close, open and extended order, to be able to move in column and deploy into line. One Captain Thomas Ramsay summed up this need when he wrote in the *Naval and Military Gazette* of April 1842 that it was actually 'quite plain that there is only one sort of infantry, and in a modern system of warfare every foot soldier is required to perform every sort of military service.'[29] As the Russians fought in a very similar manner to the French the British system, now with rifle-armed infantry, was not found wanting.

The final piece in what was something of a jigsaw of debate was the effect of the new rifles on tactics. The technological advantage of the rifle over the smoothbore might appear obvious but the development of a truly useful rifle had been problematic for decades. By the late 1840s too, some British regiments, especially those in India, were still awaiting replacement of their ancient flintlocks with percussion lock weapons. The 1800 Pattern Baker Rifle had only recently been replaced in the rifle regiments by the 1837 Pattern Brunswick, but this proved a poor weapon and did nothing to improve the chances of all infantrymen being provided with rifles. There was a view too that a longer-ranged and more accurate weapon would 'destroy that intrepid spirit which makes the British soldier always dash at his enemy.' This view of the Minié came, somewhat surprisingly, from Sir Charles Napier, who added that 'The short range and the very uncertain flight of shot from the musket begets the necessity of closing with the enemy.'[30] But Hew Strachan has postulated that he may have been motivated more by lack of knowledge of the Minié's great superiority and this superiority of the new rifles was sealed further by the arrival of the Enfield. With France and Prussia introducing their own rifles British infantry were in danger of being severely outclassed by technology and losing that great advantage that they had held for so long – superior firepower. The matter was sealed when individual marksmanship, which was so necessary for rifle-armed infantrymen, received a major boost in May 1853 with the opening of the School of Musketry at Hythe in Kent. The timespan between the opening of this school and the onset of the Crimean War was too short to bear fruit but new technology and improved tactics were driven together in the Crimea by force of circumstances.

Aside from administrative failings the Army of the East also lacked effective generalship in the field. By this we should distinguish between the higher level of command, as represented by Raglan and his staff, and the divisional level and below, the inexperienced Duke of Cambridge commanding the 1st Division perhaps falling, initially at least, in the Raglan camp. As so many times before and since, the soldiers and their regimental and brigade officers won the day. From the outset at the Alma the tough and aggressive Russians suffered the disheartening effect of a British line of two ranks coming on no matter what was thrown at them. Without doubt the British infantry knew what it was doing and the Alma provided two splendid examples of it doing its business well. The Russians watched the Light Division advancing in what looked like disordered fashion, disrupted in their advance by the river, vineyards, undergrowth and ascent, and coming on like a horde of skirmishers in 'a knotted chain' but taking the redoubts nonetheless.[31] The 7th Fusiliers in the 2nd Division were so disordered by the ground and the deadly Russian fire that the commanding officer 'was heard to utter an order that ought to have been unthinkable, "Never mind forming, for God's sake … come on, come on, men! Come on anyhow!"'[32] What the Russians had not appreciated was that the British infantry could attack in apparent lines but with each man firing at will, maybe two to three rounds a minute, rather than having to approach to within 50 or maybe 100 yards to halt to present and fire in volleys or by files. And the firing would have begun perhaps 500 yards out and well beyond the reach of the smoothbore muskets with which the bulk of the Russian infantry was armed.

Still, it took the 1st Division and especially the Guards Brigade to restore the situation at the height of the Russian counter-attack. The 1st Battalion Scots Fusilier Guards had crossed the river first and had got out of hand, attacking precipitately and falling back towards the river to cries of 'shame' as the two other Guards' battalions came up. The 3rd Battalion the Grenadier Guards and 1st Battalion the Coldstream Guards advanced in a more deliberate manner, taking their time to dress their ranks while under fire, but proceeding then to fire on the move. We might imagine their officers and non-commissioned officers providing words of encouragement but it is probably too wild to imagine the drums beating out any commands. Nevertheless, these three battalions – for the Scots had re-formed and turned again – in their red coatees and imposing bearskins would have presented a most beautiful sight. Close in, their disciplined volley fire was devastating. This rallied the 2nd Division and with the Highland Brigade coming up on the right of the line, the Russians gave way.

The most intense of infantry fights took place on 5 November 1854 during the surprise Russian attack at Inkerman and a number of accounts provide evidence of bugle calls as the British Army fought desperately to hold the Russians and then force them back. The 4th King's Own Royal Regiment in the 3rd Division recorded that 'The bugles sounded the Alarm' to hurry groups of soldiers to the heights to receive the Russian columns. For the 4th at least, the younger drummers were left out of battle for the regiment 'marched out of the camp … leaving only Mrs Evans, the drummer boys, and the sick to guard the Colours.'[33] Leaving the boys in camp must have been common enough practice and given the conditions by the early winter of 1854 most drums could well have been stored away in tents; but it was not universal practice. Some of the most desperate fighting early on took place in and around the exposed Sandbag Battery on the Kitspur, where the 41st (Welch) Regiment had rallied to their regimental call before being flung back by the Russians. The Guards Brigade, with parts of other battalions, then restored the situation and during the murderous close-quarter battle that ensued the battery at one point was abandoned and inside it 'Drummer Thomas Keep of the [3rd] Grenadiers, a boy of 10, had made a fire to brew tea for the wounded.'[34] We do not know if young Keep had carried his drum into the Battery or was acting purely as a medical orderly, but that such a youngster was with the fighting line is clear.

One allusion to the presence of drummers in the battle can be found in an account from the 20th (East Devonshire) Regiment. During the early afternoon the 20th, a regiment still armed with smoothbores, fell back through the French 7th Light Infantry, which then also began to retire. The 20th then saw the 55th (Westmoreland) Regiment come up in support and 'Someone called out (from the British lines but in French) "Drums to the front". The Drummers and the Buglers ran boldly out to the front and sounded the "Double Quick Charge" call. The whole line, British and French charged forwards.'[35] Almost certainly these drummers were carrying bugles and not drums.

We might conclude that drummers with drums became a rarity in the field in the entrenchments at Sebastopol and in the associated battles, but a number of contemporary and near-contemporary illustrations provide useful evidence of drums as well as bugles. While a number of these might be dismissed as stylised uniform studies or examples of more routine activities away from the battlefield, the existence of illustrations executed by eyewitnesses, and soldiers at that, is pretty conclusive. Lieutenant F. W. Balfour of the 2nd Rifle Brigade painted a spirited watercolour of a Rifle Brigade company extended as skirmishers, with a bugler, alongside his officer, summoning reinforcements from the supports.[36] This use of bugles by a rifle regiment is as expected but the artist P. W. Reynolds noted that, according to the clergyman and artist Joseph Ebsworth, at about the time of the Crimean War he had seen the drummers of the 7th Royal Fusiliers equipped with bugles alone. Of drummers, Vanson, a young French staff officer present in the Crimea, produced a number of important watercolours and sketches and these included a group of drummers and fifers of the Foot Guards in camp, although the location was not defined. At the outset of the campaign in the spring of 1854 he sketched a drummer of a battalion company of the 38th (1st Staffordshire) Regiment arriving at Gallipoli and carrying both drum and bugle. Even more importantly, Captain Henry Wilkinson of the 9th (East Norfolk) Regiment drew a number of sketches of life as it was in the trenches at Sebastopol in the winter of 1854–55 and one of these, entitled *The Guard parading for the Trenches*, showed the rear view of a drummer, clad in greatcoat with a hood over his head. He is also shown carrying a drum and a bugle and the date – 2 February 1855 – is important as it is evidence of the continued use of the drum in the field despite the rigours of the campaign. And for the very first time we have photographic evidence of the battlefield, with a number of

Roger Fenton's famous photographs of the war. One shows a bugler of the 68th (Durham Light Infantry) Regiment and the other a drummer, holding only a bugle, of the 3rd (East Kent) Regiment – The Buffs. This drummer is shown standing behind Brigadier General Charles von Straubenzee and is, presumably the general's orderly drummer. Queen Victoria had two albums of photographs taken in 1856 of troops who had returned from the Crimea. One of these shows the splendidly bearded Bugler Tobin of the Rifle Brigade and he carries the long bugle of the time.[37]

After the great battles of late 1854 the war in the Crimea settled down in the trenches surrounding Sebastopol until the weather improved enough for assaults on the city's defences in the summer of the following year. The intervening months were interspersed with activity and on the night of 19 April units of the Light Division conducted a raid on some Russian rifle pits. During the Russian counter-attack early the next morning Drummer MacGill of the 77th (East Middlesex) Regiment distinguished himself. We know precious little about young MacGill but he was with his commanding officer, Colonel Egerton, throughout and witnessed his death. The regimental history stated:

> Drummer MacGill, a boy of fifteen, who was orderly bugler to Colonel Egerton that night, rushed into the enemy's pit and seizing a Russian bugler held him fast till he surrendered and gave up his bugle as a trophy to his youthful conqueror; for this act MacGill received the French Medal of Valour.[38]

The Russian bugle eventually passed into the collection of the Middlesex Regiment Museum and now resides in the collection of the National Army Museum.

The war withered on and a suitable epitaph to this section might be had in the failed attempts in the summer and early autumn of 1855 on the fortifications surrounding Sebastopol. On 18 June, the anniversary of the battle of Waterloo, the British and French made concerted if poorly coordinated assaults on, respectively, the Redan and the Malakoff. They were both dismal failures and caused considerable casualties. On the far left the 3rd Division penetrated the Russian defences but failure at the Redan forced a withdrawal. When the 18th (Royal Irish) finally received the order to retire they spent a number of hours getting their wounded away. Satisfied that this was completed their commanding officer, Lieutenant Colonel Edwards, directed the remaining men to get away 'by twos and threes. Keep up a warm fire. When across the open, bugler sound the Regimental Call and the retire.'[39]

★

No sooner had the British Army withdrawn from the Crimea than it became embroiled in a fight that threatened the whole foundation of its position in the East and especially in India. While not classed as a European-type war between major powers, fighting methods on both sides during the war that Britain knows largely as the Indian Mutiny and India knows as the first war of independence were much the same as those in the Crimea. The native regiments of the armies of the three presidencies of the East India Company had all been led by British officers but they were still equipped with smoothbore percussion muskets, while the company's European regiments as well as the Queen's regiments in India had begun to be issued with the new Enfield rifle; the Minié rifle was never issued in India. The impending issue of the Enfield to the native regiments was a major catalyst for the rebellion, for the cartridges were greased with animal fat and barrack-room rumour had the Hindus believe this was cow fat while the Muslims believed it was pig fat, thus causing irreconcilable offence to both religious groups. Often greatly outnumbered, the Crown's forces were able to maintain superiority on the battlefield through their being increasingly equipped with the Enfields. Fighting was characterised by a number of desperate sieges and defences but also by much open warfare across India's vast plains and, as Michael Barthorp has summarised, 'That in a pitched battle on the plains British infantry could overcome an equal or greater number of sepoy infantry was due ... more to the superiority of the British soldier's Enfield rifle ... which enabled effective fire to be opened at greater ranges than the sepoy's musket.'[40] Discipline and steadiness both, of course, played their part too.

As ever, there is not a great deal of written evidence for drummers and buglers. Their commonplace presence and routine activities in cantonments and in the field in India are barely mentioned in contemporary documents and their close resemblance to what took place in the Crimea can be safely assumed. Like the Crimea, the bugle in India appeared to be just about entirely responsible for what was once the remit of the drum. The 61st (South Gloucestershire) Regiment, having suppressed the sepoy mutiny at its own station at Ferozepore in May 1857, had marched on Delhi the following month. Captain Charles Griffiths, commanding the Grenadier Company of the 61st, wrote a detailed account of the siege of the city. Within its pages he tells us at least that on Delhi Ridge on 9 July, during a surprise attack by some enemy cavalry, 'At 8 a.m. the bugles of the regiments on the right sounded the alarm, followed at once by the "assembly"'.[41] The regiments of mutinous sepoys, trained entirely in the British way, also used their bugles in like fashion. They went further and it would have been unsurprising, if galling, to hear their bands strike up familiar tunes. One observer besieged at Lucknow recorded that

> One of the greatest insults we received at the hands of the enemy was their playing ... regularly every morning, and sometimes of an evening, all our popular English airs. ... The disloyal rascals had even the impudence to finish their music with the loyal hymn 'God save the Queen.'[42]

They would have been aided by the fact that a number of British musicians, and amongst them company drummers in the native regiments, sided with the mutineers, either by force of circumstances to save their own lives or voluntarily. These were all Christians, the majority Anglo-Indians, who often owed their survival to the good will of their native brothers-in-arms. A number, when punished by the military authorities, were sentenced to hang but in all cases had their sentences commuted to varying terms of imprisonment or branding as deserters, the Commander-in-Chief reckoning that they had been guilty of no more than want of courage.[43]

There exist, fortunately, a handful of illuminating examples that help us materially to understand the roles and employment of the British field buglers. One such is the memoir of Captain Thomas McKenzie, who had been born into the 94th Regiment in 1830 and at the age of 11 had been enlisted as something of a special case into the 64th

(2nd Staffordshire) Regiment. His father had been persuaded to re-join the army as master tailor to the 64th but only on condition that he could bring with him his two sons. McKenzie was, many years later, to be instrumental in the training of Canada's militia and published an account in 1898 of his military life. Its importance to our story is that it contains much detail of his time as a drummer and 'Field bugler to the generals commanding in the Persian Campaign and the Indian Mutiny'.[44]

At the regiment's depot at Templemore in Ireland in 1841 the boy McKenzie 'immediately began to acquire a soldier's duty as well as to learn how to play the flute, beat the drum, and blow the bugle ... and by October, 1843, [the 64th having returned from Nova Scotia] I was considered to be perfect and able to take my place in the fife and drum band [sic] of the regiment.'[45] The following year, aged 14, McKenzie was promoted to the rank of 'full drummer' and noted that he took his place at that point as 'field bugler to the regiment.' From these simple words we might deduce the difference in status and role between the young drummer boys, held on the strength of the regimental band but not employed as drummers and buglers as such, and the older boys and men employed properly as drummers and buglers. McKenzie consistently referred to his role as a 'field bugler' and never a 'field drummer' and thus we might deduce further that in the field by about 1850 the business of signalling was done by bugle alone, as we have already supposed. By 1851 McKenzie had left the 'band' – he also consistently, if erroneously, referred to the drums as the 'band' – to be a drill corporal and then drill sergeant but retained his appointment too as a field bugler. It is of interest too that he wrote of the very regular parades and meetings where the officers and sergeants were all expected to understand and react to the various bugle calls. And it is of great interest when he described the 64th in the mid-1850s:

> In those days a regiment on parade could perform all the movements by bugle call; and as our Colonel (Stopford) had been formerly in a light infantry corps (43rd) he kept the men moving by bugle sound as much as possible.[46]

This statement further reinforces the fact that all infantry were now expected to act in the manner of light infantry.

The 64th was one of two Crown infantry regiments (the other was the 78th Highlanders) to be sent to fight in Persia in 1856. As Colonel Stopford, commanding the 64th, was appointed brigadier general he took with him from his regiment Sergeant McKenzie as his staff (that is, orderly) bugler. In the attack on the old Dutch fort at Reshire in late November 1856 Stopford was mortally wounded and, in another illuminating statement, McKenzie wrote that 'I immediately took from my haversack a bandage' in an attempt to give first aid to his dying brigadier. This proves to us that the drummers/buglers – possibly all of them – had this task even when employed in their primary role. McKenzie noted earlier in his memoir that he had learned to apply a bandage 'and during the Persian campaign and the Indian mutiny often had to do so.'[47] When major reinforcements arrived in Persia in early 1857 McKenzie was appointed orderly bugler to the army commander, Lieutenant General Sir James Outram, and wrote of his duties in sounding the assemble, the advance and the halt as required during the approach to the fortified city of Bushire and eventually sounding the cease fire at the final battle at Kooshab. Throughout this time McKenzie was mounted on horseback.

On the outbreak of the Indian Mutiny the whole Persian force sailed via Bombay for Calcutta to join Major General Havelock in the march to relieve the besieged city of Cawnpore; once again McKenzie was appointed field bugler to the commanding general. Throughout the campaign to relieve Cawnpore, the attempts and eventual success in relieving Lucknow and then the relief of Cawnpore for the second time, McKenzie served mainly in this capacity and as an aide-de-camp to Havelock (although Havelock's memoirs state that his orderly bugler was from the 78th Highlanders[48]) and then to General Sir Colin Campbell. Of Havelock's bugler, John Marshman, the editor of Havelock's memoirs and his brother-in-law, remarked that in mid-July 1857, during the first battle to relieve Cawnpore, 'As the enemy's first gun was fired, the general gave him his watch to mark the time. The bugler noted the moment before he put it into his pocket, and as the last shot was sent after the retreating enemy, took the watch out again, and coolly said, "Two hours and forty-five minutes, Sir!"'[49] Sadly, McKenzie mentioned nothing of his bugling duties in India except to state that, during the march from Calcutta, Havelock had McKenzie sound the '"grog" bugle call, which he had also done for Outram in Persia, but that it was more usual for Havelock to order him to 'sound the "coffee" call (a call I invented).' However, McKenzie also spread light on an act of gallantry by a bugler of the 64th, an act that was to lead to the bugler being awarded the Victoria Cross. In mid-July 1857, still en route for Cawnpore and during one of the fights on the road:

> ... a bugler of ours, named Flynn, was mentioned in despatches for his bravery in killing [an] artilleryman in the act of firing [a] gun. This same bugler saved Major Sterling's life afterwards at Cawnpore [Stirling (not Sterling) was acting CO] by interposing his bugle to receive the cut of a rebel cavalryman.[50]

McKenzie always stated that he himself had been recommended for the Victoria Cross by Outram but no citation appeared to have been written before Outram died. The 64th had an ambivalent relationship with the coveted cross and the circumstances for which Flynn was, eventually, awarded the cross remain clouded in mystery.[51] Drummer Thomas Flynn, like so many drummers, was born into his regiment and, like so many men of the 64th, was an Irishman. The act for which he was cited took place at Cawnpore on 28 November 1857. A depleted British force under Major General Charles 'Redan' Windham was besieged in the city and in an attempt to relieve the situation Windham had ordered an offensive against the surrounding rebel positions. Flynn's citation stated simply:

> For conspicuous gallantry, in the charge on the Enemy's guns on the 28th November, 1857, when, being himself wounded, he engaged in a hand to hand encounter two of the Rebel artillerymen.[52]

Flynn was then just 15 years and about three months old and might well be the youngest ever holder of the Cross. He is certainly the youngest British Army recipient, for Hospital Apprentice Andrew Fitzgibbon, also 15 and three months and whose cross was awarded in China in 1860, was on the strength of the Bengal Medical Establishment of the Indian Army. Flynn's actual role on the battlefield at that time is also unclear and many questioned the ability of a young drummer to bring down two artillerymen with his drummer's short sword. But he might have done and there is a near-contemporary coloured sketch of Windham's attack about this time that shows the British infantry advancing against the Gwalior Contingent, a bugler with his bugle to his lips just behind the skirmish line.[53] It was a desperate time for the British and further testament to this is a poignant memorial in the grounds of All Souls Memorial Church at Cawnpore to the bandsmen of the 64th who died there between September and November 1857. The memorial includes the names of two bandsmen who were killed also on 28 November. One of them was Band Boy Bernard Fitzpatrick whose age is not recorded but, classed as a boy, would have been 14 or under. Captain H. F. Saunders of the 70th (Surrey) Regiment, attached to the 64th, wrote that same day that 'I cannot refrain from mentioning one instance of remarkable bravery on the part of a mere boy, a drummer [sic] of the 64th; while the struggle for the guns was going on, the youth darted to the front, and thrust some brickbats into the mouth of a gun, hoping by this means to render it useless, but was cut to pieces by the rebels.'[54] One regimental historian in the 19th century noted that, in an attack on the rebel guns, 'Amongst those who were first into the battery were several armed bandsmen and drummers in the ranks, lads born and brought up in the Regiment.'[55] A more recent article in the *Bulletin of the Military Historical Society* provided a useful summary:

> The [64th's] fight was grim and prolonged, the regiment losing heavily ... Boy Fitzpatrick of the Band was cut to pieces while putting an enemy gun out of action, having taken part in a gallant attack, and would have been awarded the VC had he lived. ... Drummer Flynn was awarded the decoration for capturing two guns and slaying the gunners.[56]

In the attack on the Secundrabagh at Lucknow on 14 November a drummer of the 93rd Highlanders was one of the first through the breach blown in the wall, and one of the first to be killed in the assault. The young Lieutenant Frederick Roberts, later Field Marshal Lord Roberts VC, on entering the breach saw him and remarked that he 'found him just inside the breach, lying on his back, quite dead, a pretty, innocent-looking fair-haired lad, not more than fourteen years old.'[57] Shortly afterwards a party of Highlanders took the Shah Najaf and

Drummer Ross, purportedly just 12 years old, climbed onto the dome of the mosque and sounded the regimental call so that those besieged in the Lucknow Residency could see that relief was close. The Residency acknowledged but Ross was not done and returned to the summit of the dome. 'Holding on to the spire of the dome with his left hand, [he] blew the call known as "The Cock of the North" as a blast of defiance to the enemy!'[58]

Flynn's was not the first Victoria Cross to be awarded to a drummer. Some two months earlier in the war two Crosses were awarded for actions within 24 hours of each other during the siege of Delhi. We know very little about 27-year-old Bugler William Sutton of the 60th Rifles. His citation states simply that the award was 'For gallant action at Delhi on the 13th of September, 1857, the night previous to the Assault, in volunteering to reconnoitre the breach.' But the citation also added that on 2 August, during an attack by mutineers, Sutton 'rushed forward over the trenches, and killed one of the Enemy's Buglers, who was in the act of sounding.'[59] Sutton was one example of an award of the Victoria Cross being made when his comrades elected him for it. The following day the British besieging force at Delhi carried out its successful attack on the city. During the assault on the Kabul Gate Drummer Miles Ryan, together with Sergeant James McGuire, were waiting with their regiment, the 1st Bengal European Fusiliers of the East India Company, when a conflagration caused some stacked ammunition to explode. McGuire and Ryan 'rushed into the burning mass, and, seizing the boxes, threw them, one after the other, over the parapet into the water ... [and] by their coolness and personal daring, saved the lives of many at the risk of their own.'[60] We do not know if Ryan was actually acting at the time as an ammunition carrier, which was one of the jobs spare drummers were called upon to perform. Their regiment was to become the 101st (Royal Bengal Fusiliers) in 1861, after all the European regiments of the East India Company were brought home. Sergeant McGuire, it is sad to relate, was one of eight recipients of the Victoria Cross to forfeit his medal, McGuire for an act of theft.

On the same day another Victoria Cross was awarded to a bugler employed in his primary role. The previous day to the assault the

Kashmir Gate was assessed as the other of the two practicable breaches. But for the attack to succeed the gate itself needed to be blown in. Lieutenant Duncan Home of the Bengal Sappers and Miners led the demolition party of two sections, one of Home himself and three men and the other under Lieutenant Philip Salkeld, with six more men. Salkeld's section included 35-year-old Bugler Robert Hawthorn of the 52nd (Oxfordshire Light Infantry) Regiment and another Irishman. Of this total of 11 men just four survived the blowing open of the gate – both officers, Sergeant John Smith, and Bugler Hawthorn. Except for Hawthorn, all were Bengal Sappers and Miners. Hawthorn's citation stated that:

> On 14 September, 1857, at Delhi, India, Bugler Hawthorne, who accompanied the explosion party, not only performed the dangerous duty on which he was employed, but previously attached himself to Lieutenant Salkeld, of the Engineers, when dangerously wounded, bound up his wounds under a heavy musketry fire, and had him removed without further injury.[61]

The demolition party had gone forward at first light to carry out its task and that any of the soldiers survived was almost unbelievable. That the surviving sappers also managed to lay their charges and explode them – and survive that too – was something of a miracle. But the assault of the storming party, holding off some 700 yards away, could not begin until confirmation had been given of the destruction of the gate. Lieutenant Home, sheltering by now in the fortress ditch, ordered Hawthorne to sound the advance, which was the agreed signal for success and, to ensure its authenticity, was most likely preceded by the regimental call of the 52nd. Home feared that, with the tremendous noise of gun and musket fire, the call would go unheard and Hawthorne therefore continued to call from the centre of the ditch, where he stood exposed. Fortunately, Colonel George Campbell, commanding the storming party and also the 52nd, had his orderly bugler, Bugler Johnson, go forward to listen for the call. He picked up Hawthorne's notes and in they went.[62]

All four drummer/bugler recipients of the Victoria Cross during the Indian Mutiny were Irishmen.

The sound of the bugle could certainly bring about the best in men. At the end of 1857 the situation at Lucknow showed no sign of getting any easier. On 1 January 1858 Captain Oliver Jones of the Royal Navy found himself with the 53rd (Shropshire) Regiment about to break out from Cawnpore. He wrote the following:

> They were saying that during the night a sentry had heard a bugle and Flood, of the 53rd … with whom I was chatting, said, 'By Jove, I hear it now!' We went a hundred yards to the front to get away from the chattering, and to listen, and sure enough we heard not only the bugles sounding the advance, but the rattle of the wheels of the artillery. Flood immediately fell in his picket, and then threw them out in skirmishing order …

Later the 53rd's skirmishers made a rush forward and their commanding officer ordered, in the circumstances, the main body to advance. Definitively, here too is a solid example of a line drummer with a bugle. Captain Oliver went on:

> The advance was first sounded by a little drummer-boy of the 53rd … who stuck himself up on a mound and too-tooed away the advance and the double with all the breath in his lungs. When asked afterwards what he meant by sounding it without orders, he said, 'Please, sir, I was afraid the men would kick me if I didn't.'[63]

★

The two wars in the Crimea and in India showed the British Army in a more conventional manner than was otherwise the case for much of the 19th century. If the army that deployed to the Crimea in 1854 looked and acted, more or less, like that of Wellington's in 1815, by the war's end in 1856 much had been learned that would help with general modernisation in the decades ahead. The army that emerged from India in 1858 – an army that was, in fact, larger than the army facing the Russians – had learned valuable lessons too, if somewhat tempered by reinforced prejudices towards the rebellious sepoys. On both occasions Britain's armies had proved themselves tactically superior and masters of the field but as a result the further modernisation that was necessary proved to be a slow and evolutionary process. Rifle-armed infantry had certainly proved able to operate more loosely without losing cohesion and fire effect and use to great advantage the supersession of controlled volley firing by independent firing. Essentially, however, the British Army had continued to maintain tactical principles that would have been recognised half a century earlier. As Michael Barthorp has summarised:

> ... this meant that the two-deep line, with a battalion's companies side by side, remained the formation for firing and the charge; and the column, with each company in line but one behind the other at varying distances, the formation for manoeuvre [sic]. Against cavalry a square, or rather rectangle, with each side in four ranks, was formed from line or column. The drills to perform these evolutions had been simplified, though were still done very much as a drill; and the techniques of masking a line or column with skirmishers, formerly the preserve of Rifles and Light Infantry battalions and companies, was now, in well-trained battalions, within the competence of any company.[64]

There was, as demonstrated, no great change to the role of drummers and buglers because there appeared no necessity to do anything other than continue to evolve as circumstances demanded. In the decades ahead the British Army did not face another major challenge of the European type but, while distracted by smaller wars, it did not, fortunately, cut itself off from wider influences.

One other impact of the war in the Crimea needs to be mentioned in passing. This did not affect most drummers and buglers directly but it represented the initiation of full professionalism and set standards for music overall in the British Army. The very poor state of Army bands in the Crimea – when they did get the opportunity to play – has been mentioned. They were also ill-served by a number of bandmasters who were still civilians, and some foreigners, who elected not to deploy with their bandsmen. In 1856 the Commander-in-Chief, the Duke of Cambridge, who was genuinely interested in music, approved the formation of a Military Music Class. Its original aim was to take in musically minded soldiers and, principally, serving members of the regimental bands and turn them into bandmasters. When the first class of 85 pupils assembled in March 1857 it did so at Kneller Hall in Twickenham, which was to become the Military School of Music, and later the Royal Military School of Music. What is important to note is that the first class included two drummers from the Foot Guards, three drummers from the line regiments, one bugler from the Rifle Brigade and the drum major of the 38th Regiment.[65] The wider impact of the school was that, through Kneller Hall's gradual and successful attempts to standardise military music, the numerous regimental quick marches and other tunes were also written down and codified. It meant too, as Lewis Winstock has expounded, 'From that day forward regimental music was in the hands of soldiers, not civilians, and the bands of the Army could never again fall apart when they were needed most.'[66]

CHAPTER 9

Scarlet into Khaki

Every one must have rejoiced at the absence of bugling; there is no greater source of
mistake and confusion than perpetual company and battalion bugling in the field.

If the period represented in the previous chapter showed no great
changes on the battlefield, the period in this and the next chapter,
which cover the second half of the 19th century and the first decade of
the 20th, showed particularly marked changes. We have seen that change
was afoot and there was certainly no clear line to be drawn between the
pre-1850s and the post-1850s. But what characterised this next period
of land warfare was significant technological change – universal adoption
of breech-loading and then magazine-fed rifles and quick-firing artillery, machine guns, early wireless communications and aeroplanes – and
we might recognise these elements as the first signs of modern war.
Importantly, while the British Army was almost constantly at war and
engaged in some often very serious struggles across the Empire, it did
not fight another major power between the Crimea and the Great War.
These 'colonial' or 'small' wars, which were already making their mark
on British tactical methods, had a major effect on the way the army
did its business in the last three or four decades of the 19th century.
Nevertheless, while 'great power warfare' was not Britain's immediate
problem, her army was not immune from the lessons of far greater
struggles of the time in North America and on the European continent.
Ian Knight has provided another fitting summary:

> The British army did not exist in a vacuum, and theorists were aware of
> the implications of events in the wider world ... Yet in practical terms, the

experience of the army in the field was very different from these large-scale, industrialised, conflicts, being shaped instead by a constant round of small-scale colonial campaigning.[1]

The more imaginative, as Knight has put it, of the British military establishment watched the greater conflicts with interest and with an eye to the future. There is another embedded and incorrect view that the British Army officer was, in general, an uneducated man who took little interest in his own professional development let alone that of the army as a whole. Possessed of the greatest military and economic power the world had ever known, what incentive was there to take too much heed of lessons from elsewhere? And the British Army had to focus on fighting its own particular foes and there was little enough in the way of resources for these as it was. But the latter half of the 19th century in particular saw comprehensive changes in every single aspect of the British Army and that, by the time of the reign of Edward VII, it had become a recognisably modern beast says much for its adaptability.

This was a period characterised too by the British soldier changing his traditional scarlet tunic for one of khaki. Despite the universal adoption of khaki by British and Imperial armies overseas by the last decade of the 19th century, the army at home continued to train in scarlet and, had Britain gone to war on the European mainland at this time, it might well have done so in scarlet cloth. The shock of the second war in South Africa, referred to here as the Anglo-Boer War, between 1899 and 1902, kicked the British Army into the 20th century and in time to modernise properly for the greater struggle ahead. We shall see that there continued to be bugles and even drums in the fighting line, both at home and overseas, throughout. This seems incongruous as our story until now has described an almost complete decline in the use of the drum in the field and, as will be shown in the start of this chapter, the bugle looked as if it would follow. But the conditions in which the British Army now had to fight saw, in some places, almost a reversion to close order and a new requirement for drum as well as bugle for all purposes.

The main feature of Britain's wars in this period was that they were against, mainly, ill-equipped and indifferently organised opponents, although it would be wrong to ignore the ferocity and challenges of some of the campaigns, even if the opponents were invariably written off at the time as 'mere savages'. In one opponent at least – the Boer farmers of southern Africa – the British Army was dangerously close to being outclassed, if only in the short term and even if the experience was ultimately of great benefit in going some way to prepare the army for war in 1914. Elsewhere the British soldier showed much admiration for the extraordinary bravery and fighting prowess of his other foes.

'Small Wars' is something of a misnomer as some of these wars were far from small. But the phrase was used to classify the type of warfare between 'highly trained, armed and organised force[s]', such as the British and other European armies, and 'broadly speaking, irregulars': tribesmen and the like. The character and the lessons to be drawn from these wars were best described in Colonel Charles Callwell's very well known and widely read textbook of the same name. First published in 1896, *Small Wars* was in effect the definitive 'Tactical Textbook for Imperial Soldiers', to use Colonel Peter Walton's 1990 subtitle to his reprint of the 1906 edition.[2] The book was to remain largely extant in its field until 1939. While the tactical methods of the Great War barely influenced Britain's approach to policing the Empire, the tactical principles and methods of the soldiers of the Queen Empress Victoria had continued relevance for the soldiers of the King Emperors up to George VI. One might argue that the 'small wars' that followed the Second World War also drew just as many useful lessons from Callwell and others.

'Small Wars' covers a wide range of campaigning. Callwell had in fact taken the phrase from general use at the time and in his introduction noted that the term was 'somewhat difficult to define' and had 'no particular connection with the scale on which any campaign may be carried out.'[3] While his explanation of what the term encompassed is anachronistic and rather out-dated it does help us separate the methods used in this type of warfare from 'general war'. In his words, small wars comprised 'expeditions against savages and semi-civilised races by disciplined soldiers, … campaigns undertaken to suppress rebellions and guerrilla warfare in all parts of the world where organized armies are struggling against opponents who will not meet them in the open field.'[4] We still struggle to classify this type of warfare as it still tends to infer that the fighting is never that serious, while the contrary is more often the case.

★

The universal adoption of rifles and then breech-loaders and the introduction of such destructive long-range weapons as machine guns and rifled, breech-loading artillery, brought about a significant change to the tactical manoeuvres of the infantry. While there had been a gradual and universal adoption of extended-order/light infantry-type tactical formations across the line infantry as rifles, with their much longer effective range, became universal from the 1850s, the much increased rate of fire of the breech-loader saw increased depth in both attacking and defending formations. It should be noted that the word 'depth' is used here in the context of the depth of tactical formations as a whole and not of the firing line.

Examination of the various official publications of the time is, again, helpful when trying to follow any official change to drills but tells but half the story. As before, the drill book represented plenty of theory, and much of that informed by practice, but often struggled to keep up with developments in the field, as will be seen. When the *Infantry Manual* was reissued in 1857 there were no discernible changes from what had gone before. The same might be said for the 1859 edition of the *Field Exercise and Evolutions of Infantry*, the first revision of the manual since 1833, but for some subtle changes. The instructions for light infantry were still afforded a separate section and it was made clear, again, that 'All Regiments [are] to be instructed in Light Infantry Movements', and emphasising further that 'Although a certain number of regiments are styled "light infantry," it is necessary that every corps of infantry shall be fully instructed in this important branch of its duty.'[5] With much of the regulations still given over to close-order evolutions we might deduce that, despite the lessons of the Crimea and the Mutiny and the influence of the rifle and, indeed, longer-range artillery, there remained a need to balance the new with the old. The new regulations were certainly hardly less complicated than the earlier publications.

But what was perhaps most significant in the 1859 regulations was the much clearer direction given on the organisation and tactical arrangement of light infantry in the field. Since the earliest days of light infantry it was recognised that they were most effective if divided into a skirmish line of men, usually in pairs but sometimes in a chain of four in extended order, plus supports and reserves. This division did not change in 1859 but the clarity provided effectively established the link between, in effect, smoothbore tactics and rifle tactics, between close-order line and column and the universal adoption of open and extended order. Specifically, the 1859 regulations stated:

> When a regiment is employed as light infantry, it is usually divided into three parts, – skirmishers, supports, and reserve; but it may frequently be deemed advisable to cover the movements of a line with skirmishers and supports, or skirmishers only ... The supports should always be composed of numbers equal to the line of skirmishers; thus, each company that is extended should have a company to support it. The reserve should be at least one third part of the whole body.[6]

This laid down the basis for the fire and movement tactics that were to develop in the years ahead. Minor modifications were also made to the various bugle sounds and these rose in number from 12 to 14, with the note G again being used further to define certain movements. The main changes were that Retreat became Retire, the two sounds for Incline to the Right and to the Left were replaced by one alone for Incline, with direction defined by combinations of Gs. Alarm now was also to mean Look out for Cavalry and two additional sounds were Quick Time and Double Time. But it was re-emphasised that the bugle 'should seldom be used' as 'calls ... are liable to be misunderstood, and ... they reveal intended movements to the enemy, who will soon be acquainted to them ...' Words of command were always to be preferred and their dissemination was to be improved by employing men as 'connecting links', who were later defined as 'runners'.[7] Any proliferation of bugling was, if only advisedly, suppressed as 'The commanding officer's bugle will generally be found sufficient in light infantry drill; repeated sounds only create confusion and delay.'[8] The drum received little mention except for denoting their position in the line, which remained as two equal-sized divisions placed behind number two and number six companies in an eight-company battalion.

It is worth mentioning in passing that a further revision of the *Field Exercises and Evolutions* dated 1861 was published at Horse Guards in January 1862. The major change reflected in this revision was the inclusion of detailed manual exercises for the rifle, both 'long' (the 'three-band' Enfield) and 'short' (the 'two-band' Enfield issued to rifle regiments), and the bayonet. But it is worth recording that two more bugle calls had been added: 'lie down' and 'rise'.[9]

The full influence of long-range rifles and of long-range artillery was yet to tell but the impending arrival too of breech-loading weapons, which would increase firepower dramatically, was beginning to influence opinion. While the lessons emerging from the American Civil War were largely questioned for their relevance to a European war, the superiority demonstrated by the Prussian infantry over the Danish in the Second Schleswig War of 1864 was rather closer to home. The Prussians had been equipped with the Dreyse 'needle' rifle since 1848 but the impact of this weapon – the first effective and universally issued breech-loading rifle – was not fully appreciated until the second war against the Danes. Intelligent British military commentators such as one Colonel P. L. MacDougall prophesied about the effect of the new weapons on infantry tactics. 'One principal effect of the improved firearms' he wrote 'is to give increased importance to the movement of troops in extended order, and to the rapidity of their march, more especially in the case where they are required to assault an enemy's position.'[10] MacDougall was scathing about the existing teaching from the drill book and especially its long-repeated 'General Principles of Light Infantry'. He used as an authority the advice of Sir William Napier when commanding the 43rd Light Infantry in the Peninsula and concluded that 'The secret of success in light infantry movements [and therefore the movements now of all infantry] is, *to obtain the speed of irregularity, and yet to divest it of confusion.*'[11] MacDougall further prophesied that future battles would 'be decided principally by artillery' and if this reduced the comparative value of infantry, 'the influence on cavalry must be nearly to destroy its utility altogether as an offensive arm on the field of battle.'[12] The ultimate dilemma, which he also foresaw, was to move in as dispersed a formation as possible to reduce casualties but to be able to concentrate to effect a decision on the battlefield. The British Army was to experience a further dilemma in facing 'irregulars' in the years to come and it was not until it experienced the struggle against the Boers that it was able to grasp the full impact of modern war, to its benefit.

Any actual distinction between line infantry and light infantry was finally removed by order of the Commander-in-Chief when, in 1860, he abolished flank companies in all battalions. A useful manual detailing the equipment of the infantry, compiled under the orders of the Secretary of State for War in 1865, summarised most helpfully the situation: 'The system of having "flank companies," as they are termed, now, however, no longer exists, his Royal Highness the Field Marshal Commanding-in-Chief, having been pleased by a circular memorandum (No. 38, Horse Guards, 30th May 1860) that no selection of men is to be made for any particular companies.'[13] This same manual reaffirmed that a battalion consisted of ten 'service' companies and two 'depot' companies, the latter placed in 22 UK-based depot battalions and thus removing the need for expensive and wasteful regimental depots. A line battalion of ten companies was authorised an establishment of 1,119 officers and men and this included 20 drummers or buglers. The two depot companies had a strength of 220, including four drummers. That some regiments continued to retain titles that implied light infantry or, for that matter, fusilier status was now purely honorary, although the regulations noted that there were still to be 'Buglers only in light infantry and rifles.'[14] This really was a technical distinction on paper for the line battalions, while they might retain the rank of drummer, and were to continue to do so, employed these men more usually as buglers. Finally, in 1870, the next revision of the *Field Exercises* removed any reference whatsoever to light infantry and henceforth skirmishing – operating in extended order – was afforded a more prominent place in the manuals.

Revision of the manuals became much more frequent from the publication of the 1877 *Field Exercise and Evolutions* and, while blind obedience to any drill was not expected, we should assume that the instructions continued to give general guidance to the employment of infantry in the field. General The Viscount Wolseley – that 'Very Model of a Modern Major General' of Gilbert and Sullivan's comic operetta *The Pirates of Penzance* of 1879 – when Adjutant General and thus the army authority on changes to tactical doctrine, warned in his preface to *Infantry Drill* in 1889 that:

> [Such] regulations are based on the principle of demanding great exactitude in the simplified movements still retained for Drill, while conceding the utmost latitude to all commanders, of however small a unit, in Manoeuvre. The first must be carried out literally, the second must be observed in the spirit more than in the letter.[15]

The fact is that any concept of a universal and sudden adoption of 'fire and movement' – the two base elements of infantry manoeuvre – at the onset of this period is largely illusory, and if General Wolseley was then commenting as he did, he was recognising the fact that drill books were there to teach basic tactical methods and that commanders in the field were best placed to put theory into useful practice. The British Army was strongly influenced by the lessons of the Austro-Prussian War of 1866 and Franco-Prussian War of 1870–71, although much less so by the American Civil War of 1861–65. Given the sheer scale and length of the latter its limited impact on British Army thought may seem strange. This is even more so as a number of British officers observed the campaigns and battles and these included Wolseley. The war also attracted the serious attention of Colonel, later Major General Sir Patrick MacDougall, mentioned above and the first commandant of the British Army's Staff College, and of Colonel, later General, Sir Edward Hamley, who wrote *The Operations of War* in 1866, 'one of the most significant books ever written by a British soldier'.[16] This became the standard text book at the Staff College and continued to receive updates in revised editions up to the eve of the Great War. Mention must also be made of the works of Colonel George Henderson, Professor of Military Art and History at the Staff College in the 1890s. He hoped that through his best-known works – *The Campaign of Fredericksburg* (1886) and *Stonewall Jackson and the American Civil War* (1898) – he could turn attention away from the – to him – over-rating of the tactical lessons of the Franco-Prussian War.

The British Army was certainly not alone in its consideration throughout this period of the efficacy of bugle calls in the field. One Colonel Balck, a Prussian officer, wrote in his book *Tactics* in 1911 in his consideration of the issuing of orders that 'To prevent troops from misunderstanding signals or from obeying those not intended for them, all trumpet calls in battle, except "charge," "fix bayonet," and "attention," are forbidden.'[17] While he may be forgiven for not distinguishing between trumpet and bugle, he cited a number of examples of the effects of mistaken calls during the two wars Prussia fought against Austria and France. Some of these are worth detailing:

> During the engagement at Trautenau (27th June, 1866), the trumpet signal 'assemble,' given at another point, caused four Prussian battalions to withdraw.
>
> On the morning of June 26th, 1866 (day of rest), reveille sounded by a trumpeter was mistaken for an alarm signal. The 7th Infantry Division assembled and the signal was repeated in two other army corps.
>
> The village of Diletz (action at Gitschin, 1866) was to be evacuated at the sounding of the signal (Saxon) 'First Brigade withdraw.' The signal was, however, understood and carried out by only three battalions; two battalions, which were at the same time engaged, did not hear it at all and maintained their position until they were taken in reverse by hostile fire and forced to withdraw.
>
> In the crisis of the fight of the Fusilier Battalion of the 48th Infantry and the 1st Battalion of the 52nd at Vionville [otherwise known as the battle of Mars-la-Tour and fought on 16 August 1870], the signal 'assemble' was sounded and repeated by other trumpeters, further mischief being averted by the energetic efforts of the officers who prevented trumpeters from blowing the call and ordered them to blow 'commence firing' instead.[18]

A truly vast amount has been written on every aspect of the American Civil War and, it is unfortunate to relate, much romantic nonsense about drummers. American military development before the war was retarded by the nature of the US military, with its tiny regular army and the independent nature of state militias. A brief examination of tactical manuals shows that they demonstrated a strong French influence in all things and far less advancement beyond Napoleonic-style drills. General Winfield Scott, who was to earn fame in the Mexican-American War of 1846–48 published, in 1835, *Infantry Tactics*, and much of its detail on infantry exercises and manoeuvres almost harkened back to the English platoon fire system. For example, in consideration of firing, 'The instructor will cause the firing to cease whether by company or by two ranks (or file) by a roll of the drum; and at the instant the roll commences, the men will cease firing. The roll will always be followed by a tap on the drum.'[19] However, in listing the various drum beats and bugle calls, there being 19 of the former and 22 of the latter, the bugle would appear to have gained greater presence in the American infantry by this time. Mercifully, Colonel William Hardee's *Rifle and Light Infantry Tactics*, written in 1855 at the behest of the Secretary for War, disposed of the constraints imposed by the drum but continued to emphasise close order and firings in line by numbered companies.

All of these strictures were to be modified dramatically during the course of the war. The natural democracy inherent in the volunteer basis of the armies of both sides in the Civil War and the inclination, present to this day, of the American soldier to learn fast, added much-needed pragmatism to the early lessons wrought by rifled muskets against lines of manoeuvring infantry. Without going into detail, the presence of drummers and buglers in the field is undeniable but their part in battle is unclear. Distinctions between types of military musician are difficult to define, although there is clear evidence that two or three types were present in one form or another: what were defined as 'field musicians', that is, orderly drummers and buglers; corps of drums, which were made up of the field musicians; and brass bands. The roles of these groups were very much the same as in the British Army, with every company having 'at least two musicians, a drummer and either a fife or a bugle player.'[20]

At the same time there was certainly a blurring of distinction between corps of drums and bands and practicalities of diminishing numbers and lack of equipment, especially in the Confederacy, meant that regimental musicians tended to give way to brigade groups. As early as July 1862 Congress passed General Order Number 91 'which reduced the number of bands to one per brigade.'[21] Paddy Griffith, drawing on a work by Joshua Chamberlain who, famously, held the left of the Union line on the second day of Gettysburg on 2 July 1863, wrote in his detailed exposition of Civil War battle tactics that, while 'Bugle calls provided another vital aural clue to the ebb and flow of combat … each brigade had its own identifying signal.'[22] While there is also some evidence that bands played during some of the fighting it is apparent too that most musicians filled the role of ammunition and ration carriers or medical orderlies. Union General William Babcock Hazen reckoned in 1864 that 'the removal of wounded from the firing line was much more promptly performed by the musicians than the "ambulance corps."'[23] In conclusion, we might assume that a number of buglers were retained in the field to be used as signallers but there was little practical use for any complicated field calls once battle commenced, beyond some idealistic attempts to do so early in the war.

Certainly the view that tended to prevail in the British Army was that 'Civil War tactics [were] aberrations arising from unique conditions'[24] and should be dismissed as such, with the rugged terrain and the employment of what were seen as volunteer masses limiting the effectiveness of the attack rather than the true influence: increased firepower. 'They overlooked the basic fact, which now appears obvious – that the new tactics stemmed from an increase in firepower and that infantry now had to extend formations and dig for cover.'[25]

Notwithstanding the experience in war of other nations, for the British the dominant tactical theme for much of the latter third of the century was, and until the lasting shock of the Anglo-Boer War, focussed on fighting poorly armed and relatively poorly organised tribal masses. The significant threats posed by the Zulu and Dervish in the open spaces of Africa, and especially in the desert, required a reversion to close-order tactics and massed volleys to keep the fast-moving swarms beyond spears' length. While emphasis continued to be placed on the need to execute the attack to achieve a decision on the battlefield, the manuals remained squarely focussed on doing this against a similarly armed and organised enemy, while experience was constantly against very different enemies. British armies in the field often proved themselves to be highly adaptable to the conditions they faced, but disaster could, and did, unfold, through a combination of poor estimation of the enemy's capabilities and just as poor appreciation of the tactics required on the spot.

In general an attacking brigade or division would go forward in two lines, with a ready reserve in supporting columns. However, a battalion in the first line would deploy with two companies in extended order, each advancing alternately and covered by the fire of the other. In support would be two further companies, some 150 to 200 yards behind, moving in the most practical formation to be ready to support the firing line. About another 400 yards behind the supports would be the main body of four companies, moving in column. Always with the attack in mind, the firing line would close on its objective, being built up as necessary by the supports and, if required, the main body, until fire superiority was achieved and the order would be given to charge with the bayonet. The speed of all movement was governed by the ground, control and cohesion of the battalion being paramount, with the charge executed at the double time of 165 paces to the minute. The efficacy of the order to charge being given by the bugle can be readily appreciated. Similar formations were to be used in the defence, the principle for success being that every yard's width of ground should be covered by three men. Depending on the terrain, a battalion would thus be expected to cover about 300 to 350 yards of frontage. The three-tier formation did not, therefore, dictate that every man was in the firing line. This would be disastrous against rifle-armed enemy infantry.

It is important to remember too that, no matter which opponent was being faced, command and control in battle remained thoroughly dependent on the eyes and ears of commanders and the ability to transmit orders by voice or other audible signal. Senior officers and especially commanders of armies in the field still looked to place themselves on horseback in a prominent position close to the firing line in order to command and impose control, and this continued to persist until commanders were driven to the rear or into better cover by Boer rifles. They were accompanied by a small staff of officers able to dash off with written messages and, importantly for our study, stood next to the commander would be his orderly bugler. Mechanical means such as the heliograph (which was first used on active service in India in 1877), signalling flags (introduced in the 1860s) and even electric telegraph began to make their presence felt on the battlefield during this period but were of very little use in governing detailed movements of companies and battalions. It is little wonder, therefore, that the bugle (and the whistle, increasingly) remained to the fore as the main supplement to the voice. The use of the drum was not dead, although there is barely any evidence of its use other than as an accompaniment to marching and, possibly, charging.

Echoing the regulations there was something of a backlash against the bugle in the 1870s, which presaged in many ways the further amendment of regulations and, certainly, practice. In 1870, in commenting on field manoeuvre exercises, Major T. Lynden Bell of the 1st Battalion the 6th (Royal 1st Warwickshire) Regiment wrote: 'Lastly, dispense with bugling in light infantry exercise, for although things may not be done on the instant, they will be done better.'[26] That this debate was active was demonstrated in a lecture given to the Royal United Services Institute in June 1872 by General Sir William Codrington, having observed army manoeuvres over the previous three years. Codrington, who had commanded at brigade and divisional level in the Crimea and was Commander-in-Chief at the occupation of Sebastopol, declared that:

> Every one must have rejoiced at the absence of bugling; there is no greater source of mistake and confusion than perpetual company and battalion bugling in the field. It would almost be good for the mouth pieces of bugles to be taken possession of by an officer or a sergeant when in presence of the enemy.[27]

When considering the battalion in the attack the 1877 regulations clearly understood this conundrum and provided encouraging common sense:

> Movements in extended order must in general be regulated by word of command and signals. Commands must be repeated by the captains and every supernumerary belonging to the extended line. Calls on the bugle may occasionally be necessary as substitutes for the voice, but as they are liable to be misunderstood, and may reveal intended movements to the enemy, they should seldom be used, unless for purposes of drill. The commanding officer's bugle will generally be found sufficient; repeated sounds only create confusion and delay.[28]

That General Codrington, Major Bell and, presumably, others, had a good point was illustrated at least a little by Private John Collier of the 2nd Hampshire Rifle Volunteers, who wrote of the autumn manoeuvres of 1872 of much bugling for 'turning out, reveille, lights out, fall in and cease firing' at the end of a successful engagement. This shows that there were a number of additional calls prevalent in the army, or at least amongst the Volunteers, although these, such as Lights Out, might simply have been additional definitions applied at the time to standard calls. The confusion deprecated by General Codrington was at least intimated by Private Collier when he wrote:

> ... then all our Division came up ... where we had a sharp engagement. We could hardly see each other for smoke, and it was suffocating. The noise of the cannons, the bugle calls, and the voices of the Generals ...[29]

Whether or not young Collier was more confounded by the generals than by the bugles might be a moot point! The 1877 regulations printed some further changes to the bugle calls and there were now 17 in all, to be applied most specifically to infantry in extended order alone. This had first been laid down in the 1870 regulations but extended order was now applicable as a formation for both the attack and for skirmishing. The calls were exactly as the 16 before but with the addition now of a call for 'charge'. A number of calls were, also as before, to be further defined by sounding combinations of the note G and it is now worth quoting these in full and to speculate, in trying to understand the intent, whether these instructions by bugle alone would be heard and understood as applicable to one's own particular part of the line:

> One G sounded on the bugle will denote the right of the line; two G's the centre; three G's the left.
>
> The G, or G's, preceding any sound will denote the part of the line to which it applies. For instance: two G's before the Extend, will signify, to extend from the centre; one G, followed by the Close, to close to the right; one G, followed by the Incline, to incline to the right; three G's, followed by the Wheel, to wheel to the left.
>
> The halt annuls all previous sounds except the Fire. The Incline and Wheel must be preceded by the distinguishing G; a double Incline will signify a direct turn to the flank indicated. When the Fire is combined with any other call, it should always be the last sounded, for if the men were ordered to fire they might not hear the second call.
>
> The Alert implies unexpected danger; when it sounds, the men in movement will at once halt, and wait for further orders.
>
> When moving by sound of bugle, men will wait till the bugle has ceased before they move.
>
> Only men extended will act on bugle sounds; a support will invariably move by word of its commander.[30]

These regulations noted, again as before, that 'Every regiment should have a well marked and simple regimental call', and this was always to precede instructions being sounded by bugle. These regimental calls were to form the origin of many of the regimental quick marches that were now being written. It is worth emphasising a particular point still further that 'Companies in the extended line alone act on bugle sounds ... supports and main body invariably move by word of their commanders.'[31] The bugle was thus dedicated to the firing or attacking line only, its use elsewhere on the field of battle being deemed unnecessary.

An important 1877 addition to the means to exercise command and control was, also for the first time in the manual, the use of the whistle to sound signals or to attract attention to other signals, by which was meant the use of hand or arm signals.[32] There was no further amplification of this general instruction until the 1884 edition of the *Field Exercise*, which provided a page of musical notation for 'Notes on the Whistle'. These were limited to just five sounds: Attention, Advance, Halt, Retire and Assembly or Rally.[33] When these regulations were more fully revised in 1889 much more attention was given to whistle calls and hand signals but instructions for the use of the bugle were maintained, even if the need for stealth was given added emphasis: 'to enable the advance to be conducted as quietly as possible, there should be no unnecessary words of command and no bugle sounds.' This did not stop the further gradual proliferation of authorised bugle calls, which now numbered 22. It would help to list these for the year in question:

I. EXTEND.	XII. PREPARE FOR CAVALRY.
II. CLOSE.	XIII. QUICK.
III. ADVANCE.	XIV. DOUBLE.
IV. RETIRE.	XV. LIE DOWN.
V. HALT.	XVI. RISE.
VI. FIRE.	XVII. THE CHARGE.
VII. CEASE FIRE.	XVIII. MARCH AT EASE.
VIII. ASSEMBLE.	XIX. ATTENTION.
IX. INCLINE.	XX. ADVANCED GUARD.
X. WHEEL.	XXI. REAR GUARD.
XI. THE ALERT.	XXII. FLANK GUARD.

It would appear from this list, without it being specified in the regulations, that the bugle calls were no longer confined to troops deployed in extended order. At home and in peacetime overseas' garrisons bugle calls became an ever-present constant in regulating the day in camp and often in field exercises. *Standing Orders* for the 1st Battalion the Royal Warwickshire Regiment for 1883 show an additional 22 regimental and company bugle calls on top of those found in army regulations. They included such calls as 1st Breakfast Bugle and 1st Tea Bugle and different calls for each of the eight companies.[34] One might approve of the moral effect of the familiar bugle sounds but we might imagine too that many a young soldier, and young officer, remained befuddled by this litany of calls.

Line battalions were, at last, formally established for buglers in 1865, each company being allocated one drummer and one bugler, one of them also carrying the fife. For the first time the 1877 regulations formally relegated the majority of a battalion's drummers to other than drumming/bugling roles in the course of a battle, the commanding officer's bugler – the 'orderly' – being the sole bugler retained for providing additional means to exercise command and control. Apart, therefore, from the commanding officer's orderly bugler and for buglers alongside company commanders when acting with independent or detached companies, all other drummers and buglers were now given precise instructions to remain behind the second line of any advance (later changed, in 1896, to remaining with the reserve) to assist with resupplying ammunition.

There was very little mention at all of drummers or drums in all of the various regulations, which reflected the reality of the situation, and we might now take this opportunity to accept for good the word 'bugler' if the man himself was indeed carrying a bugle and even though his official title in the line infantry and Foot Guards was still 'drummer'. The 1877 regulations did list one drum call which, together with the 'field bugle' was the 'Infantry Call for Charge'. The detail provided was that

> On the bugles (by the order of the battalion commander) sounding 'the advance', the battalion, having fixed bayonets, will advance in one general line; on reaching charging distance, the signal for the final rush will be given by the drums of the regiment beating and the bugles sounding 'the charge' on which the men will quicken their pace and cheer.[35]

This almost resurrection of the drum to support the charge is difficult to explain, although classifying this 'musical accompaniment' to the charge as signalling is stretching definitions a little. However, we might assume that the drum's usefulness for its moral effect when manoeuvring in the face of a foe such as the Dervish tribesmen of the Sudan had been witnessed, although the reason for its appearance in the 1877 regulations can only be guessed at. But the period was also to witness a reversion to close-order formations, as intimated above, as the best means of defence and, indeed, attack when facing tribal masses moving at great speed.

The 1889 revision stated more simply that, whistles having been blown to signal the cease fire and fixing of bayonets, 'The commanding officer will then give the order to the whole to charge, upon which, with loud cheers, drums beating and bugles sounding, the position will be vigorously assaulted.'[36] This was repeated, with minor amendment to include the bagpipes, in the 1892 and 1896 editions of *Infantry Drill* until, finally, the drum disappeared for good. In *Infantry Training 1902*, with its emphasis on skirmishing as 'the all important formation in warfare against a well-armed enemy' the signal for the assault (the word 'charge' being absent here) 'should come from the senior officers present, and be sounded on the bugle ... During the delivery of the assault on the enemy's position the men will cheer, bugles be sounded, and the pipes played.' Given the hard lessons of the Anglo-Boer War this instruction might seem surprising. But the attack being the decisive act in battle, the need to carry an assault with all vigour towards an enemy position still required a good degree of shock action, to which the sound of the bugle (and bagpipe) would contribute.

So, while bugle calls in war became limited by the 1905 regulations to just the Charge and the Alarm, *Infantry Training (4-Company Organization) 1914*, published on 10 August that year, stated under 'Infantry in Attack' that 'The commander who decides to assault will order the *charge* to be sounded, the call will at once be taken up by all buglers, and all neighbouring units will join in the charge as quickly as possible. During the delivery of the assault the men will cheer, bugles be sounded, and pipes played.'[37] These regulations can be forgiven for their lack of anticipation of the conditions to come, although that the same regulations were reprinted in 1916 would seem inappropriate. The years between final victory over the Boers and the onset of the greater struggle against Imperial Germany and her allies demonstrated further evidence of that dilemma of extension versus concentration but the superiority of fire and the need for the interaction of all arms were at least confirmed in southern Africa. As one modern study has concluded:

> From 1902 to 1914, the infantry of the British Army experienced a vast overhaul of training and tactics. The B[ritish] E[xpeditionary] F[orce] of 1914 was tactically almost unrecognizable from the army that had been defeated by the Boers at Colenso, Magersfontein, and Stormberg in 1899. Whereas the Victorian infantry system had placed faith in volley firing and cumbersome, linear formations, the army of 1914 utilized flexible tactics that emphasized dispersion, intelligent use of ground, and skilful marksmanship.[38]

CHAPTER 10

Hark, I Hear the Bugle Calling

Good-bye Dolly I must leave you, Though it breaks my heart to go
Something tells me I am needed, At the front to fight the foe
See the soldier boys are marching, And I can no longer stay,
Hark, I hear the bugle calling, Good-bye Dolly Gray.

There is, in addition to the soldier's farewell implicit in the words of *Good-bye Dolly Gray*, something of a farewell to the bugle (and by associ-ation the drum) in this popular song of the Anglo-Boer War. The origins of the song are actually American, written as it was at the time of the Spanish-American War of 1898. But some of the words were changed for the British audience, 'soldier boys', for example, replacing 'boys in blue'.

The fighting across the Empire during the 19th century and up until the Great War took in everything from minor skirmishes to major battles and involved a very long list of foes. The most notable of these were the Egyptian army, Sudanese tribesmen, the formidable Zulu, the just-as-formidable tribesmen of the North-West frontier of India, and the Afghan army, if the latter can be called that. There were others of great note too, if the scope of the campaigns was less ambitious: amongst them the tribesmen of Ashante (or Asante) in west Africa, Chinamen, Maori, Abyssinian and the Fenians in Canada. Such geographical diversity suggests that matters of vastly different terrain and climate were also important considerations. The biggest challenge of all during this period came twice when British soldiers confronted the white Boer farmers of southern Africa and, as mentioned already, the second of these wars saw the most formidable challenge of all. We can piece together enough evidence of bugles and even drums to get a feel for the reality of their use on campaign and there is some photographic evidence to back this up. It would certainly seem that, as the various regulations noted above advised, there continued to be a further diminution of drumming and bugling for practical reasons and especially when a British force was attempting to conceal its intentions from the enemy. Still, there are some notable – and dramatic – examples and they can be used to illustrate practice across the whole army.

British soldiers fought in three campaigns against the Maori of New Zealand, the first between 1845 and 1847 and the second and third in the 1860s. In the First Maori War the British infantry were still armed with smoothbore muskets but by the onset of the second war in 1860 they were now armed with rifles. Yet these new weapons made little difference against a well-equipped and extremely ferocious enemy in their well-defended strong stockades, or *pah*. The challenges of command and control in forest and swamp would be the same for Britain's armies everywhere, although the Maoris usually chose to confront the British from behind their *pah* rather than outside. When these became impossible to defend against modern artillery the Maoris reverted to raiding and ambushing. Raiding had been a common feature of the fighting in the first war, where isolated European farms were particularly vulnerable targets. During May 1846 a detachment of 48 men of the 58th (Rutlandshire) Regiment, under Lieutenant George Page, was protecting Boulcott Farm, which lay about 15 miles outside Wellington on North Island. As dawn was breaking on 16 May one of the sentries was just able to get off one shot before he was cut down by Maori tomahawks. First out of the guard tent was Page's drummer, William Allen. He 'seized his bugle and managed to sound the alarm when his right arm was almost severed by the blow of a tomahawk. He seized the bugle with his left hand and bravely completed the call and continued sounding until hacked to pieces.'[1] The fight went on for over half an hour, the men of the 58th eventually gaining the upper hand. Private Joseph Hinton, writing many years later, remembered finding young Allen with 'three cuts on his right arm, four on his left, three gashes on his forehead, and his mouth cut from ear to ear, and, what's more, they stole his bugle, and we afterwards heard them sounding it in the wood.'[2] The bugle was eventually found by another regiment and the 58th had a silver bugle inscribed with a record of Drummer Allen's bravery, the bugle to be carried in perpetuity by a drummer of the regiment.

Young Allen was clearly acting in his primary role. In New Zealand in 1863 during the third war Drummer Dudley Stagpoole of the 57th (West Middlesex) Regiment was twice rewarded for gallantry when rescuing wounded men. On 25 September Stagpoole won the Distinguished Conduct Medal 'for the energy and devotion which he displayed … at the affair near Kaipakopako, in having, though wounded in the head, twice volunteered and brought in wounded men.'[3] Just seven days later the 26 year-old Irishman, together with Ensign John Down, was awarded the Victoria Cross for his conduct at Pontoko 'in rescuing a wounded comrade from the rebel Maoris.'[4] It is interesting that Stagpoole's own account related that during the campaign he acted as a rifleman in the ranks and that it was for bayonetting a Maori chief, having already 'put a bullet through him' that he reckoned he was awarded the DCM.[5]

Another Victoria Cross recipient during this period was Drummer Michael Magner of the 33rd (Duke of Wellington's) Regiment; he was another Irishman. The 33rd was amongst a force despatched from India in late 1867 to punish Emperor Tewodros II of Abyssinia. After a 400-mile approach march the only serious fighting took place at Tewodros' stronghold on the Magdala plateau. With his main army easily defeated on the plains below the Emperor withdrew into his fortress and this was then taken by storm on 13 April 1868. The 33rd, armed with the new breech-loading Snider-Enfield rifle, led the assault and were confronted by sheer walls of rock topped by thick thorn bushes. There is very little known about Drummer Magner and his original role in the assault cannot be determined. We do know he was in the very front of the attack and a watercolour sketch by Lieutenant Cornelius James, made on the spot, shows a drummer with drum at the head of the 33rd and their colours also in much evidence. The regimental history provided an account of what unfolded. Blocked by the obstacles before them,

> Private Bergin, a very tall man, stabbed a gap in the hedge with his bayonet; Drummer Magner then clambered on Bergin's shoulders, heaved himself through

the gap and on to the ledge and turning, dragged Bergin up after him ... While Bergin kept up a steady fire with his Snider on the Koket-bir gate, Magner helped others of the 33rd to gain the ledge. All this while the defenders were firing back, but miraculously none of the storming party was hit.[6]

Magner and Bergin and the others with them were able to rush the gate before it was closed and then scrambled up the escarpment to gain the second gate where, just inside, Tewodros had shot himself with the revolver presented to him by Queen Victoria. Both Drummer Magner and Private James Bergin were awarded the Victoria Cross for their gallantry.

The Abyssinian campaign provided no particular challenges save those of logistics due to the great distance covered from the Red Sea to Magdala. Five years afterwards, on the African Gold Coast, there transpired major challenges for command and control. Between 1873 and 1874 Major General Sir Garnet Wolseley subjugated the Ashante in a campaign that required a radically different approach. Against an often invisible enemy in the dark African forest Wolseley provided for a higher proportion of officers within his small force. Even 'a company proved too unwieldy a tactical sub-unit and had to be split into its four, semi-independent sections, three working ahead, the fourth between 40 and 80 yards in rear' and ready to act in support or prevent the turning of a flank.[7] The desperate and confused fighting at the end of January 1874, when Wolseley's columns were drawn onto the main Ashante army as he approached their capital at Coomassie (Kumasi) along the 'main road', demonstrated how well his regiments were trained and led, despite 'The country [being] so close that I can never collect all together into one spot.'[8] While little is known of the British tactics used, prior to the campaign Wolseley had attempted to have two infantry battalions put together for the job in hand, the officers and men to be drawn from '12 of the best battalions now at home.'[9] In each of these battalions there were to be 14 buglers, which would have provided two for each of the six companies per battalion and two orderly buglers for the staff. In the end Wolseley was forced to accept those units authorised by Horse Guards – the 2nd/23rd, the 42nd and the 2nd Rifle Brigade – but he did also receive the 2nd West India Regiment who, it was hoped, would be better acclimatised to the conditions of the Gold Coast. Wolseley being Wolseley, he would have given very clear and specific orders to ensure tight control of his army. Colonel George Greaves, his chief of staff, issued a memorandum on 20 December 1873 on behalf of his commander that gave very precise direction on the 'Mode of Fighting' to be adopted. This included the following details on the use of the bugle:

> Officers Commanding battalions and companies will not order any bugle to be sounded in camp or on the march north of the [River] Prah, except to repeat those sounded on the main road by order of the Major General Commanding; and these, if preceded by any special regimental call, will be repeated only by the battalion concerned, and by any battalion that may be operating between the main road and the corps indicated by the call. When any call is not preceded by a regimental call, it will be repeated by every bugler within hearing, except those that may be on duty with the baggage guard.
>
> Whenever the advance and double is sounded it is to be understood to order a general advance of the whole front line upon the enemy. The men will then advance cheering at a fast walk, making short rushes whenever the nature of the ground will allow of their being made.[10]

The standard and commonly understood bugle calls appear to have been present throughout all of the campaigns of the time. The North-West Frontier of India was to attract British military attention ever-increasingly in the last third of the century, and beyond – and more of which below. For example, in late 1863 in the Umbeyla campaign Colonel John Adye, the Deputy Adjutant General of the Bengal Army, wrote in a letter to his brother that, as they approached the 'Village of Umbeylah … all being ready "the advance" was sounded and away we went.'[11] In a more negative example in Zululand, at Fort Newdigate in June 1879, one of the outlying piquets 'thought they saw a Zulu creeping towards them. They promptly fired three shots, which was the recognized signal that the camp was being attacked … The "close" was sounded to bring in the outposts. Then fire opened from all faces by infantry … Orders were soon issued to cease firing, but five men of the outposts were wounded by the fire of their friends in withdrawing, when apparently there was no enemy at all.'[12]

The 24th (2nd Warwickshire) Regiment in the Zulu War of 1879 provides us with a particularly useful case study of the employment of drummers on a typical colonial campaign. The 24th Regiment had two Regular battalions at this time and, unusually, both were on foreign service and in Zululand. The presence of drummers in the ranks of both 1st and 2nd Battalions of the 24th in the Zulu War is undisputed and their activities might be taken as typical of all British infantry battalions on campaign.

There is a splendid photograph in the museum of the Royal Welsh Regiment at Brecon that shows the drummers of the 2nd/24th in South Africa.[13] The photograph is of 26 drummers in all plus an officer, and of the 26 one is clearly the drum major and one of the corporals is hanging on to an antelope, which is, presumably, a regimental mascot. The faces of the drummers demonstrate that they are of all ages; some youngsters, perhaps boys, and some much older men with beards, and a number of them are holding bugles or drum sticks. They stand and sit around some piled drums: one base drum, three or four standard side drums and two 'cheese' drums. The cheese drum was a much shallower version of the standard side drum and had been brought into service in 1858. It was meant to be a handier instrument than its big brother but was never popular amongst the drummers, although numbers remained in service into the years of the Great War. The photograph of the drummers of the 2nd/24th might also be taken as typical of a full-strength infantry battalion's corps of drums on campaign. We can assume that the drummers of both battalions assisted with daily routine in camp and on the march by sounding the required calls and might assume further that the calls really were restricted to the bugle and not the drum. There survives additional photographic evidence for the presence of drummers and buglers. One of D Company 1st Battalion the 13th Light Infantry late in the war shows a cheese drum and, somewhat incongruously, a single bandsman with a trombone. The drum itself would seem out of place in a light infantry battalion, although it might be being carried by a bandsman rather than drummer. Another photograph, of the 91st Highlanders, shows their pipers and their drummers and all of these latter appear to be carrying bugles alone.

The majority of the drummers of the 2nd/24th were fortunate that morning of 22 January in South Africa as they marched off with the bulk of the battalion. Lord Chelmsford had decided on an excursion from his camp at Isandlwana and headed towards Mangeni to try to find the Zulu army, thereby dividing his force. One company – G under Lieutenant Charles Pope – stayed behind with the remaining five companies of the 1st Battalion. With G Company were two drummers, in accordance with regulations, with an additional 12 drummers and the drum major present with the 1st Battalion. It is of note too that the band of the 2nd/24th accompanied Chelmsford's column while that of the 1st/24th also stayed in camp. But we know that the bandmaster of the 2nd/24th also stayed in camp, for he appeared on the casualty list for that fateful day.

The men were having breakfast when the first order to assemble was blown by bugle at around 7.30 a.m., the order having been given to the orderly drummer by the commanding officer of the 1st Battalion, Lieutenant Colonel Henry Pulleine, via his Adjutant, Lieutenant Teignmouth Melvill. They stood under arms close in to camp for nearly three hours before being dismissed and allowed to return to their lines. A number of reasons have been postulated for the collapse of the British position at Isandlwana and it is not for this book to detail them. The British position was over-extended – just six companies of the 24th, under 600 men, occupying a frontage of 1,500 yards without any supports or a reserve – and was quickly overwhelmed by a mass of 20,000 Zulus coming on at speed. Further evidence of the use of the bugle was provided by the late David Rattray, who did much to unearth the Zulu side of the story of the war. He produced a very atmospheric audio account of Isandlwana during which he related:

> I also believe that, in compliance with Durnford's orders [Lieutenant Colonel Anthony Durnford of the Royal Engineers was the senior officer present], Pulleine couldn't bring his line in until Durnford retired. So when Durnford began to pull back from the donga to the camp, Pulleine gave an instruction to his bugler to blow the 'retire' and the bugler, with his lips a-quiver, blew the retire. [Lieutenant] Horace Smith-Dorrien said: 'Above the row of battle I heard a bugle sound the retire.' And the Zulu accounts tell us that 'they heard one of those copper things that you British people use to make noises.' With that, as N … [indistinct] explained to us, the soldiers began to scurry about like ants as they got into retreating squares and began a fighting withdrawal back to the

camp. ... [For the officers and men on the line so far out] that bugle call must have been music to their ears.[14]

A degree of folklore surrounds this battle, much of it arising at the time and in part to try to explain the inexplicable – a calamitous British defeat at the hands of 'savages'. One story, perpetuated in the movie *Zulu Dawn*,[15] was the apparent refusal of quartermasters to hand out ammunition to men other than their own. The basis for this story may have been in an account by Simeon Nkambule, one of the African mounted auxiliaries present who was an NCO with the Edendale Contingent. According to Ian Knight, he

> described how, in the closing stages of the battle, he came across a lad whom he described as a 'drummer boy' of the 24th guarding a supply of ammunition in the camp; the Edendale men were running short of rounds and asked to be given some, but the 'drummer' refused to allow them to plunder his charge., Nkambule begged him to come away with them, as the battle was clearly lost, but the boy refused – he was later seen flinging his short regulation-issue drummers' sword at the approaching Zulus.[16]

Additional folklore, long refuted, had Zulus deliberately mutilating young British drummer boys. Zulus killed everyone on the battlefield, young and old, combatants and non-combatants, and the public of Victorian England would have been horrified by this fact. Not one drummer survived Isandlwana but two bandsmen – Privates Bickley and Wilson – did escape, being two of just ten survivors of the almost 600 officers and men of the 24th Regiment who began the day. Amongst the dead was Boy Thomas Harrington of the 1st Battalion's band. Young Smith-Dorrien also survived the battle, and the war, rising to the rank of general and commanding II Corps in France and Flanders in 1914–15. B Company of the 2nd/24th, defending the mission station at Rorke's Drift, had four drummers on strength that day – its own two drummers, Patrick Hayden and James Keefe, Drummer Keefe being slightly wounded during the battle, and at least one other, being Drummer Patrick Galgey detached from D Company 2nd/24th. One source states that Drummer John Meehan from A Company was also on the strength at Rorke's Drift.[17]

The British Army invaded Egypt in August 1882 in response to the rebellion by Colonel Ahmed Arabi Bey against the Khedive – the

Ottoman ruler – and the resulting threat to the Suez Canal. Taking and holding Egypt was to have an important influence on the British Army for the next seventy-plus years. The port of Alexandria was bombarded by the Royal Navy in mid-July and it is worth mentioning that, when two British battalions were put ashore there on 17 July to restore order to a city in turmoil, one of those battalions – the 1st Battalion the South Staffordshire Regiment – carried its colours. This was to be the very last occasion a British battalion carried its colours in the field, although the distinction of carrying colours into battle for the last time lies with the 58th (Rutlandshire) Regiment in 1879 at the battle of Laing's Nek in South Africa. Colours, as well as drums, had just about had their day in battle but it is of interest that the conditions of colonial warfare could have something of a backwards influence on tactics.

During the approach to the key battle of the Egyptian campaign at Tel-el-Kebir now Lieutenant General Sir Garnet Wolseley, the army commander, decided, for all its complications, on a night-time assault on the main Egyptian entrenchments. Consequently, Wolseley gave orders that no bugles or pipes were to be sounded when camp was struck and during the approach. Surprise was maintained until almost the last moment. This was to be an attack very much in accordance with standard principles. There had been some muddling of formations in the dark and on the left of the British line the Highland Brigade (1st Battalion the Black Watch; 2nd Battalion the Highland Light Infantry; 1st Battalion the Gordon Highlanders and 1st Battalion the Cameron Highlanders) was some way forward and just some 200 yards from the Egyptian piquets when they were spotted in the darkness. The Highlanders maintained their steady pace, fixing bayonets on the move – we might imagine this order being passed quietly down the line by officers and NCOs – until the whole Egyptian position opened fire. With all surprise now lost the bugles sounded the charge and the bagpipes and drums joined in with the yells of the men as they fought their way into the enemy lines, exactly in accordance with the regulations.

For this campaign there is a beautiful representation of the division of responsibilities for drummers in battle in Richard Caton-Woodville's 1884 painting entitled *The Guards at Tel-el-Kebir, 13 September 1882.*

This artist's realistic and dramatic representations of Victoria's army can help us reinforce our imaginations of scenes that the photographer was still unable to reach. In this most atmospheric painting the brigade (comprising 2nd Battalion the Grenadier Guards; 2nd Battalion the Coldstream Guards and 1st Battalion the Scots Guards) is seen with the men lying down to avoid the worst effects of the Egyptian artillery whilst the brigade was in reserve. In a prominent position forward of his men, His Royal Highness The Duke of Connaught, the commander of the brigade, can be seen astride his grey charger, and by his side, standing, is his orderly bugler. This would have been a senior and experienced man and quite possibly a corporal or even a sergeant provided by one of the Guards' battalions. Behind the prone Guardsmen in their lines and awaiting the order to move forward can be seen a drummer with his side drum – there is another drum and, one might assume, another drummer to his left – sitting amongst the stretchers and the wounded.

While there are no photographs of this decisive battle there are some of representative groups of soldiers taken shortly after the end of the campaign and these do help us a little more. The army in Egypt wore, universally, its red tunics, white foreign-service helmets and white leather equipment. But there is evidence of an interesting mix of the two types of side drum then in service. Caton-Woodville painted the standard side drum in his depiction of the Guards Brigade and a photograph of the 1st Battalion the Scots Guards disembarking at Alexandria on 12 August 1882, with a drummer in full equipment in the foreground, bears this out. In contrast, a photograph of the 1st Battalion the Black Watch shows young Drummer Slattie, who was present at Tel-el-Kebir, carrying the much shallower cheese drum. A further illuminating photograph, of a group from 2nd Battalion the Highland Light Infantry, has the battalion's bass drum on display, providing evidence that the light infantry regiments still retained drums on occasion and not just in their bands.[18]

The British occupation of Egypt led to embroilment further south in the Sudan during the next two decades. The vast open spaces of the desert often required defensive tactics and the all-round protection afforded by infantry in square and in close order. Volley fire would begin as far out as possible to keep the enemy at a distance, but the close order also allowed the defence to withstand the hand-to-hand fighting the swordsmen and spearmen were seeking. The square was also used to protect an advance and, with little cover afforded by the ground, cut thorn would be collected to form dense hedges, or *zareba*, to provide additional defence when static. Calling for closely coordinated ranks and disciplined volleys command and control, made easier by the flat terrain, could be usefully assisted by the bugle, and the drum added for moral effect.

During the effort in late 1884 and early 1885 under Wolseley to relieve Major General Charles Gordon, besieged by a Dervish army at Khartoum, the commander of Wolseley's desert column, Brigadier General Herbert Stewart, had seen his orderly bugler killed next to him when the Dervishes broke into the British square at the battle of Abu Klea on 17 January 1885. Previously there had been much sounding of bugles in the field during the campaign. But as the column approached Metammeh on the Nile and the location of a large Dervish force Stewart, according to the accompanying war correspondent Alex MacDonald, ordered 'that there were to be no more bugle calls that night, and forbidding all lights and loud talking' for fear of warning the enemy of their approach.[19] However, there was deemed to be much need of the bugle to help control the firing line in battle, the British and Egyptian soldiers having shown some nervousness when confronted by the onrush of the Dervish host. After Stewart was mortally wounded his successor, Lieutenant Colonel Sir Charles Wilson, used bugles to control his soldiers' fire and provide additional moral effect. The Anglo-Egyptian army stood a good chance of being annihilated at Metammeh and in the battle there, which became known as Abu Kru, it had to fight its way to water for the second time. Wilson took a great risk in dividing his force, leaving his wounded and baggage with a strong guard protected by its *zareba* while his other force advanced in square to the river. The Dervish army showed every indication of charging and Wilson halted his square as the Dervishes came on in their customary rush. MacDonald, observing from within the *zareba*, wrote later that 'As the firing at first appeared to have little effect, the bugle sounded "Cease firing," which steadied [the men]; and they then opened fire at 300 yards with such deadly effect that all the leaders with their waving banners went down at once ...'[20]

With Gordon dead and Wolseley now falling back on Egypt a further expedition was mounted from Suakin on the Sudanese coast in March 1885. Major E. A. De Cosson, who accompanied the Suakin Field Force, wrote of one alarum when he 'was roused by a hoarse cry of "Guard turn out" ... and the bugles sounding the "fall in", and "double", in rapid succession, all along the line.'[21] The battle of Tofrek, also known as 'McNeill's Zareba', followed on 28 March, the 1st Battalion the Royal Berkshire Regiment having a particularly tough time of it when they were caught beyond the square. De Cosson reported that when it was all over 'the bugles sound the "cease fire", and cheer on cheer rises from the men.'[22]

In 1896 Major General Sir Herbert Kitchener, then 'Sirdar', or Commander-in-Chief, of the Egyptian Army, was given the task of reconquering the Sudan and capturing the capital Khartoum. In the final year of the campaign in 1898 Bennet Burleigh, writing for the *Daily Telegraph*, mentioned bugles and drums being played frequently in camp and on the march, the need to boost morale being clearly in evidence.[23] At the two major battles of the Atbara and Omdurman, drums, bugles, pipes and bands accompanied the advance. Burleigh described rather colourfully of the Atbara on 8 April that 'Shortly after 8 o'clock the bugles sounded the general advance. On the instant the bands of the Khedival battalions began playing, drums and bugles went cheerily, and the pipers skirled their most stirring minstrelsy. A braver sight was not to be seen in a lifetime. An advance was begun as in review order ...'[24] Kitchener's official despatch, dated 10 April, confirmed this use of various instruments. He wrote that 'At 7.40 a.m. I sounded the general advance ... the assaulting columns ... steadily and unflinchingly bore down towards the zereba, with pipes and bands playing.'[25] Lieutenant Samuel Cox of the 1st Battalion the Lincolnshire Regiment wrote that when it was all over 'the "cease fire" sounded followed by the assembly, and we formed up the battalions outside the position. Directly the "cease fire" sounded every regiment broke into tremendous cheers.'[26]

No less a personage than Winston Churchill was acting as a journalist in the Sudan at this time and, famously, took part in the charge of the 21st Lancers at Omdurman. He too covered the fight at the Atbara, writing in his two-volume work on the campaign:

> At twenty minutes to eight the Sirdar ordered his bugles to sound the general advance. The call was repeated by all the brigades, and the clear notes rang out above the noise of the artillery ... The whole mass of the infantry, numbering nearly eleven thousand men, immediately began to move forward upon the *zeriba* ... Large solid columns of men, preceded by a long double line ... marched to the assault in a regular and precise array. The pipes of the Highlanders, the bands of the Soudanese, and the drums and fifes of the English regiments added a wild and thrilling accompaniment.[27]

After the Atbara more than three months passed while Kitchener moved his army towards Khartoum. Lieutenant Hamilton Hodgson, another young officer of the 1st Lincolns, kept a daily diary and sent extracts in a letter to his father. For 26 August he described the end of another day of arduous marching:

> After the third halt some one shouted out it was all down hill the rest of the way which was cheering, and the drums came across some better ground and started playing; in fact played us into camp. I don't think I ever appreciated drums more, they got a very long step, and soon the whole brigade were going to the step. After each tune they were applauded and cheered vociferously. Dr. Hill our show drummer, who prides himself on having a black mark the size of a penny on the centre of the vellum, got his chance occasionally with a side drum solo. Poor chap, his drumming days are over, as he is wounded in his wrist – bullet came through drum first.[28]

On the morning of Omdurman on 2 September Hodgson wrote that the army stood to arms at 3.30 a.m. and Churchill noted: 'The bugles all over the camp by the river began to sound at half-past four. The cavalry trumpets and the drums and fifes of the British division joined the chorus, and everyone awoke amid a confusion of merry or defiant notes.'[29] The Dervish army hove into view around 6.30 a.m. whence the Anglo-Egyptian army commenced section volley firing with its magazine-fed Lee-Metford rifles at 2,000 yards. In front of the British battalions no Dervish got within 800 yards of Kitchener's square. Hodgson related that 'I never could have imagined anything so cool and brave as those men were ... I was sorry for [them]; they were simply wiped out.'[30] He did not mention anything of the commands or calls given in the battle line but once the advance onto Khartoum was underway he wrote that the 10th Sudanese Battalion were 'playing away at their bugles hard.' The 1st Lincolns were the old 10th Foot so as the 10th Sudanese came up Hodgson described 'I heard a man say "Why, it's the 10th" and almost simultaneously they struck up the "Poachers" [the regimental march of the Lincolns] ... And by jove there was a howl when the old tune started, and we got in step and tried to keep pace.' Eventually 'we passed them, our drums playing ... more howls.'[31]

All of these examples make it readily apparent that the conditions of these wars in the desert allowed for and even demanded something of a return to earlier tactical methods. Charles Callwell noted that in cases like the Atbara 'the attack was delivered in line in broad daylight on formidable defence works. It was foreseen that, although the enemy was armed to a considerable extent with breech-loading rifles, the fire would not be so accurate (especially after a heavy bombardment) as to render this compact formation unjustifiable, and the order of battle ensured that the shock would be tremendous even against opponents whose *forte* was hand to hand fighting.'[32] While Hollywood cannot be taken as in any way an authority in these matters, as with *Zulu Dawn* there are sometimes snippets of film that help us understand something of the character of the time. Alexander Korda's 1939 film *The Four Feathers* was based on the 1902 novel of the same name by A. E. W. Mason. The film's depiction of the battle of Omdurman provided a realistic impression of the Anglo-Egyptian army in the field. The 1st Battalion the East Surrey Regiment was used as extras for the movie and their steadfast discipline is very evident. The use of drum rolls to accompany the order for the firing line to fix bayonets at Omdurman was quite possibly an accurate re-enactment of the event. We also have good contemporary photographic evidence of drums and bugles in the Sirdar's army. Also present was the photographer Rene Bull, reporting for the *Black and White Printing and Publishing Company* of London. One of his photographs of Egyptian troops after the ceasefire at the Atbara shows a drummer with his side drum slung over his shoulder. Another, in a series taken at General Gordon's palace, clearly shows two British buglers, one of them a Highlander (either Seaforths or Camerons), who appear to be looking for souvenirs.[33]

The tactical situation often prevailing in India during this period, with operations focussed squarely on Afghanistan and the North-West Frontier, did not permit the same use of drum and bugle or the same tactical methods. There was a constancy of presence across India by the British Army and for the most part the country was at peace. A familiar feature of the day was a battalion on the road, moving station as required and helping to display the military might of the Raj. In the early 1890s Rudyard Kipling described this in his poem *Route Marchin'*:

> We're marchin' on relief over Inja's coral strand,
> Eight 'undred fightin' Englishmen, the Colonel, and the Band;
> Ho! Get away you bullock-man, you've 'eard the bugle blowed,
> There's a regiment a-comin' down the Grand Trunk Road;[34]

Private Frank Richards, in his atmospheric memoir of his time in the 2nd Battalion the Royal Welsh Fusiliers, in India before the Great War, recorded that in March 1903 the battalion marched the 160 miles from Meerut to Chakrata. Men could pay two annas to their colour sergeant to receive 'a good meat sandwich and a pint of tea at the coffee-halt, where we had half an hour's rest.' It would have gladdened their hearts and eased their grumbling stomachs when, as they approached the coffee-halt they had 'the drums striking up with the tune of "Polly put the kettle on and have a cup of tea."'[35]

But the conditions created by the tribesmen of the North-West Frontier were another matter. Not only did the mountainous terrain call for well-developed skirmishing and tight coordination of fire and move-ment, bugling could be positively dangerous. Tactical conditions here, as had proved elsewhere in very close country or tumbling hillside, were very different. Callwell noted that 'In bush campaigns the infantry work in small groups in loose formation, each group ready to dash forward independently for a short distance at a moment's notice; no great rushes in serried ranks to the sound of pipes and drum take place as at the Atbara, cohesion is often maintained only by sound and not by sight.'[36]

Quite how this was done Callwell did not enlarge further. As Michael Barthorp has stated: 'Without any of the modern means of instant communication between widely-spread bodies of troops, tactical decisions depended greatly on the officer – often quite young – who was immediately confronted by them.' On the Frontier there was an additional problem too, for 'the meaning of field calls by bugle could well be familiar to tribesmen who had served in the Army.'[37] During the siege and relief of Chitral in March and April 1895 discipline had to be carefully maintained amongst the inexperienced Kashmiri infantry. Colonel, later General Sir, Ian Hamilton and commander of the ill-fated Gallipoli campaign of 1915, acted as Military Secretary to the commander of the relief force. He recalled later that 'Bugle calls were blown as regularly as in normal camp' but, and this would have not eased nerves, 'At first the calls had been answered by the enemy ...'[38] On 5 April, a month into the siege, 'while it was still dark, there was a great deal of noise and firing. The enemy bugler, who had suddenly reappeared, blew "Assembly", "Fire" and several other calls.'[39]

The act of retiring from contact was particularly hazardous as it was, the opportunist 'Pathan' – the then common vernacular for the Pashtun – proving extremely agile at exploiting any mistake. As Callwell summed up: The 'intention of retiring should be concealed to the last moment ... Sounding the "retire" on the bugle will rarely be a wise procedure, especially on the Indian frontier where the bugle calls are known to the tribesmen.'[40] Callwell cited an example during operations in Waziristan in 1881. In the action of Shah Alam Kaghza, the 1st Sikhs were in danger of being overwhelmed by Waziris. They were kept in hand by the resolution of their commanding officer. He ordered a charge, periodically halting his men to re-form. An eyewitness account by Lieutenant Colonel Pollack in his *Notes on Hill Warfare* stated that 'After the charge we heard the general's bugle sounding our regimental call to retire.' The commanding officer 'refused to obey the order, as he was aware that if we retired through the thick scrub before the Waziris were beaten, the result would have been a heavy loss in men.'[41]

Nevertheless, when the situation demanded it, the bugle could still be employed to good effect. In the final and desperate assault on the Dargai Heights on 20 October 1897 during the Tirah campaign the 1st

Battalion the Gordon Highlanders, supported by the 3rd Sikhs, were ordered to take the position at all costs. It had proved impossible to dislodge the Afridi tribesmen from their mountain-top positions by using company and section rushes and the Gordon's commanding officer, Lieutenant Colonel Mathias, 'called out: "Highlanders! The General says the position is to be taken at all costs. The Gordons will take it!" and as the battalion's bugles blew the charge the pipers struck up "Cock o' the North"'.[42] 'One of these, named Findlater, blowing his loudest and best, was among the first to show the way across that deadly strip of ground ... when, after traversing but a few yards, he was laid low, shot through both legs, he managed to prop himself against a boulder and continued with unabated energy to play ... animating his comrades by the familiar and stirring music of his beloved pipes.'[43] Findlater was awarded the Victoria Cross for his efforts.

Elsewhere, during what was collectively described as the Great Frontier War of 1897–98, General Sir Bindon Blood was leading the Malakand Field Force against the Mamund. Accompanying him was the young Churchill, then still an officer in the 4th Hussars but with a role, as later at Omdurman, ostensibly at least of newspaper correspondent. Churchill's own published account provides evidence of bugle calls in camp during the approach marches. In a night camp as the 2nd Brigade approached the Rambat Pass in mid-September 1897, surrounding tribesmen fired on the camp for about two hours and a number of British and Indian officers and Indian soldiers were killed and wounded. Then, 'At ten o'clock a bugler among the enemy sounded the "Retire", and the fire dwindled to a few dropping shots' until it re-commenced a half hour later.[44] This provides example enough that numbers of tribesmen, trained as soldiers by the British, on completion of their service went back to their villages and used their skills against their previous colleagues. The following day, during a close action in the Mamund Valley, a detachment of the 35th Sikhs found itself forced to retire in trying circumstances. Churchill was up with them and at the moment of most danger, with

> The Sikhs, who now numbered perhaps sixty, ... hard pressed, and fir[ing] without effect. Then someone – who it was is uncertain – ordered the bugler

to sound the 'charge'. The shrill notes rang out not once but a dozen times. Everyone began to shout. The officers waved their swords frantically. Then the Sikhs commenced to move slowly forward towards the enemy, cheering. It was a supreme moment.[45]

Colonel H.D. Hutchinson was Director of Military Education in India and in his campaign history of the Tirah produced some useful tactical lessons for those operating in such difficult circumstances. He noted that:

> strict 'formations' and precise 'manoeuvres,' as we find them described and defined in our drill-books, are impossible ... Regiments new to this savage mountain warfare, which have only practised drill-book methods of attack and retirement, find themselves seriously handicapped when brought suddenly face to face with the[se] conditions ... the drill-book was not written for frontier fighting. Yet it is the guide for us all in India, as in England, and if these are the only methods constantly practised on cantonment parade-grounds, it must be impossible to shake them off at a moment's notice.[46]

Lieutenant Colonel James Grierson, who was, as a lieutenant general, given command of II Corps in August 1914 and died of a heart attack on his way to the front, underlined in his unofficial manual of 1899, that 'Rigid systems of attack are forbidden, nevertheless the regulations lay down certain general principles.'[47] Experience and this advice against any attempt in warfare of using some hidebound tactical system in ignorance of the true situation were, sadly, not fully appreciated when the British Army faced its greatest test in half a century when war broke out again in South Africa in 1899. Before full appreciation of Boer defensive firepower was felt efforts continued to be made to use standard formations and the charge in line to carry Boer positions. At Colenso on 15 December 1899, during the so-called 'black week' of the British Army, in an example of utter ignorance Major General Arthur Fitzroy Hart, commanding the 5th (Irish) Brigade, gave his men half an hour of parade ground drill before deploying his leading battalion, the 1st Battalion the Royal Dublin Fusiliers, in line of companies in close order. His remaining three battalions were up close behind with companies at quarter column distance. In broad daylight they were all sucked in to a salient created by a sharp loop there on the Tugela River, assailed by entrenched Boer riflemen on three sides.

The Dublin's commanding officer had attempted to extend his line, only to be ordered back into close order by 'No Bobs' Hart, and by the time the brigade was finally able to extricate itself it had suffered over 500 casualties. One of these was 14-year-old Drummer John Dunne. In the midst of great difficulty, as the Dublins attempted to cross the river, Dunne sounded the advance. He received a bullet through his right arm and a chunk of shrapnel in his chest but, shifting his bugle to his left hand, continued to blow. He was eventually carried to the rear and was distressed to discover that his bugle had been thrown into the Tugela. On being invalided home he was later presented with a silver bugle by Queen Victoria and a ditty of the time began: 'Bugler Dunne, Bugler Dunne, you are missing all the fun, And another chap is bugling where the battle's being won.'[48]

There was much debate in military circles over the subject of appropriate tactics. We are too ready to judge what appears to us today to be crass stupidity by officers commanding, but the dilemmas of the time were apparent to those on the battlefield and solutions were energetically sought. But, just as in the Great War, there was no technical solution within easy reach and victory, for victory there had to be, had to be obtained by too much blood. What had worked on one battlefield could be found all too unworkable on another. One such debate by those who understood took place at the Royal United Services Institute in London on 30 April 1900. Colonel Sir Howard Vincent, in commenting on the battle of Magersfontein on 11 December 1899 and the second failure of black week, reckoned that 'seeing the broken ground … over which the Highland Brigade had to advance to the attack, on a pitch-dark night … it is quite conceivable that close formation was the only one in which the direction of attack could by any possibility be maintained.'[49] While this statement did not acknowledge the failure of Lieutenant General Lord Methuen to carry out any adequate reconnaissance or consider the inadvisability at that stage of a night march, Vincent's point demonstrated the fundamental problem here in maintaining command and control. However, Vincent made a valuable conclusion when he stated that 'Again, tactics and formations will have to be revised – the close order is done.'[50] This truism was becoming increasingly evident but Major

General Sir John Maurice, a thoroughly experienced and learned officer, responded in defence of the army and its difficulties. He noted that the deductions made from the Franco-Prussian War were just the same as those now being made. 'They refer to the necessity of not attacking in close formation and the necessities of scouting ...' In the meantime the British Army had faced mass armies of 'magnificent savages' charging in close order and 'the tactics deduced ... from the 1870 campaign [meaning the Franco-Prussian War] ... or from fighting against men with the weapons used by the Boers, would be wholly inapplicable to meet savages under those conditions ... We adopted against the Zulus an excessively extended skirmishing order. Isandula [sic] was the result.'

There was certainly much to learn but conventional tactics, applied intelligently, could work on occasion. Earlier at the storming of Talana Hill at the battle of Dundee on 20 October 1899, steadfast British infantry operating in widely extended formation, got the better of the Boers. During a lull in the firing the British line was reported as dashing forward 'with drums beating, bugles sounding' and at Elandslaagte the following day 'the bugles sounded the charge.'[51] Written up as this was in the posturing tones of the illustrated volumes that constituted *With the Flag to Pretoria* it might be ignored as fanciful and over-romanticised. But we know that 'Drum-major Laurence [of the 1st Battalion the Gordon Highlanders] dash[ed] forward [and] sounded the charge and rally.' The British troops had been exposed to intense Boer fire during their advance and had faltered when they heard what turned out to be a Boer bugler sound the 'retire'. But Laurence's bugle was soon echoed by others and 'The Devons' bugles in the valley were now ringing cheerily, their long-checked impetuosity was loosed, and with fixed bayonets they dashed up the front of the position.'[52] One of these 'buglers' wrote a vivid account to his parents a few months after the battle that fully corroborated the story. Drummer Ernest Boulden of D Company, 1st Battalion the Devonshire Regiment, described the splendid work of the Royal Artillery as the British approached the Boer entrenchments from a distance of some seven thousand yards:

> We were under fire from the enemy's guns at 5 thousand yards and we done a steady advance ... we got into 18 hundred yards of the enemy and then we

gave them a few British vollies and when we found the range correct we started independent firing ... and then we go in to 200 yards and they came the white flag trick but it did not act for, as one lot was hoisting the white flag, the others were pouring hundreds of shots into us. It did seem awful and so we came to 50 yards and the order was given, 'Prepare to charge them'. 'Charge,' I sounded 3 times and then joined in the charge and I was going to put my sword through a young Boer and I saw he was wounded so I did not stick him but he deserved to be killed for he was one of the chaps that put [up] the white flag and then act tratous but I went on with the charge and we drove them down over the hill ...[53]

Elandslaagte was also notable for a further ruse by the Boer defenders. A modern history of the Devonshire Regiment described the flank attack by the Manchesters and Gordons and the trouble and casualties they had in negotiating barbed-wire fencing 'before the bugles sounded the 'charge'. It was at this critical point in the battle that The Times correspondent reports hearing the 'cease fire' sounded whereupon, he states, there was a sudden lull in the firing ... This was apparently a ruse by the enemy.'[54]

After Elandslaagte the British force retired on Ladysmith where it was besieged by the Boers for four months. On 6 January 1900, at the height of the siege, a major Boer attack tried to force the British positions and a counter-attack at Wagon Hill by three companies of the Devons was instrumental in saving the day. In his long letter Drummer Boulden wrote that, encouraged by General Sir George White,

With a ringing cheer we fixed bayonets and dear old Captain Lafone leading on in front we charged up over the hill and the Boers were only 15 yards from us and I sounded the charge with another Drummer and then we joined the charge and I dived right in amongst them and cut and poked right and left ... and we drove the Boers right off the hill ...[55]

Drummer Boulden's letter is important for a number of reasons. The use of bugles in the way he described provides solid evidence of the moral effect – positive for the Devons and negative for the Boers – that could be obtained at decisive and critical moments. We can also deduce that companies retained their company buglers in their primary role for at least some attacks. And it provides evidence too of the character of some of these fellows. We do not know how old Ernest Boulden was but he sounds like a youngster and that he was armed only with his drummer's short sword, which he had no hesitation to 'poke' at rifle-armed Boers, says much for his bravery. It was a short sword too for the 1896 regulations had shortened its blade from 17 and a half inches to 12 and a half. When his company commander was killed in the attack his Boer assailant had 'his head blown right off his body and I could not help giving him a poke with my sword ...'[56]

The later Victorian period saw a vast proliferation of illustrated media by way of popular newspapers and magazines. There was an equal proliferation of artwork showing soldiers of Britain and her Empire and amongst all these media are ample examples of drummers and buglers. Most of the artwork might best be described as uniform studies and artists such as Richard Simkin and Harry Paine were perhaps the most notable, Simkin illustrating the British Army throughout its history. Others, like Richard Caton Woodville, experienced battle at first hand and his drawings for the *Illustrated London News* and later magnificent canvasses, represent some of the finest and most realistic depictions of the army at war. He was mentioned earlier with regard to his painting *The Guards at Tel-el-Kebir*, where he was present. Orlando Norie painted over 5,000 watercolours of military subjects and a good number showing the British Army on its field exercises between the 1860s and the 1890s have an orderly bugler standing or calling alongside his commanding officer. Norie was always at pains to be realistic and these pictures are useful evidence of buglers acting in their primary role in the field.

Photographs of British military subjects also became extremely popular in the 1890s and mention was made above of the appearance of some photographs of drummers and buglers. For the Anglo–Boer War there is a well-known photograph of a young drummer, a boy it would seem and thus serving the popular perception, sitting on the ground and writing home, using his drum as his writing table. In the tent right behind him are two somewhat older campaigners, one of them wearing the rank badge of a drum major. An increasing number of photographs showed battalions on the march and one such had the Coldstream Guards being led into Bloemfontein on 13 March 1900 by their drums and fifes. Other photographs were produced for the public to create additional support for the war and one, reproduced in the *Black and White Budget* of 5 May 1900, showed a wounded bugler being helped by a comrade. The caption read:

> The Last Call: No class of soldier is more unselfish in his devotion to duty than the British bugler. Nor is his heroism lost, for how many regiments have been, after repeated rebuffs, spurred to victory at the sight and sound of their wounded bugler blowing a final call before sinking back into unconsciousness? ... the spirit of the hero within the man alone enables him to do his duty to the bitter end.[57]

The occupation of Bloemfontein was also recorded on cine film, the Anglo-Boer War being the first time cinematography was deployed by the British in war. One clip of this film also shows marching soldiers accompanied by drums and bagpipes. Most of the still photographs and cine film do not really help our understanding of any use of musical instruments on the battlefield but there are a few tantalising snapshots that reveal telling scenes. About 15 November 1899, and at about the time Churchill was taken prisoner near Chieveley when the armoured train on which he was travelling was ambushed, a photographer took an informative picture on a nearby hilltop. This showed a detachment of infantry, their officer looking through binoculars and his orderly bugler standing behind. In fact all of the impedimenta of modern signalling is in place because to the rear a signaller is wagging a signal flag and on the ground beside him is a signalling lamp and a fellow using a telescope to read replies.[58] Even more tantalising is another clip of cine film, which appears to be the same scene, or one remarkably similar. Finally, incongruous as it may seem, given that the drum must by now have been something of an unhelpful encumbrance, a photograph of British infantry occupying Boer positions on the Modder River on 28 November clearly shows a drummer with side drum, standing just to the rear of the firing line and apparently looking across to his officer.[59]

The Anglo-Boer War proved to be a wake-up call for the British Army. As Rudyard Kipling concluded in *The Lesson*: 'We have had no end of a lesson: it will do us no end of good.'[60] The exercising of command and control on the battlefield had proven to be the biggest challenge and Lord Methuen had summed this up after Modder River: 'the truth is that when no-one can get on a horse with any safety within 2,000 yards of the enemy, orders cannot be conveyed.'[61] Bugles and officers' whistles had played a useful part as the army developed its methods in the latter part of the 19th century. They might have assumed to have achieved greater utility as extended order became the norm and maintaining visual contact with one's subordinates became increasingly difficult. But it was not as simple as this.

The disaster at Spion Kop, towards the end of January 1900, epitomised what many have written off as a thoroughly badly managed war. However, one small success before ultimate defeat was shown by the 1st King's Own when their commanding officer attempted to halt the retreat of men from another, unnamed, unit:

> At this moment Col Crofton saw a company of another unit running back from the crest towards him. He rose and shouted to the officer: 'What on earth are you doing? Advance, Sir, advance!' and as he spoke a young bugler, by name Russell, who was standing by his side, without orders stood up and sounded the Advance, which, clearly heard above the uproar, carried the whole company back into its position.[62]

CHAPTER 11

Drummers, Boys and their Other Duties

I did not like the appellation drum-boy ... if a drummer had attained the age of Methuselah, he would never acquire any other title than drum-boy.

We shall pause here in our chronological examination to consider further the drummer/bugler himself. It is an opportune moment because the military conditions of the 20th century were to alter his situation radically. In many ways today we can still recognise the drummer and bugler of the last 100 years but their duties and roles have certainly become clouded, as we shall see in subsequent chapters. These infantry musicians before the Great War were quite different and if we see a drummer today in his red tunic, or a bugler in his green, it represents something of an indistinct shadow of earlier times. Yet he does still retain the status of an icon in the British Army.

Who were these drummers and, in later years, buglers, and what was expected of them? While we have already considered many aspects of their service within the military system of the day it will help us understand the part played by all of these instrument players if we now examine them more closely.

Much was said in the opening chapters about the ideal drummer and fifer in the 17th century and his special place in the field, which could be likened at times to the herald. But by the time of Marlborough the infantry drummer had little or no pretence towards language or diplomatic skills. He had shed the role of latter-day herald and, while his status was still meant to provide for some protection when carrying out duties such as beating a parley or escorting a message, he had become simply a field signaller and musician. What he did retain was a distinct and more flamboyant form of dress, which harkened back to the days when he had to be clearly identified on the battlefield by friend and foe alike. Another entire book could be given over to the dress of infantry musicians. There follows the barest summary of the salient points and the author is indebted to the numerous books written by Michael Barthorp and his helpful correspondence over the years.[1]

From the earliest days of the British Army the drummers adopted a dress-convention that was similar to that of the pikemen in the post-Restoration army, that is, of wearing coats of reversed colours. British Army regiments were distinguished by coloured facings on their red coats until these were lost in the 1881 reforms (if partially regained in the 1920s and 1930s). The colour was selected by their founding colonel so Luke Lillingston, for example, chose yellow for what was to become the 38th Regiment. His drummers therefore wore yellow coats and when the 64th was renumbered from the 2nd/11th Foot in 1758 its colonel chose black, though the soldiers wore the green facings of the 11th for a while. Royal regiments, whose facing colour was always blue, wore the Royal livery of red and blue and drummers of regiments with red facings wore white. There were numerous variations on coat colours and facings but this is at least the gist of the matter. These coats were further distinguished by additional lace to reinforce the buttonholes, in similar form to the grenadiers. This lace was, from the time of the 1742 clothing regulations, of a unique regimental pattern and began to cover the seams of the coat-sleeves and backs. And, as with grenadiers, drummers wore a mitre cap or, from 1768, a bearskin cap until they adopted standard infantry headwear in the field in the 1790s.

As the pattern of warfare changed the drummers became increasingly vulnerable to the predations of the enemy. The very nature of bugling in the light infantry also meant that wearing distinct dress was the last thing they needed, although the rifle regiment buglers only ever wore green. An order of September 1811 stated that:

> in consequence of the duties to which trumpeters and drummers were unavoidably exposed on service, and the inconvenience attendant upon their loss in action, which was ascribed to the marked difference of their dress, their clothing may be the same colour as that worn by their respective regiments, and that the distinction which it is necessary to preserve between them and the privates may be pointed out by the lace.[2]

Reversed coats were not formally abolished until 1831 but when distinct regimental lace was abolished in 1836 drummers continued to wear their regiments' lace until the introduction of universal crown lace in 1866. All drummers wore this 'crown-and-inch' lace henceforth, with the Foot Guards retaining their blue fleurs-de-lys pattern. In 1855 and for about a year all drummers were to wear white tunics, which bandsmen had adopted in 1829 when their dress was regularised for the first time. But drummers reverted to red tunics again in 1856. From this time the dress of drummers and buglers largely conformed with the regulations for all infantrymen, allowing for the additional distinctions mentioned. The new dress regulations of 1879 provided drummers and buglers with dress and accoutrements that are, broadly speaking, recognisable to this day.

The requirement for a plentiful supply of drummers led to the recruitment of increasing numbers of boys. One of the myths surrounding British Army drummers and mentioned in the Introduction was that they were all young boys; this was never the case. But this myth, so often displayed in over-romanticised paintings, has also helped to give the British Army drummer an iconic status, especially in our national culture. Certainly there were boys in the ranks of drummers, some of them very young, and evidence suggests that, for a time at least, they were employed in the line alongside their older brother drummers. This seems to be the case for the middle years of the 18th century when battles were relatively set-piece affairs but as the role of the drum waned and its use in battle was increasingly confined to the colonel's orderly drummer alone, so too were the boy drummers relegated to other roles such as medical and ammunition orderlies. Most of the drummers in the line were older men, some of them with many years of experience, this being something of an obvious necessity.

Boys were certainly employed as drummers, fifers and buglers throughout the history of the British Army and up to 1959, when 'boy service' ceased. But most of the army's drummers, certainly the active drummers in-role, were grown men and grizzled veterans – 'not the beardless lads of popular fiction and sentimental imagery.'[3] Nevertheless, until the age of enlistment for boy soldiers was regulated in the 1870s, coinciding with the legal requirement from 1875 to register births under the Births and Deaths Act 1874, very young drummer boys were found on the strength of infantry regiments. Barty-King recorded the story of Joseph Brome, who enlisted in the Royal Artillery as a drummer at the age of eight around 1720 (although he also mentioned Joseph Eliot who was just four years old when he was taken on the strength in 1804!).[4] Brome is significant because he later rose to the rank of lieutenant general but it is supposed that, while drummer boys did not usually reach such an exalted rank, eight was not an unusual age for them to begin their service. There is evidence of some even younger than Brome. An Army Long Service and Good Conduct medal sold on 27 September 2016 at the London auction house of Dix Noonan Webb belonged to Drum Major John Darkin, late of the 2nd (Queen's Royal) Regiment. Darkin was just seven years old when he attested for the Coldstream Guards in March 1828.[5] But, it should be noted, he was not appointed drummer until 1833 when he was 13 and a broad sweep of service records allows us to conclude that, while many a pre-teen boy might have been on the strength of a regiment, they performed no official function as a drummer until they had attained sufficient years to allow them to stand alongside the older drummers. This was commonly 14 or 15 but often between 16 and 18. Many of the younger boys, as we have seen, were given other duties out of the firing line. There is a good possibility that the youngest was just five when he enlisted as a drummer in the 50th (West Kent) Regiment in 1786, having been born in the regiment and then orphaned. This boy, John Murray, continued to serve in the 50th through to the Peninsular War, attaining the rank of colour sergeant.[6]

Taking and accepting such young children into the army would pro-voke outrage today but we have to remember that these youngsters, if they were born into the regiment, had no other home. Their serving soldier fathers and their mothers provided an element of security entirely absent elsewhere in society and it would appear that boys were taken into the ranks only if both their parents had died. A mother whose husband had been killed in battle or died of other causes would very quickly find a new husband and thus stay on the strength of the regiment and continue to provide a home for her children, however grim this might appear to us today. The army also provided a sanctuary for boys orphaned or abandoned elsewhere and, certainly by the middle of the 19th century, the regiments provided for the education of all of the children in their charge, whether in uniform or not. The army proved some way ahead of other institutions and 'pioneer[ed] an educational system for its children many years before the State did the same for its own.'[7]

There is a certain degree of irony at play here for, while British society in general had long looked down on its soldiers as the sweepings of the gutter, it was also seen as a welcomed destination for abandoned and orphaned boys. In 1797, with recruiting having failed to keep up with the army's demands for more men, authority was given to turn a number of regiments of foot into experimental boy regiments for service overseas. John Shipp, an orphan from Saxmundham, reckoned that three such regiments were to be formed, one of them being the 22nd (Cheshire) Regiment then at Colchester and with whom he was to enlist. Shipp wrote that all three regiments (the 22nd, the 34th and the 56th) 'were to take one thousand boys, between the ages of ten and fifteen, off the hands of the parish authorities … [and] their service was to be for life.'[8] The age bracket given by Shipp seems unlikely as boys of this age were not, as we have seen, employed knowingly as soldiers or even as active drummers. An 1828 account of the 65th (2nd Yorkshire North Riding) Regiment stated that there were 'six boy regiments' authorised in an order dated 2 December 1797, one of them being the 65th and another the 16th, and that enlistment was 'limited to boys under 18 years of age.'[9] It would seem in fact that there were as many as eight such regiments – the 9th, 16th, 22nd, 27th, 33rd, 34th, 56th and

64th – authorised between 1795 and 1797. Elsewhere all regiments were happy to recruit boys with the definite aim of them becoming musicians. The *Ipswich Journal* of 17 December 1796 appealed thus:

> Wanted, a Number of Boys, from 12 to 14 years of age, who will answer for Drummers or Music. The Commanding Officer assures their friends that the greatest care and attention will be paid to them. Any person bringing a boy of the above description, to Lieutenant Colonel Mercer, commanding the regiment at Colchester Barracks, shall receive ONE GUINEA, if approved of.[10]

Enlistment in the army certainly helped many otherwise destitute and unemployed boys, and many men, avoid the workhouse. There were other institutions offering real relief to children and the most notable of these was the Foundling Hospital, established in London in 1739 by the generous and caring philanthropy of Captain Thomas Coram. Very many of the boys were 'apprenticed' to the army which, until 1806, could be from as young as ten but from that year was fixed at 14. The hospital had a fine musical heritage from its earliest days as the composer George Frederic Handel was one of the original benefactors and a governor. As a result 'Many foundling boys went into military bands, which were part of a musical tradition dating from the earliest days of the Foundling Hospital.'[11] Even a quick examination of the stories of some of these boys on display in the Foundling Museum today shows that a good number of these band boys went on to be drummers and buglers in infantry regiments. In 1847 John Brownlow, who had been baby number 18,607 when he was admitted in August 1800, established a juvenile band at the hospital and this 'provided a stream of recruits to military bands over the next century.'[12] Brownlow himself wrote in his 1858 *The History and Design of the Foundling Hospital* that:

> During the period the band has been formed about one hundred boys have received instruction, of this number, twenty, at their own desire, have been placed as musicians in the bands of Her Majesty's Household Troops and other regiments, and also in the Royal Navy.[13]

The problem of orphaned or abandoned children was extensive. A census in Dublin in 1765 showed that 1,400 children in that city alone had fathers serving overseas or who had died in military service.[14] Out of this suffering was born the Royal Hibernian Military School, which opened its doors in 1770 and owed its early success to the patronage of King George III. In a similar vein the Duke of York's Military School, established by Royal Charter as an 'Asylum for the orphaned children of fallen soldiers',[15] opened at Chelsea in London in 1803. 'The practice of channelling new boys into the bands seems to have been common in both establishments, for the military schools have produced an astonishing number of musicians (probably numbered in thousands) over the years.'[16] How many went into the bands or the corps of drums or bugles, or went to the corps via the bands, cannot be ascertained without further extensive research, but many would have been drummers and buglers in the infantry regiments. There is an endearing photograph in an edition of *The Navy and Army Illustrated* published on 20 December 1895 that shows the 6 feet 5 inch tall Second Lieutenant Heathcote-Amory of the Coldstream Guards looking down in a fatherly manner at a drummer boy by the name of John Maskell. Maskell, it was reported, was

> Picked up at the Manoeuvres near Swindon, in 1893, while following the troops, and found to be an orphan and a fine spirited boy, the officers of the battalion placed him in the Gordon Boy's Home. There John Maskell did well and became cornet player in the band, whence the officers of the Coldstream Guards took him into their own band as a drummer. He is a universal favorite and a good boy.[17]

We can forgive the patronizing manner of the time for this was a lifeline to boys like Maskell. History does not record what became of him but it is likely he progressed to becoming a drummer proper in his new home.

Drummer boys must have been a very common sight by the mid-18th century for the Swiss artist David Morier showed what are obviously boys in his 1746 painting of the battle of Culloden. A painting of the 3rd Regiment of Foot Guards at St James's Palace in about 1790 shows the drummers and fifers as all boys, but such works only feed the misperception that they were all just boys. In the work done recently by Steven Baule he provides evidence of ages of drummers in a number of British regiments during the American War of Independence. He noted that in the 22nd Regiment in 1778, of the 11 drummers who are documented, the average age was 34. Drummer John Hardman had been the youngest of these 11 on enlistment, having joined at the age of 12, rising to the rank of sergeant in the ranks and returning to the drums at the age of 40. The eldest enlistment had been John Peake, aged 29 and transferring to the drums a month after joining. In the 23rd (Royal Welsh Fusileers) the average age of eight drummers identified in a 1786 document was nearly 27. Documents for the 47th Foot show two rather aged drummers: William Lee, who was 44 in 1773, and Nivs Lightwood, who was 58 when he was discharged as a drummer in 1782 after 32 years' service. Lady Elizabeth Butler's painting *Steady the Drums and Fifes* of the 57th Regiment at Albuhera in 1811 has been commented on already, in Chapter 6, for its apparent romanticising of a regiment's corps of drums in the midst of a battle. Research some years ago at the National Army Museum established that the average age of the 57th's drummers at Albuhera was 26. Nevertheless, at least one drummer boy was present during the battle for 11-year-old Henry Holloway was awarded the clasp for the battle for his General Service Medal.[18] We do not know if Holloway was in the firing line on the day and Butler's depiction of him, very fine though it is, is not evidence enough. At Waterloo in 1815 the 23rd Foot had just one drummer under the age of 18 while two were over 50 – one of them being 62! Just under half these drummers had been under 18 when they enlisted.

These wide variations in age continued through much of the 19th century. A telling photograph by Roger Fenton of a battalion of the Grenadier Guards at the Curragh in Ireland in 1861 shows, amongst the older drummers, at least half a dozen boys and some of them obviously pre-teen. The important reforms of the 1870s brought an end to both extremes of the very young and the very old. During the Zulu War in 1879 the 80th Regiment had 16 drummers serving. Only one was under 18 – Drummer James Appleby, a 17-year-old Londoner. The eldest was 29-year-old Donald Ferguson. However, of these 16, eight had enlisted at the age of 14. One of A Company's drummers, 26-year-old John Leather, was killed alongside his company commander at the Intombi River disaster in March 1879. That the youngest sometimes continued to serve in the ranks on the battlefield is evidenced by the story related in the previous chapter of Drummer John Dunne of the 2nd Battalion the Royal Dublin Fusiliers, who was still just 14 when he was wounded at Colenso in December 1899. Ample photographic evidence from the last decades of the 19th century and the early 20th century show many a boy amongst the drummers of an infantry battalion.

The two most famous boy drummers, and 'a brace of the most finished little fiends that ever banged drum or tootled fife in the Band [sic] of a British Regiment", must be Jakin and Piggy Lew of Rudyard Kipling's *The Drums of the Fore and Aft*:

> Jakin was a stunted child of fourteen and Lew was about the same age. When not looked after they smoked and drank. They swore habitually after the manner of the Barrack-room ... and they fought religiously once a week. Jakin had sprung from some London gutter and may or may not have passed through Dr. Barnardo's hands ere he arrived at the dignity of drummer-boy. Lew could remember nothing except the regiment and the delight of listening to the Band from his earliest years.[19]

They were hated by the other drummers 'on account of their illogical conduct' and both of them were 'frequently birched by the Drum Major ...' But, being too young to go as drummers when the battalion was despatched to the North-West Frontier, they added themselves as supernumeraries to the band, 'the only acting-drummers to be took along.' The other drummer-boys resented this greatly for, 'Not only had they been permitted to enlist two years before the regulation boys' age – fourteen – but, by virtue, it seemed, of their extreme youth, they were allowed to go to the Front – which thing had not happened to acting-drummers within the knowledge of boy'. While 'they would much have preferred being Company buglers' they were thankful enough that they were allowed to go at all. When it came to battle the Fore and Aft did not distinguish itself, and when the Ghazis came at them the inexperienced battalion ran, the band with them. Jakin and Lew would have none of it and, emboldened somewhat by a water canteen filled with rum, stepped out onto the plain, Jakin with side drum and Lew with fife. They made 'a hideous hash of the first bars of the *British Grenadiers*' but eventually 'settled into full swing and the boys kept shoulder to shoulder, Jakin banging the drum as one possessed.' The Ghazis were greatly impressed by the display and when Jakin 'beat the long roll of the Assembly' it was enough to bring the Fore and Aft to their senses and in they went, as they should have done before. But the two boys had gone down in the first volley 'as the Fore and Aft came forward, the maledictions of their officers in their ears, and in their hearts the shame of open shame. Half the men had seen the drummers die ...'[20]

Considering that all of these boys had to carry the regulation side drum of the time, it was more normal to see boys enlist in their mid-teens, although there are plenty of examples of them being much younger. Many of these boys were also born into the regiment in which they subsequently enlisted. Archibald Brunton was ten years old when enlisted as a drummer in the 58th Foot at Quebec in 1761 and he was very likely the son of Drummer Thomas Brunton, who was then 50 years old and had enlisted at the age of 21.[21] Drummer Thomas Flynn, only 15 years old when he won the Victoria Cross in 1857, was born into the 64th Foot, his father being also one Drummer Thomas Flynn. Poor young Flynn; for much of the remainder of his service he was in trouble in some form or other and spent a total of 586 days in detention or prison until his discharge in 1869, having also been reduced from drummer to private the year before.[22]

The Dix Noonan Webb sale referred to above comprised some 188 medals of British Army 'musicians', the majority being drummers and buglers who served at some time during the 19th century. In many cases the service records of the medal awardees are known and this presents us with some useful data about ages of enlistment. There is a smattering of 12- and 13-year-olds as well as 18-year-olds and above but many, where ages are known, show boys having been attested at the age of 14 or 15. Of all of these it is rare to find any boy being promoted to the rank of drummer before his 15th birthday. One of the exceptions was Guardsman Darkin, the seven-year-old, who was promoted to drummer when he was 13 in 1834. At the other end of the scale, John Slattie enlisted in the 42nd Highlanders at the age of 18 in 1859 and was not promoted to drummer until he was 39, going on to be a drummer with the Black Watch in Egypt and the Sudan between 1882 and 1885.[23]

The guiding principles for the recruitment of drummers and fifers in the 18th century were contained in a booklet written by Captain Bennett Cuthbertson of the 5th Foot and published in Dublin in 1768. *A System for the Compleat Interior Management and Œconomy of a Battalion of Infantry* included an entire chapter on the 'Qualifications Necessary in a Drum and Fife-Major, and the Appointment of Drummers and Fifers'. This neatly encapsulates the realities of the time and is worth quoting at length:

> A handsome set of Drummers, who perform their Beatings well, being one of the ornaments of shew of a Battalion, care must be taken to inlist none, but such as promise a genteel figure, when arrived at maturity; and as few, when past fourteen years of age, attain to any great perfection on the Drum, active, ingenious lads, with supple joints, and under that age, should be only chosen: of this sort, the Soldier's children in most Regiments can afford a sufficient supply; and if so, a preference is undoubtedly to be given to them, for the sake of serving the father (if he deserves it) and because such boys, from being bred in the Regiment from their infancy, have a natural affection and attachment to it, and are seldom induced to desert, having no other place to take shelter at.

> Boys much under fourteen, unless they are remarkably stout, are rather an incumbrance to a Regiment (especially on Service) as they are in general unable to bear fatigue, or even carry their Drums upon a march ...

> The finest children that can be had, should always be chosen for the Fifers, and as their duty is not very laborious, it matters not how young they are taken, when strong enough to fill the Fife, without endangering their constitutions: if proper boys can be selected in the Regiment, it will answer best, otherwise, pains must be taken, to search the country for them: the advantage of being so particular in this point, will be very striking, when these lads advance in years, as it is probable that in them, a Regiment is rearing so many fine Recruits; and from this little nursery, if proper attention is shewn to their morals and education, there is the greatest reason to hope, that some excellent non-commission-officers may one day or other be produced ...

> Unless the size of a Battalion is remarkably tall, a set of Drummers and Fifers exceeding five feet, seven inches, is rather a disadvantage to its appearance, therefore, when they grow beyond that height, and are strong in proportion to it, the most advisable method is turning them into the Ranks; to be prepared for which, they should on first entering the Regiment, be engaged for Soldiers ...[24]

Something of the character expected of them was exposed in an anonymous pamphlet of 1782 and entitled *Advice to the Officers of the British Army.*

This tongue-in-cheek document contained some additional hints for the drummer, which is also not a little fruity in the advice it gives:

> By your profession you are evidently destined to make a noise in the world; and your party-coloured coat and drum carriage, like the zone of *Venus* ... makes you appear a pretty fellow in the eyes of the ladies. So that you may always, if not over-modest (which I own is not often the failing of gentlemen of your calling), be sure of bringing off a girl from every quarter. After infecting her with a certain disease, and selling her clothes, you may introduce her to the officers ... This will at least ensure you the thanks of the surgeon and his mate.
>
> As it is necessary that a soldier should know all the uses of his arms, permit me to observe to you, that a drum and its appurtenances, in the hands of a clever fellow, answer many good purposes besides that of being beaten on. Should a flock of geese or ducks obstruct your line of march, two or three may be safely and secretly lodged in it; and the drum case will hold peas, beans, apples and potatoes, when the haversack is full.
>
> You must inform yourself of the meaning of the different beats of the drum; and endeavour to conform to the original intention of them. Thus, *reveiller* signifies to wake. Therefore, in performing this part of your duty in garrison, you must continue beating, not only till you have awakened the sentinels and the officer of the guard, but also till you have roused all the neighbouring inhabitants.[25]

Our anonymous author of 1782, Kipling's two fiends one hundred years later and Drummer Flynn in between seem to be telling us that the drummers and buglers, young and old, were no angels. When John Lucy and his brother were settling into the depot of the Royal Irish Rifles in Belfast in 1912 one of the buglers on the depot's permanent staff made it very clear that beer and cigarettes would be the key to him helping with the recruits' adjustment to army life. That 'he was a drunkard' was apparent and when, one pay-day, the recruits 'raised about eighteen hard-earned shillings' to allow the bugler to go home on leave following the death of his mother he just drank the proceeds. 'The next morning [they] were startled by the notes of the "Rouse" alarmingly near, [the bugler] too drunk to get up, but conscientiously blowing his instrument out through an open window; with his legs and the lower part of his body still in bed.'[26] Boys, individually and especially collectively will play up and it was the job of the drum major or the bandmaster to keep them under control, which could mean administering corporal punishment. The author recalls a conversation in 1980 with Major Matt Guymer.

Given into care by his destitute parents in the 1930s he enlisted as a boy trumpeter in the 12th Lancers at the age of 14. High jinks in the barrack room ended up with him pinioning the trumpet major to the door with a lance, which Boy Guymer had hurled from the other end of the room. This got him six of the best from the cane, delivered with vigour by the wounded senior NCO!

In the latter part of the 18th century some regiments made efforts to enlist black drummers. This coincided with something of a craze for employing 'Turkish' musicians, although many modern writers and some contemporary documents too readily confuse 'negro' bandsmen with drummers. But from 1759 a clear example of the ready employment of black drummers can be found in the 29th Foot. At the surrender of Guadeloupe to the British in 1759 Admiral Edward Boscawen obtained eight or ten black boys and took them to England with him in order to provide his brother, then commanding the 29th, with black drummers. 'Fifteen years later the regiment had ten black drummers, at least three of whom were survivors of the original group. The black drummers of the 29th always came in for high praise ... They "beat and play well", said a major-general in 1774, and another said the same in 1791 ... In 1821 there were "4 men of colour" in the band, and three years later it was reported that 11 vacancies in the band were "reserved for black boys, who are on their way from Africa for this purpose".[27] While this confusion between bandsmen and drummers is apparent the surviving records give details of 41 of these men who served between the early 1760s and to as late as 1843. Many of them were shown as drummers and not bandsmen on the muster rolls, although, as was common, many may well have been originally held on the strength of the band before attaining sufficient age to be a company drummer. As drummers they did what was expected of them at the time. One Thomas Walker, listed as serving as a drummer in 1765, was present at the so-called Boston Massacre in March 1770 when he was listed as a drummer in Thomas Preston's company in the 29th. At least six of them were present with the 29th aboard Admiral Lord Howe's ships when he defeated the French fleet in the Atlantic on the Glorious First of June 1794. And a number were also present with the 29th throughout the battles of the Peninsular War, with three of them still being alive in 1847 when the Military General Service Medal was approved for issue. Peter Askins, a nine-year-old boy from St Domingo when he enlisted in Berkshire in 1800, received his medal with five bars for the battles of Rolica, Vimiera, Talavera, Busaco and Albuhera.[28]

We have to remember that when Admiral Boscawen procured those black boys for his brother slavery was still a major feature of Britain's empire in the Americas. A Major J. T. Gorman, writing to the *Sunday Times* in 1924, stated 'There are frequent records of the colonel presenting a slave to the regiment to act as a drummer.'[29] Boscawen may well have been encouraged by the example of the 38th Foot, a regiment that had languished in the West Indies since 1707 and, by sheer necessity, had recruited freed slaves into its ranks. The 38th still had three black drummers when it finally departed Antigua in 1765.[30] During the 1790s evidence suggests that all the drummers of the 7th Royal Fusiliers were black and in 1796 a black drummer of the 63rd (West Suffolk) Regiment, by the name of William Russell, found himself committed to Ipswich Gaol.[31] Black drummers were not a universal feature of infantry regiments but those who served appear more likely to have been free men or freed slaves, although their forced enlistment during the 18th century cannot be discounted. They seemed to have had a reputation for fine drumming and were not simply a fashionable novelty, as some of the black bandsmen may have been. Their presence in the English militia would suggest that a number of black men present in England voluntarily joined the army. It is suggested too that the tendency to this day for bass and tenor drummers to wear animal skins is down to the fashion in the 18th and early 19th centuries of dressing black bandsmen, who were often identified as 'black-a-moors', 'after a barbaric fashion in brilliant colours, tinselled turbans and the skins of wild beasts'.[32] Why the presence of black drummers and musicians diminished markedly from about the 1820s is open to conjecture. The abolition of slavery throughout the British Empire, enacted in 1834, may well have played its part, together with growing awareness during the preceding couple of decades and more of the rightful place in society of black people.

From the statistical evidence and from the intimations of writers such as Cuthbertson of the 5th Foot it is clear that drummers, even enlisted as such, did not necessarily remain drummers. Drummer boys might hope to rise to the rank of fully fledged drummer at the age of 18 and be paid as such. The most able and trusted could become orderly drummers to the commanding officer, a post of critical importance when the drum was in the ascendant as a signalling instrument and also beyond this time when an orderly drummer or bugler was retained at the side of the commanding officer while all other drummers would be given altogether different duties. Drummers could also be promoted as such within their corps, establishments allowing for two corporal drummers and a drum major. Some, following the establishment of the Army School of Music in 1857, could even become bandmasters. One such was William Clark, who enlisted as a boy in the 106th Bombay Light Infantry in 1877 and a year later, having reached the age of 15, went into the bugle section of the battalion. The 106th became the 2nd Battalion the Durham Light Infantry in 1881 and Clark rose to become the battalion's sergeant bugler in 1885. In 1890, after just 13 years' service, he went off to Kneller Hall and on successful completion of his course became WO1 Bandmaster of the 1st Battalion the East Surrey Regiment.[33]

But many boy drummers and buglers, once they had reached 18, passed into the ranks which, while they would suffer a reduction in pay, would afford them better opportunities for advancement. The aforementioned Drummer John Shipp, who was to rise through the ranks, twice, to end his service a lieutenant in the 87th (Prince of Wales's Own Irish) Regiment, wrote in his memoirs that he 'begged of [the captain] that I might be removed from the drummers to the ranks. I did not like the appellation drum-boy. … if a drummer had attained the age of Methuselah, he would never acquire any other title than drum-boy … In about a week after having made this request I was transferred from the drummer's room, and promoted to the rank of corporal.'[34]

After the experience of the Anglo–Boer War young boys were excluded from the ranks on active service and, while boys were still able to deceive recruiting officers as to their real age during the Great War, the official employment of boy soldiers and thus drummer boys in front-line service was at an end. Yet even after the abolition of boy service the junior soldier training units that existed between 1959 and 1993, that took in 16-year-old recruits, remained a ready source of drummers and buglers for the infantry. They were not permitted to embark on active service below the age of 17 and a half and that age was later changed to 18. But, whether they were men or boys, drummers occupied a special, and even privileged, position in the army and drummers and buglers remain something of the darlings of their battalions to this day.

Their role model in everything and, at times, their surrogate father was their drum major or bugle major. Some aspects of their early service were mentioned in Chapter 3 and their presence in a regiment has been constant, since the very foundation of the British Army and before, although their position on a regiment's establishment does not appear to have been formalised until the early 18th century. They were expected to be expert at all of the drummer's skills and more, for they were expected to instruct their drummers in everything that was expected of them. In this they were, at times, assisted by fife majors. The drum majors would all have been drummers originally and Thomas Simes advised that 'They should be men whose regularity, sobriety, good conduct and honesty can most strictly be depended upon; that are most remarkable clean and neat in their dress, that have an approved ear and taste for music and a good method of teaching without speaking too harshly to the youth or hurrying them on too fast.'[35]

In 1881 drum majors were retitled sergeant drummers and this designation persisted until it was reversed in 1928. This provided greater flexibility in their appointment as the position could henceforth be held by a good corporal drummer all the way through to a warrant officer. Their role was unchanging and a typical set of battalion standing orders, drawn from Queen's or King's Regulations, included:

1. The sergeant-drummer has the superintendence of the drummers and the acting-drummers, and will report all irregularities, etc., to the Adjutant.
2. He is responsible that all bugle calls for parades, 'Reveille,' 'Retreat,' 'Tattoo,' etc., are sounded at the proper time.
3. The drums and band are commanded by the sergeant-drummer on parade and he is responsible for marching them where required, but at all other times the band is under the particular direction of the Bandmaster or sergeant.
4. The sergeant-drummer will always be present at practice, and will exact the strictest attention from the drummers thereat.

5. He will attend when the drums play at 'Reveille,' 'Retreat,' and 'Tattoo.'
6. The sergeant-drummer is answerable to the Adjutant, for the discipline, good conduct, and correct appearance of the drummers, and for the cleanliness of their barrack-rooms.
7. He will pay the greatest attention to the dress and general turnout of the drummers, who should be an example in these respects to the whole Battalion.[36]

Off duty, drummers, fifers and, later, buglers, were a ready means in providing entertainment and in accompanying song in barracks and on campaign. But, aside from his activities on the field of battle, on the march or in regulating the day, the drummer had other important duties to perform. Because the British Army, for the greater part of its history, maintained a volunteer status, recruiting was a constantly essential activity if the strength of the army was to be maintained. It was, and still is, a struggle and it is no wonder that, in his readily identifiable and more flamboyant dress and with his drum and fife, the drummer was a natural choice for recruiting duty. The plagiarist Thomas Simes, in his collected instructions for young officers of 1776, reproduced a typical beating order of the time, which authorised the recruiting officer 'by beat of drum or other wise, to raise so many volunteers in any country or part of our Kingdom of Great Britain …'[37] These were, in effect, Royal warrants and, indeed, similar warrants were used to raise new regiments of foot, invariably with the accompanying 'beat of drum'.

Unashamedly, recruiting parties used their drummers and fifers, who were invariably young boys to heighten the appeal of the whole thing, to 'drum up' interest. Young Shipp wrote how 'One autumn morning in the year 1794 … the shrill notes of a fife, and the hollow sound of a distant drum, struck on my active ear … and I scampered off to see the soldiers … The pretty little, well-dressed, fifer was the principal object of my notice. His finery and shrill music were sufficient attractions in themselves, but what chiefly caught my fancy was the size of this musical warrior, for he was little bigger than the drum he stood by.'[38] Earlier than this James Miller, who enlisted as a teenager in the 15th Foot in 1756, reckoned that 'From the earliest recollection, the hearing of a drum beat, set the heart on fire! A soldier, in my Idea, must be the first of mortals, being the guardian of his country.'[39]

Music was to be an effective inducement to enlisting for many years, although many a 'redcoat lived to regret the snare of the siren drum which ostensibly "leads him to pleasure." as well as to fight.'"[40] Lewis Winstock further expanded:

> Music also proved valuable in maintaining the spirits of the Johnny Raws who took the shilling under the influence of the spirit-stirring drum, the recruiting sergeant's outrageous patter, or, not too rarely, an excess of drink. A lieutenant of the 31st Regiment shepherding some hundred wild Irish from Portsmouth to their base at Ashford in Kent kept them together by playing their native airs on his flute. Although, as he confessed, 'I was no great proficient,' the Irish were as enchanted as the children of Hamelin.[41]

As the 19th century progressed the relative crudeness of these recruiting parties gave way to more extravagant military spectacle as a means to encourage enlistment. The presence of regimental bands across the country provided a ready means to demonstrate military prowess and in this duty the drummers and fifers were an important augmentation as they gave a heightened degree of military might than the mere delicate music of the bands. There was added value too for 'Military spectacle simultaneously presented a cautionary threat and an attraction to the civilian population – it helped the military in its role of maintaining public order by conveying the idea of strength and military coherence.'[42] The irony, again, was that the public enjoyed the whole image of the military while still abhorring the army itself.

There were less welcome duties too. Flogging had been a standard punishment in the British Army but was greatly curtailed by order in 1858; ten years later flogging in peacetime was forbidden by Act of Parliament. In 1881 it was abolished altogether under the new Army Discipline Act, which also finally did away with the annual Mutiny Act. Before its abolition flogging was delivered by the drummers, supervised by the drum major, with other drummers beating out the timing, 25 lashes at a time in slow time. Lieutenant Barker of the 4th (King's Own) entered in his diary at Boston on 14 August 1775 the record of proceedings of a court-martial, the detail showing that two private soldiers of the 35th Regiment, found guilty of stealing flour from a store, were sentenced to receive 500 lashes and 300 lashes respectively, to be administered 'by the Drummers of the Regiment to which [they] belong.'[43] This was not necessarily the case and Rifleman Harris of the 95th while in the Peninsula remembered that 'the drummers of the 9th regiment were the inflictors of the lash.'[44]

Drum majors in 1778 were advised by Thomas Simes 'always to have with you your apparatus for punishing, as it is often found necessary to hold regimental court-martials at the drum-head.'[45] There is evidence that this 'apparatus' – the cat-o'-nine-tails – was made by the drummers themselves, from drumsticks and whipcord.[46] The viciousness of this punishment cannot be underestimated and it is said that drum majors stood behind the drummers ready to beat them with their canes should the flogging be poorly dealt.[47] The anonymous author of *Advice to the Officers of the British Army* in 1782 appealed to drum majors, again somewhat tongue-in-cheek, 'at a punishment [not to] fail to exercise your rattan on your drummers, whether they favour the delinquent or not. It will keep them to their duty.'[48] But, given that the punished, unless they had committed some particularly heinous crime against their fellow soldiers, were all comrades in arms, some leniency may have been possible. Our anonymous writer also enjoined the drummers 'When ordered to put the sentence of a Court-martial into execution [to] do it according to your opinion of the matter; and, if the prisoner should, whilst in custody, have treated you to a pot of beer, or to a dram, you know how to be grateful.'[49]

There was further advice against allowing left-handed drummers to inflict the lash due to the additional, and 'unnecessary torture' this would inflict by cutting across the stripes inflicted by right-handed drummers and, if this humiliation was not enough, soldiers sentenced additionally to be discharged with ignominy were drummed out of the barracks or encampment. The regiment would be formed up to witness the execution of the sentence and, once the prisoner had had his buttons and shoulder straps cut off,

> prisoner and escort marched down the ranks while the regimental drummers and fifers played the Rogues March. ... The climax was his ejection from the barrack gates, followed by his possessions, and a kick to the backside administered by the smallest drummer of them all. Turning an unwelcome guest out of doors became known in civvy street as 'John Drum's Entertainment' as a result.[50]

Fortescue quoted from papers describing the 1727 siege of Gibraltar, when a deserter and traitor from the 26th Foot was whipped around the fortress 'after which he was drummed out of town with the Rogue's March & rope about his neck' before being placed aboard ship to be placed into slavery in the plantations.[51] In the days when there were few barracks this must have been a common enough sight, especially as similar punishment was meted out to the less savoury elements of society who lurk on the fringes of any place where soldiers might establish a camp or were housed. The 47th Foot in garrison in Boston in 1775 escorted a pedlar out of the place, having first tarred and feathered him, with a fife and drum playing a rogues' march. When the escort passed the residence of the Commander-in-Chief he thought merely that the soldiers were 'drumming a Bad Woman through the streets'.[52] This 'Rogues' March' was clearly a well-known piece as the soldiers gave it words, as with all the beatings and calls:

> Fifty I got for selling my coat, Fifty for selling my blanket,
> If ever I 'list for a soldier again, The devil will be my sergeant.

The musicians of the infantry regiments had a role in just about every element of military life and how welcome their appearance and their playing must have been on many an occasion. In the endless days of a soldier's existence across the garrisons of the Empire both drum and fife – especially the fife – would provide entertainment and the musical accompaniment to the soldiers' songs, as Francis Markham observed way back at the beginning of the 17th century:

> When his duties in the Field are finished, if then being retired into the Tent he have the other artificiall and Musicall straines wherewith to steal away the minds and ears of his hearers, it will be a great honour to him. Neither for mine owne part have I heard more sweet or more solemn melodie than that which the Drumme and Flute hath afforded.'[53]

Amid the ever-present and all too frequent deaths by disease the beat of the muffled drum and the haunting Dead March of the fife would see the soldier laid to rest in solemn ritual amongst too many of his comrades: 'The Drumme with a sad solemnitie must bring him to his grave. For it is the only mourner for the lost and the greatest honour of Funerals.'[54]

CHAPTER 12

The Great Wars of the 20th Century

War had, till then, been regarded as a glorious thing, a thing of bugles and flashing bayonets.

There is such a great difference between the seemingly methodical nature of battlefield manoeuvres of the time before the great world wars of the 20th century and everything since that the very idea of a continued role for the bugler, let alone the drummer, would appear over-imaginative. For much of that century formed drums and bugle platoons featured ever more prominently in ceremonial events and displays and became an important addition to military band concerts and music programmes, even in wartime. But it is true to say that on the battlefield the use of either instrument was a rarity. There are, unsurprisingly, no known examples of the use of the drum in the field but there are some of the bugle – and, of course, played by drummers in so many cases. Drummers and buglers certainly retained their role of regulating the day and providing musical accompaniment to the march and on parade. Indeed, for the provision of music they came into their own once again with the gradual demise of regimental bands after the Second World War, as will be related in the next chapter.

Certainly for the British Army the progression of the Anglo-Boer War provided the writing on the wall that presaged the entire removal of the 'musick' from the battlefield. It might have come about earlier, had the lessons of the last great conflict between major European powers – the Franco-Prussian War – been absorbed properly. The shocking slaughter of charging close-packed French and Prussian infantry and cavalry at the hands of well-protected, if not entrenched, defenders armed with the first truly effective breech-loading rifles and early machine guns, should have seen the evolution of entirely new tactical methods for prosecuting the attack. But the eventual outcome, especially for the French, was an even greater emphasis on the attack by waves of men advancing 'shoulder to shoulder to the sound of drum and bugle'.[1] The problem was – and this was a sound prediction – that French and Imperial German tactical theorists predicted future war as one of masses and if a decision on the battlefield was to be effected, which could never be achieved by skulking inside fortresses (a lesson learnt very painfully by the French), then a means had to be applied to get these conscript masses off their bellies and to close with the enemy. The French 1875 regulations had forbidden close-order formations, for that is what they were, from coming within range of effective enemy fire. The infantry 'mass' was instead to be preceded by a strong skirmish line and this line was to be fed by the supporting columns to create sufficient concentration to constitute the attack. While the British Army, having experienced nothing of the sort of fighting that the French had experienced, was developing its assault tactics along similar lines, their sensible execution in the face of the Boer was written off by French commentators as 'acute Transvaalitis', which can be translated as 'paralysis by fire'.[2] Instead, therefore, and under the direction of General Joseph Joffre, the French Army entered the Great War very firmly in favour of the offensive at all costs – *l'offensive à outrance*. Infantry, in their blue coats and red trousers, would advance *en masse* with drums and bugles sounding the advance; *élan vital* would carry the day.[3] The character of the French Army was certainly impressive and the effects of the shared victory on the Aisne in mid-September 1914 led, apparently, to a battalion of the Worcestershire Regiment requesting permission 'to have French trumpets and drums, a band of French buglers and drummers' accompany them on the march. This went on for some months, the march being led by 'a little French light infantry regimental sergeant major who could blow the bugle and sound the march even better than his men.' This seems somewhat unlikely and the French author, the sociologist Marcel Mauss, did note that 'the unfortunate regiment of tall Englishmen could not march' to the French style and the Worcestershire Regiment was 'forced to give up its French buglers.'[4]

The war role of drummers and buglers did indeed change forever with the onset of the Great War. But in its early battles, which in character did in fact look more like the Franco-Prussian War, that change was not immediately evident. While drums, bugles, and fifes, helped march the British infantry up and down the roads of France and Flanders and elsewhere between 1914 and 1918, the coming of mechanisation and portable wireless post-war and the universality of these modern technical innovations by the onset of the Second World War largely finished them off for signalling purposes – almost.

There is a wealth of photographic evidence of the British infantry astride the French and Belgian *pavé*, the battalions accompanied by their drummers and buglers. What is, perhaps, surprising is that this equipment continued to be supplied throughout the war and this can only add emphasis to the importance of these instruments to unit *esprit de corps*, if not as any means of signalling. This might be assumed for the Regular battalions and the Territorial battalions, especially those that were to be classified as 'first line' when the Territorial Force was expanded in late 1914. But all battalions appear to have been so equipped and sufficient men therefore found and trained to play. There exists a very atmospheric photograph of the 8th Battalion the North Staffordshire Regiment on the march near Estaires in France in the early autumn of 1915, the battalion's drummers with their drums slung on their slings over their backs. One drummer is carrying his bugle and the bass drum is being lugged along by two men.[5] This battalion was a Service, or Kitchener (K2), battalion, K2, indicating the second tranche of volunteers raised in September 1914 for the duration, so it might be assumed that drums, bugles and fifes were provided on the equipment table across the infantry, despite the vastness of the supply problem. Whether or not the instruments were supplied at War Office expense is unknown; probably so, eventually. But battalions like the 8th North Staffords and their brothers in the 7th North Staffords benefitted from the patronage of Major Cecil Wedgwood, of that great Staffordshire potteries family and in 1914 chairman of Josiah Wedgwood and Sons. The regimental history recorded that 'it was hopeless to expect that the minor needs of a new unit could receive prompt attention. It was clear that some ready money would be essential to the well-being of the new Battalion. This was promptly provided by a donation of £150 from Mrs. Godfrey Wedgwood, followed early in 1915 by another £150 ...'[6] We cannot be sure that some of this money was spent on drums, but it would be safe to assume that this could have been the case.

Sufficient, if not extensive, anecdotal evidence exists too that described the activities of these drummers and buglers on the march and their moral effect. There is also plenty of evidence that the regimental bands played an important role when the men were resting and beyond the range of the bulk of the German artillery. One such example is from the 2nd Battalion the West Yorkshire Regiment. When the battalion came out of the trenches in November 1916 during the last days of the pitiless offensive on the Somme it was placed in a tented camp just five miles behind the front line. Lieutenant Sydney Rogerson, commanding B Company, wrote that they were enjoying a 'post-prandial snooze' after a good lunch when:

> From this we were awakened by the sound of music, and hastened to find the band of one of the Guards regiments playing in an adjoining camp. This phenomenon was proving quite a draw, and men were trekking from all points of the compass to witness a spectacle so unexpected albeit so welcome. There was something curious to us in the appearance of these trim, well-drilled bandsmen, so reminiscent even in their khaki of the Mall or the Horse Guards, as there was in the civilised or civilising effect of their music in this vast heap populated with human ants. It gave us each a secret glow of satisfaction to feel that such things could still be, to know that people were still being trained for other things than digging, bombing or bayonet-fighting. We stayed till the performance ended, then turned back to our tents with a lighter step. Music hath power as well as charms.[7]

The corps (plural) of drums played a very important part in keeping morale up, especially when units marched up to take their place in the front line and when they came out of the line, should that seem appropriate. Private Albert Conn, 8th Battalion the Devonshire Regiment, another Kitchener battalion and raised in the first, K1, tranche in

August 1914, recalled marching into the line on the Somme in 1916: 'The old drum and fifes beat out the tune of The Farmer's Boy [the tune of the regimental quick march] as A Coy ... heavily laden with packs and ammunition, made their way through the village [Meaulte] on to the straight road leading to Bécordal and Fricourt.'[8]

While no one fully predicted the siege warfare that gripped the Western Front from late 1914 onwards and the changes in tactics this would force, the emphasis on movement in all pre-war training combined with a lack of experience, especially amongst the Territorial Force, led to somewhat romanticised predictions of what would prevail. One of those Territorial battalions – the 15th (County of London) Battalion the London Regiment and better known as the Civil Service Rifles – had sent very few men to South Africa, being constrained, as were all Territorial units, by the then terms of service for volunteers. Thus their arrival in France with the 47th London Division in March 1915, even with half a year of war passed, caused some disappointment. Their regimental history recorded that, on their initiation:

> There is no doubt that this first visit to the front line was productive of a sense of disappointment. War had, till then, been regarded as a glorious thing, a thing of bugles and flashing bayonets, of courage in hand-to-hand encounters, and above all, of excitement.[9]

Until experience had been gained in the first few months of the war the battalions, brigades and divisions embarking for the Continent could be guided only by the extant training regimes and manuals. The British Army had trained for a war where movement on the battlefield was expected and when conditions stagnated and trench warfare became the universal experience on the Western Front it also took time to train for these new conditions too. Training for *the* war is invariably a somewhat different prospect than training for *a* war and it should be noted that when in 1917 the German withdrawal to the Hindenburg Line provided a sudden opportunity for the British Army to advance, the appropriate tactical methods were found wanting. This happened again in the advance to victory in 1918.

In 1914 the army's field regulations continued to provide instructions that, to Richard Holmes, looked 'no different in principle to the infantry tactics in vogue when the line was red rather than khaki.'[10] This is largely true and the most up-to-date version of *Field Service Regulations Part 1 – Operations*, published in 1909 and reprinted with amendments in 1912, does give a feel of lines of men, musketry, movement and the lurking threat of cavalry. But there is also a feel of experience and common sense and, if officers went off to war in August 1914 brandishing their swords and the gunners of the field artillery were trained to bring their guns to fire in close support of the infantry, this was what was expected. The *Field Service Regulations* contained the overarching doctrine for all training and operations and the employment of infantry was made very clear:

> The essence of infantry tactics consists of breaking down the enemy's resistance by the weight and direction of its fire, and then completing his overthrow by assault ... Troops under cover, unless enfiladed, can seldom be forced to retire by fire alone ... To drive an enemy from the field, assault, or the immediate threat of it, is almost always necessary.[11]

The reality of war in 1914 brought very major changes to tactics but the principle that decision on the battlefield could only be achieved through attack held true, as it has always done and, therefore, had to be carried through. That buglers would still have a role, albeit limited, is not surprising and the updated 1914 *Infantry Training Manual* – published coincidentally just over a week after the outbreak of the war – emphasised, much as before:

> The object of the infantry in the attack is ... to get to close quarters as quickly as possible ... The commander who decides to order the assault will order the charge to be sounded, the call will at once be taken up by all buglers, and all neighbouring units will join in the charge as quickly as possible. During the assault the men will cheer, bugles be sounded, and pipes played.[12]

The infantry battalions certainly had the necessary equipment in the field with them. The 1914 *Field Service Manual*, as amended for infantry battalions of the expeditionary force in October 1914, contained the entire list of stores and equipment authorised for all battalions as well as the detailed organisation tables. It showed that infantry battalions were authorised on establishment for one sergeant drummer/bugler and

16 drummers or buglers, at four per rifle company. Under the heading of additional equipment to be carried by dismounted men, the list shows eight bugles, one base drum, eight side drums, eight flutes (six B flat and two F) and two piccolos (one E flat and one F). Rifle and light infantry battalions were authorised to carry 17 bugles 'but are not entitled to any of the other musical instruments.'[13] This latter point may have been the case but there is sufficient photographic evidence to show that at least some rifle and light infantry regiments had drums. Drummers and buglers were instructed not to carry arms or ammunition in war – not even the dainty 1895 Pattern sword – and it is worth adding too that the band sergeant was to be left at base for 'On mobilisation the band of a Line battalion is broken up: those bandsmen not required as stretcher bearers being distributed among the companies.'[14]

Another relevant manual was *Trumpet and Bugle Sounds for the Army*, also reissued in 1914. The first edition of this book was published in 1895 and there is very little difference between the two. The 1914 book, like its predecessor, contained in the main the many different regimental calls and the large number of 'routine', or camp and quarter, calls. There are 46 different calls for infantry and mounted infantry in camp, including one call for cyclists, but the bugle field calls are limited to just five (as in 1895): 'Continue or commence firing', 'Stand fast or cease fire', 'Execute orders received', 'Charge (for bugle and drum)', and 'Alarm'. It is of particular interest that the drum call for the charge is included as this would seem extremely anachronistic even for a 1914 that did not anticipate what was to come, but the drum was also included in the 1966 edition! We will examine below the realities and practicalities that the war brought and the British armies in France, Belgium and elsewhere undoubtedly issued guidance and instruction fit for the situation. But the War Office specifically limited calls in an instruction issued on 18 May 1915:

> The following trumpet and bugle sounds are to be strictly adhered to on all occasions, and no others used in His Majesty's service. General Officers Commanding, may at their discretion, order all or any of the peace calls [meaning routine calls in camp] to be used on active service: Continue or commence firing; Stand fast or cease fire; Execute orders received.[15]

Of particular note is the absence of the calls for the charge and for the alarm; clearly neither were seen to have a place on the battlefield of the day. It does appear, however, that the bugle for signalling some commands – those limited to the five available – was used in the first few months of the war. To this end we might assume that commanding officers, at least, had alongside them an orderly bugler. In the defining battle of Mons on 23/24 August 1914, Rifleman Thomas O'Donnell, 2nd Battalion the Royal Irish Fusiliers, remembered later that 'Many of us were bare but for our trousers availing ourselves to the warm sunshine to wash and dry our shirts and socks after our long tramp through France and Belgium, [when] our bugles got orders to sound the stand to arms.'[16] Certainly this use of the bugle to get the men to assemble rapidly would seem like common sense but Rifleman O'Donnell also gave us one brief but telling example of the bugle sounding the charge. On 26 August the British Expeditionary Force stood its ground briefly to check the German onslaught. At Landrecies, 'The word was passed along the line that we were to charge. When our buglers sounded the charge, everyone went charging forward yelling like madmen' – just as the regulations demanded! However successful this tactic was that day as 'the Germans broke and ran like frightened hares in terror of hounds', their bugles were almost entirely silenced thereafter for the assault.[17]

In place of the bugle the voice was preeminent, backed up by the whistle, which every British infantry officer carried on his Sam Browne belt. So it was to their surprise that they heard the bugles of the attacking German infantry in those mass assaults that characterised German tactics at the outset of the war. At Mons, before the British Expeditionary Force conducted its epic retreat, the crude mass assault methods of the Germans met their comeuppance in the well-aimed and rapidly delivered musketry of the British infantry. German assaults were invariably preceded by intense shrapnel bombardment from German field guns and John Lucy, now Corporal, also of the 2nd Battalion the Royal Irish Rifles, recalled that, mid-afternoon on 23 August:

> Finally the shelling ceased, and we put up our heads to breathe more freely. Then we heard conch-like sounds – strange bugle calls. The German infantry, which had approached during the shelling, was in sight and about to attack us ...

> In answer to the German bugles or trumpets came the cheerful sound of our officers' whistles, and the riflemen, casting aside the amazement of their strange trial, sprang into action.[18]

The detailed war history of the Grenadier Guards contained further examples of this German trait, noting that, in late September 1914 'Another indication of a coming attack was the playing of the band [sic] of some German regiment, which was heard on one or two occasions – evidently as a stimulant for the men who were to take part.'[19] Even as late as the first battle of Ypres, with the Germans still attempting to bludgeon their way through the British positions by sheer weight of numbers, bugles were still in evidence. On the night of 2 November the Grenadiers and the 2nd Battalion the Oxfordshire and Buckinghamshire Light Infantry repelled such an attack when 'the enemy advanced with a beating of drums and blowing of horns.'[20] There are further similar examples in British regimental records of the sound of German bugle calls and that the German infantry had their bugles with them, like their British counterparts, is demonstrated in at least one published German account. Captain Walter Bloem, a company commander in the 12th Brandenburg Grenadiers (*Grenadierregiment Prinz Carl von Preussen (2. Brandenburg) Nr. 12*) wrote his account of Mons in 1916 and recorded that, pinned down by British rifle fire, alongside him was 'Pohlenz, my bugler, a bullet hole through the bugle slung on his back.'[21] Interestingly too, Bloem wrote that he and his non-commissioned officers used their whistles, though to little effect. The Germans had even attempted subterfuge when, at Le Cateau on 25 August, their buglers opposite the 2nd Battalion the King's Own Yorkshire Light Infantry sounded the British call for the cease fire. The Yorkshiremen were not to be convinced because the battalion buglers had been assigned to ration-carrying fatigues.

While use of whistles was largely confined to signalling the moment of the assault in the great offensives later on, Lucy's published account indicated that controlling whistle blasts were in universal use by the Regular British Army in 1914. Of that day at Mons, which witnessed his battalion's baptism of fire, he added that 'The satisfactory sharp blasts of the directing whistles showed that our machinery of defence was working like a drill book.' And on the following day, as the great retreat got underway, he wrote that 'We donned our gear, fell in, and marched off to a succession of whistle signals,' noting too that as they got into the rhythm of the march, 'our going brought songs to our lips. Our popular *Tipperary* and *One Man Went to Mow* marked the pace of our retirement ...'[22] Lucy provided no evidence of his battalion's drums and bugles on this march but if they were not carried they would almost certainly have been stored in the battalion's main baggage to the rear. This was not necessarily a safe haven. The 1st Battalion the South Staffordshire Regiment lost at least some of its drums in the retirement of the 7th Division on 22 October 1914 at the height of the first battle of Ypres. The regimental history recorded that 'the battalion lost the greater portion of its transport ... stores, and records.' The battalion was forward in an isolated position and 'to try to get the transport away first would have given the whole show away to the enemy.'[23] At least some kit was later recovered for the Staffordshire Regiment Museum has a drum – interestingly one of the cheese drum type – and it bears the inscription: 'This drum fell into the hands of the enemy during the first battle of Ypres, October 1914, and was recaptured a few days later.'

The retreat, like all such retreats, was a desperate business and men, completely worn out through marching and fighting rearguard actions and rarely able to eat or sleep, need strong demonstrations of leadership and personal example to keep them going. The cavalry invariably had the job of screening the withdrawal of the infantry and in shepherding stragglers. A tale was told of one incident:

> The final sweep up was made late in the afternoon by Major Tom Bridges of the 4th Dragoon Guards ... In the market place at St. Quentin he found some hundreds of men lying helpless on the ground ... they were the broken remnants of two good regiments ... [and] were past hearing the word of command or persuasion. When the reason is out of action you must call to something deeper, more instinctive. Everyone who has ever marched to a band knows how music adds to your marching power without your thinking of it. Though the War Office had forgotten this, Major Bridges had not. He looked about St. Quentin, found a toy shop, bought a toy drum and two penny whistles, got two of his men to play the whistles and fastened the drum to his own belt. Then he paraded in the square, playing the British Grenadiers ... The beat of it got into the dead

men's pulses and made them soldiers again. They staggered up and followed the toy band out of the town, and down the long dark road towards Noyon.[24]

While the stark reality of fighting conditions in those early days provided very little opportunity for bugles to be used in action they continued to be carried. The commanding officer of the 2nd Ox and Bucks made a diary entry on 24 October that recorded his going forward of his battalion on the Menin Road at Ypres 'with two buglers.'[25] Drummers and buglers did continue to carry their bugles on occasion and there is evidence of them being taken ashore at Gallipoli. Two examples have emerged, both from buglers within a day or so of landing. Bugler George Bissett of the Wellington Battalion of the New Zealand Infantry Brigade was killed on 27 April 1915, two days after landing at ANZAC Cove, his commanding officer recording that 'the bugler lad' lay unburied, 'with his bugle on his back face downwards, shot in his tracks.'[26] And the day after landing at Suvla Bay on 8 August that year, Bugler Jack Griffiths of the 1st/5th Battalion the Royal Welsh Fusiliers, wrote home to say that they had had 'a proper slashing, but … I am one of the lucky ones. My bugle was fairly riddled with bullet holes but none caught me.'[27]

Even on that most fateful day of 1 July 1916, when the British Army suffered its worst casualty rate in its history with nearly 20,000 men killed, at least one bugle was used to initiate the main attack. Drummer Jack Downs of the 10th Battalion the Royal Inniskilling Fusiliers, sounded the advance for the 36th (Ulster) Division that morning at 7.30 a.m. It is perhaps indicative of the expected conditions, that few Germans were expected to survive the days of preliminary bombardment, that a bugle, or a number of bugles, were used to augment the officers' whistle blasts as the men went over the top. Martin Middlebrook, in his famous book about the first day of the Somme attack, wrote:

> At zero hour the British barrage lifted. Bugles blew the 'Advance'. Up sprang the Ulstermen and, without forming up in the waves adopted by other divisions, they rushed the German front line … By a combination of sensible tactics and Irish dash, the prize that eluded so many, the capture of a long section of the German front line, had been accomplished.[28]

There were reports too that the German defenders, protected in their deep dugouts, were summoned to their fire steps in some places by bugles. The Ulstermen were also fuelled, in part at least, by 1 July being the anniversary of the battle of the Boyne in 1690, which turned the tide against England's last Catholic king. Exactly one hundred years on from 1916 Jack Downs' bugle sounded the advance again at a centenary commemoration at Enniskillen Castle; 'few bugles could have more resonance than that belonging to Drummer Downs.'[29]

Using bugles for command and control even in the trenches was probably not that rare an event under certain circumstances. The problems of command and control, especially in the attack, were enormous in an age before efficient and lightweight wireless sets appeared on the scene. Great emphasis was placed on 'line' – telephone cable run out between all and every unit – but it was extremely vulnerable to breakage due to shellfire and flags and lamps were equally difficult to employ efficiently. Coloured rockets played their part relatively effectively but for audible signals, just voice and whistle were usually all that existed. In one attempt to overcome these deficiencies on the Somme on 4 July 1916, in a raid launched by the 1st/15th Londons, the signal for the raiding company to return was 'the Battalion call blown by buglers in the FRONT LINE, and a series of alternate red and green rockets ...'[30] The 10th Inniskillings used a bugle to sound the retire for a raiding party that captured a machine gun at Kemmel Hill during the night of 10 September 1916. Another battalion of the London Regiment – the 13th (Kensington) Battalion – had at least some buglers directly involved in trench raiding operations and late on in the war. Private John Steward wrote a near-contemporaneous account of his life in France and Flanders between 1916 and 1918 and recalled a trench raid carried out in broad daylight in early March 1918. The raiders, well practised, rushed the German trench, shot those who resisted and grabbed some prisoners: 'Then the bugler in attendance blew a blast on his horn and the boys hopped back – except one who had been killed.'[31] It may be that, as the 13th Londons and 15th Londons were in the same division that the use of bugles in this way was a divisional standing order. But the practice was likely to be more widespread and bugles were certainly a readily available means to provide a signal that could be heard above the cacophony of the front line. They were also used to warn of gas attacks and we might assume here that, despite the War Office instruction of May 1915, the call used was the 'alarm'. Father Willie Doyle, padre to the 8th Battalion the Royal Irish Fusiliers, wrote to his father in April 1917 about a gas attack one year before. Already suffering from the effects of gas and a day anointing the dying he lay down to sleep 'only to be rudely awakened at four next morning by the crash of guns and the dreaded bugle call "gas alarm, gas alarm."'[32]

Also ignoring War Office instructions, if he had ever been aware of them, on the first day of the third battle of Ypres on 31 July 1917 the commanding officer of the 1st North Staffords ordered that bugles should sound the charge when the barrage lifted off the German first line so that his men would know to get forward as rapidly as possible. Prior to the attack eight trained buglers had to be found in the battalion and when the time came all except one were wounded in the advance. This lone survivor, Drummer William Dimmelow of D Company, did get to blow the charge but was shot in the mouth, through his bugle, in the process. Many years later a subaltern in the battalion, Lieutenant Bernard Martin, wrote a particularly scathing and somewhat unfair account of this episode. An extract captures the flavour of the situation as recalled by Martin when his commanding officer asked him his opinion:

> Platoon Commanders will know the exact moment when the barrage lifts from Jehovah Trench and you'll signal to your men to charge. I want Buglers to sound the Charge at that moment … Naturally I was flattered to be consulted … but how does a subaltern tell his Commanding Officer that his proposal is balderdash? I suppose I looked blank for the CO went on enthusiastically, 'Nothing like a bugle call to stimulate courage when it's most needed.'[33]

In fact, while Bernard Martin wrote in disparaging terms, the complexities of the attack that morning and especially of the artillery barrage, meant that the lead companies were ordered to walk from their jump-off positions, staying behind their protective barrage, until the time came when the barrage lifted off the German front line. At this juncture the men had to run and the bugle was a good means to ensure they did this all together. This was not the long waves of infantry walking to their deaths that many imagine characterised all attacks on the Western Front. By the time of Third Ypres in mid-1917 infantry tactics were far advanced from the earlier years of the war. But Bernard Martin, in old age, thought that this 'barmy idea' was because the CO had been in the trenches at most a month, while we know that Captain (temporary lieutenant colonel) Vyvyan Pope had been on the Western Front since the battalion arrived there in August 1914 and, at 25, already had a Distinguished Service Order and a Military Cross to his name. This was not some old colonel simply digging out an obsolete tradition but someone trying to find a means to get his companies forward. Bernard Martin did concede, having accepted the order to find the 'eight' buglers (it was probably just four, two each for C and D Companies) and provide them with bugle and revolver practice, that the CO 'pointed out that in a crisis men tend to be unduly aware of themselves, feel isolated, and a bugle call assures them they are not acting alone, that others are called to act with them.'[34]

Perhaps the memory of one drummer can serve to draw a line under any possible universal use of bugles to control tactical manoeuvre on the Western Front, once both sides began to dig in after the fighting on the River Aisne in September 1914. As the BEF went forward and crossed the Aisne, Drummer E. L. Slaytor of the 3rd Battalion the Coldstream Guards, recalled that on 14 September they were advancing in extended order and, coming under heavy fire, were ordered to retire to form a firing line:

> We'd just started back when a shell fell between the next man and myself. We both fell to the ground [and] as I fell, the bugle I'd carried all the way through the retreat and advance slipped off my pack and fell under my chin. What a jolt it gave me! A real thump on the jaw. What with getting tangled up in the bugle cord, and the heat and excitement of the moment, I was in a fair old state. My comrade looked round and yelled, 'Chuck the bloody thing away.' That was a heinous crime of course, but I was past caring. Anyway I hadn't blown the wretched bugle since those far off days in Chelsea Barracks (only a month before!). So I tore it off and slung it as hard as I could in the direction of the German line. I don't suppose it did the Germans much harm, but it certainly relieved my feelings.[35]

Three drummers won Victoria Crosses in the Great War, although only one of these men while acting under what might be termed his principal employment. It might be recalled from earlier chapters, however, that drummers were also told off, if they were available, to assist with ammunition resupply and helping the wounded. Near Ypres on 23 October 1914 Drummer William Kenny of the 2nd Battalion the Gordon Highlanders, rescued wounded men on five occasions, having already made a name for himself by conveying messages over fire-swept ground and saving machine guns from capture. Kenny was then 34 years old and was an Irishman who had served in the Anglo–Boer War, being then recalled to the Colours on mobilisation in 1914. Also at Ypres, 23-year-old Drummer Spencer John 'Joe' Bent of the 1st Battalion the East Lancashire Regiment, won his Victoria Cross for five days of valour and leadership which culminated in him taking command of his platoon. The battalion was reeling from an attack and Bent was taking part in a general retirement when he remembered he had left a French army cornet in the trench. He returned to the front line and discovered his platoon sergeant, who told him that no orders to retire had been given. Bent then ran back to his retreating comrades and rallied them. His citation read:

> For conspicuous gallantry near Le Gheer, on the night of 1/2 November, 1914, when, after his Platoon Sergeant and Section Commander had been struck down, he took command, and with great presence of mind and coolness succeeded in holding the position. Drummer Bent had previously distinguished himself on two occasions, 22 and 24 October, by bringing up ammunition, under a heavy shell and rifle fire, and again on the 3rd November, when he brought into cover some wounded men who were lying exposed in the open.[36]

The gallant Joe Bent had joined the army as a drummer at the age of 14, having been orphaned, and was to receive the Military Medal in 1918 in addition to his VC.

The third Victoria Cross winner was Drummer Walter Ritchie of the 2nd Battalion the Seaforth Highlanders. A degree of mythology surrounds this story and there exists a dramatic artist's impression that shows Ritchie beating a drum on the German parapet during the attack by his battalion on the first day of the battle of the Somme on 1 July 1916. This would have been a very unlikely act but was given some credence when his mother told a reporter from the *Daily Telegraph* that her son had been court-martialled for taking his drum into the front line. The facts are that Ritchie, who was a pre-war Territorial in the Scottish

Rifles, had been part of the attack by his battalion at Beaumont Hamel on that fateful day. The 2nd Seaforths had gained the German trenches but were being forced out as they began to run out of ammunition and receive increasing numbers of casualties. According to his citation, Ritchie, wounded in the knee, 'on his own initiative ... stood on the parapet of the enemy trench, and, under heavy machine gun fire and bomb attacks, repeatedly sounded the "Charge", thereby rallying men of various units who, having lost their leaders, were wavering and begin-ning to retire.'[37] Ritchie had found a German bugle in the enemy trench and it was this instrument he used to great effect.

It would be improper not to also mention Bandsman Thomas Rendle of the 1st Battalion the Duke of Cornwall's Light Infantry, who was awarded the Victoria Cross for gallantry on 20 November 1914 at Ypres. Rendle was a stretcher-bearer in the battalion and spent much of that day rescuing men in the heat of battle. He is the only bandsman ever to have been awarded the VC.

There is a poignant reminder of the drummers and buglers of the armies of the British Empire on the Menin Gate at Ypres – that mag-nificent monument to some of the men who fell in Flanders in the Great War and have no known grave. The regiments of Foot Guards listed some of their drummers and seven men's names appear for the Grenadiers, Coldstream, Scots and Irish. But there are also two names from infantry battalions of the Indian Corps, killed before the Corps departed the Western Front for Mesopotamia and East Africa towards the end of 1915. They are Bugler Deokhai Rana of the 1st Battalion the 4th Gurkha Rifles, and Bugler Zaman Ali of the 40th Pathans. There is a series of photographs that show the pipes and drums of the 40th Pathans playing in a French village in July 1915.[38]

A final word on the Great War is necessary, and it is from the United States. Rather tellingly, what has been described as 'the bugle that soun-ded the end of the First World War' was sounded by an American soldier. Following the signing of the armistice in the Forest of Compiègne early in the morning of 11 November 1918, General John Pershing, com-mander of the American Expeditionary Force, ordered Private Hartley Edwards to sound 'taps' at 11.00 a.m., to signify the end of the war.

This was not without difficulty. Edwards had joined the US Army that May and had never played the bugle in his life before but was to find himself just some months later as Pershing's personal bugler. Pershing was a stern disciplinarian and Edwards nearly missed the opportunity to play his part in history:

> When a sergeant told [Edwards] to blow 'Taps' at 11:00 a.m., he pointed out that by order of General Pershing. 'Taps' was played only at funerals or for lights-out. But the sergeant convinced him that Pershing would approve of 'Taps' being played.[39]

Hartley 'Hot Lips' Edwards subsequently became something of a celebrity, playing 'Taps' again at the victory parade at the Arc de Triomphe in Paris the following year and continuing in the role of official bugler for US Army veterans for years thereafter. In 1956 he played again at the Arc de Triomphe and this time in front of the French President, Charles de Gaulle, to mark the centenary of the late President Woodrow Wilson's birth. The French President asked that this by now famous bugle be left in France but Edwards had promised it to the Smithsonian Institute, where it now resides.[40]

★

The Second World War has not a great deal to say about the use of instruments in the field but we might begin here with the proven ubiquity of the bugle in the matter of air raid precautions. General Sir David Fraser, late of the Grenadier Guards, recalled in his published memoir his time at the Guards Depot at Caterham in 1940. The almost peacetime regularity of the day was punctuated, naturally enough, by the bugle but in the summer of 1940 this was disturbed by the sounding of air raid sirens, accompanied invariably by Hurricanes taking off from nearby Kenley Airfield and the opening up of anti-aircraft guns, all to defend the approaches to London. The Guards' recruits on the drill square hoped on such occasions to hear the 'welcome "Disperse" blown on the bugles, which meant a squad being fallen in and dismissed to the air raid shelters ... before physical activity began again with the damnable blowing of "All Clear"'. If this were to happen at night the alarm was blown 'by the drummers, bicycling rapidly through barracks, handlebars controlled by left hand, bugle held to mouth by right' and all recruits moved to the nearest shelters. This, indeed, happened on young David Fraser's first night at Caterham. Laughing and chatting in their trench in the dark with the sound of gunfire and falling bombs in the distance they were suddenly barked at by an unseen senior NCO who told them in no uncertain terms:

> Pay attention, all Recruits in here! There is a raid on! Recruits will remain here until the All Clear is blown. Thereafter recruits are to return to barrackrooms fast. Any Recruit returning to shelters without orders after the blowing of the 'All Clear' will be shot for cowardice![41]

There are some isolated examples of field use and that the armies of Britain and her Empire continued to find opportunities to put on a display of drum, bugle, fife and bagpipe should not be that surprising. There was no place for a 'corps' of drums or bugles – the increasingly common vernacular for a formed platoon – in an infantry battalion mobilised for war. However, the drummers or buglers on establishment were invariably retained as a formed body as a defence platoon for battalion headquarters and good quartermasters would ensure that their instruments were, somehow, found a place in the battalion's main baggage, even if that baggage was placed inconveniently far to the rear. This might not be far enough back and fast-moving events, such as the German attack into France on 10 May 1940, could easily deliver a battalion's baggage into enemy hands. The drums of the 5th Battalion the Gordon Highlanders, were captured in June 1940 when 51st Highland Division surrendered to General Rommel's 7th Panzer Division at St Valéry-en-Caux. One of the drums – a tenor drum – was recovered by the Americans in Germany and returned to the Gordons in a ceremony in Munich in June 1945.[42] Many battalions abandoned their surplus equipment, including their drums, in the retreat to Dunkirk. The 1st Battalion the Suffolk Regiment hid their drums in Roubaix in late May 1940. When the battalion returned there in December 1944 the British Army's town major had already recovered two of them and the local resistance helped recover a third.[43]

Organisation tables for infantry battalions during the war spread little light on where the drummers were to be found, and battalions in any case had a habit, as they do still, of organising themselves in a way that best suited themselves. That a formed body of drummers, buglers or pipers could appear seemingly miraculously when occasion demanded their presence is evident from a number of examples and proves that these 'corps' continued to exist throughout the war, if invariably differently employed.

The historian Colonel A. J. Barker has given some inkling as to how drummers and buglers were used in important wartime roles. His notes appear in his book on the Korean War but, as he states accurately, 'At the time of the Korean War both organisation and equipment were virtually the same as in 1945',[44] we can deduce the location of the drummers in some measure. It would appear that, as a group, they were retained in Headquarter Company and assigned to the 'Admin' Platoon and divided between the defence of battalion headquarters and the provision of snipers. There is some ambiguity at play in trying to decipher who exactly did what, and there is some suggestion that numbers were also assigned to the medical element as stretcher-bearers, for there were a sergeant and 20 stretcher-bearers on a battalion's establishment. At least one drummer, Lance Corporal Jim Glibbery of the 1st/4th Battalion the Essex Regiment, was awarded the Military Medal for bravery while acting as a stretcher-bearer in Tunisia in April 1943.[45] But drummers and buglers were more commonly grouped in the admin platoon and, rather more definitively, Barker wrote that the admin platoon also included 'the Drum Major, and 16 drummers or pipers who were deployed for the close defence of battalion HQ and 6 of whom were trained as battalion snipers.'[46] These six snipers – 'six privates from the Corps of Drums (HQ Coy)' – were placed under the command of a warrant officer within the Intelligence Section.[47]

The storm broke properly with the German invasion of the Low Countries and France in May 1940. For some time thereafter, with the British armies in retreat in Europe and, subsequently, in the Far East, drumming and bugling was hardly a priority. There is no doubt that they were present, as shown by the example of the drums lost by the 5th Gordons, but they would have been something of an encumbrance in retreat and could hardly have expected to find their way onto the evacuation ships at Dunkirk. However, even in the Far East, where the war against Japan began disastrously, bugles were present in the field. Drummer Arthur Lane of the 1st Battalion the Manchester Regiment had enlisted in 1935 and it was his bad fortune to be with the battalion when it surrendered to the Japanese at Singapore in February 1942. Lane was then serving in the machine-gun platoon but he had his bugle with him and during his three and a half years of captivity was 'one of a handful of buglers in the camps and played my bugle at thousands of burials for the victims of the "sons of heaven"', as he later recalled.[48] In the one theatre where, eventually by late 1942, the British offensive proved unstoppable – North Africa – there was hardly occasion for even ceremonial use until the victory parades took place in Tripoli on 4 February 1943 and in Tunis on 20 May. At the former the massed pipes and drums of the 51st Highland Division, re-formed after the original division was lost in France, were able to show off their unforgotten skills and at the latter it was reported in the war diaries of the Grenadier Guards that the assembled corps of drums quickened the beat to the 140 paces to the minute of the light infantry in order to disrupt the steady march of the battalions of Foot Guards.[49]

There was time, albeit short, to organise these major parades and for the supply chain to deliver in time for practice and execution the necessary musical instruments to the men who, in greater part, had been carrying rifle and bayonet for the better part of a couple of years. There were more impromptu displays of military music as the Allied campaigns progressed through Sicily, Italy, France, Belgium and even Germany from mid-1943 onwards and the moral effect on liberated and occupied peoples of half an hour or so of a beating or sounding, and especially if drums were joined by bagpipes, was palpable. The importance of these displays in demonstrating the ascendancy of the Allies and providing an uplifting tonic to battle-worn infantrymen helps explain how even drums found their place in a battalion's baggage.

The 1st Canadian Infantry Division had a particularly gruelling introduction to combat when it fought its way through the mountains of central Sicily in the summer of 1943. Supplying the essentials of war – ammunition, fuel, water and rations – along a tortuous logistic chain from the southern beaches and over miles of very poor and dust-laden tracks was particularly challenging. Bitter battles were fought against the Germans and none more so than in the fight for the hilltop fortress town of Agira. It fell to 2nd Canadian Infantry Brigade on the evening of 28 July 1943 and just two evenings later the drummers and pipers of the Seaforth Highlanders of Canada beat retreat in Agira's rubble-strewn square. The flawless parade was recorded for posterity by the Canadian Broadcasting Corporation, the dramatic setting highlighted by the CBC reporter pointing out that 'you can look across the sunburned valley and see the hills where the Germans are.' As the pipes and drums of the Seaforths stepped off, led by Pipe Major Edmund Essen of Vancouver, the commentary observed that 'This was the first sound of liberation ...'[50]

Another telling Canadian example came from shortly after the liberation of Rome and helps us to understand much more how a battalion's drummers coped with the varying demands of war. Captain Strome Galloway, acting second-in-command of the Royal Canadian Regiment, wrote in his somewhat cutting memoir that:

> The 'Drums' had been reactivated as soon as we arrived at Piedimonte. Since October 1943, eight months in all, the drums and bugles of The Regiment had been stored with the municipal authorities in Campobasso. ... There is a place for military music in war; if not actually when men are grappling with the enemy, then at least before and after. With this in mind The Royal Canadian Regiment managed to smuggle its bugles and drums out to the Mediterranean in June, 1943. It was not until a year later, however, that there was an opportunity to get 'The Drums' together as a body.[51]

Back together, the drums and bugles took every opportunity to practise whilst the battalion was in a rest camp outside Rome. They played at their brigade sports day just six days after being resurrected and another two days later joined with the pipers of the 48th Highlanders of Canada to play at the divisional sports meet. But Galloway was perturbed to find, on reading an article in the Canadian Division's newspaper, that the Drum Major, Sergeant Billy Beales, had then taken his nine drummers and 16 buglers into the eternal city to put on a 45-minute display of their skills. They claimed to be the first Allied military band (sic) to play in St Peter's Square and Galloway heard later that Beales had 'managed to march into the Vatican, past the Swiss Guards, playing a rather obnoxious piece usually known by the title, "The Protestant Boys are Marching to War". Hordes of Roman citizens cheered their every brassy note and drum flam. It is doubtful anyone knew they hadn't any business in Vatican Square – which was probably just as well!'[52]

The Canadian newspaper – *The Red Patch* – noted that 'drums were not on the War Establishment of an assault battalion in the invasion of Sicily' but their positive effect on morale encouraged the Royal Canadian Regiment to take them forward and they began to be used to march the rifle companies 'back from a hard fought action [until] once, while practising in an abandoned factory a few hundred yards behind the line in northern Italy they could be so clearly heard that the enemy shelled their practise area in retaliation.'[53] This is an important point. Soldiers from the Dominium armies – especially the Australians and Canadians – had a propensity to ignore what they considered petty orders from higher up, such as the forbiddance of taking their musical instruments to war. The drum, especially, was in any case a cumbersome and fragile impediment on the modern battlefield. This did not stop some units but demonstrating unit character and *esprit de corps* in the face of the enemy might be one thing. If a regimental call then brought down a torrent of enemy fire it could well reverse its morale-boosting effects. Bugles and even bagpipes were much easier to carry but these instruments did not really have any place in the forward combat zone due to the retaliation they could provoke. During the Normandy campaign in June and July 1944 a number of infantry battalions in 15th (Scottish) Division had pipers forward with the rifle companies. On 30 June, during the dying hours of Operation *Epsom*, the 2nd Battalion the Gordon Highlanders, 'had been forming up for an attack … with pipes playing, when the rousing effect of the pibroch was shattered by a mortar bombardment.' A soldier in the 10th Battalion the Highland Light Infantry, recalled that their commanding officer had formed up the survivors of the battalion to harangue the non-commissioned officers for not doing better. They were unimpressed, especially as 'The pipes were playing, saying to the Germans "here we are!"'[54] Nevertheless, as Ian Daglish has observed in one of his excellent accounts of the Normandy campaign: 'Amongst [all of a quartermaster's stores] the Pipe Band drums, pipes, and kilts, officially frowned upon but under no circumstances [were they] to be left behind.'[55]

Galloway also stated most clearly that, in his battalion of Royal Canadians, where all drummers and buglers were concerned '… their job was not all music and fancy marching. There was no "establishment" for a band [sic]. To keep them intact they were used as a protective platoon for battalion headquarters and as an ammunition-carrying detail when battle was joined.'[56] This is definitive evidence of the actual wartime employment of drummers and buglers. And that they were combat infantrymen first and foremost was demonstrated when, in an action by the battalion around Rimini in September 1944, these very men – who Strome Galloway continued to refer to as 'bandsmen' – helped in recapturing one of the company positions. One bugler, wounded by shrapnel in the cheek, was unable to blow his bugle for some time and the lead drummer, with comparable misfortune, suffered a broken wrist!

In some recompense to the somewhat flagrant Protestant zeal of the Canadian drummers and buglers it is also recorded that the massed pipes and drums of 38th (Irish) Brigade, together with formed parties from the brigade's three battalions (6th Inniskilling Fusiliers, 2nd London Irish Rifles and 1st Royal Irish Fusiliers), marched through St Peter's Square on 12 June 1944. In all, while the rest of the brigade was still fighting, 150 Catholic officers and soldiers assembled for an audience with Pope Pius XII, the pipes and drums leading them into the Vatican. The brigade war diary reported that 'It was a glorious day, the sun shining down out of a cloudless sky, the drums glinting, the hackles waving proudly in the breeze and to the tune of "The Wearing of the Green", the Brigade marched across the Piazza into the Vatican.'[57]

The drum, as has become obvious, had no place at all in the battle zone but there are some tantalising examples of the employment of bugles in battle and we might suppose that in a number of infantry battalions at least, a drum major or bugle major had secreted a bugle in his pack should an opportunity arise to use it. There are some surprising examples of the use of the bugle by British airborne forces, two being from the 6th Airborne Division on D-Day in Normandy and the other from 1st Airborne Division at Arnhem, as well as one example from a Territorial battalion in Normandy. These would indicate that the practice of using bugle calls to govern tactical manoeuvre might have been more widespread.

The complexity of airborne operations and their potential for disaster were demonstrated only too well in the airborne assault on Sicily during the start of Operation *Husky* in July 1943. Major lessons had been learned, especially in trying to assure adequate command and control. So it was that the 9th Parachute Battalion, whose task it was to eliminate the Merville gun battery on the Normandy coast ahead of the seaborne landings in the early morning of 6 June 1944, provided for a number of bugle calls in the drills for the attack on the actual battery. The paratroopers intended to land and approach the battery as silently as possible but 'If surprise is lost or if time is short CO will order bugle call "CHARGE", which will indicate "NOISY" method.' On hearing the call the fire support group of two rifle platoons, the snipers and anti-tank gunners were to open fire and B Company was to be prepared to blow breaches in the protecting wire fences. The breach was to be coordinated with the landing of gliders close by, bringing in heavy equipment to destroy the gun emplacements. 'Four and a half minutes before gliders are due to land CO orders bugle call "REVEILLE". On this call Mortar Officer orders (over telephone [the battalion would have laid line]) Mortar Pl[atoon] to change over to one det[achment] firing 3 Star Shells and whole area is lit up.' With two and a half minutes to go before the first glider touched down it was to signal the letter 'M' from its headlight. On receiving this signal or in time 'CO orders bugle-call "FALL-IN". All fire with the exception of the diversionary party and flares will then cease … When third glider is down CO orders bugle-call "LIGHTS OUT" and 3 Mor[tar] Star Shells cease fire.' Finally, for the attack, once B Company had cleared wire and mines and the way through was clear enough, 'CO orders bugle call "REVEILLE" on which area is lit up by 3 Mor[tar] Star Shells … On this call B Coy will not light any more fuses, even if all gaps have not been blown, and C Coy will assault.' There were some variations should there be no significant obstacles and C Company was therefore able to assault more rapidly and once success had been achieved and the German guns had been blown up, red-green-red 2-inch mortar flares were to be sent up 'followed by Bugle-call "STANDFAST"', which was the signal for all troops to reorganise on the position. The last call was to be 'COOKHOUSE' and all troops would begin their withdrawal from the battery.[58]

9 Para's experience that morning well suited the old adage, ascribed to Prussian Field Marshal Helmuth von Moltke, that no plan survives first contact with the enemy. It suffices here to say that, well under-strength and with just one of his machine guns, none of his other support weapons and no gliders, the commanding officer ordered the assault and the position was carried without any one of the bugle calls being sounded. We know too that in the chaos of the drop, one of the assigned buglers – Corporal Jim 'Marra' McGuinness – lost his bugle along with his rifle but at least managed to reach the battalion rendezvous. He was subsequently assigned to the one Vickers machine gun that had survived the drop and won the Military Medal for his gallantry.[59]

The history of the 7th Parachute Battalion (Light Infantry) states that, with men having become widely dispersed during the drop into Normandy, 'many troopers landed well away from the DZ and had to make their way to the rendezvous point (RV). With Private Chambers sounding the regimental call on his bugle, men made their way to the RV.'[60] 7 Para had been formed in 1942 from the best part of the 10th Battalion the Somerset Light Infantry, so the regimental call used was that of the Somersets. In the very severe fighting in July 1944 in Normandy to take Hill 112, the 4th Battalion the Dorsetshire Regiment was committed against the German defenders of the village of Etterville. In an excellent example of the moral effect of a bugle call, Major Joe Symonds, commanding B Company, wrote that 'At 0620 hrs Col. Cowie gave the long awaited signal to go by having L/Cpl. Butt sound the charge on his bugle. The battalion rose to its feet as one man, many cheered. It was a wonderful experience.'[61]

The 2nd Parachute Battalion at the battle of Arnhem in September 1944 provides another rare example of actual use of the bugle in battle. Major Digby Tatham-Warter had been an officer in the Oxfordshire and Buckinghamshire Light Infantry before volunteering for airborne forces and commanded A Company 2 Para at Arnhem Bridge. When he was interviewed in the 1980s by the historian Martin Middlebrook he professed that he had had little confidence in the radios available at the time and had therefore trained his company 'in the use of bugle calls for signalling orders and intentions in advance-guard actions', the calls being 'much the same as those used in Sir John Moore's Light Division in the Peninsular wars.' During the increasingly intensive fighting as the paratroopers fought their way to the bridge:

> ... it gave me great satisfaction to see it working perfectly under enemy fire. Each platoon and Company HQ had two buglers trained to sound the simple calls we used. While Jack Grayburn [one of the platoon commanders and who was awarded a posthumous VC for his gallantry at the bridge itself] was working round to the right of the enemy machine gun, I was joined by Colonel Frost. He had been hard on the heels of my company and now came forward, impatient at the delay, to see the situation himself. But we did not have to wait long for Grayburn's bugle call signalling that he was back on the axis road, and I sounded the call to resume the advance.[62]

It might be added that, while the sounds of bugles could hardly be concealed, the rarity of their use allowed them to be blown without any danger, certainly initially, of giving away intentions. German reaction is not recorded but their surprise can be imagined. Lieutenant Colonel Frost, who commanded the 2nd Parachute Battalion at Arnhem, famously used a hunting horn to help rally his men on the drop zone.[63] The horn had been presented to him by the Royal Exodus Hunt in Iraq in 1940 on his departure for England and he had used it in similar fashion at Oudna in Tunisia in October 1942 and in Sicily in July 1943. Frost most probably encouraged Tatham-Warter to develop bugle calls after 2 Para's experience in Tunisia where their radios failed and, unsupported, the battalion suffered a large number of casualties and was forced to withdraw.

The Far East is better known for the Japanese use of bugles in battle. It is apparent that the Imperial Japanese Army used bugles widely in the field during the war, and this deduction is helped by the large numbers of Japanese bugles that were collected on the battlefield by American servicemen. Two such bugles, one picked up at Guadalcanal in 1942 and the other at Rabaul in 1944, are in the Museum of the Pacific War in Fredericksburg, Texas. The Japanese Army was a relatively unsophisticated beast compared to British, Empire and American forces, but appreciated very quickly, and certainly once the tables began to turn against them, that announcing an attack by the blowing of company bugles was potentially disastrous. They had relied greatly on the psychological effects of bugle blowing at night and in their *banzai* charges, but these could not overcome a steadfast defence. Nevertheless bugles were still being used towards the end of the war, at times in desperation, and US Marine Dick Meadows on Saipan in June 1944 later 'recalled hearing a bugle followed by a rush of 300 to 500 Japanese soldiers.'[64] Two months later a mass breakout of Japanese prisoners of war at Cowra in Australia was heralded by a bugle call.

All of the campaigns in the Far East were notable for the massive difficulties presented for logistics and for the effects on operations of climate and terrain. These problems were present to an even greater degree in the two Chindit operations – the two long-range penetration expeditions behind Japanese lines in Burma in 1943 and 1944. One story has emerged of the use of bagpipes during the second expedition (Operation *Thursday*) to help stiffen morale, in which Piper Tim Ainslie and another piper of the 2nd Battalion the Black Watch, provided an accompaniment to the march:

> In one of the final actions marching towards Mogaung Tim took turns with the only other surviving piper to play at the head of a depleted but still proud Battalion, on a set of pipes that had been dropped by parachute for that purpose.[65]

Yet even in the difficult circumstances of operations in Burma, soldiers did keep some bugles with them. Following the crossing of the River Chindwin in October 1944 the 4th Battalion the King's African Rifles, was tasked with capturing Leik Ridge. In the first attempt on 10 October C Company carried out the attack alone, the company bugler sounding the charge and the Ugandan infantrymen bellowing their war cry. This first attack failed but was renewed half an hour later, again to the accompaniment of the bugle. The Japanese could not be dislodged and preparations were made for the whole battalion to conduct the assault on

22 October. This attempt was successful, the Ugandans attacking again to the 'sound of the "Charge" blown on the bugle'[66] and C Company's young bugler contributing to the success by blowing 'Come to the cookhouse door' as the assault went in![67]

★

Before considering the final elements of this story examination must be made of a theme that links small wars and the wars of empire with post-Second World War methods of peacekeeping. The two great wars of the 20th century were a scale apart from what had been the British Army's 'normal' business, built up over the second half of the previous century, of 'imperial policeman'. 'The first duty of Britain's armed forces', as described by the historian Lawrence James, 'had been to protect the Empire, push back its boundaries, and impose the Imperial peace on its subjects.'[68] This theme ran through the course of the first half of the 20th century and concurrent with both world wars. Until the inexorable break-up of the British Empire there was still an empire to police and the job of imperial policeman, considered especially in the inter-war years as 'proper soldiering', formed a major part of a British soldier's life. But the period after the end of the Great War was marked not so much by small wars in their traditional sense as by, in effect, policing operations, where soldiers were called out in aid of the civil power to restore order or suppress riot.[69]

It must be added too that the British Army continued to experience the challenges of 'small wars' throughout the inter-war period and these included the ever-present problem of the North-West Frontier. A major conflict broke out with Afghanistan in 1919 and there were numerous conflagrations throughout these two decades, the most notable being in Iraq and Palestine. Aside from these the canny tribesmen of the Frontier were as troublesome as before. And the tactical techniques were as before, if the infantryman was now aided by air power and even the tank. Especially on the Frontier, lack of experience could prove deadly. One helpful guide cautioned young officers about making a withdrawal from contact obvious to the enemy, remarking somewhat sarcastically that 'At one time it used to be the fashion for the piquet to blaze away ... It would have been better to bugle the "Retire"'. The author,

General Sir Andrew Skeen, had considerable experience of the Frontier and noted how 'quaint ideas crept into peace training after every frontier show, ideas which ought never to have been thought of by folk who had done the work under fire.'[70]

During the Second World War the War Office published a pamphlet entitled *Street Fighting for Junior Officers*. Included was a section detailing the actions to be taken when suppressing civil disturbances, itself taken from *The Young Officer's Guide to Military Law*. The law providing soldiers with the legal powers to act in the event of civil disorder and riot had been enacted in the reign of King George I and, while clearly intended to provide legal powers for soldiers at home, had wide application across the Empire. Certainly by 1943 the problem of civil disturbance was growing ever greater in India but the pamphlet, by inclusion of this guidance, probably had an eye on any breakdown of law at home as well as across the Empire. In all situations it was absolutely imperative that the *Riot Act* should be read out, ideally by a local magistrate, to warn rioters that measures would be taken to disperse them should they not disperse of their own accord. The reading of the act was as important for the legal protection of the local military commander – usually a young subaltern – as it was to alert the crowd to their potential fate. The pamphlet drew the following from *King's Regulations* paragraph 1279 (b): 'In order that the attention of all persons present should be called to the fact that the proclamation is about to be read, its reading should be prefaced by "The Alarm" loudly blown on the bugle or trumpet.'[71]

As ever, the reality for the soldiers on the ground could leave a big gap between what the pamphlet said and what they had to do. Growing civil unrest in India between the world wars and during the Second World War provided major challenges to the British authorities. In 1943 at the height of the war against Japan a number of Regular battalions of the British Army were withdrawn from fighting the Japanese to boost internal security in India. This was a distasteful task for British soldiers and Lieutenant H. G. Bentley-Smith of the 1st Battalion the North Staffordshire Regiment described one such occasion when he recalled that:

> The standard copybook procedure was for troops to accompany an Indian civil magistrate to the riot area if civil police had been unable to handle the situation.

The magistrate would order the rioters to disperse. A negative response and serious deterioration of civil control would prompt the magistrate, as a last resort, to sign, on the spot and perhaps under a shower of missiles, a written request for 'Military Aid to Civil Power'. This authorised the troops' commander (usually a lieutenant) to open fire if necessary. One subaltern reported the magistrate's verbal request as: 'Please Sahib, can you just fire one bullet gently?'[72]

This example helps set the context but we have further illumination from Field Marshal Sir William Slim. As a company commander in India in the 1930s he was called out to a communal riot between Hindus and 'Mohammedans' in Gurampur. As the civil police began to buckle under the violent blows of both sides Slim had the magistrate sign over his authority and then acted:

> I reckoned that if I did not act within three minutes there would be wholesale murder in the square, so I got a section, five men, on to the roof [of a bus], as fast as I could, and told them to lie down ready to fire. The bugler we had with us I ordered to blow the 'Commence Fire', the call we use on the ranges. The bugle shrilled out above the clamour, and many heads turned to look at us, but beyond that it had no effect.

Slim quickly ordered rounds to be fired at both sides of the melee, to the obvious chagrin of the Hindu magistrate.[73]

CHAPTER 13

Last Post

I told them that I will always remember that 'Last Post', eased out with lots of lip and spit to hold that last high note. Accountants can say what they like about military music, but it goes straight to a man's heart.

The late Professor Richard Holmes used these words in concluding one of the chapters of his final book, *Soldiers*, described in one review as 'a book of majestic, heart-rending humanity: a deeply affectionate portrait of British soldiers as they have existed for more than 350 years.'[1] The epigram above is a fitting epitaph too when considering drummers and buglers and, indeed, all British military music in more recent years. Richard Holmes, typically, was talking to soldiers of the 1st Battalion the Princess of Wales's Royal Regiment in Al Amarah in Iraq in 2004. He was then the Colonel of the Regiment and was describing the repatriation to England of Private 'Ray' Rayment of the battalion, who had died there that August. It was of great importance to the men of the 1st Battalion that the drummer and bearer party for the repatriation had been provided by their 2nd Battalion.

Earlier in the chapter Holmes had got to the heart of the problem facing post-Second World War military music and particularly in maintaining corps of drums in their unequal struggle against '... the dual pressures of financial retrenchment and successive operational tours ... An enthusiastic commanding officer could make a real difference, but while piping always attracted the interest of officers ... there was infinitely less concern about drumming. A forceful drum major might both attract and train drummers and protect his Corps of Drums from the adjutant's desire to post drummers off to the rifle companies.'[2]

The rot in all military music, if we might call it that, had set in early on. An article in the *British Army Journal* of July 1951 noted that, with regard to regimental marches: 'In these days of austerity regimental bands are not heard so often by the troops as formerly. It follows that official regimental marches are not played so frequently as heretofore and there may be some excuse for short-service men not recognizing their regiment's "signature tune" when they do hear it.'[3] In the immediate post-war period drummers and buglers certainly retained their official role of regulating the day but this role waned considerably in the decades that followed. There was something of a late flowering of their earlier role of providing musical accompaniment to the march and on parade, especially when drums were accompanied by flutes and even cymbals and glockenspiels. With the demise of the regimental bands in the British Army in the mid-1990s each battalion's corps of drums or bugles was the only music left under the control of the commanding officer. But maintaining these corps became an increasingly major struggle against operational commitments and manpower shortages. The two regiments of the Light Infantry and Royal Green Jackets, and their successors in the Rifles after 2007, had better success with their buglers but the demands of modern operations created an ever-increasing impression that all instruments were out of place in a modern army.

The Korean War fought against the Korean communists and their Chinese ally between 1950 and 1953 was, in character and by way of the soldiers and their equipment, largely an extension of the Second World War. In the previous chapter we noted, in quoting A. J. Barker, that there was no noticeable difference between the way drummers and buglers were organised and employed in Korea compared to the earlier war. Evidence that bugles were carried in the field is provided by the outstanding example of the 1st Battalion the Gloucestershire Regiment at the battle of the Imjin River in Korea in April 1951. This battle against vast numbers of attacking Chinese resulted in the destruction of the battalion but the heroic stand of the Glosters stemmed the Chinese spring offensive against the South Korean capital. In the desperate final stages of the fight in the early hours of 25 April and with the Glosters down to three rounds of ammunition per man the drum major of the battalion, Philip Buss, was called for. The Chinese accompanied all of their hitherto failed mass-formation attacks with much trumpeting and the Glosters' commanding officer was growing weary of the sound: 'It'll be a long time before I want to hear a cavalry trumpet playing after this.' His adjutant, Captain (later General Sir) Anthony Farrar-Hockley, responded by saying: 'It would serve them right, sir, if we confused them by playing our own bugles. I wonder which direction they'd go if they heard "Defaulters" played?' The CO took him seriously and Farrar-Hockley called down the slope to the men in their trenches and Drum Major Buss, producing his bugle from his haversack, asked the adjutant what he should play:

> 'It's getting on towards daylight,' I called back to him, 'play Reveille – the Long and the Short. And play "Fire Call" – in fact, play all the calls of the day as far as "Retreat", but don't play that!'
>
> A little way below us in the darkness, I heard a few preliminary 'peeps' as the Drum-Major warmed his instrument up. This was followed by the sound of the stones dislodged as he climbed from his slit-trench to sound the calls; for I have said that the Drum-Major was a man who knew how things should be done, and the idea of playing his bugle under cover in a slit-trench was beyond him. I could just see his tall, lean figure, topped by a cap comforter – almost a shadow in the darkness. Then he began to play. He played each 'Reveille' twice, he played 'Defaulters', 'Cookhouse', 'Officers Dress for Dinner', all the 'Orderly NCO' calls, and a dozen more besides. He always played a bugle well; that day he was not below form. The sweet notes of our own bugle, which now echoed through the valley below him, died away. For a moment, there was silence – the last note had coincided with a lull in the action. Then the noise of the battle began again – but with a difference: there was no sound of a Chinese bugle. There are not many Drum-Majors in the British Army who can claim to have silenced the enemy's battle calls with a short bugle recital.[4]

The war reached a situation of protracted stalemate in 1952 and when, on 27 July 1953, an armistice was signed between belligerents, buglers of the 1st Battalion the Durham Light Infantry, were sent forward to sound the ceasefire. One of the buglers, Lance Corporal Harry Sanson, recalled that 'At first we were told to go to the frontline forward positions' but this was considered too dangerous and was postponed twice. On the third night 'We blew [the ceasefire] from the hilltop about [a] mile or two from the front line. But the troops would have all heard it ... As we prepared to blow our bugles in the pitch black night, you heard gunfire going off all around you. When we finished blowing it just went dead. Dead quiet. All this thumping and banging just stopped.'[5]

Similar activities took place throughout the forces of the United Nations that same day. Robert Ericson, bugler of the 1st Service Battalion 1st US Marine Division, played 'taps' that night at 10.00 p.m. in the United Nations Truce Camp in Panmunjom. In 2003 the South Korean government invited Ericson – the 'ceasefire bugler' – to sound the ceasefire again in Seoul on the fiftieth anniversary.[6] Ericson recalled that his daily duties at the Freedom Village included playing the daily military bugle calls for the camp and this traditional role for British Army buglers was certainly in evidence. Harry Sanson, as one of the Durham's company buglers, would 'call morning reveille and sound the lowering of the flag' when in camp and when in the field would help 'take ammunition to troops on the front line after nightfall.'[7]

Despite economies and re-ordered priorities, the use of buglers to regulate the day in barracks and even on the firm bases of more recent operations – whether the designation of duty drummer in the line regiments and in the Foot Guards was used or not – has persisted. George MacDonald Fraser's semi-fictional Private McAuslan, J. – 'the Dirtiest Soldier in the World' – was roused to some sort of soldiering in immediate post-war North Africa 'From the moment when the Drums beat "Johnnie Cope" at sunrise ...'[8] In *McAuslan in the Rough* our narrator recalled that on six days a week, 'Reveille was sounded in the conventional way at six, by a bugler on the distant square playing the famous 'Charlie, Charlie, get out of bed ... But on Fridays it was very different. Then the duty of sounding reveille devolved on the battalion's pipes and drums, who were bound to march round the entire barrack area, playing full blast.'[9] Another example comes from early 1956 when the 1st Battalion the East Surrey Regiment, stationed at Bury St Edmunds, was warned to deploy to Cyprus as the whole of the Middle East looked like it would burst into flames after an Egyptian-inspired coup in Iraq.

Second Lieutenant Tony Thorne recalled that in the early hours of that morning, while assisting with the embarkation plan,

> a bugle blew reveille and it occurred to me that the soldiers who Dan [the Embarkation Officer] intended to despatch in fighting order within half an hour were at that moment just waking up. The bugle call was followed almost immediately by the howl of the emergency siren ... Within seconds they would discover that this time was for real.[10]

The continuation of National Service until 1962 provided the conditions for maintaining large corps of drums and bugles for the simple reason that there were large numbers of young men held on the strength of the infantry battalions. Dougie Bridges of the North Staffords, who was one such drummer, recalled that in the 1950s 'the Corps of Drums had both regular and national service soldiers serving together and the numbers in the drums would quite often be up to 30 members ...' These would be broken down into eight side drummers, two tenor drummers, one base drummer, one on the cymbals, 12 buglers and the remainder playing the flute.[11] These corps continued to be employed during training exercises in the field and in war as the battalion headquarters' defence platoon and this role allowed the corps to maintain a good degree of independence whilst in barracks, permitting regular music practice and ready availability of drummers and buglers to carry out the daily routine calls. Practice was maintained at a high standard too as the corps' offices were invariably located in barracks alongside those of the regimental band. However, by the early 1980s reduced manpower numbers – the army went through a particularly difficult period of poor recruiting in the late 1970s – meant that such independence had become an expensive luxury. As a result the drummers and buglers, if they were to be maintained as a corps, found themselves increasingly re-roled as machine gunners and this was eventually forced on all infantry battalions when separate drum and bugle platoons were removed from official battalion organisation tables. They also found themselves re-roled as rifle platoons for the very regular deployments to operations in Northern Ireland in the 1970s and 1980s. For much of this whole post-war period the commander of the drum and bugle platoons had been the battalion adjutant, with the drum major acting in effect *in loco parentis* on a daily basis due to the adjutant's all-consuming duties alongside the commanding officer. But in Northern Ireland the drum major invariably found himself 'relegated' to the appointment of platoon sergeant, with a young officer in place as full-time platoon commander. Occasionally drummers and buglers would be called upon to act as such for a special occasion but priority had to be to supporting operations across Ulster's six counties. Nevertheless, due to the long-time restriction imposed on the use of trained soldiers under the age of 18, the resident battalions in Northern Ireland — the battalions deployed for 18 months and later two years — held a number of under-18s as drummers and buglers on the strength of headquarter company. These youngsters were able therefore to be used in their traditional role until the day they attained the age of 18 and could move into a rifle platoon; it was a day for which they itched.

Echoing an earlier age, these under-18s had always provided large numbers of drummers and buglers. More correctly they were often rather younger, for boys aged 17 years could sign up as adult recruits as many of them would attain the age of 18 whilst undergoing the six months of adult recruit training. For 'juniors' it was another matter and it was these boys who provided a fertile ground for the taking in and training of future drummers and buglers. In 1957, following the publication of a report by Lieutenant General Sir Euan Miller on the organisation and administration of boys' units in the army, the rank of 'boy' was abolished and the rank of junior replaced it. Those 15- to 17-year-olds who passed the necessary tests and were deemed future NCO material went, for the infantry, to the Infantry Boys Battalion, which had been established at Tuxford in Nottinghamshire in 1952. When boys became juniors from 1957 the name of the unit was changed to the Infantry Junior Leaders' Battalion (IJLB). By 1960 the IJLB was at Oswestry in Shropshire and in 1975 it moved to Shorncliffe Camp in Kent, where it joined hands with the Junior Infantrymen's Battalion (JIB), which had been at Shorncliffe since 1967. But the main purpose of the IJLB was to train future infantry leaders and it was the junior soldiers' companies in the infantry divisional training depots that became the focus for bringing up young drummers and buglers. These companies took in the same age range and because all junior soldier training was at least 12 months in duration there was ample time to instil a great deal of expertise in the infantry's young musicians – drummers, buglers and bandsmen. In the early 1970s the junior soldiers' companies were organised into three platoons – drums, band and infantry – and the junior recruits competed for places in the platoons in that order with, as a consequence, the drummers tending to be the better soldiers and as good as the junior leaders. Nigel Brown of the Worcestershire and Sherwood Foresters Regiment was a subaltern in the Junior Soldiers' Company at the Depot of the Prince of Wales's Division at Lichfield in 1971–72 and recalled the differences between the budding drummers and bandsmen:

> The band platoon (commanded by a bandmaster) was the more delicate platoon and was treated accordingly. I recall it was decided that all juniors should take part in a milling afternoon. The bandmaster objected very strongly on the basis that the milling might damage the lips of the band platoon. There were no such concerns for the buglers in the drums.[12]

The raising of the school leaving age from 15 to 16 in 1974 began to have a detrimental effect on the recruitment of junior soldiers. This effect was not that marked initially and passing-out parades at the divisional depots continued to see large numbers of junior drummers on parade. Film footage of a parade at the other depot of the Prince of Wales's Division at Crickhowell in South Wales in 1986 showed 16 drummers (12 side drums, two tenor drums and two bass drums), two cymbals and 24 buglers/flautists. This depot served four infantry regiments at that time – the Devonshire and Dorset Regiment, the Royal Welch Fusiliers, the Royal Regiment of Wales and the Gloucesterhire Regiment – the parade demonstrating most graphically the size of the corps and the skills of these young drummers under Drum Major Tony Blackshaw of the Cheshire Regiment. But the closing down of junior soldier training in the mid-1980s was disastrous. IJLB closed in 1985 and the JIB in 1991. There then followed a succession of reorganisations that eventually led to the closure of all of the divisional depots and the concentration of all infantry recruit training at Catterick. Concurrent was the loss of all junior soldier training and, therefore, the removal of all junior musician training. The final flourishes occurred in the early 1990s when drummers and buglers could still turn out in considerable numbers. When the massed drums of the Prince of Wales's Division beat retreat at Cardiff Castle in 1992 the numbers of drummers on parade of the division's then nine regiments were practically uncountable. A similar experience was had when the massed bugles of the Light Division sounded retreat at Horse Guards in 1993.

Through all of these years and all of these changes there is, unsurprisingly, no evidence of bugles being used to provide field calls during combat and not even the example of the Glosters in Korea can really be cited. Even as late as 1966, when the third and final edition of *Trumpet and Bugle Calls for the Army* was published, it continued to list 'Field Calls for Infantry and Mounted Infantry in Field Exercise and Manoeuvre.' These numbered just three: 'Continue or Commence Firing', 'Stand Fast or Cease Fire' and 'Execute Orders Received'. An additional two calls listed under 'Field Calls for Dismounted Corps' showed 'Charge' and 'Alarm'.[13] But the reality was that the necessity for these calls had long passed with the arrival of effective field radios and their issue down to section level in the 1950s. Effectiveness is a relative term and the British Army Larkspur radio system was certainly an improvement on what had gone before. But the section set, the SR (Station Radio) A40, was a miserable thing and well into the early 1980s, until the issue of Clansman became universal, infantry platoon commanders continued to use whistle blasts to control their dispersed sections in the field. So poor was the reputation of the A40 that the author, whilst Regimental Signals Officer in his battalion as it took over its equipment in Gibraltar in 1981, watched with some horror as his sergeant major hurled an A40 over the fortress wall. As it smashed on the rocks below, he remarked 'There! You can throw it farther than you can talk on it!'

Clansman was markedly better but no guarantor of communications. In 1990 during an exercise at the British Army Training Unit Suffield in Canada the author, commanding a company of armoured infantry, became so frustrated by trying to get the attention of his reserve platoon once it had dismounted, and despite the proliferation of radios, had one of his accompanying machine gunners, Corporal Timmins of the Drums Platoon, deploy his bugle and play the regimental call. This worked, partially, but rather taken by this he decided to employ the bugle again during a dismounted night attack. The author's company had begun the attack in support and had to pass through the lead company once it had taken the initial objective. Orders were given that the company would begin the second assault on the enemy's depth position on the signal of the bugle sounding the 'Charge'. Corporal Timmins had no idea what this was so out came something remembered from a Hollywood movie and which might have been sounded by the US Cavalry as it swept down on a bunch of Apache.

Yet there were times when bugles were retained when troops deployed on the ground, if not during conventional operations. In the two decades after 1945 that saw the dissolution of the British Empire there were frequent occasions when British troops were deployed on the streets to deal with riotous mobs or to separate different groups intent on violence; the case of India before partition was described earlier. A similar situation occurred in Hong Kong in October 1956 when large numbers of Chinese nationalists, who had flooded into the colony, fought Chinese communist sympathisers for control of parts of Kowloon. Here the army was called out in support of the Royal Hong Kong Police and, while not committed in the end, was organised to conduct riot control in the traditional way. A more vicious campaign occurred in Cyprus between 1955 and 1959 when Greek Cypriots resorted to violence to try to force *enosis*, or union, with Greece. Here British forces were the target of acts of terrorism and rioting, the latter often backed by lurking terrorists armed with grenades. The 1st Battalion the South Staffordshire Regiment was deployed early on and had conducted riot control training beforehand in Egypt. As Second Lieutenant Tony Griffiths, one of the many young National Service officers in the battalion, later reflected: 'I never expected to carry out the drill for real.' In command of 3 Platoon in A Company he recalled that early attempts to quell riots entailed 'hollow square – bugler – banner – barbed wire, the lot.'[14] But such concentrations of men in narrow streets or open squares proved very vulnerable to armed attack. Similar tactics were employed at the onset of the 'Troubles' in Northern Ireland in 1969 but tactics soon changed to better cope with new conditions and bugles were no longer part of riot control equipment. Indeed, a bugle had, by the 1960s, no part to play whatsoever in the exercise of command and control in the field and its story in this respect was at an end. Military radios have continued to improve and infantry platoon commanders no longer have recourse to their whistles to control their sections. Today every man on the ground has access to a radio by way of the Personal Role Radio, a very lightweight and short-range piece of equipment that began to be issued in 2004. And if these and the larger radios fail, the mobile telephone has assumed a place all of its own.

With no operational role in which drummers and buglers would deploy their instruments the very place of these men in an infantry battalion appeared increasingly anachronistic. The impact of modern-day pressures has been mentioned already and drummers and buglers not only found it difficult to find their place in a modern battalion but it was becoming increasingly difficult too to find the numbers required. Major Richard Powell has reflected on this aspect and has cited a number of reasons for the decline of 'the army's senior music.' These included the raising of the school leaving age from 15 to 16 in 1974 and its effect on the recruiting of young soldiers, many of whom had gone into the drums as we have seen. Routine Saturday working also came to an end and, what with cheap transistor radios now providing plentiful in-barrack entertainment and every soldier being able to afford a watch, even regulating the day by bugle call was no longer absolutely necessary; more a nice-to-have. Lieutenant Colonel Rodney Bashford, who had begun his military service in the King's Royal Rifle Corps, was later bandmaster of the 17th/21st Lancers and, after retirement, curator of the museum at the Royal Military School of Music at Kneller Hall, wrote in 1997 that:

> much less is heard of the bugle's sweet sounds these days. Just dial a few numbers and you can, in a trice, summon the pioneer sergeant or rustle up a few fatigue men without aid of music ... Along with the cavalry trumpet the bugle is becoming inefficient ... it is almost inaudible against the roar of traffic, jet aeroplanes and, in battle, the cacophony of modern fire-power.[15]

At the end of 2015 the Tate Britain ran an exhibition showing 14 brass and wind instruments that had survived battles over the previous

150 years. They included the bugle blown by Lord Cardigan's orderly trumpeter, William Brittain of the 17th Lancers, to sound the ill-fated charge of the Light Brigade at Balaclava on 25 October 1854. In commenting on the exhibition Andrew Bomford of the BBC noted that, in its day 'The bugle was the wristwatch, the radio and the mobile phone of the army.'[16] But no longer. Much of this contributed to drummers and buglers becoming less inspired and, while military bands were going through something of a heyday, with military tattoos and events such as the Royal Tournament at Earls Court in London providing scope for massed bands and being extremely well attended, 'Drummers ... were learning to lurch on in the background as something of a musical afterthought, rather than in their former swift and bold manner.'[17]

An associated problem was the reduction in the size of an infantry battalion. Kipling's once 'Eight 'undred fightin' Englishmen' marching 'over Injia's coral strand'[18] remained about the same in establishment terms for an infantry battalion of the Second World War, although the 1914 war establishment had been, on paper at least, 1,007 officers and men. These figures provided more than adequate space for the drum and bugle platoons and their allotted role of battalion headquarters' defence platoon. But the further reductions in size in the decades after 1945 put greater and greater strains on this establishment and thus on finding a place for the 'musick' within the ever-changing organisations. Since the 1980s the average size of an infantry battalion has been about 650 with numbers differing plus or minus due to the battalion's role. In the 1980s these main roles were described as 'mechanised' (the battalions in the British Army of the Rhine equipped with the FV432 armoured personnel carrier) and 'airportable' (the battalions assigned to reinforce Germany). Other roles included parachute battalions, battalions assigned to public duties, battalions assigned to Operation *Banner* in Northern Ireland and battalions dotted around the planet in various overseas garrisons. All had slightly different establishments but all managed, somehow, to maintain a drum or bugle platoon. By the end of the 20th century the main roles were identified as 'armoured infantry' (in Warrior infantry fighting vehicles, with an enhanced establishment of around 740), 'mechanised' (now in the wheeled Saxon) and 'light', the latter having been sub-divided at one stage as Type A and Type B, with Type A battalions having a defined operational role and Type B battalions assigned to a rather nebulous home defence role on the British mainland. In the majority of all battalions the drummers and buglers were now kept together as the machine-gun platoon but establishment tables rarely directed this to happen. In 2002 the only type identified as having drummers or buglers was the armoured infantry battalion, a note on the establishment table stating that 'One pl[atoon] in the Bn is the Drums/Bugle Pl.'[19]

The situation was serious enough for a group of enthusiasts to get together in London in the summer of 1977 to form the Corps of Drums Society. Its foundation actually lay in the Territorial Army, which had been emasculated in post-war cuts, and in particular in the corps of drums of the Honourable Artillery Company (HAC), a London-based regiment and one of the oldest military units in the country. The Society's original aim was 'to preserve the Corps of Drums style of music as a living thing before it is too late'[20] while its principal charitable aim today has been updated: 'To promote and preserve the concept and traditions of the drum, flute and bugle corps of drums.'[21] The Territorial Army as established in 1907, with all of its intimate local connections, was broken up in 1967 (and there have been at least four major reorganisations since). All of the Territorial infantry battalions had maintained effective corps of drums and there was keen competition within the regionally grouped county organisations. But when the county Territorial regiments were all disbanded these corps struggled for a time to survive. Some Territorial drummers from the Home Counties and especially those from the Bedfordshire and Hertfordshire Regiment took matters into their own hands and joined the HAC in the late 1960s. The HAC's own corps had been dominated largely, and very effectively, by ex-drummers of the Foot Guards but now became a mixture of Guardsmen, the old Territorial infantry and members of corps from various schools. The skill and enthusiasm within the new corps were instrumental in maintaining standards and knowledge, which was to express itself effectively with the formation of the Society.

The early 1980s saw in fact something of a resurgence in drumming and in bugling in the infantry. The first issue of the society's newsletter, *The Drummer's Call*, had lamented:

> To-day it is not even necessary for the routine barrack calls to be sounded (though this is still done in many battalions) and the Corps of Drums is an entirely ceremonial body whose primary task must be their allotted military function within the battalion. On a ceremonial parade however many Corps of Drums have become merely an extension of the regimental band and very rarely parade on their own ... The Royal Military School of Music have stated that they have no jurisdiction or authority over the training or establishment of drummers, fifers, buglers, trumpeters, etc.[22]

But the drum and bugle platoons were coming back into their own as regimental bands experienced reductions in numbers of bandsmen, which brought them down in 1985 from 27 to 21. There were also greater demands on the bands. The infantry regimental bands, while they all lived with the infantry battalions of their parent regiment, had never been an integral part of those battalions ever since the days when bandsmen were recognised as soldiers and not civilians in 1803. A battalion could never, therefore, expect to have 'its' band at its beck and call. The bands were also becoming increasingly unavailable as they met the rising numbers of wider ceremonial commitments and tended to prefer to commit themselves to rising demands from civilian organisations for their services, for which they were paid extra. By contrast, the drummers and buglers were always on hand to support the battalion. When a corps of drums appeared on its own it evoked a growing sense of pride in this older tradition and the base sound that the drummers could beat, often backed by bugle pieces and flute pieces, took everyone back to something that seemed finer and grander. The corps became more musical in their own right. Corps of drums had long included bass drummers to regulate the beat for the march and for renditions of popular pieces for static displays of their skills. Quite when they began to include a cymbalist in their numbers is unknown but the 1985 *Drummer's Handbook* suggested that the instrumentation within a corps, whether it had 16 drummers or 24, included one set of cymbals.[23] While not prescribed, many a corps also had a drummer knocking out the tune on a glockenspiel.

This resurgence in drumming was accompanied by greater efforts to dress and equip the drummers of the infantry of the line more correctly. The Foot Guards, invariably consumed by the demands of public duties, had never experienced a slackening of their dress standards. But the scarlet full dress of the infantry had long been lost and, while drummers were supposed to maintain full dress, this had proved almost impossible. Starved of resources many battalions had their drummers wearing what might best be described as an economy version of full dress, the red tunics being cast-offs from the Foot Guards and the blue cloth helmets being nothing more than converted policemen's helmets. The restoration of proper tunics, properly faced and laced, and proper helmets with the correct brass fittings, owed a great deal to Colonel Peter Walton, late of the Royal Army Ordnance Corps and latterly Director of the Army Museums Ogilby Trust. He worked very closely with the Army Dress Committee to re-impose the correct standards across all of the infantry battalions and sweep away some of the more extraordinary dress inventions of some commanding officers. So successful was this initiative that the regimental bands also re-adopted full dress and set aside their blue Number One Dress tunics and caps.

In 1993 one of the impacts of the 1990 government defence review, called *Options for Change*, resulted in the sweeping away of the old regimental bands. Already the bands had suffered from diminishing numbers, which had largely prompted the 1985 reduction to 21 bandsmen. This was a number set by unit establishment tables and the reality was often very different. In 1993 the band of the Staffordshire Regiment, which had boasted a strength of nearly 40 just a decade earlier, 'had dwindled to only 13 instrumentalists' and, noted the bandmaster, WO1 Bob Meldrum, 'without the help of our TA band we would not have been able to sustain the service that we have provided in recent years.'[24] Pre-Options there had been 69 Regular Army bands but these were to reduce to 29 by April 1995 and all under the centralised control of the new Corps of Army Music. However, the cut in the number of bands was intended to be balanced somewhat by the rise in numbers of bandsmen, and now bandswomen, per band to 35. It was hoped that this increase in the size of each band would help overcome some increasingly clear shortcomings and one ex-director of music of the Irish Guards, Major Gerald Horabin, commented in early 1993 that 'Taking account of the sick, lame and weary, some regiments could only muster 16 bandsmen on parade. When 500 to 600 men are marching past you could hardly hear the music.'[25] Sadly, further cuts followed and by 2014 there were just 23 Regular bands and, in theory more than in practice, 19 Territorial bands of part-time volunteers.

While, as we have seen, drummers and buglers were not exempt from various economies, their very survival demanded extra effort outside the battalions. Some regimental bands had been generous with their time and knowledge in raising the music skills of their cousins, if not brothers, in the drum and bugle corps. Kneller Hall for a while even incorporated some corps in their five-year inspections of every band, if the corps were up to it. But the loss of the regimental bands and the vastly diminished skills of young drummers and buglers associated with the removal of all junior soldier training required a new initiative. In 1995 a Drum Company was established at the Infantry Training Centre at Catterick in North Yorkshire and there the Drumming Wing is now one of the two parts, with the All Arms Drill Wing, of the Army School of Ceremonial. As Captain Keith Hatton, who commanded Drums Company in 2001, put it: 'Most regiments no longer have a regimental band. All they have, musically, are the Drums'[26] and something had to be done to bring standards back up. The company now trains drummers, buglers and flautists of the three English regiments of Foot Guards, the English and Welsh line regiments and the Rifles. Scottish and Irish drummers are trained at the Army School of Bagpipe Music and Highland Drumming at Edinburgh. In the final analysis however, it is all, as always, down to the enthusiasm and leadership of every battalion's commanding officer. Lieutenant Colonel Peter Hollins of the Parachute Regiment commanded one of the training battalions at the Infantry Training Centre and reported that:

> most commanding officers are convinced that drums and bugle platoons are necessary for morale purposes. Yet they are reluctant to release soldiers to come on the courses ... What is really required is for the CO of each battalion to say: 'I'm going to take some pain here and release people for these courses'. Drums

platoons are the soul of a regiment or battalion and we need to give them some emphasis to raise the profile of drumming to the level it deserves.[27]

As the days are long gone when boys entered training and chose the drums as a favoured course, the Drums Company is the sole vestige of drumming and bugling standards in the modern British Army.

The playing of routine calls, whether or not for regulating the day, is one thing; sounding calls in an operational context is another, as has been demonstrated throughout this book. As noted above, battalions have continued to take their bugles and even their drums to war but their use has been confined most sensibly to semi-permanent camps and away from the battlefield proper, although these camps such as in Bosnia, Iraq and Afghanistan, have always remained vulnerable to attack and especially by some sort of artillery or missile. In some cases the drummers, otherwise employed with rifle or machine gun, and the regimental bandsmen, otherwise employed as field medical orderlies, have had the opportunity to accompany a ceremonial parade. The 1st Battalion the Staffordshire Regiment, then an armoured infantry battalion in Warrior, took its drummers and the regimental band to Saudi Arabia in 1990 at the onset of what was to become the First Gulf War. Drums platoons in infantry battalions at that time had continued to be employed in war as machine-gun platoons, their machine-gun teams, equipped with the General Purpose Machine Gun (GPMG), being divided up equally amongst the three rifle companies. This, while it gave the drummers a dual role, or triple role if one includes the fact that the drummers were also all trained riflemen, helped greatly to preserve the corps of drums or bugles in all of the infantry battalions. It also allowed, even on operations, for the concentration of the drummers for a particular occasion and on 21 December 1990 the Staffords celebrated Ferozeshah Day – their main regimental day – in the Saudi desert with their drums and their band. The band too had converted to its war role and formed the backbone of the medical support to the battalion, with bandsmen allocated to the regimental aid post and to the company medical sections. The deployment of these medical orderlies amongst men they knew proved a great fillip to morale. They treated some 60 casualties during training and during the war itself and helped provide much care to the great numbers of surrendered Iraqis ahead of the arrival of prisoner-of-war collecting units.[28]

The new armoured infantry had a particular problem in coping with the inclusion of drummers in the new establishment. The mechanised infantry in their FV (Fighting Vehicle) 432 'battle taxis' in Germany had always been the poor relation to the armoured (tank) regiments but the arrival of the Warrior in the late 1980s put the new armoured infantry battalions on a level footing with the tanks, sweeping away the rather pedestrian approach to armoured warfare that the infantry had sported hitherto and to the benefit of the combined-arms battle. Warrior rapidly proved its capability when it was deployed with 7th and then 4th Armoured Brigades during the first Gulf War to liberate Kuwait from its Iraqi occupiers. The considerably enhanced firepower provided for each infantry section by a turret-mounted 30 mm Rarden Cannon and a Hughes Chain Gun threatened to eradicate any requirement for the further employment of drummers and their GPMGs but they were able to be retained on establishments as has been demonstrated. The author's notes for a 7th Armoured Brigade briefing on Warrior in 1989 declared that 'In addition [to Warrior's weaponry] each platoon will find one SF [GPMG in the "sustained fire", that is tripod-mounted, role] – each two drummers – and a sniper. The SF deploys in the dismounted light role in the attack but on its tripod in defence.'[29] Great efforts were often made, despite local circumstances, to keep the drummers or buglers together. Sometimes force of circumstances, especially on operations, prevented this. In the 1st Battalion the Princess of Wales's Royal Regiment in Iraq in 2004 many of the drummers were trained and utilised as Warrior drivers, work which would have kept them well away from their bugles as the battalion battled the increasingly ferocious insurgency in and around Basra.[30]

It is a sad fact that lack of familiarity with the routine calls has become commonplace but to this day infantry battalions in their home stations and even, at times, when deployed on operations, continue to maintain the various calls during the day when they can and even if they are unable to maintain a fully or even partially constituted corps of drums and buglers. Alwyn Turner, in his delightful history of the sounding of the 'Last Post', was concerned that 'the daily routine of the bugle call was dropping out of use in the army. It had survived into the modern world, but by the end of the 1960s the everyday calls were becoming less familiar.'[31] A book published in the 1930s summed up, if in slightly Orwellian tones, the persistency of the calls:

> You've got to live to the bugle. That's your clock, from now on. I'll wake you up about six. I'll call you to breakfast, and warn you a quarter of an hour before each parade. I'll tell you when your dinner-time begins and ends, and when you're finished for the day. It'll warn you of air raids, and give you the All Clear when they're over. If you've got to see the company commander or the commanding officer, it'll call you out for Orders. It'll tell you when you've got to switch the lights out. Do just what the bugle says, when it says. You'll be doing right.[32]

Major John Brereton, who joined the Royal Horse Artillery as a boy trumpeter in 1932, recalled in later years something similar:

> Once upon a time every schoolboy knew that the sun never set on the British Empire. If he became a soldier he discovered there were few corners of that Empire wherein he was not summoned to his duties by the clangour of trumpet and bugle calls. Roused at some ungodly hour by *Reveille*, he was bidden to parade, to attend orderly room, even sick parade ... At 2200 hours *Last Post* warned that he had only 15 minutes before lights out commanded him to douse the barrackroom buttis and settle quickly into his cot for the night. Today there cannot be many white-haired ex-soldiers whose lives were once regulated by trumpet or bugle.[33]

Still, in those later years, if no other calls were possible during a busy day, battalions might still be woken from their slumbers by 'Reveille', might possibly hear 'Retreat' at daily guard-mounting at 6.00 p.m. each evening and be put to bed, figuratively speaking, with 'Last Post' at 10.00 p.m. This author recalls fondly these and other calls such as 'Mens' Meal' around midday and 'company sergeant majors to the RSM' at various times in a number of battalions that included the Staffords, 1st Battalion the Duke of Edinburgh's Royal Regiment, 2nd Battalion the Grenadier Guards and 3rd Battalion the Royal Green Jackets. This was during the timescale 1977 to 1997 and included a diverse series of postings: Colchester in 1977–79 and 1983–85, Londonderry in 1979–80 and Ballykelly and Aldergrove in 1985–87, Fallingbostel in Germany in the late 1980s, Tern Hill in the mid-1990s and in Hong Kong in the same period. During deployment to Gibraltar in 1981–83, the drumming, bugling and other musical skills of the Staffords were considerably enhanced by the requirement to meet very regular ceremonial commitments on the Rock, with motivation provided early on due to relieving a battalion of the Light Infantry that possessed very highly polished bugling skills. Regular images have appeared of buglers and even drummers during the wars in Afghanistan and Iraq since 2001, buglers especially being found for ceremonies to repatriate the dead or for one of the many flag-lowering ceremonies as the army withdrew its units and handed over to local forces. In 2016 1st Battalion the Mercian Regiment, as just one example, reported that 'The men of the Corps of Drums … do Duty Bugler daily on rotation'[34] when in camp and this continues to be the case for most of the infantry battalions.

The third and last edition of *Trumpet and Bugle Calls for the Army* in 1966 still listed 40 routine bugle calls.[35] The great majority of these, excepting perhaps 'School', continued to be in evidence certainly throughout the final years of the 20th century. All of the calls can be heard played to excellent effect on a website established by ex-members of the Duke of Edinburgh's Royal Regiment. The website actually lists 41 'British Bugle Calls', having added the 'Charlie Reveille' – a short reveille common in infantry regiments – and all of these may be taken as common across the whole of the infantry. All three editions of the *Trumpet and Bugle Sounds for the Army* – 1895, 1914 and 1966 (when the word 'Calls' was substituted for 'Sounds') also listed all of the regimental calls for the regiments existing prior to the 1950s amalgamations. The 1966 edition even added new calls for such regiments as the Special Air Service. This publication was eventually superseded in 1985 by the first edition of *The Drummer's Handbook*. It was two of the Corps of Drums Society's early members – Major and ex-drummer Jack Barrow of the Duke of Edinburgh's Royal Regiment and Drum Major Mike Hall of the Coldstream Guards – who, with founding members Phil Williams, Roger Davenport and the HAC's then drum major, Greg Tunesi, gave birth to the first edition of the *Handbook*. Ironically this handbook, published under the approving hand of the

then Director of Infantry, provided for the very first time comprehensive guidance and instruction on every aspect of instrument playing in
the infantry corps of drums and bugles. Significantly however, both
the 1985 handbook and its 2013 successor made no mention of any
of the regimental calls and provided only a small selection of traditional
calls and beatings, perhaps proof that many of the routine calls really
are no longer heard.[36]

The subject of familiarity with the bugle calls, other than the most
common of 'Reveille', 'Retreat' and 'Last Post', was and still is addressed
in a most pragmatic fashion by the provision of unofficial words to
the various calls. Major Michael Barthorp, a renowned historian of the
British Army, was serving with the 1st Battalion the Northamptonshire
Regiment in Trieste in 1951. British forces had been deployed to Trieste
to prevent the city's occupation by the Yugoslavs in one of the Cold
War's little-known escapades. The Northamptons were serving alongside
the 1st Battalion the North Staffordshire Regiment and many of the
Regulars in this battalion had spent years in India before the Second
World War. Michael Barthorp recalled later that:

> When we were in Trieste in the 1950s ... we used to have periodic 'turn-outs'
> when all the drummers would assemble on the square to sound the Alarm,
> whereupon the time-honoured words ... with [their] old Imperial echoes –
> 'There's a nigger on the wall' repeated ad nauseam ... would ring out from the
> barrack-rooms. In those days of course we still had a number of old [North-
> West] Frontier hands who had heard it in earnest.[37]

Today these words would have very offensive overtones of course but
they were indicative of the prejudices then inherent in the army and
in particular amongst soldiers who had served in any country where
the inhabitants had dark skins. Richard Holmes hinted at there being
authorised 'words to help soldiers remember the various calls, and
alarm was officially: "Larm is sounding, hark the sound/Fills the air
for miles around/Arm! Turn out! And stand your ground."' Holmes,
giving an example of the Hampshire Regiment in 1914, added that
these words were more commonly replaced by 'Sergeant Major's on the
run! Sergeant Major's on the run!'[38] Today soldiers would not recognise
the 'Alarm' or most of the other calls. However, some do remain familiar

and one in particular, the call for 'Mens' Meal' or the Dinner Call, the accompanying words being 'O come to the cookhouse door, boys, come to the cookhouse door.' John Brereton asked rhetorically in his 1996 article: 'How many doddery ex-buglers remember the tune for Officers' Dinner? 'Officers' wives eat puddings and pies, sergeants' wives eat skilly [soldiers' wives get nothing at all to fill their empty bellies]'.[39] While not words to calls, buglers over the decades have also found ways to judge the time between finishing 'Last Post' and sounding the 'Reveille', marked usually by a two-minute silence. This they do by singing to themselves a simple tune that they have timed to about two minutes. In 2016 a bugler playing at one of the centenary services marking the first day of the battle of the Somme in 1916 admitted he sang the children's song *Nelly the Elephant*!

This author has yet to find solid evidence that there were any officially laid down words. In all three editions of the *Trumpet and Bugle Sounds/ Calls* there is no such evidence but it can be supposed with some certainty that in a number of regimental archives their exist one or other editions of these books where the music is suitably annotated with the words common to that regiment. The United States Army did much the same thing, although the music to its bugle calls is different to British music. The words for 'Mess Call' in the US Army, for example, runs as 'Soupy, soupy, soupy, with-out a single bean; Porky, porky, porky with-out a streak of lean; Coffee, coffee, coffee; weak-est ever seen.'[40] In the British Army 'Reveille' was followed by 'Rouse', intended as the final warning to get out of bed. The 'official' words to this call 'were meant to bring to mind the phrase "Come, make a move! And show a leg! Why dil-ly dal-ly? Now don't you hear? Get out of bed, it's past re-veil-le." But other words came to mind more easily 'Get out of bed, Get out of bed, You lazy bug-gers; Get out of bed, Get out of bed, You lazy bug-gers.'[41]

For the US Army 'Reveille' contained typically irreverent words:

> I can't get 'em up, I can't get 'em up, I can't get 'em up in the morn-ing;
> I can't get 'em up, I can't get 'em up, I can't get 'em up at all.
> The corp'ral's worse than pri-vates; The sergeant's worse than corp'rals;
> Lieu-ten-ant's worse than sergeants; An' the cap-tain's worst of all![42]

Words were almost universally applied to marches from *Lilliburlero* in the late 17th century and beyond, and if not before that, and we only have to think of *British Grenadiers* or *It's A Long Way To Tipperary* to summon up familiar words and tunes. Many of these tunes continue to be played today but very many of the original regimental marches are also being lost as regiments have amalgamated time and again with, in some cases, new marches written for the new regiments or, at best, one or two marches retained from the antecedent regiments. An infantry regiment would normally have a regimental quick march and a regimental slow march, and possibly an approach march. But added to this list would be a number of tunes adopted by the regiment and usually taken into the regiment's body of music due to a significant historical incident or a particularly memorable posting. Some of these marches also had words to them with some of these words best forgotten! Lewis Winstock has written that 'The best-known tune which the British acquired in India was *Zacmi dil* or *The wounded heart*, a Pathan song of homosexual love …' This tune had been adopted by the King's (Liverpool Regiment) and the Prince of Wales's (North Staffordshire) Regiment before the Great War, due to the lengthy service of both regiments in the sub-continent. The North Staffords used this as an assembly march and as an approach march from at least 1912 and their county rivals, the South Staffords, were never slow to remind them that a translation of the words at the beginning of the tune reads: 'There's a boy across the river, With a bottom like a peach, But alas – I cannot swim.'[43]

While many of the calls and marches are forgotten an enterprising drum major or bugle major who has studied his calling can summon up a useful tune for a special occasion. Routinely at dinner nights in officers' and sergeants' messes the officers, or sergeants, and their ladies will move into the dining room to the accompaniment of suitable music after the relevant dinner call has been sounded on the bugle. The aforementioned Mike Hall recalled that in an unnamed infantry battalion in Germany in recent years the drummers, expecting a long weekend back in England, were informed at very short notice by the regimental sergeant major that they were required to play instead at the sergeants' mess dinner night on the approaching Saturday.

Come the eve of the dinner and the Corps of Drums [was] formed up in the Sergeants' Mess Dining Room. Given the first nod by the Mess Steward, they came to the ready position; upon the second nod, the drummers launched into playing the Rogue's March (alias 'Whore's March') to play the RSM's wife and all other Mess wives, into the Ladies' Dinner Night ... After dinner and further musical offerings from the drummers, the RSM ... asked 'what was the bright little tune by which the ladies had been played into dinner?' The drum major, without hesitation, replied 'It's a traditional tune reserved for such occasions as this, Sir!'[44]

In 2013 there were as many as eight roles for the 38 surviving Regular infantry battalions, which included the Foot Guards, and the 14 Territorial infantry battalions, with the Territorial Army about to be renamed the Army Reserve. These roles were: 'parachute', 'armoured infantry', 'air assault', 'heavy protected mobility' (in the Mastiff), 'light protected mobility' (in the Foxhound), 'light', 'mechanised' and 'public duties' (which are, effectively, light-role battalions). Three years later and at the time of writing, with the Regulars having lost another four battalions, all but the air assault and mechanised roles had been maintained and these are the roles defined for the infantry within the 'Army 2020' changes.[45] Fourteen of the Regular battalions have been allotted the light role, with their establishment reduced to just 501 infantry officers and men. Having also reduced each of the three rifle companies to two, instead of three, rifle platoons, the shortfall is intended to be made up by a permanent affiliation with a Reserve infantry battalion, which will produce the third platoon when it is required. However, the loss of the third Regular platoon in each company is offset, at least in terms of firepower, by creating a machine-gun platoon of six guns for each. All other types of battalion except for armoured infantry are to maintain a single machine-gun platoon within their manoeuvre support companies. But with many of these machine gunners also having to master heavy machine guns, grenade launchers and sniper rifles, it is rare to find drummers and buglers in their ranks.[46]

A survey of all of the Regular infantry battalions conducted by the author in early 2016 demonstrated that, of those battalions answering the survey – just under one third made up of two Guards' battalions, seven line battalions and one Rifles' – all maintained a corps in some form or another. With the recent resurrection of assault pioneer platoons eight battalions had double-hatted their drummers and buglers as assault pioneers and were able to keep them together in a platoon within what is called manoeuvre support company. One battalion – 2nd Battalion the Royal Anglian Regiment – placed all of its drummers in the anti-tank platoon, also in manoeuvre support company, and another battalion – 1st Battalion the Yorkshire Regiment – divided its drummers up within support company but across the assault pioneer, anti-tank and mortar platoons. Average numbers per corps, including drum and bugle majors, were 15, with the lowest being nine drummers and the highest being 20 buglers. Each corps of drums maintained side drums, bass drums, bugles and flutes, but there was no sign of tenor drums in all cases. A pair of tenor drums on the flanks of the side drummers, the tenor drummers invariably sporting draped animal skins and decoratively swirling their sticks, took much practice and coordination. It is no surprise therefore that they are now a rarity.

It is in many ways against the odds that any of the corps of drums or bugles survive in any form, but they do. While infantry battalions other than the three battalions of Foot Guards assigned to public duties at any one time do little foot drill, and even such ostensibly big ceremonial parades such as presentations of new colours have become cut-down affairs, there continues to be high demand for the infantry's remaining 'musick'. Many members of the public were surprised to hear that Lee Rigby of the 2nd Battalion the Royal Regiment of Fusiliers, who was so savagely murdered by Islamist extremists outside his barracks at Woolwich in London in May 2013, was a serving drummer and held that rank. At his military funeral his coffin was carried by his fellow drummers, resplendent in their laced drummers' tunics and fusiliers' bearskin caps. At the very least the demand for a bugler to provide a decent rendition of 'Last Post' at military funerals and at the growing number of memorial services has fuelled interest in the continuing place of drummers and buglers in the modern army. Training these musicians remains a challenge, as we have observed. Since time immemorial 'buglers of poor technique', as Rodney Bashford has put it (and adding that 'Buglers were not noted for their innate musicality'), would attempt to conceal their inadequacies and thus the consequent rebuke, if not punishment, of the regimental sergeant major, by persuading a fellow bugler or even a band trumpeter to sound the appropriate call from a hidden spot nearby. He might get away with it, but Bashford recalled that the bugler who tried to protect himself from the pouring rain by sounding from the protection of the chapel porch in the old Victoria Barracks in Belfast met his comeuppance despite the darkness of the hour. 'The Padre, who must have been at his devotions, emerged suddenly to investigate the trespass, ramming the mouthpiece and half the bugle well past the culprit's tonsils. Never did *Last Post*, with its final sighing cadence, die on such a wail and a whimper.'[47]

Perhaps the ultimate solution is automation. The US Army had a particular problem by the beginning of the 21st century, with so many veterans from the Second World War dying every day and all of them entitled to have 'Taps' sounded over their graves. With just around 500 buglers then in the army and sometimes with large numbers of veterans passing away, it became impossible to meet demand. The invention of an automated bugle helped solve the problem. 'It is a bugle discreetly fitted with a battery-operated conical insert that plays the twenty-four notes of Taps at the flick of a switch [reported the *Guardian* newspaper]. It is all digital, with no human talent or breath required. All you do is hold it up, turn it on and try to look like a bugler.'[48] Scandalous and 'typically American' might be the reaction of every drummer and bugler who has gone before. But the Royal Fusiliers trialled this instrument at the Tower of London in 2005 and reported favourably:

> We have been reluctant to use it at any regimental funeral, nor has it been used at the nightly Ceremony of the Keys here in the Tower of London. But we did sound the *Last Post* from the battlements on the roof of the Regimental Headquarters here in the Tower ... to signal the start of the official three minutes silence in memory of those killed by the tsunami.[49]

★

If one of the enduring images of the British Army is to see its men marching through our towns and cities with drums beating, colours flying and bayonets fixed with, hopefully, the drummers resplendent in their scarlet full dress or the buglers in their rifle green, another enduring image is of the stilling and mournful tones of the Last Post. Quite when the call, named as such, usurped the traditional 'tattoo', or 'last retreat' at the end of the day is unknown, but it is recorded in a letter home in the 1850s. Military funerals had long seen drummers marching in slow time with black-covered, muffled drums beating a dead march. The additional accompaniment of bugles seems to have become more evident from as early as the 1820s. No record of referring to this as Last Post is, however, evident before a soldier of the 71st Highland Light Infantry wrote home from Canada in October 1853, having witnessed a funeral of one of his colleagues. He told that 'When the coffin was deposited in the grave, the Last Post was played between every volley that was fired over it.'[50] But it was not until the years immediately following the end of the Great War that the blowing of Last Post for 'Our Glorious Dead' became established universally.

In recent years this sound has assumed a growing presence at military memorials and ceremonies across the country as, in some way, a late and guilty recognition of the service of our soldiers. Another irony is at large here: at a time of great public unpopularity of the 'wars of choice' in Iraq and Afghanistan, the British soldier has received greater public acclaim. The Last Post has been sounded in both of these two benighted countries as British soldiers have hauled down the Union Flag, their job unfinished. But it has been sounded too for those 635 servicemen and women who have died in these two wars since 2001. It is, as Alwyn Turner has reflected, 'the one piece in the bugle's repertoire that has achieved instant recognition.'[51] The original meanings of the 'retreat' and the 'tattoo' have both been transformed into latter-day symbols of military pomp, with massed drums, bugles, pipes and bands. The 'retreat', combined with additional music in a sunset ceremony, is deeply moving. But it is the sounding of the infantry's Last Post at funerals and services of remembrance that has come to symbolise some final act and a passing away of what has gone before, whether in mourning for the individual or some greater endeavour.

Drummers and buglers may no longer be the Instruments of Battle but the Last Post has not yet sounded for them. If the call may appear to represent silence and remembrance at the going down of the sun, it is never the end of the matter. As Turner has concluded:

> The order of service at a soldier's funeral does not end with that call. 'The Last Post is the Nunc Dimittis of the dead soldier. It is the last bugle call,' Stephen Graham of the Scots Guards had written in 1919, before adding: 'It is the last, but it gives promise of Reveille – of the great Reveille which ultimately the Angel Gabriel ought to blow.[52]

Sir Denis Forman's memoir of his wartime service serves as the final word. In 1943 in transit via Algeria to Italy he recalled: 'The day began with the Green Howards Reveille, the most beautiful bugle call of all, and ended with the 'Last Post' ...'[53]

Notes

Introduction

1   Glenn Williams, US Army Center of Military History, quoted in Elizabeth Collins, *The Beats of Battle: Images of Army Drummer Boys Endure*, www.soldiers.dodlive.mil.
2   Hugh Barty-King, *The Drum – A Royal Tournament Tribute to the Military Drum*, London, 1988, p 8.
3   John Selby (ed.), *The Recollections of Sergeant Morris*, Moreton-in-Marsh, 1998, p viii.
4   Selby, *ibid*, p 2.
5   Drummer Fife, *With their Musket, Fife and Drum*, www.queensroyalsurreys.org.uk.
6   Trevor Herbert and Helen Barlow, *Music & the British Military in the Long Nineteenth Century*, Oxford, 2013, p 16.

Chapter 1

1   Mark Healy, *New Kingdom Egypt*, Botley, 1992, p 60.
2   Sir J. Gardner Wilkinson, *The Manners and Customs of the Ancient Egyptians*, London, 1837, Volume I, p 297.
3   www.youtube.com/Trumpets of Tutankhamun.
4   Nic Fields, *The Spartan Way*, Barnsley, 2013, p xxxviii.
5   Thucydides, *History of the Peloponnesian War*, translated by Rex Warner, London, 1972, p 392.
6   Fields, *ibid*, pp 145–146.
7   Peter Connolly, *Greece and Rome at War*, London, 1981, p 76.
8   Aristides Quintilianus, *De musica*, in Thomas J. Mathiesen, *Apollo's Lyre – Greek Music and Music Theory in Antiquity and the Middle Ages*, Lincoln, 1999, p 230.
9   Vegetius, *De Re Militari* Book II, www.pvv.ntnu.no.
10   Flavius Romanus, *The Roman Army*, www.hillsdalesites.org.
11   A. K. Goldsworthy, *The Roman Army at War 100 BC–AD 200*, Oxford, 1996.
12   Goldsworthy, *ibid*.
13   Diodorus Siculus, *Bibliotheca historica*, Polybius, *The Histories*, quoted by Lisa Spangenberg, *Celtic Studies Resources*, www.digitalmedievalist.com.
14   Henry George Farmer, *Military Music*, London, 1950, p 10.
15   Barty-King, *ibid*, p 30.
16   Farmer, *ibid*, p 11.
17   Georges Duby, *The Legend of Bouvines:War, Religion and Culture in the Middle Ages*. Translated by Catherine Tihanyi, California, 1990. At www.deremilitari.org.

18   Sir John Froissart, *The Chronicles of England, France, Spain and the Adjoining Countries from the Latter Part of the Reign of Edward II, to the Coronation of Henry IV*, Volume II, translated by Thomas Johnes, London, 1839, p 467.
19   *The Battle of Agincourt, 1415*, www.eyewitnesstohistory.com/agincourt.
20   Anne Curry, *The Battle of Agincourt – Sources & Interpretations*, Woodbridge, 2000, p 160.
21   David Potter, *Renaissance France at War: Armies, Culture and Society, c. 1480–1560*, Woodford, 2008.
22   Potter, *ibid*, p 286.
23   Potter, *ibid*, p 285.
24   Farmer, *ibid*, p 185.
25   Christopher Gravett, *German Medieval Armies 1300–1500*, Oxford, 1985, p 17.
26   Farmer, *Military Music, ibid*, p 15.
27   Potter, *ibid*, p 286.
28   Potter, *ibid*, p 286.
29   R. J. Knecht, *Francis I*, Cambridge, 1982, p 247.
30   Potter, *ibid*, p 287.
31   Potter, *ibid*, pp 287–288.
32   Henry George Farmer, 'The Martial Fife', *JSAHR*, Volume XXIII, p 66.
33   *Celebrating British Drum & Fife Music*, Corps of Drums Society, www.corpsofdrums.com.
34   Barty-King, *ibid*, pp 32–33.
35   Francis Grose, *Military Antiquities Respecting a History of The English Army from the Conquest to the Present Time*, Volume II, London, 1788, p 247.
36   *JSAHR*, Volume XX, p 121.
37   *JSAHR*, Volume XX, p 182.
38   Farmer, *ibid*, p 67.
39   Sir John Fortescue, *A History of The British Army, Volume I*, London: Macmillan, 1899.
40   Duff Cooper, *Sergeant Shakespeare*, London, 1949, p 5.

Chapter 2

1   Keith Roberts, *Pike and Shot Tactics 1590–1660*, Oxford, 2010, for a detailed comparison of systems.
2   Charles Carlton, *Going to the Wars – The Experience of the English Civil Wars 1638–1651*, London, 1992, p 20.
3   Carlton, *ibid*, p 71.
4   G. Derbridge, 'A History of the Drums and Fifes 1650–1700', *JSAHR,* Volume XLIV p 50.
5   Barty-King, *ibid*, p 11.
6   *JSAHR*, Volume XX, 1940, p 182.
7   Barty-King, *ibid*, p 13.
8   Barty-King, *ibid*, p 14.
9   Derbridge, *ibid*, p 51.
10   Stuart Peachey, *The Mechanics of Infantry Combat in the First English Civil War*, Bristol, 1992, pp 18–19.
11   Lieutenant Colonel J. H. Leslie, 'The Points of War', *JSAHR*, Volume IX, 1930, p 108.
12   Farmer, *ibid*, p 67.
13   Leslie, *ibid*, pp 108–109.
14   *JSAHR*, Volume VII, pp 249–250.
15   *JSAHR*, Volume VII, p 250.
16   Peachey, *ibid*, p 7.
17   Anne Belsey, 'A Simple Guide to William Barriffe for Busy Officers', *The Sealed Knot Orders of the Day*, Volume 30, Issue 3, May/June 1998.
18   Maurice Cockle, *A Bibliography of English Military Works up to 1642 and of Contemporary Foreign Works*, London, 1900, p 115.

19 Farmer, '16th–17th Century Military Marches', *JSAHR*, Volume XXVIII, 1950, p 50.

20 Michael Pfeil, *Drumming in the English Civil Wars – Myths, facts and informed guesses*, Bristol, second edition, 1997, p 14.

21 Lewis Winstock, *Songs & Music of the Redcoats – A History of the War Music of the British Army 1642–1902*, London, 1970, p 17.

22 Farmer, *ibid*, p 50.

23 Farmer, *ibid*, p 50.

24 Pfeil, *ibid*, p 16.

25 Pfeil, *ibid*, p 17.

26 Pfeil, *ibid*, p 16.

27 Pfeil, *ibid*, p 21.

28 Christopher L. Scott, Alan Turton and Eric Gruber von Arni, *Edgehill – The Battle Reinterpreted*, Barnsley, 2004.

29 Keith Roberts, *Soldiers of the English Civil War (1): Infantry*, London, 1989, pp 14–15.

30 *A Worthy Speech spoken by his Excellency the E. of Essex in the head of His Armie before his arrival at Worcester, on Saturday lst, being the 24th September, 1642*, London, 1642, in British Library E 200 (64) and reproduced in Scott, Turton, von Arni, *ibid*, p 201.

31 Scott, Turton, von Arni, *ibid*, p 108.

32 Scott, Turton, von Arni, *ibid*, p 109.

33 Scott, Turton, von Arni, *ibid*, p 109.

34 Peachey, *ibid*, p 3.

35 Peachey, *ibid*, p 4.

36 Carlton, *ibid*, p 86.

37 Carlton, *ibid*, p 219.

Chapter 3

1 Barty-King, *ibid*.

2 Farmer, *Martial Fife, ibid*, p 67.

3 Henry George Farmer, *The Rise & Development of Military Music*, London, 1912, p 47.

4 Farmer, *ibid*, p 34.

5 Major Gordon Turner and Alwyn Turner, *The History of British Military Bands, Volume Two – Guards and Infantry*, Staplehurst, 1996, p 14.

6 John Tincey, *The British Army 1660–1704*, London, 1994.

7 Lieutenant Colonel Richard Elton, *The Compleat Body of the Art Military: Exactly compiled, and gradually composed for the Foot, in the best refined manner, according to the practice of the Modern Times*, London, 1650.

8 Elton, second edition, London, 1659, pp 54–55.

9 Elton, *ibid*, pp 17–18.

10 Elton, *ibid*, p 17.

11 W. Y. Carman, 'The Dress of Erle's Regiment in 1704 and 1709', *JSAHR*, Volume XLVI, p 203.

12 *JSAHR*, Volume XI, pp 176–180.

13 *38th Foot Inspection Reports 1769 and 1771*, Staffordshire Regiment Museum.

14 Barty-King, *ibid*, p 12.

15 Barty-King, *ibid*, p 12.

16 Elton, *ibid*, pp 177–178.

17 Elton, *ibid*, p 176.

18 Peter Young and Wilfrid Emberton, *The Cavalier Army – Its Organisation and Everyday Life*, London, 1974.

19 Barty-King, *ibid*, p 13.

20 Elton, *ibid*, p 178

21 Farmer, *ibid*, p 67.

22 Humphrey Bland, *Treatise of Military Discipline*, 1727, quoted by Farmer in 'The Retreat', *JSAHR*, Volume XXV, p 119.

23 Bland, *ibid*, p 120.

24 J. A. Houlding, *Fit for Service: The Training of the British Army 1715–1795*, Oxford, 1981.

25 David Blackmore, *Destructive and Formidable – British Infantry Firepower 1642–1765*, London, 2014.

26 Blackmore, *ibid*, p 167.

27 *An Abridgement of the English Military Discipline By His Majesties permission*, London, 1676, pp 20–21.

28 *English Military Discipline, ibid*, pp 69–71.

29 *An Abridgement of the English Military Discipline, Compiled by the Late Duke of Monmouth*, London, 1690 edition, pp 82–86.

30 D. G. Chandler (ed.), *A Journal of Marlborough's Campaigns During the War of the Spanish Succession 1704–1711 by John Marshall Deane*, Society for Army Historical Research, Special Publication Number No 12, 1984, pp 110, 114.

31 Chandler, *ibid*, p 48.

32 John Millner, *A Compendious Journal Of all the Marches, Famous Battles, Sieges, etc, of the Triumphant Armies, Of the ever-glorious Confederate High Allies, etc*, 1733.

33 Soldier John Scot, *The Remembrance: A Metrical Account of the War in Flanders 1701–12* in James Ferguson (ed.), *Papers Illustrating the History of the Scots Brigade in the Service of the United Netherlands 1572–1782*, Volume III, Edinburgh, 1901, p 497.

34 Quoted in James Falkner, *Marlborough's Wars – Eyewitness Accounts 1702–1713*, Barnsley, 2005, p 97.

35 Falkner, *ibid*, p 49.

36 Houlding, *ibid*, pp 174–175.

37 Houlding, *ibid*, p 190.

38 Houlding, *ibid*, p 160.

39 Humphrey Bland, *A Treatise of Military Discipline; In which is Laid down and Explained The Duty of the Officer and Soldier, Thro' the several Branches of the Service*, London, 5th Edition, 1743, p 41.

40 Bland, *ibid*, p 6.

41 Bland, *ibid*, p 14.

42 Bland, *ibid*, pp 74–87.

43 Bland, *ibid*, pp 132–133.

44 Bland, *ibid*, pp 270–271.

45 Bland, *ibid*, p 249.

46 Brigadier General Richard Kane, *Campaigns of King William and Queen Anne; From 1689, to 1712. Also a New System of Military Discipline, for a Battalion of Foot on Action; etc*, London, 1745, p 109.

47 Kane, *ibid*, p 114.

48 Kane, *ibid*, pp 115–116.

49 Barty-King, *ibid*, p 44.

50 Kane, *ibid*, pp 116–119.

51 Kane, *ibid*, pp 119–120.

Chapter 4

1 Colonel H. C. B. Rogers, *The British Army of the Eighteenth Century*, London, 1977, p 204.

2 Kane, *ibid*, 109–110.

3 Rogers, *ibid*, p 202.

4 Houlding, *ibid*, p 351.

5 Houlding, *ibid*, p 351.

6 Houlding, *ibid*, p 351.

7 Sir John Fortescue, *A History of The British Army*, Volume II, London, 1899, p 97.

8   Houlding, *ibid*, p 358.
9   Major General Sir Henry Everett, *The History of The Somerset Light Infantry*, London 1934, p 88.
10   Blackmore, *ibid*, p 130.
11   *General Wolfe's Instructions to Young Officers: Also His Orders for a Battalion and an Army, etc*, London, 1768, p 35.
12   *Wolfe, ibid*, p 49.
13   Stephen Brumwell, *Redcoats – The British Soldier and War in the Americas, 1755–1763*, Cambridge, 2002, p 225.
14   Reginald Hargreaves, *This Happy Breed*, London, 1951, p 42.
15   Sir John Fortescue, *Following the Drum*, London, 1931, pp 32–33.
16   Fortescue, *ibid*, p 491.
17   Trevor Royle (ed.), *A Dictionary of Military Quotations*, London, 1990, p 188.
18   *Wolfe, ibid*, p 39.
19   Tobias Smollett and David Hume, *Compleat History of England*, London, 1827, p 247.
20   Andrew Cormack and Alan Jones (eds.), *The Journal of Corporal Todd 1745–1762*, Stroud, 2001, pp 76–77.
21   Houlding, *ibid*, p 205.
22   Houlding, *ibid*, p 205.
23   Francis Grose, *Military Antiquities of the English Army*, Volume 1, 1786, quoted by Farmer, *JSAHR*, Volume XXIII, p 68.
24   Notes in *JSAHR*, undated, p 82.
25   WO 27/1 quoted in Houlding, *ibid*, p 278.
26   Houlding, *ibid*, p 278.
27   Alan J. Guy (ed.), *Colonel Samuel Bagshawe and the Army of George II 1731–1762*, London, 1990, p 226.
28   Brumwell, *ibid*, pp 194–195.
29   Houlding, *ibid*, p 279.
30   Winstock, *ibid*, p i.
31   Henry George Farmer, '16th–17th Century Military Marches', *JSAHR*, Volume XXVIII, 1950, p 49.
32   Winstock, *ibid*, p 19.
33   Winstock, *ibid*, p 18.
34   Farmer, *ibid*, p 52.
35   Winstock, *ibid*, p 25.
36   Winstock, *ibid*, p 43.
37   Henry George Farmer, 'Our Regimental Bands', *JSAHR*, Volume XLII, p 158.
38   Herbert and Barlow, *ibid*, p 36.
39   Herbert and Barlow, *ibid*, p 38.
40   Fortescue, *ibid*, p 583.
41   Herbert and Barlow, *ibid*, p 53.
42   Herbert and Barlow, *ibid*, p 55.

Chapter 5

1   Houlding, *ibid*, p 375.
2   Houlding, *ibid*, p 183.
3   Houlding, *ibid*, p 215.
4   Stephen Brumwell, *Redcoats – The British Soldier and War in the Americas, 1755–1763*, Cambridge, 2002, p 12.
5   Brumwell, *ibid*, p 3.
6   Brumwell, *ibid*, p 209.
7   Brumwell, *ibid*, p 254.
8   Earl John Chapman and R. Paul Goodman, 'Quebec, 1759: Reconstructing Wolfe's Main Battle Line From Contemporary Evidence', *JSAHR*, Volume XCII, 2014, p 28.

9   Stephen Brumwell, 'Rank and File: A Profile of One of Wolfe's Regiments', *JSAHR*, Volume CXXIX, 2001, p 17.

10   Houlding, *ibid*, p 355.

11   David L. Preston, *Braddock's Defeat – The battle of the Monongahela and the Road to Revolution*, Oxford, 2015, p 112.

12   Preston, *ibid*, p 257.

13   Preston, *ibid*, p 269.

14   Ian McCulloch and Tim Todish, *British Light Infantryman of the Seven Years' War – North America 1757–63*, Oxford, pp 10–11.

15   Houlding, *ibid*, p 129.

16   Houlding, *ibid*, p 205.

17   Houlding, *ibid*, p 218.

18   Thomas Simes, *A Military Course for the Government and Conduct of a Battalion Designed for their Regulations in Quarter, Camp or Garrison*, London, 1777, p 18.

19   Simes, *ibid*, pp 25–26.

20   Simes, *ibid*, p 177.

21   Gary Vorwald and Erik Lichack with Paul Ackermann (ed.), *Military Music of the American Revolution – A Collection of Authentic Signals, Camp Duties, Marches, and Favorite Airs for the Fife and Drum*, Brigade of the American Revolution, 2007, p 2.

22   Mathew H. Spring, *With Zeal And With Bayonets Only – The British Army on Campaign in North America, 1775–1783*, Norman, 2008, p xii.

23   Spring, *ibid*, p xii.

24   Vorwald and Lichack, *ibid*.

25   Steven M. Baule, 'Drummers in the British Army During the American Revolution', *JSAHR*, Volume LXXXVI, 2008, p 22.

26   *Commons Journal*, pp 613–4 and 616.

27   Mark Urban, *Fusiliers,* London, 2007, p 101.

28   'The Diary of Lieutenant John Barker, Fourth (or The King's Own) Regiment of Foot, From November 1774 to May 1776', *JSAHR*, Volume VII, 1929, p 152.

29   Nathaniel Philbrick, *Bunker Hill – A City, A Siege, A Revolution*, London, 2013, p 99.

30   Vorwald and Lichack, *ibid*, p 10.

31   Vorwald and Lichack, *ibid*, p 10.

32   *The American Magazine of Useful and Entertaining Knowledge*, Volume II, Boston, 1836, p 496.

33   Baule, *ibid*, p 21.

34   Don N. Hagist, *British Soldiers American War*, Yardley, 2012, p 255.

35   Letter from Michael Grenier to author dated 6 January 2002.

36   Baule, *ibid*, p 21.

37   David Hackett Fischer, *Paul Revere's Ride*, New York, 1994, pp 59–60.

38   Fischer, *ibid*, p 181.

39   Fischer, *ibid*, pp 204–5.

40   Fischer, *ibid*, p 199.

41   Philbrick, *ibid*, p 132.

42   Philbrick, *ibid*, p 132.

43   Fischer, *ibid*, p 240.

44   Major H. FitzM Stacke, 'Princeton 1777', *JSAHR*, Volume XIII, 1934, p 224.

45   Urban, *ibid*, p 118.

46   Raoul F. Camus, *Military Music of the American Revolution,* Chapel Hill, 1976, p 73.

47   Urban, *ibid*, p 124.

48   Reproduction in John Mollo, *Uniforms of the American Revolution*, London, 1975, Plate 95.

49   Peggy Beach, *Battle of King's Mountain*, 1977, www.co.cleveland.nc.us.

50   Spring, *ibid*, p 247.

51 Spring, *ibid*, p 190.
52 *Evolution of the Military Bugle in the Nineteenth Century*, www.middlehornleader.com.
53 James Frassett, *The Battle of Saratoga – Freeman's Farm*, www.revolutionaryarchives.org.
54 *Diary of Bernardus Swartout, 2nd New York regiment, 10 November 1777 to 9 June 1783*, in John U. Rees, "'Bugle Horns", "Conk Shells", and "Signals by Drum'", *Journal of the Brigade of the American Revolution*, 1996.
55 *General Orders, 24 August 1779*, in Rees, *ibid*.
56 Joseph Trudeau, *Music in the Continental Army*, MA Thesis, American Public University System, Charles Town, 2014.
57 Don H. Hagist (ed.), *A British Soldier's Story – Roger Lamb's Narrative of the American Revolution*, Baraboo, 2004, p 26.
58 Hagist, *ibid*, pp 15, 37.
59 Sir A. Campbell, *Journal of an Expedition against the rebels in Georgia etc, 1778*, in Spring, *ibid*, p 90.
60 Spring, *ibid*, p 102.
61 Spring, *ibid*, p 140.
62 Spring, *ibid*, p 141.
63 Spring, *ibid*, p 143.
64 Spring, *ibid*, p 160.
65 Spring, *ibid*, p 147.
66 Richard M. Ketchum, *Saratoga – Turning Point in America's Revolutionary War*, London, 1999, p 204.
67 Ketchum, *ibid*, pp 204 and 496.
68 Spring, *ibid*, pp 216–217.
69 Spring, *ibid*, p 146.
70 Spring, *ibid*, p 156.
71 Spring, *ibid*, p 159.
72 Spring, *ibid*, pp 159 and n 133 p 321.
73 Spring, *ibid*, p 221.
74 Spring, *ibid*, p 229.
75 Spring, *ibid*, p 180.
76 Spring, *ibid*, p 237.
77 Spring, *ibid*, p 239.
78 John Milsop, *Continental Infantryman of the American Revolution*, Oxford, 2004, p 19.
79 www.let.rug.nl/usa/documents/1776-1785.

Chapter 6

1 Philip Haythornthwaite, *British Napoleonic Infantry Tactics 1792–1815*, Oxford, 2008, p 5.
2 Peter Snow, *To War With Wellington – From the Peninsula to Waterloo*, London, 2010, p 173.
3 David Dundas, *Principles of Military Movements Chiefly Applied to Infantry*, London, 1788, pp 9–12.
4 *General Regulations, and Orders for His Majesty's Forces*, Adjutant General's Office, 12 April 1786, pp v–vi.
5 *General Regulations 1786, ibid*, p 60.
6 Dundas, *ibid*, pp 27–29.
7 Dundas, *ibid*, p 43.
8 *General Regulations 1786, ibid*, pp 10–11.
9 Dundas, *ibid*, p 61.
10 Dundas, *ibid*, pp 13–14.
11 David Dundas, *Principles of Military Movements*, Dublin 1789, p 107.
12 Dundas, *ibid*, p 110.
13 *Rules and Regulation for the Formations, Field Exercise, and Movements of His Majesty's Forces*, War Office 24 June 1801, p 68 and p 78.
14 *General Orders and Observations on the Movements and Field Exercise of the Infantry*, Horse Guards, 1 September 1804, p 13.

15 *General Orders 1804, ibid*, p 6.

16 *General Orders 1804, ibid*, p 8.

17 Richard Holmes, *Redcoat – The British Soldier in the Age of Horse and Musket*, London, 2001, pp 9–11.

18 Count Henry D'Ideville, *Memoirs of Marshal Bugeaud, From his Private Correspondence and Original Documents, 1784–1849*, translated and edited by Charlotte M. Yonge, London, 1884, pp v–vi.

19 Henry George Farmer, 'Our Bands in the Napoleonic Wars', *JSAHR*, Volume XL, 1963, p 33.

20 Paddy Griffith, *French Napoleonic Infantry Tactics 1792–1815*, Oxford, 2007, p 63.

21 Griffith, *ibid*, p 56.

22 'Operations of the Fifth or Picton's Division in the Campaign of Waterloo' by an Officer of the Division, *United Service Magazine*, June 1835, p 182.

23 Captain Sir John Kincaid, *Adventures in the Rifle Brigade and Random Shots from a Rifleman*, 1830 and 1835, facsimile reprint Glasgow, 1981, p 238.

24 Charles Oman (ed.), *William Grattan – Adventures with the Connaught Rangers, 1809–1814*, London, 2003, pp 34–35.

25 *The Standing Orders for the 33rd (1st Yorkshire West Riding) Regiment*, 1798.

26 *JSAHR*, Volume XIII, 1934, pp 50–52.

27 Urban, *ibid*, pp 13–14.

28 Barty-King, *ibid*, p 91.

29 *JSAHR*, Volume XXIX, 1951, p 19.

30 David Gates, *The British Light Infantry Arm c. 1790–1815 – its creation, training and operational role*, London, 1987, p 55.

31 Gates, *ibid*, p 55.

32 *Regulations for the Exercise of Riflemen and Light Infantry and Instructions for their Conduct in the Field*, London: Horse Guards 1798, reprinted 1814, plates 7 and 8.

33 *Regulations for the Exercise of Riflemen and Light Infantry and Instructions for their Conduct in the Field*, War office, 1814 edition, pp 18–20.

34 *Regulations for Riflemen, ibid*, p 21.

35 Major General J. F. C. Fuller, 'Two Private Letters From Major-General Sir John Moore', *JSAHR*, Volume IX, 1930, p 163.

36 Major General J. F. C. Fuller, 'Sir John Moore's Light Infantry Instructions of 1798–1799', *JSAHR*, Volume XI, pp 68–75.

37 Oman, *ibid*, p 145.

38 Barty-King, *ibid*, pp 83–84.

39 Kincaid, *ibid*, pp 165–166.

40 Alwyn Turner, *The Last Post – Music, Remembrance and the Great War*, London, 2014, p 30.

41 www.royal-irish.com.

42 Captain B. H. Liddell Hart (ed.), *The Letters of Private Wheeler 1809–1828*, Moreton-in-Marsh, 2000 edition, p 122.

43 Farmer, *ibid*, pp 33–34.

44 Farmer, *ibid*, p 35.

45 Herbert and Barlow, *ibid*, p 55.

46 *General Orders Relative to Soldiers Acting as Musicians*, London, 5 August 1803.

47 Jonathan Crook, *The Very Thing – The Memoirs of Drummer Bentinck, Royal Welch Fusiliers, 1807–1823*, London, 2011, pp 29–30. Note that the spelling 'Welch' instead of 'Welsh' was granted only in 1920.

48 Crook, *ibid*, p 54.

49 Haythornthwaite, *ibid*, p 21.

50 Charles James, *The Regimental Companion; Containing the Relative Duties of Every Officer in the British Army*, London, 1799, p 238.

51 'Memoirs of Edward Costello in Portugal and Spain', *United Service Journal*, 1839, Part II.

52 Captain Alex M. Delavoye, *Records of the 90th Regiment (Perthshire Light Infantry)*, London, 1880, p 40.

53 Haythornthwaite, *ibid*, p 5.

54 Rory Muir, Robert Burnham, Howie Muir and Ron McGuigan, *Inside Wellington's Peninsular Army 1808–1814*, Barnsley, 2014, p 28.

55 Muir et al, *ibid*, p 37 n 49.

56 Stuart Reid, *British Redcoat (2) 1793–1815*, London, 1997, p 26.

57 Haythornthwaite, *ibid*, p 45.

58 Captain T. H. Cooper, *A Practical Guide for the Light Infantry Officer: Comprising Valuable Extracts from all The Most Popular Works on the Subject*, London: T. Egerton, 1806, p 98.

59 Muir etc, *ibid*, p 117.

60 Fuller, *Two Private Letters, ibid*, p 163.

61 Cooper, *ibid*, p 98.

62 Christopher Hibbert (ed.), *The Recollections of Rifleman Harris*, Moreton-in-Marsh, 2000, pp 15–16.

63 Arthur Bryant, *Jackets of Green*, London, 1972, p 52.

64 Liddell Hart, *ibid*, p 82.

65 Urban, *ibid*, p 76.

66 'Two Months Recollections of the Late War in Spain and Portugal by a Private Soldier', *United Service Journal*, 1830, p 417.

67 'The Journal of Lieut. P.K., 88th Regt', *United Service Journal*, 1837.

68 W. F. K. Thompson, *An Ensign in the Peninsular War*, London, 1981, p 264.

69 *JSAHR*, Volume XLVIII, 1970, p 159.

70 *JSAHR*, Volume XXXIX, 1961, p 108.

71 Holmes, *ibid*, p 215.

72 Muir etc, *ibid*, p 149.

73 Colonel K. H. Leslie, *Military Journal of Colonel Leslie, K.H., of Balquhain, Whilst Serving with the 29th Regt in the Peninsula, and the 60th Rifles in Canada, &c. 1807–1832*, Aberdeen, 1887, p 147.

Chapter 7

1 Michael Barthorp, *The British Army on Campaign 1816–1902 (1): 1816–1853*, London, 1987, p 3.

2 Ian Knight, *Go to Your God Like a Soldier – The British Soldier Fighting for Empire, 1837–1902*, London, 1996, p 12.

3 Huw Strachan, *From Waterloo to Balaclava – Tactics, Technology, and the British Army, 1815–1854*, Cambridge, 1985.

4 *United Service Journal*, 1845, Part III, p 100.

5 Strachan, *ibid*, p 14.

6 Barty-King, *ibid*, pp 92–93.

7 *Field Exercise and Evolutions of the Army*, as revised in 1824, London, 1824, p iii.

8 *Field Exercise 1824, ibid*, p v.

9 *Field Exercise 1824, ibid*, p v.

10 *Field Exercise 1824, ibid*, pp 131–132.

11 *Field Exercise 1824, ibid*.

12 *Field Exercise 1824, ibid*, p 138.

13 *Field Exercise 1824, ibid*, p 71.

14 *Field Exercise 1824, ibid*, p 218.

15 *Field Exercise 1824, ibid*, p 219.

16 *Field Exercise 1824, ibid*, p 219.

17 *Field Exercise 1824, ibid*, p 219.

18 *Field Exercise 1824, ibid*, p 220.

19 *Field Exercise 1824, ibid*, pp 222–223.

20 *Field Exercise 1824, ibid*, p 265.

21 *Field Exercise and Evolutions of the Army, as Revised in 1833*, London, 1833, pp 1–2.

22 *Field Exercise 1833, ibid*, pp iii–iv.

23   *Memoranda by Lieut.-General Lord Frederick Fitzclarence, for the Use of Young Officers Assembled in Poona*, quoted in Strachan, *ibid*, p 18.

24   Strachan, *ibid*, p 18.

25   *Field Exercise 1833*, *ibid*, p 127.

26   *Field Exercise 1833*, *ibid*, p 198.

27   *Field Exercise 1833*, *ibid*, p 209.

28   *United Service Journal 1830*, Part II, p 606.

29   *Ibid*.

30   *Field Exercise 1833*, *ibid*, pp 256–260.

31   *Field Exercise 1833*, *ibid*, p 273.

32   *United Service Journal*, 1832, Part II.

33   Major C. Leslie, *Instructions for the Application of Light Drill to Skirmishing in the Field*, Dublin, 1831, pp 22–23.

34   *General Orders 28 December 1816*, London: Horse Guards.

35   Samuel Potter, *The Art of Beating of the Drum with the Camp Garrison & Street Duty by note*, Westminster, 1815.

36   *The King's Regulations and Orders for the* Army, Adjutant-General's Office, Horse Guards, 1st June 1837, p 147; The *Queen's Regulations and Orders for the Army*, Adjutant-General's Office, Horse Guards, First of July, 1844, p 140.

37   *United Service Journal*, 1839, Part II.

38   *The Infantry Manual … Containing an Abstract of the Field Exercises and Evolutions of the Army*, Adjutant General's Office, Horse Guards, London, 1 March 1847.

39   *JSAHR*, Volume XXXIV, 1956.

40   City of Liverpool Museums.

41   *JSAHR*, Volume XXXIII, 1955.

42   National Army Museum.

43   *JSAHR*, Volume XLVII, 1969.

44   Michael Barthorp, *British Infantry Uniforms Since 1660*, Poole, 1982, p 68.

45   Major M. C. Spurrier, 'The Paulet Group', *JSAHR*, Volume XLVI, 1968.

46   Barthorp, *Infantry Uniforms*, *ibid*, p 76.

47   Jeremy Archer, *The Old West Country Regiments (11th, 39th and 54th) From Plassey to the Somme*, Barnsley, 2011, p 174.

48   *Recollections of the Campaign in Spain. By a Captain of the Late British Auxilliary Legion*, *United Service Journal*, 1838, Part II.

49   *Recollections*, *ibid*, 1838, Part III, pp 89–90.

50   *Recollections*, *ibid*, p 93.

51   'Assault on Ghuznee, From the Letter of an Officer of the Army of the Indus', *United Service Journal*, 1840, Part I, p 146.

52   Major W. Hough, *A Narrative of the March and Operations of the Army of the Indus, in the Expedition to Afghanistan in the Years 1838–1839*, London, 1841, pp 175–176.

53   'Despatch of Lieutenant General Sir John Keane to the Governor-General of India, headquarters camp, Ghuznee, July 24, 1839', *United Service Journal*, 1839, Part III.

54   'Memorandum of the Engineers' Operations Before Ghuznee, in July 1839', *United Service Journal*, 1840, Part I.

55   'The Campaign of Afghanistan. In a Series of Letters, By an Officer of the Queen's', *United Service Journal*, 1840, Part II.

56   Alwyn W. Turner, *The Last Post: Music, Remembrance and the Great War*, London, 2014, p 13.

57   James Lunt (ed.), *From Sepoy to Subedar, being the Life and Adventures of Subedar Sita Ram, a Native Officer of the Bengal Army written and related by himself*, London, 1988, p 124.

58   Ian Knight, *Queen Victoria's Enemies (3): India*, London, 1990, p 13.

59   Letter of Lieutenant J. P. Robertson in *History of The East Surrey Regiment*, Volume 1, London, 1916, pp 178–182.

60   Robertson letter, *ibid*, p 183.

Chapter 8

1   Knight, *Go to Your God, ibid*, p 35.

2   Henry Farmer, *'Bands in the Crimean War', JSAHR*, Volume XLI, 1964, p 20.

3   Lieutenant Colonel P. L. Binns, *A Hundred Years of Military Music*, Gillingham, 1959, p 20.

4   *The King's Regulations and Orders for the Army*, Adjutant General's Office, Horse Guards, 1st June 1837, p 146.

5   Trevor Herbert and Helen Barlow, *Music & the British Military in the Long Nineteenth Century*, Oxford, 2013, p 64.

6   Farmer, *ibid*, p 21.

7   *General Order [Army of the East]. – 10th May, 1854. No. 1.*

8   Alexander Kinglake, *The Invasion of the Crimea: Its Origin, and an Account of its Progress*, Volume II, London, 1865, p 427.

9   Farmer, *ibid*, p 23.

10   Farmer, *ibid*, p 23.

11   Farmer, *ibid*, p 23.

12   Farmer, *ibid*, p 23.

13   Michael Barthorp, *Heroes of the Crimea – The Battles of Balaclava and Inkerman*, London, 1991, p 30.

14   *General Orders [Army of the East]. – Bivouac on the Bouljanak River, 19th September 1854. No. 3 and No. 4.*

15   Farmer, *ibid*, p 23.

16   Farmer, *ibid*, p 24.

17   Farmer, *ibid*, p 24.

18   Farmer, *ibid*, p 24.

19   Farmer, *ibid*, p 24.

20   Farmer, *ibid*, p 25.

21   Turner, *ibid*, p 12.

22   Colonel Cowper (ed.), *The King's Own*, Volume II, Oxford, 1939, p 94.

23   Alastair Massie, *The National Army Museum Book of the Crimean War*, London, 2005, p 45.

24   A. W. Kinglake, *The Invasion of the Crimea*, Volume III, London, 1866, pp 151–152.

25   William Howard Russell, *The Great War with Russia – The Invasion of the Crimea; A Personal Retrospect of the Battles of the Alma, Balaclava, and Inkerman, and of the Winter of 1854–55*, 1895, Cambridge, 2012 Edition, p 67.

26   Jay Luvaas, *The Education of an Army – British Military Thought, 1815–1940*, London, 1965, p 34.

27   Huw Strachan, *From Waterloo to Balaclava – Tactics, Technology, and the British Army, 1815–1854*, Cambridge, 1985, p 19.

28   Strachan, *ibid*, pp 22–23.

29   *Naval and Military Gazette*, 9 April 1842, p 230.

30   Strachan, *ibid*, p 43.

31   Barthorp, *ibid*, p 31.

32   Kinglake, *ibid*, p 22.

33   Cowper, *ibid*, p 106.

34   Barthorp, *ibid*, p 103.

35   *XXth Regiment, Crimean War 1854 The Battle of Inkerman*, www.lancs-fusiliers.co.uk.

36   Michael Barthorp, *The British Army on Campaign 1816–1902 (2): The Crimea 1854–56*, London, p 10.

37   Major A. F. Flatow, 'A Crimean Photograph of the Rifle Brigade', *JSAHR*, Volume XXXVIII, 1961, p 155.

38   Charles Kingsford, *The Story of the Duke of Cambridge's Own (Middlesex Regiment)*, London, 1916, p 124.

39   Massie, *ibid*, p 206.

40   Michael Barthorp, *The British Army on Campaign 1816–1902 (3): 1856–1881*, London, 1988, p 7.

41   Charles John Griffiths, *A Narrative of The Siege of Delhi With an Account of the Mutiny at Ferozepore In 1857*, published as *Sepoys, Siege & Storm: The Experiences of a Young Officer of H.M. 61st Regt. At Ferozepore, on Delhi Ridge and at the Fall of Delhi During the Indian Mutiny*, Leonaur Edition, 2006, p 63.

42   L. E. Ruutz Rees, *A Personal Narrative of the Siege of Lucknow*, third edition, London, 1858, p 343.

43   John Fraser, 'Europeans who Sided with the Mutineers in India 1857–9: The Christian Bandsmen of the Native Infantry Regiments', *JSAHR*, Volume LXXIX, 2001, pp 119–130.

44   Captain Thomas McKenzie, *My Life As A Soldier*, St John, 1898.

45   McKenzie, *ibid*, p 3.

46   McKenzie, *ibid*, p 7.

47   McKenzie, *ibid*, p 9.

48   John Clark Marshman, *Memoirs of Major-General Sir Henry Havelock*, London, third edition, 1867, p 310.

49   Marshman, *ibid*, p 310.

50   McKenzie, *ibid*, p 39.

51   Brigadier J. Tanner, 'The Youngest VC? Drummer Thomas Flynn and the 64th (2nd Staffordshire) Regiment at the Relief of Cawnpore, 1857', *Soldiers of the Queen – The Journal of the Victorian Military Society*, Issue 145, June 2011, pp 3–12. This article was written before knowledge of Captain McKenzie's passage about Flynn came to light.

52   *The London Gazette*, 12 April 1859.

53   *Gallant Attack of Windham's Small Force on the Gwalior Contingent, 26 November 1857*, Anne S. K. Brown Military Collection, Brown University Library.

54   Tanner, *ibid*, p 8.

55   Major H. G. Purdon, *An Historical Sketch of the 64th (Second Staffordshire) Regiment and of the Campaigns Through Which They Passed*, undated book, Staffordshire Regiment Museum, p 199.

56   Joseph S. Honan, 'The Youngest Victoria Cross – 3406 Drummer Thomas Flynn VC', *Bulletin of the Military Historical Society*, February 1989, p 124.

57   A. W. Cockerill, *Sons of the Brave – The Story of Boy Soldiers*, London, 1984, p 119.

58   W. H. Fitchett, *The Tale of the Great Mutiny*, New York, 1901, p 233.

59   *The London Gazette*, 20 January 1858.

60   *The London Gazette*, 24 December 1858.

61   *The London Gazette*, 27 April 1858.

62   Roger Perkins, *The Kashmir Gate. Lieutenant Home and the Delhi VCs*, Chippenham, 1983, pp 26–30.

63   Captain Oliver J. Jones RN, *Recollections of a Winter Campaign in India in 1857–58*, first published in 1859, Portsmouth: Royal Navy Museum, 1989, pp 68–69, 74–75.

64   Barthorp, *Crimea, ibid*, p 11.

65   Lieutenant Colonel P. L. Binns, *A Hundred Years of Military Music, being the story of the Royal Military School of Music Kneller Hall*, Gillingham, 1959, pp 48–50.

66   Winstock, *ibid*, p 170.

Chapter 9

1   Knight, *ibid*, p 13.

2   Colonel C. E. Callwell, *Small Wars: Their Principles and Practice*, London, 1906 edition, re-published with an introduction by Colonel Peter S. Walton, as *Small Wars – A Tactical Textbook for Imperial Soldiers*, London, 1990.

3   Callwell, *ibid*, p 21.

4   Callwell, *ibid*, p 21.

5   *The Field Exercises and Evolutions of Infantry, 1859*, London, 1859, p 205.

6   *Field Exercises 1859, ibid*, pp 205–206.

7   *Field Exercises 1859, ibid*, pp 209–212.

8   *Field Exercises 1859, ibid*, p 213.

9   *Field Exercises and Evolutions of Infantry, 1861*, London, January 1862, p 380.

10   Colonel MacDougall, *Modern Warfare as influenced by Modern Artillery*, London, 1864, p 414.

11 MacDougall, *ibid*, p 418.

12 MacDougall, *ibid*, pp 14–15.

13 *Army Equipment, Part V, Infantry*, London, 1865, p 21.

14 *Army Equipment, ibid*, p 24.

15 Colonel P. S. Walton, *Simkin's Soldiers – The British Army in 1890, Volume II, The Infantry*, Chippenham, 1987, p 15.

16 Luvaas, *ibid*, p 165.

17 Colonel Balck, *Tactics*, Translated by Walter Krueger, London, 1911, p 41.

18 Balck, *ibid*, p 42.

19 Major General Scott, *Infantry Tactics, Or, Rules for the Exercise and Manoeuvres of the United States Infantry*, New York, 1835, pp 118–119.

20 Maureen Manjerovic and Michael J. Budds, *More Than A Drummer Boy's War: A Historical View of Musicians in the American Civil War*, College Music Symposium, 1 October 2002.

21 Manjerovic and Budds, *ibid*.

22 Paddy Griffith, *Rally Once Again – Battle Tactics of the American Civil War*, Marlborough, 1987, p 58.

23 Manjerovic and Budds, *ibid*.

24 Jay Luvaas, *The Military Legacy of the Civil War – The European Inheritance*, Lawrence, 1988, p 46.

25 Luvaas, *ibid*, p 46.

26 Major T. Lyndon Bell, letter dated 29 June 1870, *RUSI Journal*, Volume XIX, 1871.

27 General Sir William J. Codrington, *Autumn Manoeuvres Abroad and at Home 1869–1871*, lecture given to the Royal United Services Institute, 19 June 1872.

28 *Field Exercise and Evolutions of Infantry 1877*, p 209.

29 Private Collier, *The Autumn Manoeuvres of 1872*, unsourced document, pp 222–233.

30 *Field Exercise 1877, ibid*, pp 91–92.

31 *Field Exercise 1877, ibid*, p 210.

32 *Field Exercise 1877, ibid*, p 92.

33 *Field Exercise and Evolutions of Infantry 1884*, p 422.

34 *The Standing Orders of the 1st Battalion Royal Warwickshire (late 6th) Regiment*, Chatham: Gale & Polden, 1883, pp 81–82.

35 *Field Exercise 1877, ibid*, p 228.

36 *Infantry Drill 1889*, p 374.

37 *Infantry Training (4-Company Organization) 1914*, London, 1914, p 146.

38 Spencer Jones, *From Boer War to World War – Tactical reform of the British Army, 1902–1914*, Norman, 2012, p 112.

Chapter 10

1 Tom Gibson, *The Maori Wars – The British Army in New Zealand 1840–1872*, London, 1974, pp 66–67.

2 Michael Barthorp, *To Face the Daring Maoris – Soldiers' Impressions of the First Maori War 1845–1847*, London, 1979, pp 153–154.

3 *London Gazette*, 23 September 1864.

4 *London Gazette, ibid*.

5 *No. 2843, Drummer Dudley Stagpool, VC DCM*, Lummis VC Files, National Army Museum.

6 J. M. Brereton and A. C. S. Savory, *The History of the Duke of Wellington's Regiment (West Riding) 1702–1992*, Huddersfield, 1993, p 190.

7 Michael Barthorp, *The British Army on Campaign 1816–1902 (3): 1856–1881*, London, 1988, p 10.

8 Ian F. W. Beckett, *Wolseley and Ashanti – The Asante War Journal and Correspondence of Major General Sir Garnet Wolseley 1873–1874*, Stroud, 2009, pp 360–361.

9 Beckett, *ibid*, p 55.

10 Beckett, *ibid*, p 284.

11 Brigadier General H. Biddulph, 'The Umbeyla Campaign of 1863 and the Bhutan Expedition of 1865–66 – Contemporary Letters of Colonel John Miller Adye', *JSAHR*, Volume IXX, 1940, p 41.

12 Callwell, *ibid*, p 464.

13 Lieutenant Colonel Mike Snook, *How Can Man Die Better – The Secrets of Isandlwana Revealed*, London, 2005.

14 David Rattray, *The Day of the Dead Moon,* Audio CD 1997.

15 *Zulu Dawn*, American Cinema Releasing, May 1979.

16 Ian Knight, *Gutted Like Sheep – The Questionable Fate of the 24th's Drummer Boys at iSandlwana*, www.ianknightzulu.com, 7 June 2015.

17 See www.rorkesdriftvc.com.

18 All three photographs are in the Royal Collection and are printed in Michael Barthorp, *War on the Nile – Britain, Egypt and the Sudan 1882–1898*, Poole, 1984.

19 Alex Macdonald, *Too Late for Gordon and Khartoum*, London, 1887, p 257.

20 MacDonald, *ibid*, p 276.

21 Major E. A. De Cosson, *Days and Nights of Service with Sir Gerald Graham's Field Force at Suakin*, London, 1886, p 59.

22 De Cosson, *ibid*, p 153.

23 Bennet Burleigh, *Sirdar and Khalifa or the Re-Conquest of the Sudan 1898*, London, 1898.

24 Burleigh, *ibid*, pp 232–233.

25 Burleigh, *ibid*, p 292.

26 John Meredith (ed.), *Omdurman Diaries 1898 – Eyewitness Accounts of the Legendary Campaign*, Barnsley, 1998, p 88.

27 Winston S. Churchill, *The River War*, London, 1899, New English Library edition, 1973, p 227.

28 Ernest J. Martin (ed.), 'The Lincolnshires at Omdurman, September, 1898 – Diary of Lieutenant Hamilton Hodgson', *JSAHR*, Volume XXI, p 73.

29 Churchill, *ibid*, p 259.

30 Martin, *ibid*, p 77.

31 Martin, *ibid*, p 79.

32 Callwell, *ibid*, p 380.

33 *Black and White War Albums Soudan No. 1: Omdurman* and *Soudan No. 2: Atbara, Snapshots by Rene Bull, Special Correspondent to 'Black and White'*, London: Black and White Publishing Company, undated.

34 Rudyard Kipling, *Barrack-Room Ballads and Other Verses*, London, 1892, pp 68–69.

35 Private Frank Richards, *Old Soldier Sahib,* Uckfield, 2003, p 110.

36 Callwell, *ibid*, p 381.

37 Michael Barthorp, *The Frontier Ablaze*, London, 1996, p 20.

38 General Sir Ian Hamilton, *Listening for the Drums*, London, 1944, pp 141–142.

39 Hamilton, *ibid*, p 153.

40 Callwell, *ibid*, p 329.

41 Callwell, *ibid*, pp 328–329.

42 Barthorp, *ibid*, p 102.

43 Colonel H. D. Hutchinson, *The Campaign in Tirah, 1897–1898 – An Account of the Expedition Against the Orakzais and Afridis*, London, 1898, p 74.

44 Winston S. Churchill, *The Story of the Malakand Field Force – An Episode of Frontier War*, London, 1898, p 119.

45 Churchill, *ibid*, pp 128–129.

46 Hutchinson, *ibid*, pp 227, 229.

47 James Moncrieff Grierson, *The British Army by a Lieutenant-Colonel in the British Army*, London, 1899. Republished *Scarlet into Khaki – The British Army on the Eve of the Boer War* with a preface by Colonel Peter Walton, London, 1988, p 137.

48 *Bugler Dunne – Dublin Fusiliers*, angloboerwarmuseum.com.

49 Colonel Sir Howard Vincent, 'Lessons of the War: Personal Observations and Impressions of the Forces and Military Establishments now in South Africa', lecture given at the Royal United Services Institute, Monday 30 April 1900, *RUSI Journal*, Volume XLIV, June 1900, p 613.

50 Vincent, *ibid*, p 635.

51 H. W. Wilson, *With the Flag to Pretoria*, Volume 1, London, 1900, pp 25, 29.

52 George Clarke Musgrave, *In South Africa with Buller*, Boston, 1900, p 112.

53 Jeremy Archer, *The Old West Country Regiments (11th, 39th and 54th) From Plassey to the Somme*, Barnsley, 2011, pp 366–367.

54 W. J. P. Aggett, *The Bloody Eleventh – History of the Devonshire Regiment, Volume II, 1815–1914*, Exeter, 1994, p 310.

55 Archer, *ibid*, p 389.

56 Archer, *ibid*, p 389.

57 Stereoscopic photograph by Underwood and Underwood, *Black and White Budget*, 5 May 1900, p 150.

58 H. W. Wilson, *With the Flag to Pretoria – A History of the Boer War of 1899–1900*, Volume I, London, 1900, p 78.

59 Wilson, *ibid*, p 168.

60 Rudyard Kipling, *The Lesson*, 1901.

61 Spencer Jones, *From Boer War to World War – Tactical Reform of the British Army, 1902–1914*, Norman, 2012, p 41.

62 Colonel L. I. Cowper (ed.), *The King's Own – The Story of a Royal Regiment, Volume II 1814–1914*, Oxford, 1939, p 235.

Chapter 11

1 See in particular Michael Barthorp, *British Infantry Uniforms Since 1660*, Dorset, 1982.

2 Lieutenant Colonel M. B. Savage, 'Uniform of the 38th Foot', *'The Knot' – Journal of the South Staffordshire Regiment*, Number 7, August 1954, pp 5–6.

3 Richard Holmes, *Soldiers, ibid*, p 482.

4 Barty-King, *ibid* , p 72.

5 The Collection of Medals to Musicians formed by the late Llewellyn Lloyd, Dix Noonan Webb, 27 September 2016.

6 Frogsmile at victorianwars.com, 20 May 2011.

7 Colonel N. T. St John Williams, *Tommy Atkins' Children – The Story of the Education of the Army's Children 1675–1970*, London, 1971, p 3.

8 C. J. Stranks (ed.), *The Path of Glory – Being the Memoirs of the Extraordinary Military Career of John Shipp, Written by Himself*, London, 1969, p 10.

9 'Record of the Services of British Regiments: Sixty-Fifth (Second York North Riding) Regiment of Foot', *The Naval and Military Magazine*, Volume IV, Number VII, September 1828, London, 1828, p 65.

10 Cockerill, *ibid*, p 71.

11 www.coram.org.uk/foundling-hospital/foundlings-war.

12 Coram.org, *ibid*.

13 John Brownlow, *The History and Design of the Foundling Hospital, With a Memoir of the Founder*, London, 1858, Cambridge University Press Edition, 2015, p 91.

14 Cockerill, *ibid*, p 57.

15 Cockerill, *ibid*, p 75.

16 Cockerill, *ibid*, p 96.

17 *The Navy and Army Illustrated*, 20 December 1895, p 18.

18 www.armytigers.com/artefacts/"steady-the-drums-and-fifes".

19 Rudyard Kipling, *The Drums of the Fore and Aft*, in *Wee Willie Winkie and Other Stories*, Allahabad, 1888, p 67.

20 Kipling, *ibid*, pp 91–92.

21 Brumwell, *Rank and File, ibid*, p 16.

22 Tanner, *ibid*, p 10.

23 Llewellyn Lloyd Medals, *ibid*.

24 Captain Bennett Cuthbertson, *A System for the Compleat Interior Management and Œconomy of a Battalion of Infantry*, Dublin, 1768, pp 14–16.

25 Anon, *Advice to Officers of the British Army*, 1782, pp 87–90.

26 Lucy, *ibid*, pp 26–28.

27 J. D. Ellis, 'Drummers for the Devil? The Black Soldiers of the 29th (Worcestershire) Regiment of Foot 1759–1843', *JSAHR*, Volume LXXX, 2002, p 187.

28 Ellis, *ibid*, pp 199–201.

29 *JSAHR*, Volume XXI, 1926, Note 204.

30 J. Paine, 'The Negro Drummers of the British Army', *Royal Military College Magazine and Record*, Number 32, 1928.

31 *JSAHR*, Volume XXI, *ibid*.

32 *JSAHR*, Volume XXI, *ibid*.

33 Mike Boxall, '"An Excellent Bandmaster" – BM William Clark, 1st Bn. The East Surrey Regt', *Soldiers of the Queen – Journal of the Victorian Military Society*, Issue 157, September 2014, pp 19–20.

34 Stranks, *ibid*, p 80.

35 Barty-King, *ibid*, p 49.

36 *The Standing Orders of the 1st Battalion South Staffordshire Regiment (38th Foot)*, Aldershot: Gale & Polden, 1912, pp 21–22.

37 Thomas Simes, *The Military Guide for Young Officers, Volume I*, Philadelphia, 1776, p 207.

38 Stranks, *ibid*, p 2.

39 Brumwell, *ibid*, p 80.

40 Winstock, *ibid*, p 90.

41 Winstock, *ibid*, pp 90–91.

42 Herbert and Barlow, *ibid*, p 218.

43 *Diary of Lieutenant John Barker, ibid*, p 153.

44 Hibbert, *Rifleman Harris, ibid*, p 67.

45 Barty-King, *ibid*, p 53.

46 W. G. F. Boag, letter to the author, 6 October 1995.

47 R. M. Barnes, *A History of the Regiments and Uniforms of the British Army*, London, 1967, p 125.

48 *Advice to the Officers, ibid* p 84.

49 *Advice to the Officers, ibid*, p 88.

50 Barty-King, *ibid*, p 54.

51 Fortescue, *ibid*, p 20.

52 Fischer, *ibid*, p 70.

53 Francis Markham, *Five Decades of Epistles of War 1622*, quoted in Barty-King, *ibid*, p 54.

54 Markham, *ibid*, p 43.

Chapter 12

1 Richard Holmes, *The Last Hurrah: Cavalry on the Western Front, August–September 1914*, in Hugh Cecil and Peter Liddle (eds.), *Facing Armageddon – The First World War Experience*, Barnsley, 2003, p 281.

2 Holmes, *ibid*, p 281. He was quoting General Langlois, the founder of the *Revue Militaire Générale*.

3 Holger H. Herwig, *The Marne, 1914*, New York, 2009, p 57.

4 Marcel Mauss, *Techniques of the Body*, in Margaret Lock (ed.), *Beyond the Body Proper – Reading the Anthropology of Material Life*, London, 2007, p 52.

5 Anon, *History of the 8th North Staffords*, Longton, 1921, p 18.

6 *8th North Staffords, ibid*, p 10.

7 Sidney Rogerson, *Twelve Days On The Somme – A Memoir of the Trenches, 1916*, London, 2006, p 107–8.

8   Jeremy Archer, 'The Devonshires Held This Trench – The Devonshires Hold It Still', *Stand Tó! – The Journal of the Western Front Association*, Number 88, April/May 2010, p 5.

9   Anon, *The History of the Prince of Wales' Own Civil Service Rifles*, London, 1921, p 60.

10 Holmes, *ibid*.

11 *Field Service Regulations Part 1 – Operations, 1909*, Reprinted with Amendments 1912, War Office, 29 July 1912.

12 *Infantry Training (4-Company Organization) 1914*, War Office, 10 August 1914.

13 *Field Service Manual 1914 – Infantry Battalion (Expeditionary Force)*, issued with Army Orders dated 1 October 1914, p 22.

14 *Field Service Manual 1914*, *ibid*, p 10.

15 War Office, 18 May 1915.

16 Mathew Richardson, *1914: Voices From The Battlefields*, Barnsley, 2013, p 36.

17 www.firstworldwar.com/diaries/monsandloos.

18 John F. Lucy, *There's A Devil In The Drum,* Uckfield, 1993 edition, p 113.

19 Lieutenant Colonel Sir Frederick Ponsonby, *The Grenadier Guards in the Great War of 1914–1918*, London, 1920, p 78.

20 Ponsonby, *ibid*, 162–163.

21 Walter Bloem, *The Advance From Mons 1914 – The Experiences of a German Infantry Officer*, Leipzig, 1916, re-published by Helion, 2004, p 44.

22 Lucy, *ibid*, pp 121–122.

23 James P. Jones, *A History of the South Staffordshire Regiment (1705–1923)*, Wolverhampton, 1923, p 146.

24 Harry Newbolt, *Tales of the Great War*, London, 1916, pp 183–184.

25 www.lightbobs.com/1914.

26 www.armymuseum.co.nz/kiwis-at-war. The museum has Bugler Bissett's shattered bugle in its collection.

27 www.wrexham.gov.uk/english/heritage/mentioned_in_dispatches.

28 Martin Middlebrook, *The First Day on the Somme 1 July 1916*, London, 1971, pp 174–175.

29 *Somme Bugle to sound the 'Advance' 100 years on*, www.inniskillingsmuseum.com, 24 June 2014.

30 *War Diary 1st/15th London Regiment 4 July 1916*, National Archives, WO 95/2732.

31 Andrew Robertshaw and Steve Roberts (eds.), *The Platoon – An Infantryman on the Western Front 1916–1918*, Barnsley, 2011, p 157.

32 www.fatherdoyle.com/2015/04/27.

33 Bernard Martin, *Poor Bloody Infantry: A Subaltern on the Western Front 1916–17*, London, 1987, p 154. Drummer Dimmelow's damaged bugle is in the Staffordshire Regiment Museum.

34 Martin, *ibid*, 155.

35 Lyn MacDonald, *1914: The Days of Hope*, London, 1989.

36 H. L. Kirby and R. R. Walsh, *Drummer Spencer John Bent, VC*, Museum of the Queen's Lancashire Regiment.

37 www.qohldrs.co.uk/html/drummer_walter_ritchie_vc.

38 British Library, www.searcharchives.bl.uk, Photos 24/(44) and (45).

39 Sue Vander Hook, *The United States Enters World War I*, Edina: Abdo, 2010, p 81.

40 Kelly Whitson, at www.americanhistory.si.edu/blog/2013/11/the-bugle-that-sounded-the-end-of-the-world-war-i.html.

41 David Fraser, *Wars and Shadows – Memoirs of General Sir David Fraser*, London, 2002, pp 149–150.

42 See photograph of Corporal Willie Simm on the front cover of *The War Illustrated*, Number 212, 3 August 1945.

43 Colonel W. N. Nicolson, *The Suffolk Regiment 1928 to 1946*, Ipswich, undated, p 139.

44 A. J. Barker, *Fortune Favours The Brave: The Battles of the Hook, Korea 1952–53*, London, 1976, p 151.

45 'Lance-Corporal Jim Glibbery', Obituaries, *Daily Telegraph*, 30 July 2005.

46 Barker, *ibid*, p 154.

47 Barker, *ibid*, p 152.

48 Julian Ryall, *Daily Telegraph*, 11 November 2014.

49 Post on www.ww2talk.com, 22 Dec 2010.

50 Mark Zuehlke, *Operation Husky – The Canadian Invasion of Sicily, July 10–August 7, 1943,* Vancouver, 2008, p 367.

51 Strome Galloway, *Bravely Into Battle – The Autobiography of a Canadian Soldier in World War Two,* Toronto, 1988, p 200.

52 Galloway, *ibid*, p 201.

53 Galloway, *ibid*, p 202.

54 Ian Daglish, *Over the Battlefield – Operation Epsom*, Barnsley, 2007, pp 228–229.

55 Daglish, *ibid*, p 226.

56 Galloway, *ibid*, p 202.

57 *War Diary 38 (Irish) Brigade Headquarters, 12 June 1944*, National Archives, WO 170/606.

58 Appendix B to 9 Para Bn Op Order No. 1.

59 Corporal Jim McGuinness interview by David Hay, *Whitehaven News*, 17 January 1983, reproduced in www.bbc.co.uk/history/ww2peopleswar.

60 7thbn6thabn.com/History.

61 Patrick Delaforce, *The Fighting Wessex Wyverns – From Normandy to Bremerhaven with the 43rd Wessex Division*, Stroud, 1994, p 57.

62 Martin Middlebrook, *Arnhem 1944 – The Airborne Battle*, London, 1994, p 145.

63 John Waddy, *A Tour of the Arnhem Battlefields*, Barnsley, 1999, p 53.

64 Rebecca Kheel, in www.ocregister.com.

65 'Obituary of Pipe Major Tim Ainslie BEM', www.pipesdrums.com, 31 August 2006.

66 Lieutenant Colonel H. Moyse-Bartlett, *The King's African Rifles*, Naval and Military Press reprint 2012, p 633.

67 www.medalofkar.com/medalofhonour.

68 Lawrence James, *Imperial Rearguard – Wars of Empire, 1919–85*, London, 1988, p 1.

69 See Chapters 1 and 2 of Gwynn, Major General Sir Charles, *Imperial Policing*, London, 1934.

70 General Sir Andrew Keen, *Passing It On: Short Talks on Tribal Fighting on the North-West Frontier of India*, Aldershot, 1932, re-published, with an introduction by Robert Johnson, as *Lessons in Imperial Rule – Instructions for British Infantrymen on the Indian Frontier*, Barnsley, 2008, p 59.

71 *Street Fighting for Junior Officers*, London, 1944.

72 H. G. Bentley-Smith, undated typed notes, Museum of The Staffordshire Regiment.

73 Field Marshal Sir William Slim, *Unofficial History*, London, 1959, pp 83–85.

Chapter 13

1 Dan Jones, *Daily Telegraph*, 3 September 2011.

2 Richard Holmes, *Soldiers – Army Lives and Loyalties from Redcoats to Dusty Warriors*, London, 2011, p 486.

3 Major T. J. Edwards, 'Regimental Marches', *British Army Journal*, Number 6, July 1951, p 66.

4 Captain Anthony Farrar-Hockley, *The Edge of the Sword*, London, 1954, pp 55–56.

5 Gavin Engelbrecht, 'Nothing But Silence', *The Northern Echo*, 4 November 2011.

6 Joseph Newkirk, *Bob Ericson: Korean War's 'ceasefire bugler'*, www.whig.com, 26 July 2012.

7 Engelbrecht, *ibid*.

8 George MacDonald Fraser, *The Complete McAuslan*, London, 2000, p 32.

9 MacDonald Fraser, *ibid*, p 219.

10 Tony Thorne, *Brasso, Blanco and Bull*, London, 2000 edition, p 233.

11 Lieutenant Colonel D. G. Bridges, notes to author, September 2015.

12 Colonel Nigel Brown, email to author dated 27 September 2015.

13 *Army Code 14163, Trumpet and Bugle Calls for the Army*, London: HMSO, 1966, pp 62–63.

14 A. B. Griffiths, 'Two Years of National Service – A Subaltern's Tale', *The Stafford Knot*, Number 75, 2003, p 27.

15 Rodney Bashford, 'Is it the call I'm seeking?', *Soldier*, 1997 and published in full in www.rgjband.com

16 Andrew Bomford, PM programme, BBC Radio 4, 19 November 2015.

17 Major Richard Powell, *The Drums from Napoleon to the 1980s*, unpublished notes dated 6 October 1995.

18 Rudyard Kipling, *Barrack-Room Ballads and Other Verses*, London, 1900 Edition, p 68.

19 'Armoured Infantry Battalion (Unit Establishment)', *Headquarters* Infantry Issue1.0:Jul 02, p 1-57-1.

20 Holmes, *ibid*, p 486.

21 www.corpsofdrums.com/about/our-aims.

22 In Holmes, *ibid*, p 486.

23 *Army Code 71333, Infantry Training – The Drummer's Handbook*, Ministry of Defence, 1985, pp 1–4.

24 *The Stafford Knot – The Journal of The Staffordshire Regiment*, Number 65, 1993, p 52.

25 Mary Braid, 'Military Music Sounds Note of Regret: Army Bands Are Being Halved in Defence Cuts', *The Independent*, 19 April 1993.

26 Ray Routledge, 'Don't Lose The Beat', *Soldier*, June 2001, p 51.

27 Routledge, *ibid*, p 52.

28 'Regimental Band Knot Notes', *The Stafford Knot – The Journal of the Staffordshire Regiment*, Number 63, 1991, p 39.

29 Author's notes, B Company 1 STAFFORDS, 14 April 1989.

30 Richard Holmes, *Dusty Warriors – Modern Soldiers at War*, London, pp 287, 297, 330.

31 Turner, *ibid*, p 176.

32 Anon, *Britain's Modern Army Illustrated*, London, undated, pp 9, 12.

33 John Brereton, 'Trumpeters Ready … Sound', *Soldier*, 14 October 1996, p 18.

34 1 Mercian, *Instruments of Battle Questionnaire for Line Battalions*, March 2016.

35 *Army Code 14163, ibid*, pp 82–94.

36 *Army Code No. 71333 – Infantry Training – The Drummer's Handbook*, Ministry of Defence, 1985 and *Army Code 71333 – Infantry Training – The Drummer's Handbook*, Ministry of Defence, August 2013.

37 Major M. J. Barthorp, letter to the author, 8 June 1995.

38 Holmes, *Soldiers, ibid*, p 65.

39 Brereton, *ibid*, p 18.

40 Arthur Edward Dolph, *'Sound Off!' – Soldier Songs From Yankee Doodle to Parley Voo*, New York, 1929, p 75.

41 Holmes, *Soldiers, ibid*, p 526.

42 Dolph, *ibid*, pp 73–74.

43 Winstock, *ibid*, p 205.

44 Major Mike Hall, *With Trumpet, Drum and Fife – A Short Treatise Covering the Rise and Fall of Military Musical Instruments on the Battlefield*, Solihull, 2013, p 100.

45 James Tanner, *The British Army Since 2000*, Oxford, 2014, p 32.

46 www.armedforces.co.uk/army.

47 Bashford, *ibid*, pp 14–15.

48 Turner, *ibid*, p 185.

49 *Soldier*, August 2005, p 15.

50 Turner, *ibid*, p 27.

51 Turner, *ibid*, p 24.

52 Turner, *ibid*, p 194.

53 Denis Forman, *To Reason Why*, London, 1991, p 65.

Bibliography and Sources

Magazines, Journals and Newspapers

British Army Journal
British Army Review
Bulletin of the Military Historical Society
Commons Journal
Drummers Call – The Newsletter of the Corps of Drums Society
Journal of the Royal United Services Institute (RUSI Journal)
Journal of the Society for Army Historical Research (JSAHR)
Naval and Military Gazette
Soldier
Soldiers of the Queen – The Journal of the Victorian Military Society
Stand To! – The Journal of the Western Front Association
The American Magazine of Useful and Entertaining Knowledge
The Daily Telegraph
The Independent
The London Gazette
Military Illustrated
The Naval and Military Magazine
The Northern Echo
The Stafford Knot – The Journal of the Staffordshire Regiment (The Prince of Wales's)
The War Illustrated
United Service Journal

Websites

7thbn6thabn.com
americanhistory.si.edu
angloboerwarmuseum.com
armedforces.co.uk
armymuseum.co.nz
armytigers.com
bbc.co.uk
co.cleveland.nc.us
coram.org.uk

corpsofdrums.com
deremilitari.org
digital medievalist.com
eyewitnesstohistory.com
fatherdoyle.com
firstworldwar.com
hillsdalesites.org
ianknightzulu.com
inniskillingsmuseum.com

let.rug.nl
lightbobs.com
medalofkar.com
middlehornleader.com
ocregister.com
pipesdrums.com
pvv.ntu.no

qohldrs.co.uk
revolutionaryarchives.org
searcharchives.bl.uk
victorianwars.com
whig.com
wrexham.gov.uk
ww2talk.com

British Army Orders and Official Publications

An Abridgement of the English Military Discipline, 1676.

An Abridgement of the English Military Discipline, 1685.

An Abridgement of the English Military Discipline, 1690.

[The Duke of Marlborough's] Exercise of the Foot with the Evolutions, c. 1690.

Exercise for the Horse, Dragoons and Foot Forces, 1728.

A New Exercise, to be Observed by His Majesty's Troops on the Establishment of great-Britain and Ireland, 1756.

Manual Exercise as Ordered by His Majesty, [extracts] 1758.

New Manual and Platoon Exercise, 1764.

General Regulations, and Orders for His Majesty's Forces, 1786.

Rules and Regulations for the Field Exercise and Movements of the Army in Ireland, 1789.

Rules and Regulations for the Formations, Field Exercise, and Movements, of His Majesty's Forces, 1792.

Regulations for the Exercise of Riflemen and Light Infantry and Instructions for their Conduct in the Field, 1798.

Rules and Regulations for the Formations, Field Exercises, and Movements of His Majesty's Forces, 1801.

General Orders Relative to Soldiers Acting as Musicians, 1803.

General Orders and Observations on the Movements and Field Exercise of the Infantry, 1804.

Regulations for the Exercise of Riflemen and Light Infantry and Instructions for their Conduct in the Field, 1814 Edition.

General Orders 28 December 1816, 1816.

Field Exercise and Evolutions of the Army, as Revised in 1824, 1824.

Field Exercise and Evolutions of the Army, as Revised in 1833, 1833.

The King's Regulations and Orders for the Army, 1837.

The Queen's Regulations and Orders for the Army, 1844.

The Infantry Manual – Containing an Abstract of the Field Exercises and Evolutions of the Army, 1847.

General Order, [Army of the East], 10 May 1854.

General Orders [Army of the East] – Bivouac on the Bouljanak River, 19 September 1854.

The Infantry Manual, 1857.

The Field Exercises and Evolutions of Infantry, 1859, 1859.

The Field Exercises and Evolutions of Infantry, 1861, 1862.

Army Equipment, Part V, Infantry, 1865.

Field Exercise and Evolutions 1870.

Field Exercise and Evolutions of Infantry 1877.

Field Exercise and Evolutions of Infantry 1884.

Infantry Drill 1889.

Field Exercise and Evolutions 1889.

Infantry Drill 1892.

Infantry Drill 1896.

Infantry Training 1902.

Infantry Training 1905.

Field Service regulations Part 1 – Operations, 1909, reprinted with amendments, 1912.

Infantry Training (4-Company Organization) 1914, 1914.

Field Service Manual 1914 – Infantry Battalion (Expeditionary Force), 1 October 1914.

Street Fighting for Junior Officers, 1944.

Army Code 14163, Trumpet and Bugle Calls for the Army, 1966.

Army Code No. 71333 – Infantry Training, the Drummer's Handbook, 1985.

Armoured Infantry Battalion (Unit Establishment), July 2002.

Army Code No. 71333 – Infantry Training, the Drummer's Handbook, 2013.

Books and Articles

Ackerman, Paul (ed.), Vorwald, Gary and Lichack, Erik, *Military Music of the American Revolution – A Collection of Authentic Signals, Camp Duties, Marches, and Favorite Airs for the Fife and Drum*, Brigade of the American Revolution, 2007.

Aggett, W. J. P., *The Bloody Eleventh – History of the Devonshire Regiment, Volume II, 1815–1914*, Exeter: Devonshire and Dorset Regiment, 1994.

Anon, *Advice to the Officers of the British Army*, London, 1782, 1946 edition.

Anon, *Britain's Modern Army Illustrated*, undated.

Anon, *History of the 8th North Staffords*, Longton: Hughes & Harber, 1921.

Anon, *History of the East Surrey Regiment*, Volume 1, London: 1916.

Anon, *The History of the Prince of Wales' Own Civil Service Rifles*, London: P.W.O. Civil Service Rifles, 1921.

Anon, *The Standing Orders of the 1st Battalion Royal Warwickshire (late 6th) Regiment*, Chatham: Gale & Polden, 1883.

Anon, *The Standing Orders of the 1st Battalion South Staffordshire Regiment (38th Foot)*, Aldershot: Gale & Polden, 1912.

Archer, Jeremy, *The Old West Country Regiments (11th, 39th and 54th) From Plassey to the Somme*, Barnsley: Pen & Sword, 2011.

– 'The Devonshires Held This Trench – The Devonshires Hold It Still', *Stand To! – The Journal of the Western Front Association*, No 88, April/May 2010.

Balck, Colonel, *Tactics*, translated by Walter Krueger, London, 1911.

Barker, A. J., *Fortune Favours the Brave: The Battles of the Hook, Korea 1952–53*, London, 1974, Pen & Sword edition, 2002.

Barnes, R. M., *A History of the Regiments & Uniforms of the British Army*, London: Seeley Service & Co., 1967.

Barthorp, Michael, *To Face the Daring Maoris – Soldiers' Impressions of the First Maori War 1845–1847*, London: Hodder & Stoughton, 1979.

Barthorp, Michael, *Marlborough's Army 1702–11*, London: Osprey, 1980.

Barthorp, Michael, *The Zulu War – A Pictorial History*, Poole: Blandford Press, 1980.

Barthorp, Michael, *British Infantry Uniforms Since 1660*, Poole: Blandford Press, 1982.

Barthorp, Michael, *War on the Nile – Britain, Egypt and the Sudan 1882–1898*, Poole: Blandford Press, 1984.

Barthorp, Michael, *The British Army on Campaign (1) – 1816–1853*, London: Osprey, 1987.

Barthorp, Michael, *The British Army on Campaign (2) – The Crimea 1854–56*, London: Osprey, 1987.

Barthorp, Michael, *The British Army on Campaign (3) – 1856–1881*, London: Osprey, 1988.

Barthorp, Michael, *The British Army on Campaign (4) – 1882–1902*, London: Osprey, 1988.

Barthorp, Michael, *Heroes of the Crimea – The Battles of Balaclava and Inkerman*, London: Blandford, 1991.

Barthorp, Michael, *The British Troops in the Indian Mutiny 1857–59*, London: Osprey, 1994.

Barthorp, Michael, *The Frontier Ablaze*, London: Windrow & Greene, 1996.

Barty-King, Hugh, *The Drum*, London: The Royal Tournament, 1988.

Bashford, Rodney, 'Is it the call I'm seeking?', *Soldier*, 1997.

Baule, Steven M., 'Drummers in the British Army During the American Revolution', *JSAHR*, Volume LXXXVI, 2008.

Beach, Peggy, *Battle of King's Mountain*, www.co.cleveland.nc.us.

Beckett, Ian F. W., *Wolseley and Ashanti – The Asante War Journal and Correspondence of Major General Sir Garnet Wolseley 1873–1874*, Stroud: The History Press for the Army Records Society, 2009.

Belsey, Anne, 'A Simple Guide to William Barriffe for Busy Officers', *The Sealed Knot, Orders of the Day*, Volume 30, 1998.

Biddulph, Brig-Gen H., 'The Umbeyla Campaign of 1863 and the Bhutan Expedition of 1865-66 – Contemporary Letters of Colonel John Miller Adye', *JSAHR*, Volume IXX, 1940.

Binns, Lieutenant Colonel P. L., *A Hundred Years of Military Music, being the story of the Royal Military School of Music Kneller Hall*, Gillingham: Blackmore Press, 1959.

Blackmore, David, *Destructive and Formidable – British Infantry Firepower 1642–1765*, London: Frontline, 2014.

Bland, Humphrey, *A Treatise of Military Discipline; In which is Laid down and Explained The Duty of the Officer and Soldier, Thro' the several Branches of the Service*, Fifth Edition, London, 1743.

Bloem, Walter, *The Advance from Mons 1914 – The Experiences of a German Infantry Officer*, Leipzig, 1916, Helion edition, 2004.

Boxall, Mike, 'An Excellent Bandmaster' – BM William Clark, 1st Bn The East Surrey Regt, *Soldiers of the Queen – Journal of the Victorian Military Society*, Issue 157, September 2014.

Braid, Mary, 'Military Music Sounds Note of Regret: Army Bands Are Being Halved in Defence Cuts', *The Independent*, 19 April 1993.

Brereton, J. M. and Savory, A. C. S., *The History of the Duke of Wellington's Regiment (West Riding) 1702–1992*, Huddersfield: Amadeus Press, 1993.

Brereton, John, 'Trumpeters Ready … Sound', *Soldier*, 14 October 1996.

Brownlow, John, *The History and Design of the Foundling Hospital, Wit a Memoir of the Founder*, London, 1858, Cambridge University Press Edition, 2015.

Brumwell, Stephen, *Redcoats The British Soldier and War in the Americas 1755–1763*, Cambridge: Cambridge University Press, 2002.

Brumwell, Stephen, 'Rank and File: A Profile of one of Wolfe's Regiments', *JSAHR*, Volume LXXIX, 2001.

Bryant, Arthur, *Jackets of Green*, London: William Collins Sons & Co, 1972.

Buckley, Roger (ed.), *The Napoleonic War Journal of Captain Thomas Henry Browne 1807–1816*, London: Bodley Head for the Army Records Society, 1987.

Burleigh, Bennett, *Sirdar and Khalifa or the Re-Conquest of the Sudan 1898*, London: Chapman & Hall, 1898.

Callwell, Colonel C. E., *Small Wars – A Tactical Textbook for Imperial Soldiers*, London, 1906. Reprinted London: Lionel Leventhal, 1990.

Camus, Raoul F., *Military Music of the American Revolution*, Chapel Hill: University of North Carolina Press, 1976.

Carlton, Charles, *Going to the Wars – The Experience of the English Civil Wars 1638–1651*, London: Routledge, 1992.

Carman, W. Y., 'The Dress of Erle's Regiment in 1704 and 1709', *JSAHR*, Volume XLVI, 1969.

Carman, W. Y., *Richard Simkin's Uniforms of the British Army – Infantry, Royal Artillery, Royal Engineers and other corps*, Exeter: Webb and Bower, 1985.

Chandler, D. G. (ed.), *A Jornal of Marlborough's Campaigns During the War of the Spanish Succession 1704–1711 by John Marshall Deane*, Society for Army Historical Research, Special Publication No. 12, 1984.

Chapman, Earl John and Goodman, R. Paul, 'Quebec, 1759: Reconstructing Wolfe's Main Battle Line from Contemporary Evidence', *JSAHR*, Volume XCII, 2014.

Churchill, Winston S., *The Story of the Malakand Field Force – An Episode of Frontier War*, London: Longmans, Green & Co., 1898.

Churchill, Winston S., *The River War*, London: Eyre & Spottiswoode, 1899, New English Library Edition, 1973.

Cockerill, A. W., *Sons of the Brave – The Story of Boy Soldiers*, London: Leo Cooper, 1984.

Cockle, Maurice, *A Bibliography of English Military Works up to 1642 and of Contemporary Foreign Works*, London: Simpkin, Marshall, Hamilton, Kent, 1900.

Collins, Elizabeth, *The Beats of battle: Images of Drummer Boys Endure*, www.soldiers.dodlive.mil.

Connolly, Peter, *Greece and Rome at War*, London: Macdonald Phoebus, 1981.

Cooper, Duff, *Sergeant Shakespeare*, London: Rupert Hart-Davis, 1949.

Cooper, Captain T. H., *A Practical Guide for the Light Infantry Officer: Comprising Valuable Extracts from all The Most Popular Works on the Subject; with further Original Information*, London: T Egerton, 1806.

Cormack, Andrew and Jones, Alan (eds.), *The Journal of Corporal Todd 1745–1762*, Stroud: Sutton Publishing for the Army Records Society, 2001.

Cowper, Colonel (ed.), *The King's Own*, two volumes, Oxford, 1939.

Cramer, James, *Military Marching – A Pictorial History*, Tunbridge Wells: Spellmount, 1992.

Crook Jonathan, *The Very Thing – The Memoirs of Drummer Bentinck, Royal Welch Fusiliers, 1807–1823*, London: Frontline, 2011.

Curry, Anne, *The Battle of Agincourt – Sources & Interpretations*, Woodbridge: Boydell Press, 2000.

Cuthbertson, Bennett, *A System for the Compleat Interior Management and Œconomy of a Battalion of Infantry*, Dublin, 1768.

Daglish, Ian, *Over the Battlefield – Operation Epsom*, Barnsley: Pen & Sword, 2007.

De Cosson, Major E. A., *Days and Nights of Service with Sir Gerald Graham's Field Force at Suakin*, London: John Murray, 1886.

Delaforce, Patrick, *The Fighting Wessex Wyverns – From Normandy to Bremerhaven with the 43rd Wessex Division*, Stroud: Alan Sutton Publishing, 1994.

Delavoye, Captain Alex M., *Records of the 90th Regiment (Perthshire Light Infantry)*, London: Richardson & Company, 1880.

Derbridge, G., 'A History of the Drums and Fifes 1650–1700', *JSAHR*, Volume XLIV, 1967.

D'Ideville, Count Henry, *Memoirs of Marshal Bugeaud, From his Private Correspondence and Original Documents, 1784–1849*, translated and edited by Charlotte M. Yonge, London: Hurst and Blackett, 1884.

Dolph, Arthur Edward, *'Sound Off!' – Soldier Songs from Yankee Doodle to Parley Voo*, New York: Cosmopolitan Book Corporation, 1929.

Drummer Fife, *With their Musket, Fife and Drum*, www.queensroyalsurreys.org.uk.

Duby, George, *The Legend of Bouvines: War, Religion and Culture in the Middle Ages*, translated by Catherine Tithanyi, 1990, www.deremilitari.org.

Duckers, Peter, *British Military Rifles 1800–2000*, Princes Risborough: Shire Publications, 2005.

Dundas, David, *Principles of Military Movements Chiefly Applied to Infantry*, London, 1788.

Dundas, David, *Principles of Military Movements*, Dublin, 1789.

Edwards, Major T. J., 'Regimental Marches', *British Army Journal*, Number 6, July 1951.

Engelbrecht, Gavin, 'Nothing But Silence', *The Northern Echo*, 4 November 2011.

Ellis, J. D., 'Drummers for the Devil? The Black Soldiers of the 29th (Worcestershire) Regiment of Foot 1759–1843', *JSAHR*, Volume LXXX, 2002.

Elton, Lieutenant Colonel Richard, *The Compleat Body of the Art Military: Exactly compiled, and gradually composed for the Foot, in the best refined manner, according to the practice of the Modern Times*, second edition, London, 1659.

Everett, Major General Sir Henry, *The History of the Somerset Light Infantry*, London, 1934.

Falkner, James, *Marlborough's Wars – Eyewitness Accounts 1702–1713*, Barnsley: Pen & Sword, 2005.

Farmer, Henry George, *The Rise & Development of Military Music*, London: W. M. Reeves, 1912.

Farmer, Henry George, 'The Martial Fife – The Bi-Centenary of its Reintroduction', *JSAHR*, Volume XXIII, 1945.

Farmer, Henry George, 'The Old Drum and Fife Calls of the Scottish Regiments', *JSAHR*, Volume XXIV, 1946.

Farmer, Henry George, 'The Retreat – A Suggested Origin of the Modern ceremony', *JSAHR*, Volume XXV, 1947.

Farmer, Henry George, *Military Music*, London, 1950.

Farmer, Henry George, '16th–17th Century Military Marches', *JSAHR*, Volume XXVIII, 1950.

Farmer, Henry George, 'The Earliest British Trumpet and Bugle Sounds', *JSAHR*, Volume XXIX, 1951.

Farmer, Henry George, 'Our Bands in the Napoleonic Wars', *JSAHR*, Volume XL, 1963.

Farmer, Henry George, 'Bands in the Crimean War', *JSAHR*, Volume XLI, 1964.

Farmer, Henry George, 'Our Regimental Bands', *JSAHR*, Volume XLII, 1964.

Farmer, Henry George, 'The Martial Music of the Georges', *JSAHR*, Volume XLII, 1964.

Farmer, Henry George, *British Bands in Battle*, Hinrichsen Edition 1482, 1965.

Farmer, Henry George, 'The King's Trumpets', *JSAHR*, Volume XLIV, 1967.

Farrar-Hockley, Captain Anthony, *The Edge of the Sword*, London: Frederick Muller, 1954.

Ferguson, James (ed.), *Papers Illustrating the History of the Scots Brigade in the Service of the United Netherlands 1572–1782*, three volumes, Edinburgh: Scottish History Society, 1899–1901.

Fields, Nic, *The Spartan Way*, Barnsley: Pen & Sword, 2013.

Fischer, David Hackett, *Paul Revere's Ride*, New York: Oxford University Press, 1994.

Fitchett, W. H., *The Tale of the Great Mutiny*, New York: Charles Scribner's Sons, 1901.

Flatow, Major A. F., 'A Crimean Photograph of the Rifle Brigade', *JSAHR*, Volume XXXVIII, 1961.

Flavius Romanus, *The Roman Army*, www.hillsdalesites.org.

Fletcher, Ian, *In Hell Before Daylight – The Siege and Storming of the Fortress of Badajoz, 16 March to 6 April 1812*, Staplehurst: Spellmount, 1994.

Fletcher, Ian, *'A desperate Business' – Wellington, The British Army and the Waterloo Campaign*, Stroud: Spellmount, 2001.

Forman, Denis, *To Reason Why*, London: André Deutsch, 1991.

Fortescue, Sir John, *A History of the British Army*, 13 volumes, London: Macmillan, 1899–1930.

Fortescue, Sir John, *Following the Drum*, Edinburgh and London: Wm. Blackwood & Sons, 1931.

Fraser, General Sir David, *And We Shall Shock Them – The British Army in the Second World War*, London: Hodder & Stoughton, 1983.

Fraser, General Sir David, *Wars and Shadows – Memoirs of General Sir David Fraser*, London: Allen Lane, 2002.

Fraser, John, 'Europeans who Sided with the Mutineers in India 1857–9: The Christian Bandsmen of the Native Infantry Regiments', *JSAHR*, Volume LXXIX, 2001.

Frassett, James, *The Battle of Saratoga – Freeman's Farm*, www.revolutionaryarchives.org.

French, David, *The British Way in Warfare 1688–2000*, London: Unwin Hyman, 1990.

French, David, *Military Identities – The Regimental System, the British Army and the British People, c. 1870–2000*, Oxford: Oxford University Press, 2005.

Froissart, Sir John, *The Chronicles of England, France, Spain and the Adjoining Countries from the Latter Part of the Reign of Edward II to the Coronation of Henry IV*, Volume II, translated by Thomas Johnes, London: William Smith, 1839.

Fuller, Major General J. F. C., 'Two Private Letters from Major-General Sir John Moore', *JSAHR*, Volume IX, 1930.

Fuller, Major General J. F. C., 'Sir John Moore's Light Infantry Instructions of 1798–1799', *JSAHR*, Volume XI, 1932.

Galloway, Strome, *Bravely Into Battle – The Autobiography of a Canadian Soldier in World War Two*, Toronto, Gazelle Book Services, 1988.

Gates, David, *The British Light Infantry Arm c. 1790–1815 – Its Creation, Training and Operational Role*, London: Batsford, 1987.

Gibson, Tom, *The Maori Wars – The British Army in New Zealand 1840–1872*, London: Leo Cooper, 1974.

Goldsworthy, A. K., *The Roman Army at War 100 BC–AD 200*, Oxford: Oxford University Press, 1996.

Gravett, Christopher, *German Medieval Armies 1300–1500*, Oxford: Osprey, 1985.

Grierson, Lieutenant Colonel James, *The British Army 'by a Lieutenant Colonel in the British Army'*, London: Sampson Low, Marston & Company, 1899. 1988 edition introduced by Colonel Peter Walton and published as *Scarlet into Khaki – The British Army on the Eve of the Boer War*, London: Greenhill Books, 1988.

Griffith, Paddy, *French Napoleonic Infantry Tactics 1792–1815*, Oxford: Osprey, 2007.

Griffith, Paddy, *Rally Once again – Battle Tactics of the American Civil War*, Marlborough: Crowood Press, 1987.

Griffiths, Colonel A. B., 'Two Years of National Service – A Subaltern's Tale', *The Stafford Knot – The Journal of the Staffordshire Regiment*, Number 75, 2003.

Griffiths, Charles John, *A Narrative of The Siege of Delhi With an Account of the Mutiny at Ferozepore In 1857*, published as *Sepoys, Siege & Storm: The Experiences of a Young Officer of H.M. 61st Regt. At Ferozepore, on Delhi Ridge and at the Fall of Delhi During the Indian Mutiny*, Leonaur Edition, 2006.

Grose, Francis, *Military Antiquities Respecting a History of the English Army from the Conquest to the Present Time*, two volumes, London, 1786.

Guy, Alan (ed.), *Colonel Samuel Bagshawe and the Army of George II 1731–1762*, London: Army Records Society, 1990.

Gwynn, Major General Sir Charles, *Imperial Policing*, London: Macmillan and Co., 1934.

Hagist, Don N., *A British Soldier's Story – Roger Lamb's Narrative of the American Revolution*. Baraboo: Ballindalloch Press, 2004.

Hagist, Don N., *British Soldiers American War – Voices of the American Revolution*, Yardley: Westholme Publishing, 2012.

Hamilton, General Sir Ian, *Listening for the Drums*, London: Faber, 1944.

Hamley, Colonel Edward, *The Operations of War Explained and Illustrated*, sixth edition updated by Major General L. E. Kiggell, Edinburgh and London: Blackwood, 1914.

Hall, Major Mike, *With Trumpet, Drum and Fife – A Short Treatise Covering the Rise and Fall of Military Musical Instruments on the Battlefield*, Solihull: Helion & Company, 2013.

Hargreaves, Reginald, *This Happy Breed*, London: Skeffington and Son, 1951.

Haythornthwaite, Philip, *British Napoleonic Infantry Tactics 1792–1815*, Oxford: Osprey, 2008.

Haythornthwaite, Philip and Embleton, Gerry, *British Infantry Musicians in the 18th Century, Parts One and Two*, Military Illustrated.

Healy, Mark, *New Kingdom Egypt*, Botley: Osprey, 1992.

Herbert, Trevor and Barlow, Helen, *Music & the British Army in the Long Nineteenth Century*, Oxford: Oxford University Press, 2013.

Herwig, Holger H., *The Marne, 1914*, New York: Random House, 2009.

Hibbert, Christopher (ed.), *The Recollections of Rifleman Harris*, Moreton-in-Marsh: Windrush Press, 2000.

Holmes, Richard, *Redcoat – The British Soldier in the Age of Horse and Musket*, London: Harper Collins, 2001.

Holmes, Richard, *The Last Hurrah: Cavalry on the Western Front, August-September 1914*, in Hugh Cecil and Peter Liddle (eds.), *Facing Armageddon – The First World War Experience*, Barnsley: Pen & Sword, 2003.

Holmes, Richard, *Soldiers – Army Lives and Loyalties from Redcoats to Dusty Warriors*, London: Harper Press, 2011.

Honan, Joseph S., 'The Youngest Victoria Cross – 3406 Drummer Thomas Flynn VC', *Bulletin of the Military Historical Society*, February 1989.

Hopton, Richard, *The Battle of Maida 1806 – Fifteen Minutes of Glory*, Barnsley: Pen & Sword, 2002.

Hough, Major W., *A Narrative of the March and Operations of the Army of the Indus, in the Expedition to Afghanistan in the Years 1838–1839*, London: Wm H Allen, 1841.

Houlding, J. A., *Fit for Service – The Training of the British Army 1715–1795*, Oxford, 1981.

Howard, Dr Joseph H., *Drums in the Americas*, New York: Oak Archives, 1967.

Howell, Caro, *The Foundling Museum*, London: The Foundling Museum, 2014.

Hutchinson, Colonel H. D., *The Campaign in Tirah 1897–1898 – An Account of the Expedition Against the Orakzais and Afridis under General Sir William Lockhart*, London: Macmillan and Co, 1898.

James, Charles, *The Regimental Companion containing The Relative Duties of Every Officer in the British Army and rendering the Principles of System and Responsibility familiar*, London: T. Egerton, 1799.

James, Lawrence, *Imperial Rearguard – Wars of Empire 1919–85*, London: Brasseys, 1988.

Jones, James, *A History of the South Staffordshire Regiment (1705–1923)*, Wolverhampton: Whitehead Brothers, 1923.

Jones, Captain RN Oliver J., *Recollections of a Winter Campaign in Indian 1857–58*, published 1859, Portsmouth: Royal Navy Museum, 1989.

Jones, Spencer, *From Boer War to World War – Tactical reform of the British Army, 1902–1914*, Norman: University of Oklahoma Press, 2012.

Kane, Brigadier General Richard, *Campaigns of King William and Queen Anne; From 1689, to 1712. Also a New System of Military Discipline, for a Battalion of Foot on Action, etc.*, London, 1745.

Keen, General Sir Andrew, *Passing It On: Short Talks on Tribal Fighting on the North-West Frontier of India*, Aldershot: Gale & Polden, 1932, re-published, with an introduction by Robert Johnson, as *Lessons in Imperial Rule – Instructions for British Infantrymen on the Indian Frontier*, Barnsley: Pen & Sword, 2008.

Ketchum, Richard M., *Saratoga – Turning Point in America's Revolutionary War*, London: Pimlico, 1999.

Kincaid, Captain Sir John, *Adventures in The Rifle Brigade and Random Shots from a Rifleman*, 1909 combined edition, Glasgow: Richard Drew Publishing, 1981.

Kinglake, Alexander, *The Invasion of the Crimea: Its Origins, and an Account of its Progress*, eight volumes, London: William Blackwood, 1863–1887.

Kingsford, Charles, *The Story of the Duke of Cambridge's Own (Middlesex Regiment)*, London, 1916.

Kipling, Rudyard, *Barrack-Room Ballads and Other Verses*, London: Methuen and Co., 1892.

Kipling, Rudyard, *Wee Willie Winkie and Other Stories*, Allahabad: A. H. Wheeler, 1888. 1988 facsimile edition introduced by Philip Mason.

Kirby, H. L. and Walsh, R. R., *Drummer Spencer John Bent VC*, Museum of the Queen's Lancashire Regiment, undated.

Knecht, R. J., *Francis I*, Cambridge: Cambridge University Press, 1982.

Knight, Ian, *Queen Victoria's Enemies (3): India*, London: Osprey, 1990.

Knight, Ian, *Go To Your God Like A Soldier – The British Soldier Fighting for Empire, 1837–1902*, London: Greenhill Books, 1996.

Knight, Ian, *Gutted Like Sheep – The Questionable Fate of the 24th's Drummer Boys at iSandlwana*, www.ianknightzulu.com, 7 June 2015.

Leslie, Lieutenant Colonel C., *Instructions for the Application of Light Drill to Skirmishing in the Field*, Dublin, 1831.

Leslie, Lieutenant Colonel C., *A Treatise on the Employment of Light Troops on Actual Service; Containing General Principles, Compiled from Eminent Practical Authors, etc*, Brighton, 1842.

Leslie, Lieutenant Colonel J. H., 'The Points of War', *JSAHR*, Volume IX, 1930.

Leslie, Colonel K. H., *Military Journal of Colonel Leslie, K. H., of Balquhain, Whilst Serving with the 29th Regt in the Peninsula, and the 60th Rifles in Canada, 7c. 1807–1832*, Aberdeen: University Press, 1887.

Liddell-Hart, Captain B. H. (ed.), *The Letters of Private Wheeler 1809–1828*, Moreton-in-Marsh: Windrush Press, 2000.

Lucy, John F., *There's A Devil In The Drum*, London: Faber and Faber, 1938.

Lunt, James (ed.), *From Sepoy to Subedar, being the Life and Adventures of Subedar Sita Ram, a Native Officer of the Bengal Army written and related by himself*, London: Macmillan, 1988.

Luvaas, Jay, *The Education of an Army – British Military Thought, 1815–1940*, London: Cassell, 1965.

Luvaas, Jay, *The Military Legacy of the Civil War – The European Inheritance*, Lawrence: University of Kansas, 1988.

MacArthur, Roderick, 'British Army Establishments During the Napoleonic Wars, Part 1 – Background and Infantry', *JSAHR*, Volume LXXXVII, 2009.

Macdonald, Alex., *Too Late for Gordon and Khartoum*, London: John Murray, 1887.

MacDonald Fraser, George, *The Complete McAuslan*, London: HarperCollins, 2000 edition.

MacDonald, Lyn, *1914: The Days of Hope*, London: Penguin, 1989.

MacDougall, Colonel, *Modern Warfare as Influenced by Modern Artillery*, London: John Murray, 1864.

Mackesy, Piers, *British Victory in Egypt – The End of Napoleon's Conquest*, London: Routledge, 1995.

Manjerovic, Maureen and Budds, Michael J., *More Than A Drummer Boy's War: A Historical View of Musicians in the American Civil War*, College Music Symposium, 1 October 2002.

Markham, Francis, *Five Decades of Epistles of War*, 1622.

Marshman, John Clark, *Memoirs of Major-General Sir Henry Havelock*, London: Longmans, Green, Reader, and Dyer, Third Edition, 1867.

Martin, Bernard, *Poor Bloody Infantry: A Subaltern on the Western Front 1916–17*, London: John Murray, 1987.

Martin, Ernest J. (ed.), 'The Lincolnshires at Omdurman, September, 1898 – Diary of Lieutenant Hamilton Hodgson', *JSAHR*, Volume XXI, 1943.

Massie, Alastair, *The National Army Museum Book of the Crimean War – The Untold Stories*, London: Sidgwick & Jackson, 2004.

Mauss, Marcel, *Techniques of the Body*, in Margaret Lock (ed.), *Beyond the Body Proper – Reading the Anthology of Material Life*, London: Duke University Press, 2007.

Maxwell, Colonel Leigh, *My God – Maiwand! Operations of the South Afghanistan Field Force, 1878–80*, London: Leo Cooper, 1979.

May, Robin and Embleton, Gerry, *The British Army in North America 1775–1783*, London: Osprey, 1997.

McCulloch, Ian and Todish, Tim, *British Light Infantryman of the Seven Years' War – North America 1757–1763*, Oxford: Osprey, 2004.

McKenzie, Captain Thomas, *My Life as a Soldier*, St John: J & A McMillan, 1898.

Meredith, John (ed.), *Omdurman Diaries 1898 – Eyewitness Accounts of the Legendary Campaign*, Barnsley: Leo Cooper, 1998.

Middlebrook, Martin, *The First Day on the Somme 1 July 1916*, London: Allen Lane, 1971.

Middlebrook, Martin, *Arnhem 1944 – The Airborne Battle*, London: Viking, 1994.

Milner, John, *A Compendious Journal Of all the Marches, Famous Battles, Sieges, etc., of the Triumphant Armies, Of the ever-glorious Confederate High Allies, etc.*, 1733.

Milsop, John, *Continental Infantryman of the American Revolution*, Oxford: Osprey, 2004.

Mollo, John, *Uniforms of the American Revolution*, London: Blandford Press, 1975.

Moore, Sir John, *Instructions Given to the Battalions of Light Infantry of Irish Militia Under My Command in Ireland, in 1798–1799*.

Moyse-Bartlett, Lieutenant Colonel H., *The King's African Rifles*, Naval and Military Press reprint, 2012.

Musgrave, George Clarke, *In South Africa with Buller*, Boston: Little, Brown, and Company, 1900.

Muir, Rory; Burnham, Robert; Muir, Howie and McGuigan, Ron, *Inside Wellington's Peninsular Army 1810–1814*, Barnsley: Pen & Sword, 2006.

Muir, Rory, *Wellington – The Path to Victory 1769–1814*, New Haven and London: Yale University Press, 2013.

Muir, Rory, *Wellington – Waterloo and the Fortunes of Peace 1814–1852*, New Haven and London: Yale University Press, 2015.

Newbolt, Harry, *Tales of the Great War*, London, 1916.

Newkirk, Joseph, 'Bob Ericson: Korean War's "ceasefire bugler"', www.whig.com, 26 July 2012.

Oakes-Jones, Captain H., 'The Old March of the English Army', *JSAHR*, Volume XXIII, 1927.

Oman, Charles (ed.), *William Grattan – Adventures with the Connaught Rangers, 1809–1814*, London: Greenhill Books, 2003.

Paine, J., 'The Negro Drummers of the British Army', *Royal Military College Magazine and Record*, Number 32, 1928.

Palmer, Roy (ed.), *The Rambling Soldier – Military Life Through Soldiers' Songs and Writings*, London: Penguin, 1977.

Peachey, Stuart, *The Mechanics of Infantry Combat in the First English Civil War*, Bristol: Stuart Press, 1992.

Perkins, Roger, *The Kashmir Gate – Lieutenant Horne & the Delhi VCs*, Chippenham: Picton Publishing, 1983.

Pfeil, Michael, *Drumming in the English Civil Wars – Myths, Facts and Informed Guesses*, Bristol: Stuart Press, 1997, second edition.

Philbrick, Nathaniel, *Bunker Hill – A City, A Siege, A Revolution*, London: Doubleday, 2013.

Ponsonby, Lieutenant Colonel Sir Frederick, *The Grenadier Gurads in the Great War of 1914–1918*, London: Macmillan & Co., 1920.

Potter, David, *Renaissance France at War – Armies, Culture and Society c. 1480–1560*, Woodbridge: Boydell Press, 2008.

Potter, Samuel, *The Art of Beating of the Drum with the Camp Garrison & Street Duty by note*, Westminster, 1815.

Preston, David L., *Braddock's Defeat – The Battle of the Monongahela and the Road to Revolution*, New York: Oxford University Press, 2015.

Purdon, Major H. G., *An Historical Sketch of the 64th (Second Staffordshire) Regiment and the Campaigns Through Which They Passed*, undated.

Quintilianus, Aristides, 'De musica', in Thomas J. Mathiesen, *Apollo's Lyre – Greek Music and Music Theory in Antiquity and the Middle Ages*, Lincoln: University of Nebraska Press, 1999.

Rattray, David, *The Day of the Dead Moon*, Audio CD, 1997.

Rees, John U., '"Bugle Horns", "Conk Shells", and "Signals by Drum": Miscellaneous Notes on Instruments During the American War for Independence', *The Brigade Dispatch – The Journal of the American Revolution*, Volume XXVI, Number 4, Winter 1996.

Reid, Stuart, *British Redcoat (2) 1793–1815*, London: Osprey, 1997.

Richards, Private Frank, *Old Soldier Sahib*, Uckfield: Naval & Military Press, 2003 Edition.

Richardson, Mathew, *1914: Voices from the Battlefields*, Barnsley: Pen & Sword, 2013.

Roberts, Keith, *Soldiers of the English Civil War (1): Infantry*, London: Osprey, 1989.

Roberts, Keith, *Pike and Shot Tactics 1590–1660*, Oxford: Osprey, 2010.

Robertshaw, Andrew and Roberts, Steve (eds.), *The Platoon – An Infantryman on the Western Front 1916–1918*, Barnsley: Pen & Sword, 2011.

Rogers, Colonel H. C. B., *The British Army of the Eighteenth Century*, London: George Allen & Unwin, 1977.

Rogerson, Sidney, *Twelve Days on the Somme – A memoir of the Trenches, 1916*, London: Greenhill Books, 2006.

Routledge, Ray, 'Don't Lose The Beat', *Soldier*, June 2001.

Royle, Trevor (ed.), *A Dictionary of Military Quotations*, London: Routledge, 1990.

Russell, William Howard, *The Great War with Russia – The Invasion of the Crimea; A Personal Retrospect of the Battles of the Alma, Balaclava, and Inkerman, and of the Winter of 1854–55*, 1895, Cambridge: Cambridge University Press, 2012.

Ruutz Rees, L. E., *A Personal Narrative of the Siege of Lucknow, From its Commencement to its Relief by Sir Colin Campbell,* third edition, London: Longman, Brown, Green, Longmans, & Roberts, 1858.

Savage, Lt Col M. B., 'Uniform of the 38th Foot, 1st Battalion the South Staffordshire Regiment', *The Knot – Journal of the South Staffordshire Regiment*, Number 7, August 1954.

Scheer, George E., *Private Yankee Doodle – Being the narrative of Some of the Adventures, Dangers and Sufferings of a Revolutionary Soldier by Joseph Plumb Martin*, Eastern National, 2012 edition.

Scott, Christopher; Turton, Alan and von Arni, Eric, *Edgehill – The Battle Reinterpreted*, Barnsley: Pen & Sword, 2004.

Scott, Major General Winfield, *Infantry Tactics, Or, Rules for the Exercise and Manoeuvres of the United States Infantry*, New York, 1835.

Selby, John (ed.), *The Recollections of Sergeant Morris*, Moreton-in-Marsh: Windrush, 1998.

Simes, Thomas, *The Military Guide for Young Officers, Volume I*, Philadelphia, 1776.

Simes, Thomas, *A Military Course for the Government and Conduct of a Battalion Designed for their Regulations in Quarter, Camp or Garrison*, London, 1777.

Slim, Field Marshal Sir William, *Unofficial History, London: Cassell, 1959.*

Smollett, Tobias and Hume, David, *Compleat History of England*, London, 1827.

Snook, Lieutenant Colonel Mike, *How Can Man Die Better – The Secrets of Isandlwana Revealed*, London: Greenhill Books, 2005.

Snook, Lieutenant Colonel Mike, *Like Wolves on the Fold – The Defence of Rorke's Drift*, London: Greenhill Books, 2006.

Snow, Peter, *To War With Wellington – From the Peninsula to Waterloo*, London: John Murray, 2010.

Spring, Mathew H., *With Zeal and With Bayonets Only – The British Army on Campaign in North America, 1775–1783*, Norman: University of Oklahoma Press, 2008.

Spurrier, Major M. C., 'The Paulet Group', *JSAHR*, Volume XLVI, 1968.

Stacke, Major H. FitzM, 'Princeton 1777', *JSAHR*, Volume XIII, 1934.

Strachan, Huw, *From Waterloo to Balaclava – Tactics, Technology and the British Army, 1815–1854*, Cambridge: Cambridge University Press, 1985.

Stranks, C. J. (ed), *The Path of Glory, Being the Memoirs of the Extraordinary Military Career of John Shipp, Written by Himself*, London: Chatto & Windus, 1969.

Tanner, Brigadier J., 'The Youngest VC? Drummer Thomas Flynn and the 64th (2nd Staffordshire) Regiment at the relief of Cawnpore, 1857,' *Soldiers of the Queen – The Jornal of the Victorian Military Society*, Issue 145, June 2011.

Tanner, Brigadier J., *The British Army Since 2000*, Oxford: Osprey, 2014.

Thompson, W. F. K., *An Ensign in the Peninsular War*, London: Michael Joseph, 1981.

Thorne, Tony, *Brasso, Blanco and Bull*, London: Constable & Robinson, 2000 Edition.

Thucydides, *History of the Peloponnesian War*, translated by Rex Warner, London: Penguin, 1972.

Tincey, John, *The British Army 1660–1704*, London: Osprey, 1994.

Tourtellot, Arthur Bernon, *William Diamond's Drum – The beginning of the War of the American Revolution*, London: Hutchinson, 1960.

Trudeau, Joseph, *Music in the Continental Army*, MA Thesis, Charles Town: American Public University System, 2014.

Turner, Alwyn W., *The Last Post – Music, Remembrance and the Great War*, London: Aurum Press, 2014.

Turner, Major Gordon and Turner, Alwyn, *The History of British Military Bands, Volume One – Cavalry & Corps*, Staplehurst: Spellmount, 1994.

Turner, Major Gordon and Turner, Alwyn, *The History of British Military Bands, Volume Two – Guards & Infantry*, Staplehurst: Spellmount, 1996.

Turner, Major Gordon and Turner, Alwyn, *The History of British Military Bands, Volume Three – Infantry & Irish*, Staplehurst: Spellmount, 1997.

Urban, Mark, *Rifles*, London: Faber and Faber, 2003.

Urban, Mark, *Fusiliers*, London: Faber and Faber, 2007.

Vander Hook, Sue, *The United States Enters World War I*, Edina: Abdo, 2010.

Vegetius, *De Re Militari*, Book II, www.pvv.ntnu.no.

Vincent, Colonel Sir Howard, 'Lessons of the War: Personal Observations and Impressions of the Forces and Military Establishments now in South Africa', *RUSI Journal*, Volume XLIV, June 1900.

Vorwald, Gary and Lichack, Erik with Ackermann, Paul (ed.), *Military Music of the American Revolution – A Collection of Authentic Signals, Camp Duties, Marches, and Favorite Airs for the Fife and Drum*, The Brigade of the American Revolution, 2007.

Waddy, John, *A Tour of the Arnhem Battlefields*, Barnsley: Leo Cooper, 1999.

Walton, Colonel P. S., *Simkin's Soldiers – The British Army in 1890, Volume II, The Infantry*, Chippenham: Picton Publishing, 1987.

Wilkinson, Sir J. Gardner, *The Manners and Customs of the Ancient Egyptians*, London: John Murray, 1837.

Williams, Colonel N. St John, *Tommy Atkins' Children – The Story of the Education of the Army's Children 1675–1970*, London: HMSO, 1971.

Wilson, H. W., *With the Flag to Pretoria*, two volumes, London, 1900 and 1901.

Winstock, Lewis, *Songs & Music of the Redcoats – A History of the War Music of the British Army, 1642–1902*, London: Leo Cooper, 1970.

Wood, Stephen, *By Dint of Labour and Perseverance – A journal recording two months in northern Germany kept by Lieutenant-Colonel Adolphus Oughton, commanding 1st battalion 37th Regiment of Foot, 1758*, Society for Army Historical Research Special Publication No. 14, 1997.

Young, Peter and Emberton, Wilfrid, *The Cavalier Army – Its Organisation and Everyday Life*, London: Allen & Unwin, 1974.

Younghusband, Captain G. J., *Indian Frontier Warfare*, London: Kegan Paul, Trench etc, 1898.

Zuehlke, Mark, *Operation Husky – The Canadian Invasion of Sicily, July 10–August 7 1943*, Vancouver: Douglas & McIntyre, 2008.

Index